CAESAR'S COIN

Then the Pharisees went off and began to plot how they might trap Jesus in speech. They sent their disciples to him, accompanied by Herodian sympathizers, who said: "Teacher, we know you are a truthful man and teach God's way sincerely. You court no one's favor and do not act out of human respect. Give us your opinion, then, in this case. Is it lawful to pay tax to the emperor or not?" Jesus recognized their bad faith and said to them, "Why are you trying to trip me up, you hypocrites? Show me the coin used for the tax." When they handed him a small Roman coin, he asked them, "Whose head is this, and whose inscription?" "Caesar's," they replied. At that he said to them, "Then give to Caesar what is Caesar's, but give to God what is God's." Taken aback by his reply, they went off and left him.

Matthew 22:15–22

CAESAR'S COIN

Religion and Politics in America

RICHARD P. McBRIEN

MACMILLAN PUBLISHING COMPANY
NEW YORK

Collier Macmillan Publishers
LONDON

To Theodore M. Hesburgh, C.S.C.
President, University of Notre Dame (1952–1987)
With admiration and gratitude

Macmillan Publishing Company
866 Third Avenue, New York, N.Y. 10022

Collier Macmillan Canada, Inc.

Library of Congress Catalog Card Number: 86-18177

Printed in the United States of America

printing number
1 2 3 4 5 6 7 8 9 10

Library of Congress Cataloging-in-Publication Data

McBrien, Richard P.
  Caesar's coin.

  Bibliography: p.
  1. Church and state—United States.   2. United
States—Church history.   I. Title.
BR516.M376 1987   332'.1'0973   86-18177
ISBN 0-02-919720-1

CONTENTS

PREFACE

"FOURSCORE and seven years ago," President Abraham Lincoln began, "our fathers brought forth on this continent a new nation, conceived in liberty, and dedicated to the proposition that all men are created equal." This is a book about the American Proposition as it applies to the issue of religion and politics.[1]

My interest in the subject of religion is self-evident. I am a professionally active theologian. My interest in politics, on the other hand, requires some explanation.[2] I have been fascinated by American political history since high school, where my awakening was more or less coincident with the Eisenhower-versus-Stevenson presidential election campaign of 1952, marked as it was by hotly contested caucuses, primaries, and national conventions. I began subscribing to *The Congressional Record* for a while in college, and did a seminary MA thesis on right-to-work laws.

My early professional interest in theology moved along socio-political lines. My specialization then, as now, was ecclesiology, an area of theology that focuses on the nature and mission of the Church. The "nature" of the Church includes its organizational structure, the distribution of power, and the exercise of authority—all political issues of sorts; while the "mission" of the church includes its engagement in the temporal order, that is, the world of economics, law, international relations, and, of course, politics.

In 1973 I published *The Remaking of the Church*,[3] an interdisciplinary work involving both ecclesiological and political analyses, and during the 1975–76 academic year I served as the first Visiting Fellow at the John Fitzgerald Kennedy School of Government, Harvard University. In September 1984 I inaugurated a religion-and-politics lecture series at the University of Notre Dame, with Governor Mario M. Cuomo of New York, as the first speaker. Governor Cuomo's address generated an extraordinary amount of comment and discussion. It was clear that people were acutely interested in the topic, but just as acutely dissatisfied with the way it was being treated by candidates, commentators, and clergy alike.

The 1984 presidential election campaign disclosed a very large measure of confusion about the relationship between religion and politics. We weren't even sure about the primary terms, *religion* and *pol-*

itics. Parson Thwackum, in Henry Fielding's *Tom Jones*, knew what *he* meant: "When I say religion I mean the Christian religion, and when I say the Christian religion I mean the Church of England." A Thwackum syndrome seemed to prevail in some Protestant corners of the campaign, much to the discomfort of "Jews, Turks, and Infidels."[4]

But confusion was evident even within the Catholic community, in spite of Catholicism's long experience with, and highly developed doctrine on, matters of church and state and the much broader issue of church and society.[5] The controversy surrounding the exchange between Governor Cuomo and New York's Cardinal John J. O'Connor was a striking case in point. Catholics, and other interested observers, seemed eager to choose sides without much apparent regard for the complexity of the argument or its historical antecedents.

The issue of religion and politics is not about to diminish in importance. It will surely resurface in future election campaigns, including the 1988 presidential race, and during the bicentennial observances of the drafting and ratification of the U.S. Constitution (1987–89) and the Bill of Rights (1991). In the meantime, the issue will be kept alive by various decisions of the U.S. Supreme Court and ongoing debates inside and outside the Congress about such diverse matters as abortion, gay rights, pornography, school prayer, aid to parochial and other private schools, religious access to public schools, evolution versus creationism in the curriculum, Nativity scenes on courthouse lawns, the sanctuary movement, sabbath laws, legislative and military chaplains, diplomatic relations with the Vatican, and the role of religious leaders in politics, including the public pronouncements of the U.S. Catholic bishops and others on economic and foreign policy and on the strategy of nuclear deterrence.

First, in Chapter 1, the book defines and distinguishes among each of the issue's basic components: religion (including the distinctively American concepts of public religion and civil religion), church, sect, mysticism (religious individualism), politics, community, society, nation, state, and government. Then, in Chapter 2 it examines the relationship between religion and politics in context of other fundamental relationships: morality/moral values and politics, church and state, church and society, and clergy and politics.

These first two chapters have a boundary-setting function. They are designed to provide readers with a map of the territory, or as a kind of do-it-yourself kit for making up their own minds once they enter, or re-enter, the debate. These chapters might even stand alone as a general introduction or primer on the topic. They are not intended, in any case, to be provocative or polemical. My own point of view, as well as the principles which inform and shape it, will not begin explicitly to influence the discussion until the third chapter. It is my hope that, even then, objectivity will not be diminished or compromised.

Thereafter, the book focuses its attention exclusively on the American experience, probing, in Chapter 3, the issue of religion and politics first from the *political* side, with particular emphasis on constitutional and extra-constitutional notions of establishment, free exercise, separation (Jeffersonian "walls" and Madisonian "lines" alike), pluralism, and consensus, and then, in Chapter 4 from the *religious* side, with particular emphasis on the Protestant experience in America, on the place of Jews and other religious minorities, and on the content and development of Catholic theology and doctrine concerning religious liberty, church and state, and church and society.

The political and religious principles that guide this inquiry, and that are summarized at the end of Chapter 4 and again in Appendix I, are applied, in chapters 5 and 6, to pertinent cases as they arise in various contexts: the family, the school, the sanctuary, the public square, the military, the government, the economy, and the world at large. The story of the 1984 presidential election campaign is retold in relation to "the hardest case," abortion, in Chapter 5. The effort there, and in Chapter 6, is not so much to "solve" any of these cases as it is to clarify the terms of the discussion and thereby to contribute in some modest way to their eventual resolution.

Throughout the book the *political* point of reference remains always the United States of America, although passing references are also made to situations in other countries and regions of the world. The *religious* point of reference is more broadly ecumenical, taking into account Protestantism, Catholicism, Judaism, and humanism alike, but with special attention to the Catholic tradition (for reasons I hope will become clear).[6]

All of these traditions are connected somehow by what has come to be known as public and/or civil religion, in other words, by their common commitment to "civic republicanism" and to that "public virtue" which seeks "to promote the political and social involvement of all citizens, to some extent at least, in the larger interests of the public weal."[7] It is this "public good, the real welfare of the great body of the people," James Madison insisted, which is the final measure of any form of government and to which "the voice of every good citizen" must be reconciled.[8]

Despite copious notes, the book is not aimed primarily at scholars in the fields of American history, political science, constitutional law, or theology. It is intended for intelligent nonspecialists, and especially those for whom devotion to "the public good" is no idle pursuit—the kind of audience for whom such books as Walter Lippmann's *The Public Philosophy*,[9] George Wills' *Statecraft as Soulcraft*,[10] and John

Courtney Murray's *We Hold These Truths: Catholic Reflections on the American Proposition*,[11] were written.

To be sure, these three authors would not always be of one mind on every political or religious issue of consequence. The first was liberal and Jewish, the second is conservative and Protestant, the third was a liberal conservative and Catholic—a Jesuit at that. But their books have more in common than not: an abiding concern for the public good, the realm of the sacred, the lessons of human history, and the tradition of civility.

I am attempting herein to update and move beyond the extraordinary achievement of Murray's work especially, now that we find ourselves in a universe of moral, religious, and political discourse so different already from his own. I do so, however, not from any Olympian heights of special knowledge and wisdom, but as a humble companion with each reader on the lengthy, and often arduous, path to greater political and religious understanding.

This book is simply a vehicle for sharing with others something of what I myself have had to struggle to learn. Although I shall be walking the reader systematically through the material, we won't necessarily come out at the same place in the end. I should hope, however, that the book will be of some enduring value, even for those who cannot accept all of its conclusions.

There remains only the agreeable task of acknowledging my indebtedness to those who helped me in this project: the University of Notre Dame, and especially its president, Theodore M. Hesburgh, C.S.C., for granting and generously funding a full year's sabbatical leave; Martin E. Marty, of the Divinity School, University of Chicago, for reading the entire manuscript and offering many excellent bibliographical and editorial suggestions; J. Bryan Hehir, of the United States Catholic Conference and Georgetown University, for intelligent guidance on Catholic social thought and on the work of John Courtney Murray in particular; Paul R. Nelson, a doctoral student at Notre Dame, for tracking down documents, checking references, and organizing the material on U.S. Supreme Court cases for the Appendix; my secretary, Donna Shearer, for keeping everything else in order while I tried to concentrate my attention and energy on this project; and Anne Fearing, administrative assistant in the department of Theology, for always being there when needed. I am grateful, finally, to everyone at Macmillan, especially Charles E. Smith, Vice President and Publisher, Professional Books Division, who encouraged me in this project and who managed the production of what you now have in hand.

Notre Dame, Indiana
June, 1986

PART I

Religion and Politics:
The Issue

ONE

THE TERMS

THE subject of religion tends to generate a mixture of reactions. The major television networks, for example, assign commentators to politics, business, medicine, law, entertainment, and sports, but none to religion. They worry about demands for equal time from various religious groups, and about boycotts if these demands are rejected. When religion does gain air time, it often is relegated to Sunday morning slots or is placed on a pay-as-you-go basis, which means that the airwaves are dominated by those who can afford to pay the price. In the present circumstances, the clear winners in the competition for access are Protestant fundamentalists, who occupy almost every pulpit in the so-called electronic church.[1]

For others, however, fear of controversy has little or nothing to do with a policy of caution. Religion is, for them, simply irrelevant to serious human concerns. It is a matter of private taste and practice.[2] That may explain why religion pieces in many of the nation's newspapers are confined to a special Saturday page, along with the advertisements for church and synagogue services, and why the articles are usually more concerned with the internal affairs of local religious communities than with the religious dimension of major news events and issues.

On the other hand, it would seem self-evident that one cannot fully understand many major news events without taking the religious factor into account. The emergence of Islamic fundamentalism, especially in Iran, has changed the social and political character of the Middle East, and Islam generally has had a significant political impact on such diverse countries as Pakistan, Saudi Arabia, Libya, Turkey, India, Ma-

3

laysia, Indonesia, Afghanistan, Nigeria, the Sudan, Egypt, Syria, Iraq, Burma, Chad, Ethiopia, Cyprus, Lebanon, Thailand, and the Philippines.[3]

When Jihan Sadat, widow of Egypt's President Anwar el-Sadat, returned home after a five-month stay in the United States in 1985, she expressed shock at the changes that had occurred during her absence.

What had particularly troubled her was the Egyptian Supreme Court's recent abolition of the women's rights law that she had championed and her husband had decreed in 1979. The law required a man to tell his wife if he married another woman, made his second marriage grounds for divorce, and gave the first wife custody of young children in the couple's home.

Mrs. Sadat warned that the government's apparent strategy of trying to co-opt fundamentalists by incorporating them into the political process and meeting some of their demands was a serious error.

"These people are fanatics," she said. "They've been brainwashed. You can't change them, so the government must stand up to them."[4]

But fundamentalism is on the rise in much of the Arab world, according to some scholars and journalists, primarily because other "isms" have failed. Within the last 40 years, Egypt alone tried monarchism, colonialism, pan-Arabism, socialism, and Sadat's capitalism. Fundamentalism appeals to the region's Islamic roots and holds out promises of restoring Arab dignity and of resolving pressing problems. "At the present, the few who dare challenge the fundamentalists do so at their peril."[5] But it may be equally true that those who try to make sense of developments in the Arab world without a sustained effort to understand Islam, in both its fundamentalistic and nonfundamentalistic forms, also do so at their peril.

Compelling evidence of the link between religion and major political events also turns up in other countries and on other continents, particularly where Catholicism has a strong foothold. A few samples will suffice.

On June 3, 1985, the Vatican and the Italian government ratified an historic pact ending the Catholic Church's status as a state religion. The new concordat replaced the Lateran Treaty of 1929, which was negotiated by Mussolini and created the independent state of Vatican City on 109 acres of the city of Rome.

For 11 centuries the papacy had exercised secular authority over the Papal States, across central Italy. The Vatican was deprived of this land, however, in 1870 as part of the unification of Italy under the royal house of Savoy. Pope Pius IX refused to recognize the new situation, and the issue was not finally resolved until 1929 with the signing of the Lateran Treaty.

The new concordat reaffirms the independence of Vatican City, but also guarantees religious freedom for non-Catholics and ends Rome's status as a "sacred city." This title had given the Church power to ban offensive plays, books, and business enterprises. The new treaty also establishes stricter rules on tax exemptions for religious institutions and gradually phases out state subsidies for clergy. Another provision ends compulsory Catholic instruction in public schools.

Pope John Paul II said that the new treaty was a sign that Catholicism respected Italy's independence, but he added that the Church reserved the right to speak out on political and moral issues. "Today opens a new period in the institutional relations between the Church and the state in Italy," he declared.

But Italy offers only one model. In Ireland, where the union of church and state has been equally close, the hierarchy continues to resist the trend toward secularization. For example, the Archbishop of Dublin, Kevin McNamara, vigorously opposed efforts to liberalize the nation's divorce laws. When the state permits second and third marriages in violation of the commandments of God and the Church, he argued, it cloaks these morally unlawful unions with a kind of legitimacy that leads society eventually to accept marriage as provisional rather than permanent.[6] On June 26, 1986, the Irish voted overwhelmingly to keep the nation's ban on divorce.

Chile and Poland, in their turn, offer yet another model. Here, the bone of contention is not secularization but political repression. These two countries are useful examples because their situation is representative of much of Latin America and Eastern Europe.

In Chile the most consistent opposition force to the government of General Augusto Pinochet has been the Catholic Church. The Church's capacity to exercise effective political power was demonstrated in late 1985 when, under the leadership of Cardinal Juan Francisco Fresno, Archbishop of Santiago, it successfully promoted the first multi-party agreement on the steps necessary to end military rule. So strong is the Church's position, stronger indeed than that of any of the opposition parties, that one lawyer has suggested that the only one who could defeat Pinochet in an election would be a bishop. Visiting members of the U.S. Congress and the State Department have left with the same impression.

The Church's popularity is broadly based, in the affluent neighborhoods of Santiago as well as the poor ones. It feeds the poor, supports youth groups, denounces official violence, and speaks out in defense of human rights.

In Chile the Catholic Church is nose-to-nose against a right-wing government, as it was in the Philippines and in Haiti when, in early 1986, it contributed significantly to the political downfalls of Presidents

Ferdinand Marcos and Jean-Claude ("Baby Doc") Duvalier respectively. In Poland, as in Nicaragua, repression comes from the left, in
the Marxist regime of General Wojciech Jaruzelski. And there is another difference. The struggle is three-sided: the Polish state, the
Catholic Church, and the outlawed Solidarity movement.

Although the nation's primate, Cardinal Josef Glemp, has followed
a more moderate course than his predecessor, Cardinal Stefan
Wyzsinski, he has defended the Church against charges of meddling
in national politics, and has criticized government controls over education, the media, and religious life. The Marxist regime, he insists,
is postponing the final confrontation with the Church only as "a strategy . . . caused by circumstance and not good will."[7]

Cardinal Glemp has been especially critical of the government's
ban against the participation of Catholics in politics. Religion in Poland
is "so widespread," he has insisted, "that the believers should be included in the political life of the country."

If Cardinal Glemp's support of the Solidarity movement has been
marked by caution, the attitude of other high-ranking prelates has not.
After celebrating Mass at the shrine of the Black Madonna in Czestochowa for more than 50,000 industrial workers, Cardinal Henryk
Gulbinowicz called out, "Hang in there, as we are hanging in."[8] At
the altar, the Cardinal spoke with the aged parents of Father Jerzy
Popieluszko, the pro-Solidarity priest who had been murdered in 1984
by secret police officers. Later he joined Lech Walesa, the founder of
Solidarity, in sending a telegram to the Pope in the name of Polish
workers. It was on this same occasion that the abbot in charge of the
shrine personally introduced Lech Walesa to the crowd, and another
bishop, Tadeusz Goclowski, of Gdansk, attacked the government for
trying to blame its own policy failures on the Polish people, and for
its attempts to take away the nation's religious motivation.

The case of South Africa presents yet another sort of problem. The
situation is similar to Chile's and to Poland's, in one sense, but to
Italy's and to Ireland's, in another. The non-white, and especially black,
majority of the population feels itself oppressed by a hostile government and political system, and the church (in this instance, an ecumenical consortium of churches) functions as one of the principal
agents of criticism and advocates of reform. The winner of the 1984
Nobel Peace Prize, Desmond M. Tutu, the first black archbishop of
Cape Town and titular head of the Anglican Church in South Africa,
has played an important and well-publicized role in this struggle for
political equality. So, too, has the Rev. Beyers Naude, an Afrikaner,
who is Bishop Tutu's successor as general secretary of the South Af-
rican Council of Churches. On the other hand, most whites belong to
the Dutch Reformed Church, which has enjoyed a politically favored

status and which has been inclined over the years to support the nation's system of apartheid, even with arguments drawn from the Bible. Indeed, a 229-page report of the Human Sciences Research Council characterized the Dutch Reformed Church as "extraordinarily insensitive to the suffering which existing social structures inflicted on non-whites."[9] The council's report was considered remarkable because Afrikaner theologians were among its principal authors and the study itself was government-sponsored.

Other examples of the interplay of religion and politics are plentiful, inside and outside the familiar world of Western Christianity: Iran, Lebanon, Israel, Nicaragua, Brazil, El Salvador, India, and even tiny Switzerland. In June 1985 Swiss voters rejected a proposal that would have severely limited abortions and banned some contraceptives. A constitutional amendment had been supported by conservative Catholics and Protestant fundamentalists. The contest had been bitter.

In Israel, meanwhile, the debate continues over the meaning of a Jewish state. For Rabbi Meir Kahane, a member of the Kach Party in the Knesset, the issue is clear: "the State of Israel was created by Jews, Zionists, as the Jewish state, and this can mean only one thing: a state with a guaranteed majority of Jews ... [in which] Jews and gentiles are separate and apart.... The Westernized, secular Jewish liberal cannot bear it, for 'Kahanism' forces him to ask the question: Why be Jewish at all?"[10]

At the same time, Orthodox Jews continue to apply pressure to the government to enforce religious laws (the *halacha*) in everything from archaeological excavations and Saturday football games to non-kosher establishments and the construction of a Brigham Young University extension center in Jerusalem. They have burned bus stop shelters with advertisements they find offensive and have stoned motorists driving on the Sabbath. The influential daily, *Ha'aretz*, has deplored their behavior: "Jerusalem, perhaps more than any other city, is identified with freedom of worship for all faiths."[11]

Leading Reform Jews in the United States and Canada, represented by the Union of American Hebrew Congregations, have also challenged the Israeli religious establishment. A delegation of 35 members went to Tel Aviv in May 1986 to convey their concerns to Prime Minister Shimon Peres. Charles J. Rothschild, chairman of the Union's board of trustees, told a news conference in Israel, "We believe the principle of religious pluralism is a matter of right, not of numbers. In other democracies such as the United States and Canada, Jews are a small minority yet enjoy the rights guaranteed to every citizen."[12]

The issue of religion and politics was particularly prominent, of course, in the 1984 U.S. presidential election campaign. Both major candidates delivered speeches devoted to their religious convictions, indicating how those convictions were related to public office. In the Catholic community the debate was often sharp, pitting at times New York's Governor Mario M. Cuomo against New York's Cardinal John J. O'Connor, with other Catholic officeholders and bishops joining in. Editorial comment on the debate was voluminous and there was extensive television coverage. The terms of the issue, however, were not always clearly understood and articulated, nor were the arguments surrounding the issue consistently marked by insight, wisdom, and balance. Several political and religious leaders said off-the-record that, after the election, the issue should be sorted out and analyzed in a more leisurely, less partisan manner.[13] This is one modest attempt to do so.

Religion and its Varieties

Religion may have one thing in common with pornography. It's very difficult to define, but you're supposed to know it when you see it.[14] It doesn't usually work out that way, in either case.

Catherine Albanese likens it to an elephant in the dark.[15] Her reference is to a story that Buddhists and some Muslims tell about an elephant and a group of blind men who had never before encountered one. Each of the blind men felt the mysterious beast and later talked with one another about their experience. Those who had touched the head claimed that the elephant was just like a pot. Others had felt the ear and thought it like a harvest basket used to separate grain. Still others had touched the elephant's tusk and confidently announced that the elephant was part of a plow. Finally, those who had patted the elephant's trunk thought the elephant was a plow, whole and complete. The moral of the story is that each of us tries to fathom the secrets of life and the universe from a place of personal darkness. Each describes the portion experienced, and none can speak about the whole.[16]

Religion is difficult to define, Albanese contends, because definitions have to do, literally, with boundaries, and religion has no boundaries. It encompasses the whole of life, both here and beyond the boundary of this world. Therefore, we can only describe it, or at least try to.

She distinguishes between ordinary and extraordinary religion. The former is more or less synonymous with culture. (As we shall see, most sociologists and theologians would not call this "religion" in the strict sense of the word.) Ordinary religion shows people how to live well within boundaries. The latter helps people to transcend their everyday culture and concerns. Extraordinary religion brings people across boundaries and ultimately into contact with God.[17]

In the United States, as elsewhere, ordinary and extraordinary religion are often difficult to separate. In Judaism, for example, the most repeated ritual of extraordinary religion is the weekly Sabbath meal, in which a formal framework of prayer and blessings is joined to ordinary conversation and enjoyment around the dinner table. Catholicism, too, emphasizes the intimate connection between the sacred and the secular. The sacraments sanctify ordinary elements (for example, bread and wine, water, oil, fire) and the liturgical year sanctifies days, seasons, and time itself. Much of Catholic devotional life is permeated with ethnic traditions and customs. Albanese suggests that Protestantism, more than any other religious movement, tried to establish a clear distinction between the ordinary and the extraordinary. The cult movements of recent years are an example of this separationist tendency. Many cultists seek a radical break with their former ordinary lives in favor of a total commitment to extraordinary concerns.

Religion in the United States, she notes, is also marked simultaneously by manyness and oneness. The manyness, or pluralism, of religion in America is self-evident; its oneness is not. To the extent that there is a more or less unified American religion, it is, or at least has been, that of white, Anglo-Saxon Protestants, with a generous dash of Northern European immigrants. Although this religion of oneness inherits the concerns of extraordinary religion from its Protestant heritage, "it is, above all, the ordinary religion of American culture that comes to us through the media, the public-school system, government communications, and commercial networks."[18] This is also known as our civil religion and/or public religion (see the section that follows).

An assertive minority of sociologists, following in the footsteps of one of the founders of modern sociology, Emile Durkheim,[19] would tend to agree with the inclusivist approach of historians like Catherine Albanese. They insist that religion is broad enough to include scientific humanism, Marxism, and other nonsupernatural philosophies.[20] Clifford Geertz's definition of religion as a cultural system is, of course, well known. He defines it as "(1) a system of symbols which acts to (2) establish powerful, pervasive and long-lasting moods and motivations in men by (3) formulating conceptions of a general order of existence and (4) clothing these conceptions with such an aura of factuality that (5) the motivations seem uniquely realistic."[21]

The U.S. Supreme Court has also taken this inclusive view. Justice Hugo Black contributed a famous footnote to a 1961 case, *Torcaso* v. *Watkins,* in which he observed that "among religions in this country which do not teach what would generally be considered a belief in the existence of God are Buddhism, Taoism, Ethical Culture, Secular Humanism and others."[22] The Court maintained this wider view in two cases involving conscientious objectors, in 1965 and again in 1970.[23]

Even though Jesuit theologian John Courtney Murray held a more traditional, and therefore restrictive, understanding of religion, he did include nonreligious humanism (what he called "secularism") among America's four conspiracies: Protestant, Catholic, Jewish, secularist. He took the word conspiracy in its original Latin sense, as a "breathing together." Citing Cicero, Murray noted that civil society is formed by action in concert on the basis of a consensus regarding the action's purposes *("conspiratione hominum atque consensu")*. Civil society is by definition a conspiracy, *"conspiratio plurium in unum."* Only by conspiring together do the many become one: *E pluribus unum.*[24]

Most sociologists, however, have a different approach. They limit the term religion to those systems of thought embodied in social organizations that do indeed posit the existence of the supernatural.[25] They insist, in fact, that "a religion lacking supernatural assumptions is no religion at all" and that "the differences between supernatural and nonsupernatural (or naturalistic) systems are so profound that it makes no more sense to equate them than to equate totem poles and telephone poles."[26] This has been the view of those engaged in the social scientific study of religion since the discipline began to take shape in the nineteenth century, Durkheim's dissent notwithstanding. The debate is not without constitutional implications, for example, in the determination of exemptions from taxation and from military service.

One can understand the interest in broadening the definition (or description) of religion, given the plethora of recognized religions in the United States alone. But the inclusivist approach is not without serious problems. If everything is religious, then nothing in particular is religious, and sociologists themselves lose the conceptual tools to explore and sort out the real and profound differences that exist among groups, movements, and ideologies.

If it is the case, for example, that modern science is a form of religion, in what way is modern science different from what has been called religion by everyone else, including those engaged in the scientific study of religion? One can substitute any number of other social realities for "modern science" and generate the same question.

A choice has to be made. One cannot embrace at the same time the inclusivist and the restrictive notions of religion. On practical grounds alone the latter notion is to be preferred, even for a sociological definition of religion.[27] But without prejudice to the need for, and value of, sociological definitions (not to mention philosophical, anthropological, psychological, phenomenological, and cultural definitions), a definition of religion must, in the end, be theological unless we are to sever all connection between religion and God (the sacred, the holy, the transcendent, the supernatural). Most people, in fact, who would describe themselves as religious or who would be identified as religious according to standard philosophical, sociological, and psychological categories, attest to their own conviction, however vaguely or incoherently stated, that God (or some corresponding word) is on the "other side" of their religious relationship and that somehow God has managed to reach across the "infinitely qualitative distance" (Soren Kierkegaard) between the divine and the human to communicate with them through some act or process of revelation.

But this is not to say that the inclusivist notion of religion is without merit. Religion, even theologically conceived, has to do with the whole of human existence, and not merely some special sector of it. God's presence touches the whole person in the totality of the person's relationships not only with God but with all other persons, and with the whole cosmic order as well. In Catholicism this is known as the principle of sacramentality. God is present to, and active in, all created reality.[28]

I should define *religion*, therefore, as *the whole complexus of attitudes, convictions, emotions, gestures, rituals, symbols, beliefs, and institutions by which persons come to terms with, and express, their personal and/or communal relationship with ultimate Reality (God and everything that pertains to God).* The word *Reality* has been capitalized to insure that religion will not be confused with any "philosophy of life." In the act of religion, persons deliberately reach out toward God (the sacred, the holy, and so on). They perceive God in the persons, events, and things they see, that is to say, sacramentally. Religion presupposes and flows from faith, that is, a personal belief in, and commitment to, God. One is not religious who does not think there is more to reality than meets the eye. The religious person believes himself or herself to be in touch with another dimension, with what Dietrich Bonhoeffer called "the 'beyond' in the midst of our life."[29]

This does not mean, however, that every person of faith is also religious. It is possible to have only *implicit* faith in God. Even a person who thinks of himself or herself as an atheist might be a person of implicit faith. Such persons might be rejecting false notions of God, as the Second Vatican Council admitted.[30] In any case, they may be oriented to God through their firm commitment to love, justice, and similar virtues. It is not *explicit* faith in God which saves, but only that faith, explicit *or* implicit, which issues forth in obedience to God's will.[31] On the other hand, the actions of a person with implicit faith alone cannot be called religious except in the widest sense of the term. Religion is a personal, social, and institutional expression of some *explicit* faith in God.[32]

Public Religion

Religion is more than a denominational reality. It can, and often does, become part of a wider culture, transcending denominational and other traditional boundaries, where it assumes a special kind of public character. This has been particularly true of religion in the United States.

Benjamin Franklin may have been the first of the founding fathers to call attention to the public character of religion. In his 1749 *Proposals Relating to the Education of Youth in Philadelphia,* he stressed the study of history, because it would "afford frequent Opportunities of showing the Necessity of a *Publick Religion,* from its Usefulness to the Publick; the Advantages of a Religious Character among private Persons; the Mischiefs of Superstition, &c. and the Excellency of the CHRISTIAN RELIGION above all others antient or modern."[33]

Although one cannot say precisely what Franklin meant by the term "Publick Religion," it is highly probable, given the influence of the Enlightenment on him, that he thought of it as a kind of nonestablished religious culture unencumbered by sectarianism and superstition and dedicated at the same time to freedom and the common weal.[34] Public religion, therefore, was the expression of "enlightened" religious values which are widely shared among citizens of the republic. Its theological and doctrinal content was thin: belief in God, the need to do good, immortality, and rewards and punishments. Franklin viewed these as "essentials of every religion."[35] Together they provided the foundation for what came to be known as The American Way of Life.

Although Franklin and the evangelical Protestants were at some spiritual distance from one another, the latter responded positively to the notion of a public religion. They saw it as a useful vehicle for their project to make America a Christian nation in substance if not in law. The strategy and tactics they employed in pursuit of their goal have been reviewed in various major studies by Ernest Lee Tuveson,[36] Martin E. Marty,[37] and Robert T. Handy.[38]

These Protestants viewed the American republic as the pure political expression of Christianity. For them, although certainly not for Franklin, Christianity was the public religion, or the religion of the republic. This was to be a "nation with the soul of a church"[39] But the Civil War tested this proposition to its extremes. Because the nation itself was perceived as a church, Americans had no recourse to an alternate society ("the" Church). Moreover, the individual churches had already split along sectional lines a decade or more before the war.

Abraham Lincoln articulated the moral dilemmas of such a nation, making of the Union "a virtually mystical cause."[40] His death (on Good Friday!) was even looked upon as a kind of propitiatory event, cleansing the nation of its sins. Throughout the nineteenth century, therefore, (Protestant) Christianity was generally regarded as that public religion which Franklin had thought necessary for any society.

Alexis de Tocqueville had already taken note of this in his widely celebrated *Democracy in America*. "Christianity reigns without obstacles, by universal consent," he wrote. "Thus, while the law allows the American people to do everything, there are things which religion prevents them from imagining and forbids them to dare." Therefore, even though religion "never intervenes directly in the government of American society," it is "the first of their political institutions." And, beyond that, religion is regarded as "necessary to the maintenance oi republican institutions. That is not the view of one class or party among the citizens," Tocqueville concluded, "but of the whole nation; it is found in all ranks."[41] He was especially struck by the fact that his fellow Catholics, including members of the clergy, also favored the arrangement.

In the twentieth century, however, "this cultural hegemony of republican Protestantism in the public realm"[42] was called into question and began to disappear. Many factors were involved: the substantial increase in the Catholic population through immigration, the failure of Woodrow Wilson's essentially Protestant crusade to make the world safe for democracy, the ill-conceived, unenforceable, and Protestant-inspired Prohibition Amendment, the emergence of the Jewish community as co-equal with the Protestant and Catholic communities, the need for pulling together during the Second World War and, therefore, for a more broadly-based public religion, described in Will Herberg's *Protestant-Catholic-Jew*,[43] and, of course, the election of John F. Kennedy as the first Catholic president of the United States in 1960. Over the next 15 years it was this newly ecumenical, and increasingly liberal, public religion which engaged itself in the civil rights and anti-Vietnam War movements and which seemed to countenance a more permissive moral stance toward such issues as abortion, culminating in the 1973 *Roe* v. *Wade* decision of the U.S. Supreme Court.

"As the nation approached the bicentennial celebration of its independence," John Wilson has observed, "it was for the first time manifestly plural in religion and genuinely secular in government."[44]

Many view the vigorous political activity of Protestant fundamentalists in recent years as an attempt to reverse this trend and to install their own version of Protestantism as the religion of the republic.

The new religious right has encountered strong resistance from nonreligious humanists, Jews, mainline Protestants, and Catholics (although many conservative Catholics are sympathetic, and even politically and financially supportive). The Reverend Jerry Falwell and others point out, in their turn, that many who are opposed to the political activities of religious conservatives did not oppose the political activities of liberal clergymen like Martin Luther King, Jr., or William Sloane Coffin, Jr., nor did they object on constitutional grounds to the 1984 presidential candidacy of the Reverend Jesse Jackson.

On the other hand, the religious right has had to be reminded that public religion, whatever its composition, is always an expression of public values. Representatives of the religious right, however, seem still to base their public claims on private values, on what *they* regard as the Word of God according to what *they* regard as its true meaning. "The integrity of the political process requires that such a proposal be resisted," Richard John Neuhaus has written. "Public decisions must be made by arguments that are public in character. A public argument . . . is not derived from sources of revelation or disposition that are essentially private and arbitrary."[45]

Neuhaus has observed that the fundamentalist leaders who rail against secular humanists for creating what he calls the naked public square are themselves collaborators in that creation. "By separating public argument from private belief, by building a wall of strict separationism between faith and reason," he writes, "fundamentalist religion ratifies and reinforces the conclusions of militant secularism."[46]

Their response is the same one that liberal Christians made in an earlier time; namely, that there is, in fact, a core consensus on what is moral, a "moral majority," if you will. But such an approach "won't wash now," Neuhaus asserts. The resolution of major social and political issues requires a public discussion of really fundamental truths. "Such resolution requires a public ethic that we do not now possess," Neuhaus concludes.[47]

John Courtney Murray would not have agreed completely. "The whole premise of the public argument," he insisted, "is that the consensus is real, that among the people everything is not in doubt, but that there is a core of agreement, accord, concurrence, acquiescence. We hold certain truths; therefore we can argue about them. . . . There can be no argument except on the premise, and within a context, of agreement."[48] But Murray, of course, wrote those words at a very different moment in American history: before the social, cultural, political, and religious upheavals of the 1960s and 1970s, that is, before the civil rights movement, before the assassinations of John F. Kennedy, Martin Luther King, Jr., and Robert F. Kennedy, before the anti-Vietnam War protests, before Watergate, before *Roe* v. *Wade,* before the political ascendancy of the religious right, or indeed before *Playboy* became just another magazine on the rack.

If there *is* a public religion in America today, it is impossible to define and difficult to describe. This may explain why the focus of discussion seems to have shifted to a cognate phenomenon, civil religion.

Civil Religion

Benjamin Franklin added the term *public religion* to the American political vocabulary. Jean Jacques Rousseau, philosopher of the French Enlightenment, may be ultimately responsible for its cousin, *civil religion.*[49] The sociologist Robert N. Bellah transplanted it here some 200 years later, in the face of the vast social and cultural transformations of the 1960s.[50]

Bellah had become increasingly concerned about the gradual, then sudden, erosion of traditional American values and wondered aloud how the American experiment could be sustained without them. He called for a return to the true and original meaning of the now-broken covenant between God and the American nation, and to the old dreams and visions by which the republic was born.

Bellah had studied various presidential inaugural addresses, especially John F. Kennedy's, and found in them the basis of a civil religion. There were three places in Kennedy's brief address where the president mentioned God. He referred, first, to the oath he swore "before you and Almighty God," then to God, not the state, as the source of "the rights of man," and, finally, to our duty to make "God's work" here on earth truly our own. In each instance, according to Bellah, President Kennedy was sounding the themes of what had been heretofore an essentially Protestant civil religion: the sovereignty of God over the republic,[51] and our call, individually and collectively, to carry out the divine will on earth. That such themes should have been enunciated by the first Catholic president seemed to Bellah to underline how deeply established they were in the American outlook.

From the earliest years of the American republic, Bellah argued, this civil religion existed as a collection of beliefs, symbols, and rituals with respect to sacred realities. While not antithetical to Christianity, and indeed while sharing much in common with it, the American civil religion was neither sectarian nor in any specific sense Christian. In fact, there was "an implicit but quite clear division of function between civil religion and Christianity."[52] Civil religion was for the public life of the nation, and to that extent came within the provenance of the government. The wide sphere of personal piety and voluntary social action were left to the churches. The churches were neither to control the state nor be controlled by it. Government officials, regardless of their private religious convictions, were to operate under the rubrics of the civil religion whenever they functioned in an official capacity. "This accommodation," Bellah suggested, "was undoubtedly the product of a particular historical moment and of a cultural background dominated by Protestantism of several varieties and by the Enlightenment, but it has survived despite subsequent changes in the cultural and religious climate."[53]

Until the Civil War, the American civil religion focused above all on the event of the Revolution, which was the nation's Exodus from the land across the waters. An age never before known in history was initiated. This was a new millennium.[54] Americans were the Chosen People and America the Promised Land, the New Jerusalem, with a "manifest destiny" to expand its territory and influence throughout North America. The Declaration of Independence and the Constitution were its sacred scriptures and George Washington its divinely appointed Moses who led his people out of the hands of tyranny.

With the Civil War new themes of death, sacrifice, and rebirth entered the civil religion, particularly in the speeches and then in the Good Friday "martyrdom" of Abraham Lincoln. Gettysburg National Cemetery and Arlington National Cemetery became hallowed monuments of the civil religion. The establishment of Memorial Day gave ritual expression to the new themes, and integrated local communities into the national cult. Thanksgiving Day, institutionalized in Lincoln's presidency, served to integrate the family into the civil religion. Veteran's Day (originally Memorial Day) and Washington's and Lincoln's birthdays became minor feasts on civil religion's "liturgical calendar." And nowhere more deliberately than in the public school system was the civil religion transmitted and celebrated. Little wonder that the schoolhouse has become a primary battleground in the current debate about religion and politics in America, a land where the founding fathers must vie with pop music stars for heroic status and where the sports stadium has become the new sacred space.

Is there a difference, finally, between public religion and civil religion? There is—many points of similarity notwithstanding. Public religion refers to the ethico-religious value system *of* the nation, while civil religion refers to the ethico-religious value system that is centered *on* the nation itself.[55] Civil religion is a form or aspect of public religion. In summary, religion is the genus, public religion is a species, and civil religion a subspecies.[56]

Whether civil religion has any greater chance than public religion of surviving the twentieth century will depend, in large measure, on the historical-mindedness of the American people. As the nation's founders and the revolutionary events they inspired recede further into the past, many Americans find it increasingly difficult to relate to the myths that are at civil religion's core. Such myths are alien to some Americans (many Native Americans and blacks, for example) and meaningless to many of the newer and more diverse immigrants. Still other Americans, especially Catholics and Jews, see the new interest in civil religion as "a nostalgic yearning for something that happened to be importantly Protestant."[57]

Church and Sect

It should be unmistakably clear by now that the terms religion and church are not coextensive. The point is theologically and sociologically self-evident, but it cannot be taken for granted in the United States of America, given its history. Neither, if the truth be told, can it be taken for granted within the theological and sociological communities. There are, and always have been, Christian theologians who hold that there is only one, true religion. And if Thomas Luckmann is correct, there are also sociologists who identify religion and church. He himself seems to broaden the definition of church to include all forms of organized and institutionalized religion.[58]

The working assumption here, however, is that religion is a universal category (genus) and that Christianity is one of its particular forms (species), without prejudice to Christianity's traditional truth claims. In this context, therefore, it should be clear that the issue of church and state is narrower than the issue of religion and politics.

But that hardly settles the matter, because Christianity itself is not an undifferentiated religion. There are Catholics (Roman and Eastern-rite alike), Protestants, Anglicans, Orthodox (for example, Russian and Greek), and Oriental Christians (for example, Copts). "The Church" includes all Christians. Within "the Church" there are many churches (Catholic, Lutheran, Presbyterian, Russian Orthodox, Disciples of Christ, and so on). There are still further divisions within those churches (for example, the Lutheran Church in America, the American Lutheran Church, the Lutheran Church–Missouri Synod, the Association of Evangelical Lutheran Churches).

The noun *church*, therefore, can have many different meanings. It can refer to the building in which a congregation worships. It can refer to the religious organization or to the religious community. It can refer simply to the clergy or other church professionals. It can refer to a parish, a diocese, a national body, or to the entire international network of churches of a particular denomination. It can refer, furthermore, not only to a particular denomination but also to the Christian movement and the Christian tradition as a whole.

Sociologists and theologians also make a distinction between church and sect. This distinction is particularly important for our inquiry because it emerges from the effort to understand the relationship between Christianity and the world. The classic study of this relationship was done by Ernst Troeltsch, the German historian and sociologist.[59]

Troeltsch noted that the central ideals and values of Christianity "cannot be realized within this world apart from compromise." The history of Christianity, therefore, "becomes the story of a constantly renewed search for this compromise, and a fresh opposition to this spirit of compromise."[60] Accordingly, the history of the Christian church is best understood in terms of two contradictory yet complementary tendencies: compromise with the world and rejection of the world, accommodation and protest against accommodation. These tendencies, of course, are not peculiar to Christianity. They exist within every movement, religious or political, that bases itself upon an ideal that ethically transcends contemporary conditions and is, as a result, incapable of being realized without some (at least temporary) compromise. For example, no one finds pure Communism even in the Soviet Union.

Compromise or accommodation is embodied in the church; the spirit of rejection of the world and of compromise with it finds expression in the sect. Alongside these two basic forms of religious organization, Troeltsch points to a third—mysticism. This is an individualized response to the conflict between ideals and reality, although it may come to involve small groups of people without permanent form.

The church is an institutional, hierarchical reality; the sect is a voluntary, egalitarian society; and mysticism is a purely personal and experientially inward expression of Christian faith. The church is for all the masses; the sect is for the few; and mysticism seems to fall somewhere in between. The church adjusts itself to the world; the sect stands apart from the world; and mysticism remains generally indifferent to the world as we know it, since its world is the world of the spiritual. Finally, the church possesses and disposes of the objective treasures of grace and redemption; the sect locates these in the future and, for the present, stresses moral law over grace; and mysticism focuses on Christian piety, without regard for specific liturgical forms, doctrines, or traditions.

Catholicism and mainline Protestantism are examples of the church type; the Mennonites and Quakers are examples of the sect type; and individuals like Thomas Paine ("My mind is my church"), Thomas Jefferson, Ralph Waldo Emerson, Henry David Thoreau, and Walt Whitman are examples of the mysticism type, which seems to have developed into a major form in the late twentieth century.[61] This is not to say, however, that Catholicism, for example, is without sectarian impulses, or that sectarian groups are without bureaucracy, or that mysticism types are without any semblance of organization or common purpose. For Troeltsch and for us these are simply convenient categories ("types") that help us identify and sort out differences within Christianity.

Politics

When people say, "The Church should stay out of politics," or, "Religion and politics don't mix," what do they mean? How are they using words like *Church* and *religion?* We've seen already that these terms have different levels of meaning. Are they saying only that clergy ought to stay out of politics, but that laity can legitimately be involved? Do they mean that religious leaders ought never to address public policy issues, or simply that they ought not to engage in certain ("political") public policy debates?

And what do they mean by "politics"? Former Congressman Robert Drinan, a Jesuit priest, was certainly involved in politics, but hasn't Pope John Paul II also been involved: for example, in his application of moral, ecclesiastical, and diplomatic pressures on his native Poland, on Nicaragua, and on Italy? Does politics have to do only with the holding of elective office, as in Father Drinan's case, or does it also include the overt support of candidates, as in the Reverend Jerry Falwell's case?

No member of the National Conference of Catholic Bishops in the United States has ever run for public office, nor has the Conference ever endorsed or supported candidates for office. On the other hand, the Catholic bishops' pastoral letters on the nuclear arms race and on the economy have engaged the attention of public officeholders, diplomats, cabinet officials, business leaders, economists, political commentators, and the news media generally—which is exactly what the bishops had hoped. Are these pastoral letters political? Are all public pronouncements by religious leaders political or only those statements that touch upon foreign policy and the economy? What about interventions on behalf of government aid to private and parochial schools, or initiatives against abortion, pornography, the Equal Rights Amendment, and anti-discrimination statutes affecting homosexuals? Are they not political issues?

The word *politics* is derived from the Greek word *polis,* or city. Although polis was first applied to a large fortified settlement, from the tenth century B.C. the word denoted the Greek city-state, which was small enough to permit face-to-face discussion among all its citizens *(politeis)*.[62]

The word politics, therefore, pertains fundamentally to the affairs of the city. Politics has to do with the public forum and with the process of decision making that occurs there. A political community is one in which its members are "locked together in argument."[63] Running for public office—and all else related to it—is only one aspect of politics. To equate the two would be as inaccurate as equating religion with Lutheranism, and with the American Lutheran Church at that.

A simple definition of politics, however, will not suffice. We need also to take fuller account of its purpose. Otherwise, we cannot begin to understand how there could be any relationship at all between politics, on the one hand, and moral values, religion, and the churches, on the other.

A sweeping review of political theory from Plato to the present discloses a remarkably broad consensus on the purpose of politics. Politics is for the sake of justice. Right from the start, however, in Plato's *Republic,* we have disagreements about the meaning of justice. For Plato justice has to do with the right order of the soul. Thus to understand what he means by justice, we have to take "another and longer road around" to see what he means by the soul.[64]

Whatever justice might be, it is secured only when every member of the polis is doing what he or she is best suited to do. Those who are best suited to do the ruling, for example, are philosophers. (We need offer no other evidence to support the conventional view that Plato's republic is an abstract ideal!)

Aristotle was more the political realist, but he, too, argued that the polis exists to promote the good life, a life of virtue. If Plato's republic was an ideal where harmony reigned, Aristotle's state was marked by inevitable conflicts of interest. Inequality, he argued, is "generally at the bottom of internal warfare in states, for it is their striving for what is fair and equal that men become divided."[65] The good which the state must aim at, therefore, is justice, "and that means what is for the good of the whole community. Now it is pretty clear," Aristotle continues, "that justice in a community means equality for all."[66] Therein is the essential difference between democracy and oligarchy, where inequality in wealth, for example, leads to absolute inequality. In a democracy, all claim equal participation in everything; in an oligarchy, some claim a larger share because "more" is unequal.[67]

With Cicero the field of argument expanded beyond philosophy to theology. There is an unchanging, universally applicable natural law (a law of "right reason in agreement with Nature") which governs even politics, Cicero maintained. The author of that law, and, therefore, the ultimate ground for all political authority, is God, "its promulgator and its enforcing judge."[68]

This shift in the argument was especially pronounced, of course, in Judaism and early Christianity. Judaism saw itself as a people chosen by God and subordinate to the divine will, embodied not only in the Law and the prophets but in the kingship as well. The city of Jerusalem held a central place, because it was here that God chose to dwell (Deuteronomy 12:5,11). It became increasingly the symbol both of religious faith and also of national independence and greatness. It was indeed a holy city (Isaiah 48:2; 52:1; 66:20), the city of God (Psalm 46:4; 48:1,8; 87:3). Even after it had been destroyed, just as the prophets had warned (Ezechiel 22:2–4), the people looked toward a new and better Jerusalem, created not by human hands but by the power of God (Isaiah 60). Significantly, for Christians, too, Jerusalem is more than an earthly city. It is a symbol for the kingdom of God for which Jesus asked his disciples to pray daily. "In the earthly liturgy," the Second Vatican Council's Constitution on the Sacred Liturgy declared, "we share in that heavenly liturgy which is celebrated in the holy city of Jerusalem toward which we journey as pilgrims, and in which Christ is sitting at the right hand of God. . . ."[69]

The essence of Jesus's "political philosophy" is usually reduced to a kind of aphorism: "Render to Caesar the things that are Caesar's, and to God the things that are God's" (Mark 12:17; Matthew 22:21; Luke 20:25). The simplest interpretation of the first half of the saying is that since Caesar's image is on the coin, it must be his. Another explanation is that since some Jews regarded it as unlawful for them even to carry or to look at coins with images of any kind, Jesus was merely saying that such a coin was fit only for Gentiles to handle. A pious Jew should hand it over. The second half of the saying, however, is the more significant. Because "the things that are God's" are much more important than "the things that are Caesar's," his disciples must take care that God is not deprived of what is God's due, whether by giving it to Caesar or to any other person or cause. Accordingly, Jesus not only avoided the dilemma with which he had been confronted, but he turned it to his own advantage to reemphasize the central theme of his whole ministry: "But seek first his kingdom . . ." (Matthew 6:33; also Mark 1:15).[70]

The tradition was carried forward by Paul: "Let every person be subject to the governing authorities. For there is no authority except from God, and those that exist have been instituted by God" (Romans 13:1). Even though Christians are citizens of another world (Philippians 3:20) and enjoy a new freedom in Christ (Galatians 5:1), they are to obey civil authority because it is from God. Paul insists on the divine origin of civil authority three times in the Romans passage (13:1–7).

The distinction between the earthly city and the heavenly city, or kingdom of God, is drawn most sharply in Augustine. Although justice remains the overriding concern of politics, no human state can provide it, and certainly not the recently fallen Roman Empire. Instead, we are all pilgrims on the way to the heavenly kingdom. As followers of Christ and as worshippers of the true God, we belong already to the city of God. This is not to say, however, that the city of God is identical with the Church. Some members of the Church do not belong to the city of God, and some are within the city of God who are not members of the Church. "For in the ineffable foreknowledge of God," he declared in his tract on baptism, "many who seem to be outside are within: many who seem to be within are outside."[71] The earthly city, on the other hand, is guided by self-love and lives according to the flesh. In this life the two cities are inextricably mixed, like the wheat and the tares in the parable. But this is not a wholly negative fact. Even though one can only achieve peace and happiness as a member of the city of God, we still need civil society to procure and administer the material goods we require and which can be used as instruments of the soul. Citizenship in the city of God, therefore, does not abrogate, but preserves and complements, citizenship in a temporal society.[72]

Aristotle's *Politics* and *Ethics* were translated for the first time into Latin during the lifetime of Thomas Aquinas, who modified and re-shaped them in light of Christian revelation and the earlier tradition of Western political thought. Aquinas agreed that men and women are political by nature. The city which we inhabit is more than the sum of its parts and its end is more than the sum of its members' individual interests. The city exists to provide for the common good, which is the promotion of the good life, or virtue, among its citizens. However, because the city is ultimately oriented to the kingdom of God, civil society is not uniquely responsible for the cultivation of moral virtue. It is itself judged by a higher standard to which all human beings must conform themselves.[73]

Among the reformers, John Calvin was closer to Aquinas than was Martin Luther. Calvin agreed that our "true country" is in heaven and that we are only pilgrims on this earth. But we have needs while on pilgrimage and the civil government can provide for them.[74] Luther, on the other hand, had a more negative outlook on civil society ("for the natural world cannot receive or comprehend spiritual things").[75] Like Augustine he drew a sharp distinction between the kingdom of God and the earthly kingdom. The authority exercised by the latter is necessary, otherwise "evil is given free rein and the door is opened for every kind of knavery."[76] But Christians themselves should not "go to law nor use the secular sword among themselves."[77]

With Niccolo Machiavelli, however, political philosophy took a decisive turn away from this classical tradition. Now neither natural nor supernatural virtue would govern the body politic. The idea of the kingdom of God he regarded as the conceit of visionaries. In its place he substituted the principle of expediency. He advised his prince, for example, to inflict all his injuries at once so that he wouldn't have to renew them every day. Then the prince can win over his subjects when he confers benefits. Machiavelli scoffs at "dreamed up republics and principalities which have never in truth been known to exist. . . . The fact is that a man who wants to act virtuously in every way necessarily comes to grief among so many who are not virtuous. Therefore," he concludes, "if a prince wants to maintain his rule he must learn how not to be virtuous, and to make use of this or not according to need."[78]

And so the epithet "Machiavellian" entered the political vocabulary. At the same time, a new, more cynical kind of political theory had been given birth. It shows up almost immediately in Thomas Hobbes, then in Benedict Spinoza and John Locke, and thereafter in many other, less celebrated philosophers, even into our own day.

Hobbes was particularly influential in giving rise to a purely contractual notion of political association. We are not naturally political. We create "cities" out of fear and anxiety. The "state of nature" is so utterly barbaric (where life is "nasty, brutish, and short") that personal safety and property are constantly at risk. We surrender our natural rights and submit to the absolute authority of a sovereign as a preferable alternative to violence and social chaos.

John Locke, who among philosophers had perhaps the greatest single impact on the constitutional shape of the American republic, modified Hobbes's position only slightly. The "state of nature" was good and pure, not evil and wretched. Nor do we cede all of our natural rights to government. On the contrary, government is always to be restrained by a system of checks and balances. But Locke agreed with Hobbes that political association has its origin not in neighborliness or shared values but in expediency. We enter a social contract simply to regulate and preserve property and for the common defense against outside enemies.

Somewhere in between the classical and the contractual, and influenced by both, lies the Enlightenment (in its various forms) and the ideological origins of the American Revolution. The colonists repeated the familiar utopian phrases of the Enlightenment and of English libertarianism, so that what they were saying by 1776 "was familiar in a general way to reformers and illuminati everywhere in the Western world; yet it was different. Words and concepts had been reshaped in the colonists' minds in the course of a decade of pounding controversy—strangely reshaped, turned in unfamiliar directions, toward conclusions they could not themselves clearly perceive."[79]

Whether, and to what extent, the medieval Catholic tradition had any influence on the constitutional history of the United States cannot be established here. John Courtney Murray did argue, however, that constitutionalism was part of a cluster of "ancient ideas, deeply implanted in the British tradition at its origin in medieval times."[80]

There is a blending of ideas and traditions in the Declaration of Independence, the Constitution, and *The Federalist* papers. The Declaration of Independence grounds human and political rights in natural and divine law alike ("the Laws of Nature and of Nature's God"). The Constitution declares in its Preamble that governments exist for justice. And so, too, *The Federalist:* "Justice is the end of government. It is the end of civil society. It ever has been and ever will be pursued until it be obtained, or until liberty be lost in the pursuit."[81]

But some of the particulars are not out of the classical tradition. There is a fundamental distrust of every kind of authority, including religious. Each person must be free, even free to be wrong. Freedom more than order is vulnerable to assault, and vigilance is its price. The use of power over human lives, therefore, is to be jealously guarded and severely restricted. "It was only where there was this defiance, this refusal to truckle, this distrust of all authority, political or social, that institutions would express human aspirations, not crush them."[82]

Politics is concerned with such matters. And so, too, is religion.

Community, Society, Nation, State, Government

There remains only the task of sorting out some of politics' principal components. Politics, we said, pertains to the city (the polis). Is the city the same as society? Is it a community? Is it a nation?

The fundamental component of every political entity is the individual person, whose personality, however, is radically qualified and defined by a relationship with, or some orientation toward, others. This is a somewhat roundabout way of saying that human beings are social beings. Language and sexuality confirm this otherwise self-evident fact.

Families are the basic social unit. They are expressions of what the sociologists call *Gemeinschaft*, which means they are communities. Communities are characterized by "emotional cohesion, depth, continuity, and fullness."[83] They are groups of "people who are socially interdependent, who participate together in discussion and decision making, and who share certain *practices* that both define the community and are nurtured by it."[84]

A nation is also a community, or, more precisely, a community of communities. It is what Bellah calls a "community of memory," a people who do not forget their past, who become aware of themselves through their common history, and who are bound together by a common appreciation for certain exemplary individuals from that past.[85]

Society *(Gesellschaft)*, on the other hand, is systemic. It is a system of interaction. Three people chatting on a street corner do not constitute a society, but three people stranded on an island certainly do. Size, therefore, isn't the crucial variable, even though sociologists think of society as denoting a large complex of human relationships (social, political, cultural, religious, and economic) that are impersonal and contractual, but that are necessary for full human development.[86] In other words, we don't simply decide to live in society. We cannot live apart from it.

More important for our purposes than the distinction between community and society, however, is the distinction between society and state. John Courtney Murray emphasized that the American Proposition rested originally on the principle that the state is distinct from society and is limited in its offices toward society.[87]

Society is composed of many diverse communities and groups: families, voluntary associations, colleges and universities, small businesses, corporations, labor unions, religious organizations and communities, and even governmental agencies. Society, therefore, includes the body politic, of which the state is only the "topmost part."[88] It is the part concerned with the maintenance of law, the promotion of the common welfare, the administration of public affairs, and so forth.

Accordingly, there is a distinction between the common good of society, which all persons and communities within society are morally bound to pursue, and the narrower juridical notion of public order, which is the proper (and limited) concern of the state. The primary reason society needs the state is to instill and maintain justice. The primary duty of the state, therefore, is the enforcement of social justice, "to make up for the deficiencies of a society whose basic structures are not sufficiently up to the mark with regard to justice."[89]

In the so-called modern tradition (post-Machiavelli, Enlightenment), the people are sovereign, but not the state. In the classical tradition, neither the people nor the state is sovereign. God alone is sovereign. But also in the classical tradition the state exists for the people, not vice versa.[90]

There is just one final distinction to make, between the state and the government, or the regime. The government is that portion of the state which exercises the day-to-day responsibility of carrying out the purposes of the state. Governments come and go; states remain. In some countries, like France, there is a distinction between the head of state, the president, and the head of government, the prime minister. In the United States of America the president is both head of state and head of government.

*   *   *

How and in what contexts religion and politics interrelate, and where their interrelationships fit within a broader framework of relationships (for example, between morality and politics, and between church and state) are among the questions addressed in the next chapter.

TWO

CONNECTIONS AND CONTEXTS

THE religion-and-politics relationship is only one of several *kinds*. Working from the general to the particular: there is, first of all, the fundamental relationship between morality and moral values, on the one hand, and politics, on the other.[1] Then there is the somewhat narrower relationship between religion and politics—"narrower" because it is possible to have moral convictions and to behave morally without being religious. President Reagan (and, before him, George Washington) has spoken as if morality and religious faith were inseparable.[2] It is never clear, however, *which* religious faith is supposedly essential to morality.[3]

Thirdly, there is the relationship between a specific religion and politics. Wherever the connection with politics involves Christianity or one of the Christian denominations, the relationship is that of church and state and/or church and society. Fourthly, there is the relationship between religious professionals (for example, priests, ministers, rabbis, nuns, mullahs) and politics.

Issues of church and state and of church and society, therefore, do not necessarily coincide with issues of religion and politics, nor do the latter necessarily coincide with issues of morality and politics. If someone urges an incorporation of moral values in public life, that person isn't necessarily making a case for religious values in public life.[4] Similarly, if someone urges a wider role for religion in public life, that person's argument isn't necessarily limited to the role of the church in politics. Morality is broader than religion, and religion is

27

broader than church. So, too, the church embraces more than its clerical minority.

But not only are there different *kinds* of relationships; there are also different *modes* of relationships. A morally sensitive constituency or a formally religious group could find itself (1) in *opposition* to a given state and/or society (for example, the Bahais in Iran, Christians in many Muslin nations, Jews in medieval Spain); (2) in *union* with a given state and/or society (for example, Iran, Saudi Arabia, Israel, Vatican City State); or (3) in a relationship of greater or lesser *neutrality*, (for example, France, Canada, the United States of America).

Finally, there are different *contexts* for these various kinds and modes of relationships. A given state and/or society may be overtly *secularistic* (the Soviet Union), *theocratic* (Iran), or *secular* and/or *pluralistic* (the United States). Each of these contexts will shape the nature and mode of the relationships between morality and politics, religion and politics, church and society, church and state, and religious professionals (especially clergy) and politics.

This chapter will identify, and distinguish among, the principal layers of the issue addressed in this book, that is, the relationships that exist between morality/moral values and politics, religion and politics, church and society, church and state, and clergy and politics, keeping in mind all the while that these relationships are always affected by variations in mode and context.

Morality/Moral Values and Politics

"The principles of true politics," Edmund Burke wrote, "are those of morality enlarged."[5] On this point, Burke is in the classical tradition of Plato, Aristotle, Augustine, and Aquinas, each of whom argued that the polis exists to enable citizens to become virtuous and lead good lives. Concern for moral values, therefore, is intrinsic to political life.[6]

Few today bother to challenge this principle head-on. They may have little stomach for "philosophical" arguments. Instead many draw a distinction between public and private (or personal) morality. To categorize a moral issue as private is to remove it from the agenda of public debate.

For example, Henry Siegman, executive director of the American Jewish Congress, grants that religious bodies have "not only a right but also an obligation to explicate how moral principles apply to questions of public policy. The constitutional separation of church and state was never intended to insulate questions of public policy from moral considerations."[7]

"Whatever differences exist on such issues as civil rights and war and peace," he continues, "no one questions their character as issues of legitimate public concern. . . . Where Government must legislate for the public good—as distinguished from the private good—religious groups (and nonreligious groups) have every right to seek to influence public policy according to their own understanding of moral imperatives. If they are in disagreement, it is in the free marketplace of ideas that the conflict must be resolved."

Abortion, however, is not self-evidently a matter of public morality, Mr. Siegman argues. Because of our traditions of personal freedom and religious pluralism, therefore, "our religious communities must accept restraints on their political behavior." One notices that he does not repeat the parenthetical reference to nonreligious groups when calling for restraints on political behavior. Is there an assumption here that private, or personal, morality is always and only religious, while public morality may be religious and/or nonreligious? Does political activity against abortion necessarily seek "the vindication of one religious tradition . . . at the expense of another"?

The point here is not to disparage Mr. Siegman's concern or to make light of his argument (in this instance, against an October 1984 statement of the U.S. Catholic bishops, in which the bishops declared that abortion is "a matter of public, not merely private, morality"). But his approach does illuminate an avenue someone might want to take as an escape route from the classical tradition. Label a moral issue "private" or "personal" and you automatically activate the separation-of-church-and-state principle. When religious groups involve themselves in a public debate about such issues of "private" or "personal" morality, they can be accused of seeking to vindicate "one religious tradition . . . at the expense of another." Meanwhile, nonreligious groups that also have a strongly-held position on matters of "private" morality are left waiting somewhere in the wings.

Vice-presidential candidate Geraldine Ferraro and the Senator from Massachusetts Edward M. Kennedy took positions similar to Mr. Siegman's during the 1984 presidential election campaign. Because abortion is an issue of "private" morality, they argued, it "can be settled only in the depths of each individual conscience." Both the state and the church (and religious bodies generally) must respect the "logical line of separation between private morality and public policy."[8]

One of this century's outstanding Protestant theologians, Reinhold Niebuhr, is at least partially responsible for this tendency to draw too sharp a line between public and private morality. His celebrated work, *Moral Man and Immoral Society*,[9] suggested that religious ideals are concerned only with the private sector, and that the highest religious ideal is unselfishness. But unselfishness simply doesn't work as an operating principle of political morality, guided as it is by justice. Indeed, "the religious ideal in its purest form [unselfishness] has nothing to do with the problem of social justice."[10] Moreover, whenever there is an attempt to bring this religious ideal to bear in the public sector, "it results in policies which, from the political perspective, are quite impossible. . . . . It would therefore seem better to accept a frank dualism in morals than to attempt a harmony between the two methods which threatens the effectiveness of both."[11] Many politically liberal people, with little or no formal religious commitment, found this approach highly agreeable. Niebuhr readily won their respect.

An even more radical view is that morality—private *or* public— has nothing to do with politics. This is a position known as liberal constitutionalism or philosophical liberalism (to be distinguished always from political liberalism, with which politicians like Senator Kennedy have been identified). With its philosophical roots in Hobbes, Locke, Hume, and Adam Smith, liberalism holds that a good society can result from the actions of citizens motivated by self-interest alone (particularly economic self-interest). It is the so-called contract theory of politics, to which we have already referred. Its exponents stand at various points on the political spectrum: from political liberals like John Rawls and Lawrence Kohlberg to political conservatives like Robert Nozick and Milton Friedman.[12] They understand social and political relations as contracts entered into by individuals seeking personal security and gain. The state exists to enforce the terms of the contract with fairness.

Robert Bellah has characterized the contract theory of politics as "the most wildly utopian idea in the history of political thought,"[13] and his colleague, William M. Sullivan, agrees. He labels it "a highly utopian teaching masquerading as common sense."[14] In a world of limited resources, various groups are struggling to increase their own relative advantage.[15] Accordingly, the improvement in the condition of the less advantaged can no longer be left to market forces unguided by a political commitment to the general welfare. "The ambiguity of America's greatness," Sullivan argues, "has always been the coexistence of an economic life of private self-interest with a public commitment to justice and the common welfare."[16]

Between the classical view of Plato, Aristotle, Augustine, and Aquinas, and the contract theories of Hobbes, Locke, Hume, and Adam Smith (and absorbing something from each) lies the theory of republican virtue, or civic republicanism. The republican tradition, while historically friendly to religion and religious values, has been able to separate morality from religion. Unlike President Reagan and many others, the republican tradition does not assume that morality depends on religion for its very existence, and, unlike the philosophical liberals, it does not reduce life in the polis to merely contractual and procedural arrangements. The republican tradition denies the liberal notion that individuality exists outside of, or prior to, social relationships. Furthermore, the protection of human dignity depends upon the moral quality of social relationships. Citizenship is a matter of shared initiative and responsibility among persons committed to mutual care.

The relationship between morality and politics, therefore, is not the same as the relationship between religion and politics, because concern for morality and moral values in politics is not dependent upon some religious faith or commitment. The ancients, Plato and Aristotle in particular, wedded morality and politics, without rooting the former in any religious tradition.[17] "A state," Aristotle wrote, "is also something more than a pact of mutual protection or an agreement to exchange goods and services. . . . that which is genuinely and not just nominally called a state must concern itself with virtue."[18]

Religion and morality are separable. No one has made the argument more forcefully than John Stuart Mill, the nineteenth-century British philosopher. First, he separated morality from the Christian religion. Many "essential elements of the highest morality," he wrote, were not provided for, nor intended to be provided for, "in the recorded deliverances of the Founder of Christianity." It is "a great error," therefore, "to persist in attempting to find in the Christian doctrine that complete rule for our guidance which its Author intended it to sanction and enforce, but only partially to provide."[19] He broadened the argument in his *Utilitarianism* to include all religion.

For Mill morality is determined by the consequences of human acts. An action is right if, and only if, it brings about a greater balance of good over bad consequences than any other act open to the agent. He also believed that only pleasure is intrinsically good and only pain intrinsically bad. Belief in the supernatural origin of morality may once have helped it to gain acceptance, but it is no longer needed or even effective in maintaining this acceptance. Indeed, "whatever aid religion, either natural or revealed, can afford to ethical investigation, is as open to the utilitarian moralist as to any other."[20] Morality and religion were also separated by the American philosopher John Dewey.[21]

The founding fathers seem to have held to the same idea. Whether or not they were influenced more by the Scottish Enlightenment than by John Locke,[22] the common philosophical source was the Enlightenment, for which "the universe was comprehensible by reason and becoming more so."[23] "We hold these Truths to be self-evident," the Declaration of Independence declared, "that all Men are created equal, that they are endowed by their Creator with certain unalienable Rights, that among these are Life, Liberty, and the Pursuit of Happiness. . . ." Rights that can be known only through revelation are not self-evident.

This confidence in reason's power to decipher the moral code of the universe was part of the new nation's moral and intellectual state, what Tocqueville called "the habits of the heart."[24] It is a heart that "easily inclines toward benevolence. . . . What had been calculation becomes instinct. By dint of working for the good of his fellow citizens, he in the end acquires a habit and taste for serving them."[25]

No religious tradition may seem more alien to the utilitarianism of Mill, the situationalism of Dewey, or the enlightened reasoning of the founding fathers than Catholicism. The Catholic tradition, however, agrees fully with them on the fundamental principle that morality and religion are separable.[26] There is indeed a source of moral insight which is independent of revelation and religious doctrine. That source is called natural law.

John Courtney Murray had even insisted that the American Republic "was conceived in the tradition of natural law" and that "it furnished the basic materials for the American consensus."[27] As we reflect on this law "written on [our] hearts" (Romans 2:15), we may deduce many political principles, for example, that the community is the source of all political authority, or that the ruler's authority is limited to the political order, because the whole of human life is not absorbed in the polis.

But natural law cannot provide a detailed blueprint for personal or political behavior. That is not its function. Nor can it settle enormously complicated technical problems, especially in the economic order. It is only a "skeleton law," Murray suggested. Flesh and blood must be added to it "by that heart of the political process, the rational activity of man, aided by experience and by high professional competence."[28] This "dynamic order of reason in man, that clamors for expression with all the imperiousness of law, has its origin and sanction in an eternal order of reason whose fulfillment is the object of God's majestic will."[29]

Few Catholic philosophers of Murray's generation gave so spirited defense of natural law as Jacques Maritain did. In *Man and the State*[30] he argued that natural law alone can provide the rational justification for such documents as the United Nation's International Declaration of Rights, published in 1948, and even for democracy itself. Indeed, the history of human rights is bound to the history of natural law.[31]

Nowhere, however, has the Catholic tradition's affirmation of natural law been more explicit than in Pope John XXIII's 1963 encyclical, *Pacem in Terris*. Significantly, it was the first such papal letter to be addressed not only to Catholics but "to all men of good will." The pope could presume to do so because he grounded his teachings not on the Bible or on Catholic doctrine alone but on that law which is written on all human hearts.

The opening section is a virtual bill of rights, rooted in the dignity of the human person. From that principle of human dignity follows the right to life and to a worthy standard of living; the right to respect and to a good reputation; the right to freedom in the search for truth and in expressing and communicating opinions; the right to a basic education; the right to worship God, publicly and privately; the right to choose freely one's state of life; the right to work and to proper working conditions; the right to private property; the right of assembly and of association; the right to move about and take up residence within one's own country, and the right to emigrate to other countries; the right to take an active part in public affairs and to a juridical protection of one's rights.

In Catholic social doctrine, however, with every right there is a correlative duty: "And rights as well as duties find their source, their sustenance and their inviolability in the natural law which grants or enjoins them. . . . Now an order of this kind, whose principles are universal, absolute and unchangeable, has its ultimate source in the one true God, who is personal and transcends human nature."[32]

Although some Catholic theologians have questioned the capacity of the natural-law ethic to engage the interest of those outside the Catholic theological tradition,[33] there was evidence at Murray's, Maritain's, and John XXIII's time, as there is today, of a parallel concern for the development or the reconstruction of a public philosophy.[34]

Walter Lippmann, for example, deplored the "eclipse" of the public philosophy, which he identified with natural law.[35] Its "sovereign principle" is "that we live in a rational order in which by sincere inquiry and rational debate we can distinguish the true and the false, the right and the wrong."[36] Lippmann and Murray agreed that the free political institutions of the Western world were conceived and established by those who believed that "honest reflection on the common experience of mankind would always cause men to come to the same ultimate conclusions."[37] The crisis of the liberal democracies, he suggested, was precipitated by a memory loss. They had forgotten the wisdom of the ancients, the tradition of civility. And yet "a society can be progressive only if it conserves its traditions."[38]

William M. Sullivan issued a similar call for a public philosophy some 27 years later.[39] He defined it as "a tradition of interpreting and delineating the common understandings of what the political association is about and what it aims to achieve. . . . [and] this requires developing anew the understanding that dignity, mutual concern, and a sense of responsibility shared by all members of the society are essential to a morally worthwhile life."[40]

A public philosophy becomes "republican" at the point where people realize that "this is necessarily a public concern, precisely because human life is interdependent, requiring mutual trust even for individual survival."[41] By contrast, Sullivan argued, a liberal philosophy takes "legal equality as a means to enforce fairness in the competition for gain in civil society and as a bulwark against arbitrary rule." It draws "a firm distinction between public and private realms, thereby gaining autonomy for religious and intellectual as well as economic pursuits." But it also clears the public realm of all but those formal institutions which exist to umpire and negotiate conflicts of interest within civil society, thereby "draining public life of intrinsic morality and significance."[42]

The argument is advanced with equal force in the widely discussed *Habits of the Heart*, co-authored by William Sullivan, Robert Bellah, and others. "The search for common moral understandings continues even in the face of the assertion that they are impossible," they observe.[43] The therapeutically inclined American, they suggest, stoutly defends expressive individualism. Because each individual is utterly unique, there can be no common moral ground and, therefore, no public relevance of morality outside the sphere of minimal procedural rules and obligations not to injure someone else. But there is "no moment when the therapeutically inclined sound more similar than when they are asserting their uniqueness. In thinking they have freed themselves from tradition in the pursuit of rationality and personal authenticity, they do not understand the degree to which their views are themselves traditional. Nor do they realize that their minimalist insistence on justice, fairness, and respect for individuals is rooted in a much richer defense of the same things in the religious and civic philosophical traditions."[44]

In summary: morality and politics do mix, and without necessarily involving religion at all. The question is: *whose* morality, and by what process is it to be incorporated into the legal structures of the polis? It is clear that only that morality which society accepts as its own has a realistic chance of being translated into public policy—unless, of course, an unresponsive state refuses to do so or seeks to impose an alternative.

This is not to say that society's morality is beyond challenge, or that minority views are to be absorbed by the majority. When Mario M. Cuomo, governor of New York, was criticized for his major address on the subject of religion and politics at the University of Notre Dame, he sought to clarify this very point. "I did *not* say that anyone's religious values or moral codes should be surrendered to a popular consensus in order to avoid disagreement and foster harmony," he insisted at St. Francis College in Brooklyn some two weeks later. "I did *not* say that what is popular must be good. Nor that the community's consensus on what is right or wrong should never be challenged.

"What I *did* say," he continued, "and what I repeat is that if we are serious about making certain values a part of the public morality, part of the statutes and laws that bind everyone, there must first be a public consensus; that's the way laws are made in a democratic society."[45]

And what of the moral responsibility of trying to create that consensus? Or of the consensus that already exists against abortion-on-demand? These are the points on which some observers, particularly Catholic pastoral leaders and theologians, had challenged Governor Cuomo. They argued that a public official who is firmly convinced of a particular moral principle, but who believes that it cannot feasibly be translated into law at the present, nevertheless has an obligation to attempt to persuade others to his or her view, and also to exploit whatever measure of consensus already exists. Otherwise, the public official is guilty of "public passivity."[46]

If the reply is that we cannot impose our "religious" views on others, the argument moves back to the beginning. There is a distinction between morality and religion.

Religion and Politics

According to Finley Peter Dunne's Mr. Dooley, "Religion is a quare thing. Be itself it's all right. But sprinkle a little pollyticks into it an' dinnymite is bran flour compared with it. Alone it prepares a man f'r a better life. Combined with pollyticks it hurries him to it."

Mr. Dooley's sentiments are probably shared by millions of Americans, especially after the 1984 presidential election campaign. Millions of others, not sharing his point of view *or* his sense of humor, might resent the implication. Religious people, they would insist, have as much right to participate in the political process as any other citizens. If religious people think that moral values which are based solely on their own understanding of divine revelation ought to be embodied in law or public policy, they have every right to try to make a case.

This argument may be consistent with the letter of the Constitution (unless, of course, the public embodiment of certain religious values were shown to constitute the establishment of a particular religion and to infringe upon others' "free exercise" of religion), but it clearly violates its spirit. It would inject religious factionalism into the affairs of the polis.

James Madison had warned against factionalism as the great enemy of public peace. He defined a faction as "a number of citizens, whether amounting to a majority or a minority of the whole, who are united and actuated by some common impulse of passion, or of interest, adverse to the rights of other citizens, or to the permanent and aggregate interests of the community."[47]

Because factionalism is rooted in human nature, its causes cannot be removed, only its effects. In a pure democracy, if a faction happens to include a majority, the public good and the rights of other citizens can be sacrificed to its ruling passion or interest. Only in a republic can factionalism properly be contained, because government is administered by a small number of representatives elected by the rest and, secondly, because there are a greater number of citizens and a greater extent of territory than in a pure democracy. The larger the sphere, the greater the variety of parties and interests. In a republic, even if one faction did assume great strength, it would still be very difficult for that faction to discover that strength and for its members to act in unison with one another.

Madison included religious groups in his concern about factionalism, and his solution for religious factionalism was more or less the same: the encouragement of a multiplicity of religious bodies within a republican form of government. "A religious sect may degenerate into a political faction in part of the Confederacy," he noted, "but the variety of sects dispersed over the entire face of it must secure the national councils against any danger from that source."[48]

In light of Madison's analysis, it would seem that religious groups can best support the republican experiment by distinguishing always between moral values whose validity is grounded in their own confessional understanding of revelation, and moral values whose validity can be established, in principle, by reasoning and argument unrelated to sacred texts and doctrines. Here again, the distinction between morality and religion is shown to be crucial. But it is a distinction more often neglected than honored.

J. Bryan Hehir is right: "For a society like ours . . . the topic religion and politics is shorthand for the relationship of moral argument and public policy."[49] That is not the way it should be. Indeed, that failure to perceive the difference between morality and religion is at the root of most of the confusion in debates about religion and politics in general, and about specific issues like abortion. This was especially the case in the 1984 presidential election campaign.

What, then, is the relationship between religion and politics? Edmund Burke declared, in agreement with Cicero, that "religion is the basis of civil society, and the source of all good and comfort."[50] For Burke, however, that meant the establishment of Protestantism as the state religion.[51] Is it impossible, therefore, to talk about the relationship of religion and politics without limiting the term *religion* to one particular religion, in this case Protestant Christianity? If it is all too common to confuse the issue of morality and politics with the issue of religion and politics, is it not also common to confuse the issue of religion and politics with the issue of church and state? The term *church,* after all, is a Christian term.

Alexis de Tocqueville did not limit his own discussion to the Christian religion when he wrote admiringly of the place of religion in nineteenth-century American political life. Although religion never intervenes directly into the government of American society, he observed, it is nevertheless "the first of [America's] political institutions."[52] "I do not know," he continued, "if all Americans have faith in their religion . . . but I am sure that they think it necessary to the maintenance of republican institutions. That is not the view of one class or party among the citizens, but of the whole nation; it is found in all ranks."[53]

Tocqueville, like George Will, regarded religion as in a kind of partnership with politics. Both religion and politics have as their purpose "the steady emancipation of the individual through the education of his passions."[54] Equality, on the one hand, brings with it the temptation to pursue one's own interests at the expense of others', while religion inspires "diametrically contrary urges."

"Every religion," Tocqueville observed, "places the object of man's desires outside and beyond worldly goods and naturally lifts the soul into regions far above the realm of the senses." Furthermore, religion imposes on its adherents some obligations toward the rest of humankind, drawing the religious person away from self-centeredness. "Thus religious peoples are naturally strong just at the point where democratic peoples are weak. And that shows how important it is for people to keep their religion when they become equal."[55]

But Tocqueville is not without his critics. George Armstrong Kelly, for example, has suggested that Tocqueville underestimated the strength and lasting impact of sectarianism: the Millerites, the Pentecostalists, and the Mormons.[56] He also seemed to believe that an essentially Calvinist rigor in religious belief and training, tempered by the civil doctrines of the Enlightenment, was a necessary moral ingredient in American political and social life. Kelly thinks that Tocqueville may have been mistaken about this even in his own time. In any case, Tocqueville's analysis would surely not apply to America today, where, as Robert Bellah and others have shown in their *Habits of the Heart* report, individualism is far more powerful a social force than civic republicanism. Robert Coles has described the current condition as one where "politics becomes, along with everything else, a matter of impulse, whim, fancy, exuberant indulgence, bored indifference, outright angry rejection."[57] Tocqueville, Kelly concludes, would have been "disquieted" by the results we have obtained and by the way we have gotten here.

Accordingly, Professor Kelly is more favorably disposed to Max Weber's analysis than Tocqueville's. Religion and politics together are afflicted with "disenchantment." Hobbes' philosophy has triumphed in the spaces of society. There are no "mysterious incalculable forces" that come into play either in religion or in politics. Everything can be mastered in principle by calculation.

What Weber perceived to be going on in the world at large proceeded more slowly in America for various reasons, not least of which was the nation's early insulation from international strain and its "characteristic resistance to higher flights of the intellect." But now disenchantment has, by stages, visited America. Religion and politics alike have been privatized and secularized. Thus, religion is most easily marketed when it can be shown to be relevant to one's private life and when emptied of theological and doctrinal content. Citizenship, on the other hand, has been reduced to a "cheap commodity." We speak easily and naturally of the "private citizen." In the interest of rational predictability administration has been substituted for government, and justice has been devalued from a civic virtue to a matter of procedural fairness.

Pessimistic appraisals of this sort were already circulating in the mid-1960s. Many discussions at the time were shaped by a theory of secularization, most prominently articulated in Bryan Wilson's *Religion in Secular Society*.[58] If religion had any continuing impact at all, according to this theory, it was in the private sectors of life: in family affairs and in personal lifestyles, for example.

"Twenty years later," Benton Johnson has argued, "it is clear that this broad picture of the retreating influence of religion in American life is seriously distorted."[59] Peter Berger agrees: "Modernity may not be as antagonistic to religion as had previously been asserted. . . . Both the extent and the inexorability of secularization may have been exaggerated by earlier analysts."[60] Berger cites several instances of what he calls "countersecularity": the upsurge of religious movements in the Third World, the revival of religion in the Soviet Union, the counterculture movement in the United States, and the resurgence of Evangelical Protestantism in America. Harvey Cox makes a similar argument for "antimodernity" in his *Religion in the Secular City*,[61] focussing his attention on a newly resurgent Protestant Fundamentalism and on Latin American liberation theology.

Martin Marty takes a sensible middle course. There are in the United States today *both* an all-pervasive religiousness *and* a persistent secularity. Unless theorists and theologians reckon with this fact, he warns, they will always "be left stranded with each cultural shift, in search of theories to match their perceptions."[62] Legally, America is a secular, nonreligious culture, albeit pluralistic. But that culture houses an impressive number of religious institutions that attract the loyalties of three out of five citizens, and two out of five participate in weekly religious services. To be sure, the old consensus is gone, but a new one hasn't as yet taken its place. As we await it, traditionalist religion thrives. "Through it all," Marty concludes, "a paradigm that seems ambivalent and equivocal, combining as it does both religious and secular elements, does justice to the viscous aspects of American cultural life."[63]

The relationship between the religious and the secular is not the same as the relationship between the religious and the political, but there is a close parallel between them. Both religion and politics are "indifferently anchored" in both society and culture and "cut across these boundaries."[64] The First Amendment has to be read in this light. It only holds that religious institutions are to expect neither discrimination nor favoritism in the exercise of their civic responsibilities. Insofar as there is any element of *separation* (a word which does not appear in the Amendment), it applies only to religious bodies as institutions and to the state as an institution. "It was never intended to separate [religion] from the wider society or religion from culture,"[65] Cardinal Joseph Bernardin has argued. Accordingly, there is "a legitimate secularity of the political process, and there is a legitimate role for religious and moral discourse in our nation's life."[66] The challenge, therefore, is to recognize and respect the existence of the two spheres (religious and secular/political), without confusing or absolutely separating them. This had been Walter Lippmann's concern in *The Public Philosophy*. According to Lippmann, "the radical error of the modern democratic gospel is that it promises, not the good life of this world, but the perfect life of heaven. The root of the error is the confusion of the two realms."[67] In the "traditions of civility," an expression central to Lippmann's philosophy, the two realms are "inseparable but disparate." We must work out our destiny "in the balance, which is never fixed finally between the two."[68] This tradition, he argued, is challenged from many sides: by hedonists who would withdraw wholly *into* the realm of existence without regard for higher values; by ascetics who would withdraw *from* the realm of existence, waiting for the end of the world and their own release from mortality; by primitive Chiliasts who live in the expectation that the millennium is near at hand; and by modern perfectionists who believe that by their own revolutionary acts men and women can make themselves the creators of heaven on this earth. Each of these errors stems from the same fundamental disorder: the failure to recognize that the two realms cannot be fused or separated.[69]

John Courtney Murray, working out of a similar philosophical framework, applied this reasoning even more deliberately to the First Amendment. Its provisions regarding religion ("no . . . establishment," and "free exercise") were not articles of faith but articles of peace, Murray insisted.[70] They are the work of lawyers, not theologians or even of political theorists. And they were good law. Many Americans were nonbelievers who would have been placed at a political disadvantage had religion, any religion, been legally established. Moreover, there were already many denominations (a fact that James Madison applauded, of course). Which denomination would be preferred?

For Murray, as for Lippmann, therefore, "the root of the matter is this distinction of the spiritual and temporal orders and their respective jurisdictions."[71] The distinction is to be neither exaggerated nor abolished. Government is not a judge of religious truth, and parliaments are not to play the theologian. Government represents the truth of society as it is. The truth is that American society is religiously pluralist. As representative of a pluralist society, wherein religious faith is necessarily free, government undertakes to represent the principle of freedom.[72]

It might be illuminating, finally, to compare the views of two important politicians representing different generations of American Catholics: John F. Kennedy and Mario M. Cuomo. In his address on church and state before the Greater Houston Ministerial Association on September 12, 1960, candidate Kennedy adopted a strongly separationist position. "I believe in an America," he said, "where the separation of church and state is absolute. . . ."[73] (One notices again the taken-for-granted equation of "religion" with "church.") "I believe in a President," he continued, "whose views on religion are his own private affair. . . ."[74]

Kennedy, of course, spoke at a different time and in a different context from Cuomo. His audience of Protestant ministers was opposed to the mixing of religion and politics, even for themselves and their own churches. They wanted to be reassured by John Kennedy that his Catholic faith would not interfere with his constitutional obligations. He gave them reassurances in abundance. Some commentators, in fact, have argued that he went too far, exaggerating the gap between religion and politics by overemphasizing the private character of faith.[75] President Kennedy's former speech writer, Theodore C. Sorensen, expressed a different point of view during the 1984 presidential election campaign, in the midst of the controversy over the place of religion in politics: "How ironic," he wrote, "that the same pious preachers who extracted these pledges from John F. Kennedy now embrace Ronald Reagan for violating every one of them."[76]

Governor Cuomo's address came nearly 25 years later before a friendly audience of fellow Catholics at the University of Notre Dame.[77] But that was only a minor difference. The political situation which Cuomo faced was almost 180 degrees from the one which Kennedy had confronted. By 1984 many Protestant ministers had become deeply engaged in the political arena: Jerry Falwell, Marion G. (Pat) Robertson, and Jesse L. Jackson, for example. They were either active candidates themselves, as in Jackson's case, or were openly supportive of candidates, as in Falwell's and Robertson's cases. And a few Catholic prelates also seemed to draw close to the line: New York's Archbishop John J. O'Connor and Boston's Archbishop Bernard F. Law (both of whom were promoted to the rank of cardinal the following year). Although neither had actually endorsed anyone, their public statements were interpreted as clear nonendorsements of certain candidates.

Governor Cuomo offered a more nuanced position than candidate Kennedy.[78] "We are a religious people," he said at Notre Dame, "many of us descended from ancestors who came here expressly to live their religious faith free from coercion or repression. But we are also a people of many religions, with no established church, who hold different beliefs on many matters."[79] This doesn't mean that religion has to be kept completely separate from public life, as John F. Kennedy had implied. "That values happen to be religious values," Governor Cuomo argued, "does not deny them acceptability as a part of [a public] consensus. But it does not require their acceptability, either."[80] Accordingly, "all religiously based values do not have an *a priori* place in our public morality."[81] It is the community that decides whether and when religiously based values should be incorporated into public policy. But this cannot happen in the absence of a consensus.

"Way down deep," he continued, "the American people are afraid of an entangling relationship between formal religions, or whole bodies of religious belief, and government. Apart from constitutional law and religious doctrine, there is a sense that tells us it is wrong to presume to speak for God or to claim God's sanction of our particular legislation and His rejection of all other positions."[82]

Some Catholics who applauded Governor Cuomo's articulation of the principles nonetheless criticized the way he applied them to the abortion issue. Abortion is neither a Catholic issue nor a religious issue, they insisted. Opposition to abortion is rooted not in Catholic doctrine but in natural law.[83] The complaint, in other words, was that Governor Cuomo had tended to confuse a morality-and-politics issue with a religion-and-politics issue.[84] If he had, he was certainly not alone in doing so.

Church and State/Church and Society

The 1984 presidential election campaign confused rather than clarified the issue of religion and politics. Key terms were thrown together without proper distinctions: morality, religion, church, state, society.

We have made the point that morality is not identical with religion. It is possible to be moral without being religious (just as it is possible, of course, to be religious without being moral).

If morality has been confused with religion, so has religion been confused with church.[85] Again and again, participants in the debate about religion in U.S. public life have cast the discussion in church-and-state terms, as if religion were identical with Christianity.[86] This has been true not only of politicians and journalists but of religious leaders as well, some of whom believe that the United States of America is a Christian nation or at least one founded on so-called Judeo-Christian principles.[87]

The confusion has not been limited to the morality/religion/church side of the dialectic. State and society have also been collapsed into one. The separation of church and *state* has been understood as the separation of church and *society,* even though the state is only a part of society. The church-and-state relationship is of a much more limited kind. It governs the juridical relationship of the institution of the church and the institution of the state.

Beyond the church-and-state relationship there exists a whole range of issues governing the church's presence and role in the wider society. The activity of the U.S. Catholic bishops on nuclear weapons and abortion, for example, is often directed toward policies which are established by the state, but the bishops' involvement in these issues occurs in and through the channels a democratic society provides for public debate.

In such a society voluntary associations play a key role, providing a buffer between the state and the citizenry as well as a structured means of influencing public policy. In the U.S. political system the church itself is a voluntary association. As such it raises and addresses the moral dimensions of public issues, and also facilitates the engagement of its own members in the public discussion of these issues. Accordingly, the U.S. Catholic bishops consciously addressed two distinct, but overlapping, audiences in their pastoral letters on peace and the economy: the wider civil community and the ecclesiastical community of fellow Catholics. Precisely as a voluntary association the church is situated to join the public debate in this dual fashion.[88]

We take it as a matter of constitutional principle that Christians in the United States have as much right as any other citizens to participate fully in the public life of the nation and in U.S. society generally. We also take it as a matter of constitutional principle that the church in the United States has as much right as any other voluntary association to participate fully in the public life of the nation and in U.S. society generally.[89] Therefore, what is primarily at issue here is the relatively narrow relationship of church and state, not the broader relationship of church and society. But it is practically impossible to separate completely the former from the latter.

There are various typologies, schemata, or models that help identify the different kinds of church-and-state (as well as church-and-society) relationships. As we have already seen, Ernst Troeltsch proposed three great types of Christian religious institutionalization: church, sect, and mysticism. The church-type adjusts to the state, the sect-type resists the state, and the mysticism-type is generally indifferent to the state. The church-type has always been present in the United States, but it has never been dominant in pure form. Catholicism, for example, is clearly of the church-type, but it had to function for a long while as a kind of sect because of cultural alienation and bigotry. The sect-type has also been present from the beginning and has been in many ways the dominant mode of American Christianity. The mysticism-type, finally, is also not new, but it has burgeoned as a major form in the late twentieth century. The first is politically accommodationist, the second is politically dissident, and third is politically diffident.[90] For Troeltsch, the church-type is superior to the other two.[91]

H. Richard Niebuhr's classic study, *Christ and Culture*,[9] offers a larger schema, but one that has to be adapted to fit the church-and-state problematic: Christ against culture, Christ of culture, Christ above culture, Christ and culture in paradox, and Christ as transformer of culture. The first is the sectarian option, to which Troeltsch also referred. The second is the liberal option, an extreme form of the church-type. Accommodation becomes compromise with, even surrender to, the prevailing political and cultural values. The third is a synthesis of two strands: the church, like Christ, is at the same time of this world and not of this world. It can adapt to a given culture (what is called today "inculturation") and yet not become completely identified with it. Niebuhr identifies this type with St. Thomas Aquinas and the Catholic tradition generally. The fourth is dualistic, sharply dividing one realm from the other. There are two separate and distinct kingdoms, one of God and the other of humankind. The church's attention must focus on the former, not the latter. Niebuhr links this view with St. Paul and Martin Luther. The fifth is conversionist. The church is a change agent, healing and renewing what sin has wounded. Niebuhr associates this approach with the Fourth Gospel, St. Augustine's *City of God*, and John Calvin.[93]

Catholics have also developed models. For John Courtney Murray there are two: one dualistic, the other monistic.

Dualism distinguishes between church and state. One type insists on the primacy of the church over the state (because the spiritual order has primacy over the temporal), without prejudice to the integrity of each. There is a relationship that admits of cooperation. A second type subordinates one to another. Still another keeps them completely apart.

Monism collapses the distinction entirely. Either the state becomes an adjunct of the church (as in some forms of medieval Christendom) or the church becomes a department of the state (as in some Communist nations).

Murray argued that dualism isn't natural, indeed that its establishment involved a certain dislocation of the natural order, wherein political power would be stronger without the competing power of the church. "This is why," he suggested, "the tension produced by the dualism has constantly shown a tendency to dissolve into some manner of monism."[94]

Murray rejected monism of either kind, that is, the absorption of the state into the church as well as the absorption of the church into the state. His acceptance of dualism, however, was nuanced. He rejected both absolute separation, as in the case of Continental Liberalism, and union, in the sense of the *ancien régime*. He prefered *relation* over *separation*, a term he called meaningless, and over *union*, a term he called misleading.

"The relation of Church and State," he wrote, "is not constitutive of the being of either or of a third being somehow distinct from both. The relation is in the order of action. It implies a dynamic relatedness of distinct purposes and of distinct lines of action toward these purposes . . . a co-operation that respects the integrity of both operative principles and of their specific operations . . . towards one common . . . end and good, which is the perfection of man in the distinct but related orders of nature and grace."[95]

In his later work, *We Hold These Truths*, Murray argued that the American Republic rejected Jacobin Liberalism in favor of the way of cooperation. The American thesis is that government is not juridically omnicompetent. Its powers are limited. It is a theory that is "recognizably part of the Christian political tradition, and altogether defensible in the manner of its realization under American circumstances."[96] If it can be said that the American constitutional system exaggerates the distinction between church and state by its self-denying ordinances, Murray concluded, it must also be said that "government rarely appears to better advantage than when passing self-denying ordinances."[97]

Avery Dulles's *Models of the Church*,[98] like H. Richard Niebuhr's *Christ and Culture*, has to be adapted if it is to illuminate the various levels and kinds of church-state relationships. (Both, however, are more immediately applicable to the relationship between church and society.) Dulles proposes five models: church as institution, church as mystical communion, church as sacrament, church as herald, and church as servant.

The institution model emphasizes the church's self-sufficiency over against other institutions, including the state, and tends to sharpen the distinction between the saved of the church and the unsaved of the world outside. Because of its strongly hierarchical and clerical bias, this model has tended to reduce the church-and-state relationship to one of hierarchy and state. The institution model is similar to Troeltsch's church-type and H. R. Niebuhr's Christ-above-culture category.

The mystical communion model understands the church as a vast network of interpersonal relationships, created and sustained by the Holy Spirit. Although not explicitly anti-political, this model is open to an apolitical form of Christian existence. It bears some resemblance to Troeltsch's mysticism-type and to H. R. Niebuhr's Christ and culture in paradox.

The sacrament model presents the church as "a reality imbued with the hidden presence of God" (to use the words of the late Pope Paul VI at the beginning of the second session of the Second Vatican Council), a visible sign of an invisible reality. Its mission is to convert the world primarily through its own example, that is, by allowing the hidden divine reality it embodies to be seen and experienced by others. The sacrament model, which is the most Catholic of the five, corresponds to no single one of Troeltsch's types, but to all three. At the same time it is closest in meaning to H. R. Niebuhr's Christ of culture.

The herald model is, for Dulles, the most Protestant of the five. According to this model, the primary mission of the church is the proclamation of the Word of God to the whole world. It is a view associated especially with the late Karl Barth, for whom the church always stands apart from the world, announcing a God who is "wholly other" than the world. The church, therefore, has no political agenda. This model bears some similarities to Troeltsch's sect-type and to H. R. Niebuhr's Christ against culture and Christ and culture in paradox.

Finally, there is the servant model, which is the most overtly political of all. The church exists for the sake of the kingdom of God, and that kingdom is one of justice and peace as well as of personal holiness and grace. This understanding of the church is reflected in liberation theology. The church is prepared to work with or against the state in the pursuit of its missionary agenda. The servant model is perhaps closest to Troeltsch's church-type and exactly parallels H. R. Niebuhr's Christ-the-transformer-of-culture approach.

Dulles later added a sixth model, the church as a community of disciples.[99] On the surface, this model seems closest to Troeltsch's sect-type and mysticism-type, and to H. R. Niebuhr's Christ against culture and Christ above culture. But Dulles' sixth model is more comprehensive. He shows how the community-of-disciples model actually retrieves and synthesizes the positive features of the other five models without carrying forward their respective liabilities.[100]

Finally, there are four distinctively Catholic models proposed by David J. O'Brien, of the College of the Holy Cross, Worcester, Massachusetts.[101] He calls them "options." The first is that of "subcultural restoration," which hopes for a return to pre-Vatican II Catholicism and its traditional missionary agenda. Those who prefer this option would not want to jettison completely the American political experience, but their theological sentiments are closer to John Courtney Murray's enemies than to Murray himself.[102]

The second option is that of "evangelical radicalism," which is the new Catholic sectarianism. Using the language of discipleship, it counsels opposition to, and withdrawal from, the world. This option has proved to be especially attractive to Catholics in the peace movement as well as to those involved in the charismatic renewal.[103]

The third option O'Brien calls "comfortable denominationalism," an option that is basically accommodationist. It implicitly supports a privatization of religion and a political marginalization of the church. Its spirit is reflected in the lay letter, written in 1984 under the joint leadership of Michael Novak and former Treasury Secretary William E. Simon, in response to the first draft of the U.S. Catholic bishops' pastoral letter on the economy.[104]

The fourth option is that of the "public church," following Martin Marty's lead. This understanding of the church-and-state relationship is expressed in the Catholic bishops' pastorals on nuclear war and the economy, and is faithful to the thinking of Pope John XXIII and the Second Vatican Council's document on "The Church in the Modern World" *(Gaudium et spes)*. This option uses words like vocation, citizenship, and democratic participation, and leaves ample room for diverse styles. It always seeks to change the world through concrete policies and institutional ways. It criticizes subcultural restoration and evangelical radicalism as primarily expressions of alienation from America and modernity rather than as genuine efforts toward the recovery of Catholic orthodoxy or biblical prophecy. The public church option understands and accepts the need for an evangelical style in a pluralistic and free society, but would retain solidly Catholic ideas like mystical body, inclusiveness, sacramentality, social justice, common good, and dialogue. It sees Catholics as insiders, not outsiders, with a responsibility for what is and not just for what might be. The public church option is suspicious of all language that exaggerates the distinction between the church and the world. It draws its theological, philosophical, and political inspiration from Tocqueville, Cardinal Newman, the early Lamennais, Luigi Sturzo, Frédéric Ozanam, Emmanuel Mounier, and Jacques Maritain.

In summary: the problems of church and state and of church and society are not the same as that of religion and politics. They have to do only with the relationship between *Christianity* and politics That is a more limited, although not at all less-complicated, relationship, as we have just seen. Within Christianity there are, and always have been, different ways of understanding that relationship. No single approach can be canonized as the one, true Christian approach. This is not to suggest, however, that coherent and compelling answers are beyond reach. Catholicism, perhaps more than any other Christian tradition, has been able to develop a compelling, if not always coherent, theological and doctrinal body of thought on the subject. But that is for a later discussion.

Clergy and Politics

The word *clergy* usually applies only to those who have been officially designated by their religious organizations or communities to exercise some role of pastoral leadership. Within the Christian churches, the clergy consists of ordained ministers, priests, and deacons. We are using the term here in a wider sense to include anyone whose actions in the public forum could reasonably be construed as somehow representative of the churches to which they belong. By broadening the definition we can include Catholic religious women (nuns and sisters) in our discussion.

The point here is not to argue the merits of clerical involvement in politics, but simply to describe how that involvement occurs.

One level of involvement is through participation in the public debate over issues. Among the examples are the pastoral letters of the U.S. Catholic bishops on nuclear war and the economy, designed to help shape national policy. Lobbying for or against specific legislation, local ordinances, and constitutional amendments is another.

A second level of involvement is through personal association with officeholders, with the intention of influencing their political behavior, directly or indirectly. The Reverend Billy Graham, on the Protestant side, and Francis Cardinal Spellman, on the Catholic side, are cases in point.[105]

A third level of involvement is through public action designed to call attention to deficiencies in the political system. The Reverend

Martin Luther King, Jr.'s, participation in marches, demonstrations, and sit-ins on behalf of civil rights in the 1960s and the activities of the Berrigan brothers, Philip and Daniel, in the anti-Vietnam War movement are clear examples.

A fourth level of involvement is through the leadership of organized religio-political movements with a broadly based agenda of social and political issues. Father Charles Coughlin, of Royal Oak, Michigan, founded the National Union of Social Justice in 1934 to lobby on behalf of legislation (and in 1936 formed a third party in opposition to President Franklin D. Roosevelt), and the Reverend Jerry Falwell founded Moral Majority in 1979 and the Liberty Federation in 1986.

A fifth level of involvement is through active support of, or opposition to, candidates for public office by means of voter registration drives, fund raising, direct mailings, endorsements from the pulpit, and the like. Several Baptist pastors in North Carolina were actively involved in the campaign to reelect Senator Jesse Helms in 1984, and, of course, many other (black) Baptist pastors were supportive of the presidential candidacy of the Reverend Jesse Jackson in the same year.[106]

A sixth level of involvement is through indirect support of, or opposition to, candidates for public office by means of public appearances and public statements of various kinds. The public criticism of Democratic vice-presidential candidate Geraldine Ferraro by New York's Archbishop O'Connor and Scranton's Bishop James Timlin, in the heart of a national election campaign, was taken by many as an indirect message to Catholics not to vote for the Democratic ticket, whether the two bishops intended that or not. Indirect endorsements were read into the appearance of Philadelphia's Cardinal John Krol at the 1972 Republican National Convention in Miami, at the conclusion of which he stood prominently between President Richard Nixon and Vice-President Spiro Agnew, and also into the cardinal's explicit praise of President Reagan's policies during a Reagan campaign visit to the National Shrine of Our Lady of Czestochowa in Doylestown, Pennsylvania, on September 9, 1984.

A seventh level of involvement is through the acceptance and exercise of appointive public office. Sister Agnes Mary Mansour, a member of the Sisters of Mercy in Detroit, was, in fact, forced out of her religious community because she would not resign her post as head of Michigan's Department of Social Services. The late Monsignor Geno C. Baroni served as an assistant secretary in the Department of Housing and Urban Development in the Carter administration. No American clergyman, however, has been asked to serve in various appointive posts so often as Father Theodore Hesburgh, president of the University of Notre Dame: the chairmanship of the U.S. Commission on

Civil Rights and of the U.S. Select Commission to Study Immigration and Refugee Policy are chief among them.[107]

An eighth, and final, level of involvement is through active candidacy for, and service in, elective political office. Scores of Protestant ministers have served in the Congress of the United States since the founding of the Republic. Senator John Danforth of Missouri, for example, is an ordained Episcopal priest. And the Reverend Jesse Jackson ran for the presidency itself in 1984. Candidacies on the Catholic side usually receive greater public attention because they are so much more the exception to the rule. The most celebrated case in recent years was that of Father Robert F. Drinan, S.J., who served five terms in the U.S. House of Representatives in the 1970s, until compelled to withdraw from his campaign for reelection in 1980 under pressure from the Vatican. In 1984 two Rhode Island nuns resigned from their religious communities rather than abandon their political careers: Elizabeth Morancy, a state representative, and Arlene Violet, who was later elected the state's attorney general.

Therefore, when people argue that clergy should "stay out of politics," it's not always clear what they mean. As we have just seen, there are at least eight different levels of political involvement by the clergy. The Catholic Church's Code of Canon Law does not forbid involvement at all eight levels. Canon 285 stipulates only that clerics cannot hold public office, elective and appointive, "without the permission of their ordinary," that is, their bishop. Nor are they to have an active role in political parties. The rest is governed by prudence rather than by law.[108]

*   *   *

Pope John Paul II visited Canada in the midst of the 1984 U.S. presidential election campaign. By mid-September the campaign had been thoroughly permeated with controversy over the place of religion in politics. Speaking to reporters on his flight home, the pope was asked about the debate going on in the United States. "The church cannot be involved in politics as such," he said, "but the church has a duty to express itself—herself—in all moral problems and developments."

Asked what he saw to be the duties of a Catholic involved in politics, the pope replied, "He should follow his Christian conscience." As The New York *Times* reported the next morning, the pope's comments on the question of religion and politics "were not without ambiguity."[109] Given the complexity of the issue and the diversity of its components, as reviewed thus far, that should not have been surprising.

PART II

Religion and Politics in America

THREE

"CONGRESS SHALL MAKE NO LAW . . ."

WILL Herberg's *Protestant-Catholic-Jew* published in 1955 has been called by Martin Marty "the most influential account of postwar American faith by a member of any religious group."[1] Almost at once critics, in particular religious groups, faulted Herberg for leaving them out: 3 million Eastern Orthodox Christians were overlooked; conservative evangelical Protestants were neglected; marginal groups like Jehovah's Witnesses and Mormons were underestimated.

A book of the same title would provoke even greater criticism today. In just three decades the religious landscape has changed dramatically with the waves of new immigrants from Africa, the Middle East, and especially Asia. This is a nation not only of Catholics, Eastern Orthodox, Anglicans, Mormons, Jehovah's Witnesses, Jews, and countless varieties of Protestants, but of Muslims, Buddhists, Hindus, Shintoists, and blendings thereof—like Sun Myung Moon's Unification Church. This may be indeed "the most pluralistic religious and social experiment in human history."[2]

The authors and original supporters of the U.S. Constitution could not have foreseen this extraordinary religious diversification, but even in their own time they were alert to the threat to the public peace posed by religious factionalism. No one was more sensitive to that danger than James Madison.

"As long as the reason of man continues fallible, and he is at liberty to exercise it," he wrote, "different opinions will be formed. . . . The latent causes of faction are thus sown in the nature of man. . . ."

"A zeal for different opinions concerning religion," he continued, ". . . [has], in turn, divided mankind into parties, inflamed them with mutual animosity, and rendered them much more disposed to vex and oppress each other than to co-operate for their common good."[3]

For Madison a republican form of government is the best insurance against the ill effects of factionalism. A republic, he argued, enjoys two principal advantages over a pure democracy. In a republic the government is delegated to a small number of citizens elected by the rest. This serves to "refine and enlarge the public views by passing them through the medium of a chosen body of citizens, whose wisdom may best discern the true interest of their country and whose patriotism and love of justice will be least likely to sacrifice it to temporary or partial considerations."[4]

The other, and more significant, point of difference from a pure democracy is the greater number of citizens and extent of territory that a republican form of government can accommodate. The smaller the number of citizens, the smaller the number required to constitute a majority. The smaller the territory, the more easily such a majority can discover its own strength and act in unison against the interests of others. "A religious sect," Madison concluded, "may degenerate into a political faction in a part of the Confederacy; but the variety of sects dispersed over the entire face of it must secure the national councils against any danger from that source."[5]

How did the new nation propose to deal with its community of sects? By establishing no religion(s) as the religion(s) of the state and by guaranteeing freedom of religion to all. How that was done and how the "establishment" and "free exercise" clauses have been interpreted and applied constitute the subject matter of this chapter.

A fair warning, however. The territory we are about to cross has not been mapped out. More accurately, there is no *single* map to follow. There are several, and each different from the other.[6]

The U.S. Supreme Court itself admits the problem (it could hardly deny it!). "Candor compels the acknowledgment that we can only dimly perceive the boundaries of permissible government activity in this sensitive area," Chief Justice Burger has written.[7] Justice Byron White was no less candid a decade later when he noted, "Establishment Clause cases are not easy; they stir deep feelings; and we are divided among ourselves, perhaps reflecting the different views on this subject of the people of this country."[8]

As noted previously, the quality of the debate about the relationship between politics and religion has suffered from a lack of precision in

the use of such key terms as *religion* and *church,* and from a failure
to make the necessary distinctions between various components of the
issue, for example, church and state and church and society.

The Jeffersonian "wall of separation between church and state,"
for example, is frequently substituted for the Constitution's charge in
its First Amendment that "Congress shall make no law respecting an
establishment of religion, or prohibiting the free exercise thereof. . . ."

The "wall of separation," in fact, is not part of the First Amendment.
Jefferson's metaphor was not even coined until more than a decade
after the First Amendment was approved and none of those who were
active in framing the Bill of Rights, including Madison, said anything
at the time in support of an absolutely separationist view.[9] Not without
reason, many in the United States have drawn from the metaphor all
sorts of legal and constitutional implications. Although the "wall of
separation" is not found in the Constitution, neither is the "right to a
fair trial."

But to concede that the "wall of separation" metaphor has legal,
even constitutional, standing is not to accept at the same time a given
interpretation of the metaphor, in particular the one that assumes that
the state is to have no interest in, or concern for, religion. According
to this strictly separationist interpretation, the state must be not only
absolutely neutral, but supremely indifferent as well. It should touch
nothing religious whatsoever, whether to approve it or to disapprove
it, whether to support it or to impede it. Justice Hugo Black's opinion
in *Everson* v. *Board of Education* is a blunt statement of that view,
arguing that the First Amendment's establishment clause was intended
precisely to erect the Jeffersonian "wall of separation" between church
and state.[10]

However, there is no historical evidence that the founders, with
the exception of a few extreme deists and agnostics among them, ever
interpreted the principles of nonestablishment and uncoerced consent
to mean that government ought to be completely indifferent to religion.
On the contrary, they said again and again that religion provided truths
that were essential for public order and stability. Their point was that
responsibility for inculcating these truths rested with the churches
alone, to be carried out in whatever manner the churches deemed
appropriate, and that the churches should rely upon their own powers
of persuasion, not upon the government's coercive power.[11]

Neither is this absolutely separationist view consistent with the
actual life and experience of the nation, where, for example, the motto
"In God We Trust" appears on the currency, where chaplains open
each session of federal and state legislatures with a prayer, where the
U.S. Supreme Court itself uses the invocation, "God save the United

States and this Honorable Court," where religious holidays are enforced, where religious property is exempted from taxation, and clergy from the military draft.

Separationists, however, tend to discount these examples because, in their view, these practices have either lost their original religious meaning or have acquired the status of a long-standing civil custom, thereby becoming "part of the fabric of our society."[12] Leo Pfeffer, for example, calls them "marginal and of little significance,"[13] but his argument fails the test of logic. An "absolute" wall of separation cannot accommodate *any* breaches, even minor and marginal ones. The fact is that such an impregnable wall has never existed in the entire history of the nation.

The issue, therefore, is not so much the *separation* of religion from the state as it is the matter of their *relationship*. And to understand the nature of that relationship, Madison offered the more serviceable metaphor: a line rather than a wall. He referred to it as "the line of separation between the rights of religion and the Civil authority."[14] We'll return to the Madisonian metaphor in due course.

"No . . . Establishment of Religion"

"The establishment of religion had been a problem for Americans almost from the first years of settlement," Bernard Bailyn has reminded us.[15] Most of the early settlers had brought with them traditional assumptions concerning the state's responsibility for supervising and enforcing orthodox religious institutions and behavior.

But there were difficulties from the outset. In some places, like Virginia, the population was scattered and the settlers were thousands of miles from the ecclesiastical centers of Europe. Elsewhere, as in Massachusetts, religious feelings ran high and the demands for purer and purer forms of orthodoxy led to schismatic challenges to the established church. Still elsewhere, as in New York, there were simply too many different kinds of religious groups to permit the establishment of any one of them. Only in Pennsylvania did "systematic, principled opposition to establishments survive to shape the character of instituted religion in the eighteenth century."[16] Otherwise the pattern of establishments was, like so much else in the colonies, unsystematic and pragmatic.

What is clear, therefore, is that the European form of establishment was not the only form in colonial America, nor was the European meaning of establishment the only meaning in America. Indeed, at the time the First Amendment was adopted, all state establishments that still existed were general or multiple establishments of all the churches of each state, something unknown in the Europe where the established religion was always a single church. No American state, in fact, maintained an establishment in the European sense of having an exclusive or state church designated by law.[17] In no state or colony, of course, were any except a Christian (that is, Protestant) denomination established, which may explain the widespread tendency of Americans to equate the relationship of religion and politics with that of church and state.

In the Virginia of Jefferson's youth, where the Church of England was established, the law requiring nonconformist organizations to register with the government was often ignored, especially in those western counties where the settlement of dissenters was actively promoted by the government. In Massachusetts and Connecticut tolerance in worship and relief from church taxation had been extended to the major dissenting groups early in the century, prompting John Adams to describe the arrangement as "the most mild and equitable establishment of religion that was known in the world, if indeed [it] could be called an establishment."[18]

The tradition of establishment had been weakened in these pre-Revolutionary days by direct opposition. In New York, for example, a group of lawyers conducted a sustained campaign in the pages of the *Independent Reflector* against the privileges accorded the Church of England. One development brought the issue to a head. An Anglican college was founded with the financial support of the provincial government of New York. The lawyers advanced for the first time in American history the notion that public institutions, precisely because they were public, should be at least nondenominational, if not secular. But such opposition, in these early years, was scattered and uncoordinated. The government in New York succeeded in silencing the *Reflector,* whose leadership and ideas "lost their identity in the tumbling chaos of factional disputes."[19]

But anti-establishment sentiment would not disappear because it was, from the earliest pre-Revolutionary years, intermingled with constitutional arguments against parliamentary power. Two events in particular brought the issue of church-state relations once again to the public's attention.

In 1759 Virginia passed the Two-Penny Act, which drew protests from the clergy against what they claimed was an illegal devaluation of their salaries. Parliament disallowed the act and the bishop of London denounced the people of Virginia for their disrespect for the Church of England and their laxness in dealing with dissenters. Richard Bland and Landon Carter vigorously defended the legislation and attacked not only the clergy's leader, the Reverend John Camm, but the clergy in general and the bishop of London as well. Camm countercharged that the attack against the clergy was tantamount to an attack against the crown itself.

The last word in the controversy, however, was neither Bland's nor Camm's, but Patrick Henry's. In one of the Parsons' Cause cases, Henry defended a parish which had been sued by its rector for wages lost through the Two-Penny Act. In an hour-long speech before the jury, Henry called the king a tyrant who had forfeited all rights to obedience and characterized the clergy as rapacious harpies who, in opposing the Act, had acted with complete disregard for the public good. The only use of an established church, he argued, "is to enforce obedience to civil sanctions." Instead of being useful members of the state, the clergy should be regarded as "enemies of the community . . . [who] deserved to be punished with signal severity."[20]

The second event occurred in Massachusetts where, in 1759, the Church of England established in Cambridge, under the shadow of Harvard College, a mission of its Society for the Propagation of the Gospel. The man assigned to direct the mission, East Apthorp, was inexperienced, contentious, and triumphalistic. He built for himself a palatial residence, which won no friends, and was drawn into a war of intemperate words with opponents of the mission. In his rebuttal he forged a link between Christian orthodoxy and the episcopacy and equated New England nonconformity not only with superstition and fanaticism, but with "popery or Mohammedanism" as well. He insisted, furthermore, that the Society was "above censure" and "incapable of wrong motives in the application of its liberality."[21] Apthorp's pamphlet played into the persistent fears of non-Anglicans everywhere in the colonies, especially in New England, that an American episcopate was about to be established.

Jonathan Mayhew, pastor of Boston's West Church, launched a vigorous counterattack against Apthorp. Mayhew argued that the founders of the Society for the Propagation of the Gospel had gathered all Protestants, not just Anglicans, under the orthodox umbrella. Furthermore, they had not intended that the Society's funds should be used to support Episcopal clergymen in locales where adequate provision was already being made for the clergy of other denominations. Indeed, the sending of missionaries to places like Cambridge was a violation of the Society's charter and resulted only in "setting altar against altar," evidently in the hope that the nonconformists in New England would eventually submit to the establishment of the Church of England. If this were to occur, Mayhew warned, the colonists would be taxed, just as the English themselves were taxed, to support bishops and their "underlings." Neither Parliament nor the crown had the right to extend the ecclesiastical laws of England to America or to reach into the internal affairs of the colonies in any way. In the end, it was this connection between the political and the religious that dominated the controversy.

But the arguments of the local leaders in both of these cases proved to be a two-edged sword. What they had said in opposition to the home authorities was, in due course, used against them with even greater force by radical sectarians in their own midst: New Light Presbyterians, Separate Baptists, and Strict Congregationalists. Many of them were "fiercely belligerent, acutely sensitive to slights, and indefatigable in righting every wrong done them."[22]

The most advanced pre-Revolutionary arguments for disestablishment were, therefore, "unstable compounds of narrow denominationalism and broad libertarianism."[23] But the arguments in the end were irrefutable, and eventually prevailed. As the Massachusetts Baptists pointed out, the same persons who protest "year after year against being taxed without their consent and against the scheme of imposing episcopacy upon them . . . impose cruelly upon their neighbors, and force large sums from them to uphold a worship which they conscientiously dissent from."[24] The Baptists, however, made no mention of Catholics and Jews, who were also victims of discrimination, from which the Baptists and their sectarian allies profited.

In June 1776 the Virginia Assembly, with key phrases written by James Madison and influenced by the claims of the Presbyterians and Baptists as well as by Enlightenment ideals, passed the Virginia Declaration of Rights, stating that religion "can be directed only by reason and conviction" and that "all men are equally entitled to the free exercise of religion according to the dictates of conscience."[25] The next logical step was complete disestablishment, , and this occurred a decade later in Jefferson's Act for Establishing Religious Freedom and the disestablishing legislation that surrounded it.

Although most attention has always been focused on the Virginia story because the sources are uniquely ample and the main actors unusually prominent, anti-establishment pressures continued to be applied in other colonies as well, including an acutely embarrassed Massachusetts, where a partial establishment of religion was allowed to persist for a time. But the ultimate conclusion everywhere was clear.[26]

The impulse toward the nonestablishment of religion and "the free exercise thereof" had been shaped by many factors, and three in particular. First, although a substantial majority of citizens had roots in some form of puritanism, no single denomination approached majority status. Congregationalists and Presbyterians were the largest denominations when the Constitution was ratified, followed by Baptists, Episcopalians (reconstituted from the Church of England at the end of the Revolution), Reformed Christians (Dutch and German Calvinists),

Lutherans, and Catholics. There were also some Quakers, recently organized Methodists, various German pietist sects, and Jews. Even established churches, like the Congregational Church in all the New England colonies except Rhode Island, were torn by internal conflicts. Rationalists who opposed the evangelicals left to form an independent Unitarian Church. Under the circumstances, the selection of any single denomination as the established national church was out of the question.

Secondly, the nation's leaders were also troubled by the tendency of established churches to generate bigotry and persecution. While they saw merit in government support of religion at the state and local levels, they regarded as potentially harmful any kind of direct relationship between religion and the state at the national level.

Thirdly, the founders believed that religious liberty is itself a religious value. Coerced religion is an obstacle, not an aid, to genuine faith. The Second Vatican Council's Declaration on Religious Freedom would make the same point, nearly two centuries later.

Accordingly, the Constitution which was agreed to in Philadelphia in 1787, unlike the Declaration of Independence, contained no reference to God. The only mention of religion in the original document occurs in Article VI, Section 3, which declares that "no religious test shall ever be required as a qualification to any office or public trust under the United States."[27]

George Mason, the principal author of Virginia's Declaration of Rights, proposed, however, that the new Constitution be prefaced with a Bill of Rights. Roger Sherman, of Connecticut, protested on grounds that a Bill of Rights was unnecessary, such declarations of rights already being in force in the several states. Mason's motion failed.

Opponents of the Constitution seized upon the vote to urge its rejection by the states. The tactic was at least partially successful. Various state conventions discussed the issue and some produced resolutions demanding that the new federal government adopt a declaration of fundamental rights.

Elected a member of the first House of Representatives, James Madison spearheaded a move to enact a Bill of Rights. He warned on June 8, 1789, that further delay might "occasion suspicions" among the public that "we are not sincere in our desire to incorporate such amendments in the constitution as will secure those rights which they consider as not sufficiently guarded."[28]

Madison introduced nine amendments. "The civil rights of none," the first clause of his fourth amendment began, "shall be abridged on account of religious belief or worship, nor shall any national religion be established, nor shall the full and equal rights of conscience be in any manner, or on any pretext, infringed."[29] His fifth amendment was directed at the states, and provided that "No state shall violate the

equal rights of conscience. . . ." Some have interpreted this as a proposal for eliminating the remaining state establishments, even though
none of the defenders of the state establishments, who were numerous
in the House during the debate, raised any objection.

All the amendments were referred to a special committee. On August 15, the committee reported a new amendment: "No religion shall
be established by law, nor shall the equal rights of conscience be infringed." Peter Sylvester, of New York, expressed the fear that the
amendment might have the effect of abolishing religion altogether.
Elbridge Gerry, of Massachusetts, suggested that the amendment be
changed to prohibit only the establishment of "religious doctrine,"
thereby limiting the force of the amendment to questions of theology
and ecclesiastical organization. Roger Sherman continued to argue that
the amendment was unnecessary because Congress had no constitutional authority in the first place to make religious establishments.
Alexander Hamilton had made the same argument in *The Federalist*,
no. 84: "For why declare that things shall not be done which there is
no power to do?"[30]

Madison's own intervention, as reported in the *Annals of Congress*
for August 15, 1789, is worth reproducing here:

> Mr. Madison said, he apprehended the meaning of the words to be, that
> Congress shall not establish a religion, and enforce the legal observation
> of it by law, nor compel men to worship God in any manner contrary to
> their conscience. Whether the words are necessary or not, he did not mean
> to say, but they had been required by some of the State Conventions, who
> seemed to entertain an opinion that under the clause of the constitution,
> which gave power to Congress to make all laws necessary and proper to
> carry into execution the constitution, and the laws made under it, enabled
> them to make laws of such a nature as might infringe the rights of con-
> science, and establish a national religion; to prevent these effects he pre-
> sumed the amendment was intended, and he thought it as well expressed
> as the nature of the language would admit.

When Benjamin Huntington, of Connecticut, expressed his concern
that the amendment might be construed to exempt those who profess
no religion at all from providing for the support of local ministers and
the building of meetinghouses, Madison tried a further change in language, inserting once again the adjective "national" before "religion"
in order to "point the amendment directly to the object it was intended
to prevent." But this provoked another outbreak of argument about
federalism, and the motion was withdrawn.

Samuel Livermore, of New Hampshire, yet another establishment
state, moved that the amendment be put in this form: "Congress shall
make no laws touching religion, or infringing the rights of conscience."
The motion, which limited the restrictive effect of the amendment to
Congress and also avoided any explicit prohibition of establishment,

even at the national level, was passed by the House, acting as a Committee of the Whole, by a vote of 31–20.

Five days later, when the House took up the report of the Committee of the Whole, Fisher Ames, of Massachusetts, who was actually against the very idea of a Bill of Rights, offered yet another compromise that seems to have been worked out and accepted in advance, because it passed with the necessary two-thirds vote without further discussion: "Congress shall make no law establishing religion, or to prevent the free exercise thereof, or to infringe the rights of conscience." The House then passed, also without debate, Madison's amendment restricting the states. The Senate completed action on the amendments, which became the Bill of Rights, on September 9. The separate amendment on the states was dropped, reflecting perhaps the abiding resistance to federal power over the states on such matters.

That part of Madison's original fourth amendment dealing with religion was combined with a part concerned with freedom of speech and the press to form a single amendment. It began: "Congress shall make no law establishing articles of faith or a mode of worship, or prohibiting the free exercise of religion. . . ." This pleased supporters of state establishments and government aid to religion even at the national level, because it limited the ban to acts that prefer one denomination over others, in other words, that establish a single state church, and prohibited only the government's involvement in matters of theology and ritual.

The House asked for a conference, and named Madison as chairman of its three conferees. The House members refused to accept the Senate's version of the amendment on religion, and indicated that the House would not be satisfied with merely a ban on the preference of one sect or religion over others. The Senate conferees abandoned the Senate version and the amendment was redrafted into its present form: "Congress shall make no law respecting an establishment of religion, or prohibiting the free exercise thereof."

Although constitutional scholars like Leonard Levy insist that the history of the drafting of the First Amendment provides us with little understanding of its meaning and intent, at least one point does seem clear: the amendment was intended to apply exclusively to the federal government. "*Congress* shall make no law. . . ." Religion as a subject of legislation was to be reserved to the states, and the amendment itself would not directly affect them. Indeed, the various state establishments were only gradually eliminated, and always voluntarily: South Carolina in 1790, Maryland in 1810, Connecticut in 1818, New Hampshire in 1819, and lastly Massachusetts in 1833, after it became clear to the once-dominant Congregationalists that their tax money was flowing to parish after parish controlled by new majorities of dissident Unitarians.[31]

It is a matter of debate, on the other hand, whether the amendment also prohibited "any act of public authority favorable to religion in general," a view strongly resisted by what Levy calls a "formidable school of nonpreferentialists," including Edward S. Corwin[32] (this century's foremost American constitutional scholar), Walter Berns,[33] and Robert L. Cord.[34]

It is extremely important, however, that the terms of that debate be clear. The debate is not about the formal establishment of one or several religions as the official religion(s) of the state. No one seriously contends that such establishment would be within the limits of constitutional authority. Nor is the debate about the right of religious people and of religious institutions to participate in discussions concerning public policy or to attempt to shape public policy through legal means. No "wall of separation" can deny citizens who happen to be religious the rights that belong to all other citizens under the law.

The debate is about the power of the state (in the first instance, the federal government, and in the second instance, the individual states) to pass any legislation whatever regarding religion, either to support it or to impede it. What is under discussion is the validity of Leo Pfeffer's view, shared by many others and reflected in various decisions of the U.S. Supreme Court, that the intent of the First Amendment was "not merely to prohibit the establishment of a state church but to preclude any government aid to religious groups or dogmas."[35]

Pfeffer and others argue that government aid to religion, even on a nonpreferential basis, violates the "no . . . establishment of religion" clause. That view has now been embodied in various Court decisions, most notably the 1947 decision in *Everson* v. *Board of Education*, in which Justice Hugo Black, writing for the majority, referred directly to Thomas Jefferson's "wall of separation" metaphor to support his contention that the First Amendment prohibits both the federal government and the states from aiding one religion or all religions, or from preferring one religion over another. "No tax in any amount, large or small," Justice Black declared, "can be levied to support any religious activities or institutions, whatever they may be called, or whatever form they may adopt to teach or practice religion."[36]

Is this what the First Amendment intends? Is this what the "wall of separation" requires?

Jefferson's "Wall of Separation"

It was in a letter to the Baptist Association of Danbury, Connecticut, written on New Year's Day 1802, that President Thomas Jefferson introduced his now-famous "wall of separation" metaphor: "I contemplate with sovereign reverence that act of the whole American people which declared that their legislature should 'make no law respecting an establishment of religion, or prohibiting the free exercise thereof,' thus building a wall of separation between church and State."[37]

Some have tried to soften the effect of Jefferson's words by suggesting that they were not written with any care for legal precision, or that Jefferson was concerned only with the rights of conscience, or that he was simply having some fun at the expense of the Congregationalist-Federalist hierarchy of Connecticut. Moreover, his actions as president, particularly his support a year later of the Kaskaskia Indian Treaty in which money was pledged for the building of a Catholic church and the support of its priest, make an absolutist interpretation impossible.[38]

But there is a theological as well as a constitutional issue here. The paragraph in which the metaphor appears begins in this way: "Believing with you that religion is a matter which lies solely between man and his God. . . ." Whatever else Jefferson's words might suggest, they express a theological judgment with which most mainline Christian theologians would not agree.

The sentence immediately following the reference to the "wall of separation" is indicative of Jefferson's practical intent; namely, to restate his own support of "the supreme will of the nation on behalf of the rights of conscience." Jefferson, therefore, seems to have been enunciating in this letter a theological view that religion is an entirely private matter, as well as a practical, political view that everyone, as a consequence, should be allowed to follow whatever religion he or she prefers without fear or favor.

His position was essentially identical with the one he had espoused 20 years earlier in his *Notes on the State of Virginia:* "But our rulers can have authority over such natural rights only as we have submitted to them. The rights of conscience we never submitted, we could not submit. We are answerable for them to our God. The legitimate powers of government extend to such acts only as are injurious to others. But it does me no injury for my neighbor to say there are twenty gods, or no god. It neither picks my pocket nor breaks my leg."[39]

Jefferson's ecclesiology was highly individualistic: "I am a sect myself."[40] Religion pertains only to the sphere of the private. Government should not intrude upon that sphere, nor should religion abandon its sanctuary of privacy and seek to intrude upon government's territory.

But what of that dimension of religion which is not purely private? What of the nature and mission of the church itself? Did Jefferson intend that the churches, and other religious bodies, should not participate, for example, in public debates concerning public policy or

to exercise their constitutional rights to participate in the political process itself? Was his "wall of separation" so absolute as to exclude every
form of interaction between religious bodies and the state?

Alexis de Tocqueville picked up on the "wall of separation" metaphor in his *Democracy in America,* where he expressed astonishment
that all of the Catholic priests he had encountered in the United States
thought that "the main reason for the quiet sway of religion over their
country was the complete separation of church and state. I have no
hesitation in stating that throughout my stay in America," Tocqueville
reported, "I met nobody, lay or cleric, who did not agree about that."[41]

As he reflected on the American situation and compared it with
the European, he noted how often religion suffers after a revolution:

> I am profoundly convinced that this accidental and particular cause is the
> close union of politics and religion.
>
> Unbelievers in Europe attack Christians more as political than as re-
> ligious enemies; they hate the faith as the opinion of a party much more
> than as a mistaken belief, and they reject the clergy less because they are
> the representatives of God than because they are the friends of authority.
>
> European Christianity has allowed itself to be intimately united with
> the powers of this world. Now that these powers are falling, it is as if it
> were buried under their ruins. A living being has been tied to the dead;
> cut the bonds holding it and it will arise.[42]

Tocqueville is saying nothing here about legal or constitutional
matters. He applauds only the habit of American religious bodies to
shun political power and close identification with political authorities.
On the other hand, he is a Catholic, not a sectarian Protestant, like
Roger Williams, for example. Tocqueville's own religious tradition
would have led him to acknowledge that the church must be a leaven
in society. It cannot refuse to participate in its life, even its public
life, on the assumption that the world is evil and bent always on the
church's destruction. Catholicism, on the contrary, places strong emphasis on the doctrines of creation, redemption, and sanctification. God
created the world, redeemed it in Christ, and sustains it by the power
of the Holy Spirit.

Accordingly, while the "wall of separation" may keep some things
apart, it cannot keep everything apart. It is not, and never has been,
impregnable.

Madison's "Line of Separation"

It was in a letter to the Reverend Jasper Adams in 1832 that James
Madison admitted that "it may not be easy, in every possible case, to
trace the line of separation between the rights of religion and the Civil

authority with such distinctness as to avoid collisions & doubts on unessential points."

He continued: "The tendency to a usurpation on one side or the other, or to a corrupting coalition or alliance between them, will be best guarded against by an entire abstinance of the Government from interference in any way whatever, beyond the necessity of preserving public order, & protecting each sect against trespasses on its legal rights by others."[43]

Madison's metaphor is more accurately descriptive of the actual situation in the United States than Jefferson's. Jefferson talks about "church" and state, but "religion" is broader than "church," which, after all, applies only to the *Christian* religion. Madison's "rights of religion" is on the mark.

Even the word *state* raises problems. Sidney Mead insists that "there is no 'state' in the meaning of the word during the centuries when national religious uniformity was the ideal and Establishments existed."[44] The "state" is a conceptual abstraction. Furthermore, does "state" refer to the federal government or to an individual state? Again, Madison's "Civil authority" is closer to the mark.

Finally, Madison's "line," unlike Jefferson's "wall," does not suggest something solid and unchanging, cemented in place once and for all by the nation's founders. A line has length, but not breadth. It can move constantly, even zigzag. Therefore, it is not easy to trace "with such distinctness as to avoid collisions & doubts on unessential points."

If we think of the American situation with Madison's concepts of religious sects, "Civil authority," and a "line" between them, "the image is fluid, its elements constantly changing shape and moving into different relationships with each other," Mead observes. "Religious 'sects' may and have appeared in hundreds of different forms, and 'Civil authority' under our Constitutional Federalism may wear hundreds of different masks."[45]

Jefferson's "wall" metaphor, on the other hand, sets the two sides at odds with one another, as antagonists. The defender of the wall says, with Robert Frost, "Good fences make good neighbors." The attacker of the wall replies, also with Robert Frost, "Something there is that doesn't love a wall, That wants it down."[46]

The cases that have actually come before the U.S. Supreme Court, and continue to come, are not simple ones. And anyone who studies the complete record with even a semblance of care realizes soon enough that the Court has decided them all without benefit of a single doctrinal principle.[47] Its several theoretical appeals to the "wall of separation" notwithstanding, the Court has adopted, *in practice*, the Madisonian rather than the Jeffersonian metaphor.

"The boundary at which the conflicting interests balance cannot be determined by any general formula in advance," Chief Justice Charles Evans Hughes once noted, "but points in the line, or helping to establish it, are fixed by decisions that this or that concrete case falls on the nearer or farther side."[48]

The "line" metaphor has been used in several different cases since Justice Black's famous appeal to Jefferson's "wall" in *Everson* v. *Board of Education* (1947). In *Abington School District* v. *Schempp* (1963), Justice William Brennan, in a concurring opinion, wrote: "The fact is that the line which separates the secular from the sectarian in American life is elusive." Nevertheless, there is a "line we must draw between the permissible and the impermissible."[49] In *Board of Education* v. *Allen* (1968), Justice Byron White observed that "*Everson* and later cases have shown that the line between state neutrality to religion and state support of religion is not easy to locate."[50] Chief Justice Warren Burger, in *Walz* v. *Tax Commissioner of New York City* (1970), acknowledged that the "course of constitutional neutrality in this area cannot be an absolutely straight line. . . . No perfect absolute separation is really possible."[51] And, again, in *Lemon* v. *Kurtzman* (1971), the Chief Justice conceded that the Court "can only dimly perceive the lines of demarcation in this extraordinarily sensitive area of constitutional law. . . . In the absence of precisely stated constitutional prohibitions, we must draw lines. . . ."[52]

If one adopts the Madisonian "line" metaphor rather than the Jeffersonian "wall" metaphor, the absolutely separationist view is set aside. The question is no longer *whether* there will be any element of accommodation between religion and the civil authority, but *how* that accommodation will be realized without violation of the establishment and free exercise clauses of the First Amendment.

"No State Shall Make or Enforce Any Law. . . ."

However one links the First Amendment with the Jeffersonian "wall of separation between church and State" or with the Madisonian "line of separation between the rights of religion and the Civil authority," it is clear now that the amendment's restrictive provisions no longer apply exclusively to the federal government.[53] The turning point occurred in 1868 with the ratification of the Fourteenth Amendment (the so-called "equal protection" amendment): "No State shall make or enforce any law which shall abridge the privileges or immunities of citizens of the United States; nor shall any State deprive any person of life, liberty, or property, without due process of law;

nor deny to any person within its jurisdiction the equal protection of the laws."

Until the passage of the Fourteenth Amendment matters of religion and religious freedom were left entirely to the states. In 1833, in the case of *Barron* v. *Baltimore*, the U.S. Supreme Court handed down a landmark decision that the Bill of Rights applied only to the federal government and, therefore, placed no restrictions on the states. As late as 1838 a popular lecturer against religion was jailed for 60 days in Massachusetts on the charge of blasphemy. This states' rights position collapsed, however, under the weight of the Civil War. The main objective of the Fourteenth Amendment, of course, was to extend full rights of citizenship to the former slaves who had been freed under the Emancipation Proclamation and the Thirteenth Amendment.

But did the framers of the Fourteenth Amendment intend its provisions to impose on the states the same limitations previously imposed on the federal government alone? There is no evidence whatever to support such an assumption.[54] On the other hand, some scholars have argued that the language of the Fourteenth Amendment's due process clause allows for this extension. They refer to this way of interpreting the Constitution as the incorporation doctrine, that is, the Fourteenth Amendment incorporates the rights protected by the First Amendment.[55] But what may be debated among legal scholars is no longer a matter of debate within the Court itself.

In 1940, in *Cantwell* v. *Connecticut*, the U.S. Supreme Court explicitly incorporated the free exercise of religion clause into the Fourteenth Amendment, and, without elaboration, the establishment clause as well.[56] In the 1947 *Everson* v. *Board of Education* case the Court agreed that the Fourteenth Amendment did incorporate the establishment clause. "Neither a state nor the Federal Government can set up a church," Justice Black wrote for the majority. "Neither can pass laws which aid one religion, aid all religions, or prefer one religion over another."[57]

Even the dissenting judges endorsed the principle. Justice Wiley Rutledge declared that the First Amendment intended "to create a complete and permanent separation of the spheres of religious activity and civil authority by comprehensively forbidding every form of public aid or support for religion."[58] Robert L. Cord refers to the Rutledge opinion as "virtually reckless in its disregard of the indisputable facts of American history regarding the Establishment Clause of the First Amendment."[59] Indeed, Cord argues, if Rutledge and the absolute separationists are right about the intentions of the nation's founders, how did Madison and his allies persuade the states with religious establishments to ratify such an amendment in the first place?

"Original Intent"

If the Rutledge opinion, quoted above, represents one pole of the argument about "original intent," Attorney General Edwin Meese III represents the other. In a speech before the American Bar Association's House of Delegates, meeting in Washington, D.C., on July 9, 1985, Mr. Meese declared that the framers of the Constitution would have found "bizarre" the U.S. Supreme Court's interpretation that the First Amendment requires government to maintain "strict neutrality" toward religion.

"Far too many of the Court's opinions, on the whole, have been more policy choices than articulations of long-term constitutional principle," he said. Among the decisions to which he objected were those involving school prayer, government aid to religious schools, and a law giving employees an absolute right to a day off to observe their Sabbath. The attorney general announced that the Reagan administration would urge the Court to follow "a jurisprudence of original intention," which would seek to "resurrect the original meaning of constitutional provisions" rather than reading the policy preferences of the justices into the Constitution.[60] Mr. Meese's criticisms of the Court were vigorously rebutted three months later by Justices William Brennan and John Paul Stevens. Brennan assailed the "original intent" view as "little more than arrogance cloaked as humility," and Stevens characterized the attorney general's historical account as "somewhat incomplete."[61]

The attorney general left out of his prepared remarks a reference to the theory, or doctrine, of incorporation: "Nowhere else," his text stated, "has the principle of federalism been dealt so politically violent and constitutionally suspect a blow as by the theory of incorporation." When asked afterward whether he questioned the Court's decisions incorporating provisions of the Bill of Rights into the Fourteenth Amendment, thereby applying the First Amendment to the states, he replied: "I do not have any particular quarrel at this stage of the game with what the Court has done" on that issue.

The more important point, he said, was "to go back to the original intentions of the framers and that was, I believe, in religion cases to be sure that there was no preference given to any religion; it was not to put religion on the same par constitutionally as nonreligion."

The same view is expressed, perhaps more moderately, by A. James Reichley. "Some ambiguity was no doubt present in the meaning of the establishment clause from the start," he concedes. "But there is nothing in it inconsistent with the virtually unanimous view among the founders that functional separation between church and state should be maintained without threatening the support and guidance received by government from religion."[62]

Irving R. Kaufman, a judge of the United States Court of Appeals for the Second Circuit, has tried to mark out a legally sensible, centrist position, drawn from actual court experience. "In the ongoing debate over original intent," he writes, "almost all Federal judges hold to the notion that judicial decisions should be based on the text of the Constitution or the structure it creates. Yet, in requiring judges to be guided solely by the expressed views of the framers, current advocates of original intent seem to call for a narrower concept."[63]

Judge Kaufman acknowledges that it has often been difficult for him, as a federal judge, to ascertain the "intent of the framers," and even more problematic to try to dispose of a constitutional question by giving great weight to the intent argument. "Indeed, even if it were possible to decide hard cases on the basis of a strict interpretation of original intent, or originalism," he insists, "that methodology would conflict with a judge's duty to apply the Constitution's underlying principles to changing circumstances." Furthermore, in raising questions about the incorporation doctrine which applies the Fourteenth Amendment to the Bill of Rights, "the intent theory threatens some of the greatest achievements of the Federal judiciary."

Ultimately, Judge Kaufman argues, the debate centers on the nature of judicial review, or "the powers of the courts to act as the ultimate arbiters of constitutional meaning," a responsibility acknowledged since *Marbury* v. *Madison* in 1803, in which Chief Justice John Marshall struck down a congressional grant of jurisdiction to the Supreme Court not authorized by Article III of the Constitution.

But even if judges were to be guided primarily by "original intent," the task would be formidable. There is very little documentation available. The official minutes of the Philadelphia Convention of 1787 and James Madison's famous notes of the proceedings, published in 1840, are, as Judge Kaufman points out, "terse and cursory, especially in relation to the judiciary." The congressional debates over the proposed Bill of Rights, which became effective in 1791, are "scarcely better." *The Federalist* papers, generally regarded as the earliest constitutional commentary, did not discuss the Bill of Rights nor, of course, did they anticipate the Civil War amendments, including the Fourteenth Amendment.

Moreover, before one can determine "original intent," one has to identify the framers themselves. But that isn't an easy task. Were they the delegates to the Philadelphia Convention and the congressional sponsors of subsequent amendments? Or does the word "framers" also include those who debated and then ratified the constitutional provisions in state conventions and legislatures on behalf of the people they represented? "Is the relevant intention, then, that of the drafters, the ratifiers or the general populace?" Judge Kaufman asks.

The elusiveness of the framers' intent leads to another, "more telling problem." Those who argue on behalf of "original intent" presume that "intent can be discovered by historical sleuthing or psychological rumination. In fact, this is not possible. Judges are constantly required to resolve questions that 18th-century statesmen, no matter how prescient, simply could not or did not foresee and resolve."

Constitutional phrases are often grand and cryptic, embodying "majestic generalities." "The use of such open-ended provisions," Judge Kaufman observes, "would indicate that the framers did not want the Constitution to become a straightjacket on all events for all times." By contrast, when the framers did have a clear intention, they didn't mince words. Thus, Article II specifies a minimum age of 35 for the nation's president. It does not merely require "maturity" or "adequate age."

Judge Kaufman warns against the threat of abuse of power posed by a lifetime judiciary, and admits that judges are not immune to the temptation of usurping authority better left to the other two branches of government. But the "truth is that no litmus test exists by which judges can confidently and consistently measure the constitutionality of their decision." Only the judicial process itself "limits the reach of a jurist's arm."[64]

Religion and the Courts

Religion-related cases adjudicated by the U.S. Supreme Court since the ratification of the Fourteenth Amendment fall into three general categories: those concerned with the disposition of church-related property, those concerned with the First Amendment's "free exercise" clause, and those concerned with its "no . . . establishment" clause. The third category has proved far more complex and controversial than the second. Religion-related cases are no longer decided as matters of conflicting property rights.

What follows is a series of thumbnail sketches of the more important cases, but with some effort to set them in their appropriate historical context. For quick reference to these cases, in alphabetical and chronological order as well as by subject matter, see the Appendixes.

THE PROPERTY CASES

Although some law school casebooks on constitutional law begin their section on the First Amendment religion clauses with the 1947

Everson v. *Board of Education*, the Court's experience with religion and the law began in the nineteenth century. The earliest conflicts had to do with the ownership of church property (Who owned what once a congregation broke up?) and unorthodox religious practice.

The first property-related case was not exactly a First Amendment case, but it had First Amendment repercussions. Presbyterianism, like other denominations, had been split by the Civil War into northern and southern branches. A parish in Louisville, Kentucky, reflected this national division. A minority of the congregation, with southern loyalties, seized physical control of the building and the Kentucky courts upheld them because the General Assembly had departed from original Presbyterian doctrine in passing a resolution condemning slavery. For the state court, this constituted a meddling in civil affairs.

The northern faction appealed to the U.S. Supreme Court which ruled, in *Watson* v. *Jones* (1872), that the General Assembly of the national Presbyterian Church held the general governing power and was the proper agency to determine property rights in this instance. The approach of *Watson* had the general effect of placing religious associations on a legal plane with other private associations. In deciding for the right of the General Assembly to determine property ownership of one of its own parishes, the Court in effect removed itself from dealing with internal doctrinal controversies and limited itself instead to questions of fact.[65]

The *Watson* doctrine was confirmed in two later cases. In *Kedroff* v. *St. Nicholas Cathedral* (1952), the Court ruled that ownership and control of the Russian Orthodox Cathedral in New York belonged legitimately to the Patriarchs of Moscow.[66] And in *Presbyterian Church in the United States* v. *Mary Elizabeth Blue Hull Memorial Presbyterian Church* (1969), the Court also decided in favor of the preexisting governing authority (the Presbyterian Church) and against a breakaway congregation.[67]

Two important cases, in 1922 and 1925 respectively, tested the constitutional status of private schools, but both were decided also on the basis of property rights rather than on First Amendment principles. The cases surfaced at a time when both anti-Catholic and anti-German feelings were running high in the nation, the latter intensified by the First World War.

The first case had nothing directly to do with religion, but it was resolved in such a way that it would have an enormous impact on religion-related cases for the remainder of this century. The case in question was *Meyer* v. *Nebraska* in which the Court ruled unconstitutional a Nebraska law, passed in the aftermath of World War I, forbidding the teaching of any modern languages except English before the ninth grade and mandating that all subjects be taught in English.

Other states in the Middle West had also moved to suppress the teaching of the German language, with the effect of forcing students out of Catholic schools which had a strong German cultural coloration.

The Court's ruling was based on the incorporation doctrine; namely, that First Amendment rights apparently guaranteed only at the federal level were, by reason of the Fourteenth Amendment, now applicable in the states as well. Even Justice Oliver Wendell Holmes, in a dissenting opinion, acknowledged that the case turned on whether "the means adopted deprived teachers of the liberty secured to them by the Fourteenth Amendment."[68]

But it also turned on the matter of property rights. In *Meyer* the teacher-plaintiff had a property interest, according to the Court, in his capacity to teach German.

In 1925 the Court, in *Pierce* v. *Society of Sisters*, ruled unconstitutional an Oregon law requiring all children between the ages of 8 and 15 to attend public schools, effectively outlawing church-related schools for all except college students. In finding for the nuns, the Court declared that a child is "not the mere creature of the State; those who nurture him and direct his destiny have the right coupled with the high duty, to recognize and prepare him for additional obligations."[69]

Property rights were also at issue in this second case. The school was seen as the established livelihood of those who ran it. To interfere with the right of educators to sell their services and the right of parents to buy them was ruled an unacceptable restriction on economic activity.

Philip B. Kurland refers to this case as probably "the most abused citation in the construction of the first amendment."[70] The principle by which the case was decided is "as applicable to the military academy as to the parochial school and, in no way, rested on any concept of 'freedom of religion.' "[71] The Court decided no church-state issue in *Pierce* v. *Society of Sisters*.

THE "FREE EXERCISE" CASES

THE MORMON CASES

The first major First Amendment cases following ratification of the Fourteenth Amendment had to do with unorthodox religious behavior, involving the Mormons and their practice of polygamy. In 1862, with the Mormons in mind, the U.S. Congress had outlawed polygamy in the territories. A Mormon named Reynolds was arrested and convicted on charges of bigamy. Reynolds argued that the criminal bigamy statute interfered with his constitutional right to the "free exercise of religion." The case was appealed to the U.S. Supreme Court, which rendered a unanimous decision against him in 1878. Chief Justice Morrison Waite, speaking for the Court, noted that under the First Amendment, "Congress was deprived of all legislative power over mere opinion, but was left free to reach actions which were in violation of social duties or subversive of good order." Polygamy was a social act, not a religious opinion, and so was subject to legal prohibition.[72]

In the course of his decision, however, Chief Justice Waite gave official recognition for the first time to Jefferson's "wall of separation" metaphor. The metaphor served Waite's purposes here because Jefferson had coupled it with the argument that "the legislative powers of the government reach actions only, and not opinions," a corollary to the distinction Waite was making.[73]

A second Mormon case, decided in 1890, upheld an election law in the state of Idaho, which required that voters swear not only that they don't practice bigamy or polygamy, but that they don't belong to any group that favors it. A Mormon named Davis took the oath and then was arrested and convicted for falsely swearing. He appealed to the U.S. Supreme Court and he, too, lost. Justice Stephen Field, speaking also for a united Court, maintained that the First Amendment protects opinions, not actions. If a religious group believed in human sacrifice, for example, the civil government must have the right to prohibit the practice. "Crime is not the less odious," he wrote, "because sanctioned by what any particular sect may designate a religion."[74] Thus, the "secular regulation" rule was firmly in place.

The issue resolved itself extrajudicially when, in the same year, the Mormons received "a new revelation" that multiple marriages were not, after all, required by divine commandment. The main barrier to statehood disappeared, and Utah was admitted to the Union in 1896.

THE JEHOVAH'S WITNESS CASES

In 1940 the incorporation doctrine was applied for the first time to a major religion-related case, in *Cantwell* v. *Connecticut*.[75] The Court overturned a breach-of-the-peace conviction of a Jehovah's Witness for playing an anti-Catholic record in a public street, and for lacking a religious solicitor's license. According to the Court, Cantwell's right to say or play what he pleased about other religions and denominations was guaranteed by the First Amendment, which was applied to the states by the Fourteenth.

But there was a second important innovation in Justice Owen Roberts' opinion; namely, his departure from the accepted distinction between protected belief and unprotected behavior, which had been articulated in the Mormon cases. The state did indeed have the power to regulate action, but not in such a way "unduly to infringe the protected freedom."[76]

Just two weeks later, in *Minersville School District* v. *Gobitis*, the

Court ruled against another Jehovah's Witness whose children had been expelled from public school for refusing to salute the flag. At that very moment Hitler was on the march in Europe and patriotism was running high. Justice Felix Frankfurter, speaking for the Court, found an overriding state interest in instilling patriotic loyalty among the nation's youth. An outbreak of violence and discrimination against Witnesses, adults and children alike, followed the decision.

In 1943, in *West Virginia State Board of Education* v. *Barnette,* the Court reversed itself in the name of freedom of expression, which included nonparticipation in flag-saluting exercises, rather than on the right to free exercise of religion. The Court may have been influenced by the hostility its previous decisions had engendered against Jehovah's Witnesses.

The same year, in *Murdock* v. *Pennsylvania,* the Court had ruled that Jehovah's Witnesses must be exempted from a local ordinance requiring itinerant solicitors to pay a license fee. "Those who can tax the exercise of this religious practice," the Court declared, "can make its exercise so costly as to deprive it of the resources necessary for its maintenance."[77]

In 1944, in *Prince* v. *Massachusetts,* the Court upheld the conviction of another Witness for bringing her nine-year-old niece along on sidewalk campaigns to sell the Witness publication, *Watch Tower.* This was in violation of a Massachusetts law against using a minor to sell periodicals or other articles of merchandise in a public place. The Court ruled that the state has wider power over the conduct of children than over adults.

In 1980, the Court declined to hear an appeal from a lower court decision approving the firing of a Jehovah's Witness as a teacher in Chicago for refusing to teach the pledge of allegiance to the flag or the words to patriotic songs. But in 1981, in *Thomas* v. *Review Board,* the Court voted 8–1 to overturn lower court decisions which barred a Witness from receiving unemployment compensation after he was fired for refusing to work on the production of weapons for war.[78]

SABBATH-RELATED CASES

In *Braunfeld* v. *Brown,* in 1961, the Court denied the plea of an Orthodox Jewish merchant to remain open on Sunday since his religion required him to close on Saturday. The Sabbath law, according to Chief Justice Earl Warren, was enacted to advance the state's "secular goals." The statute, therefore, was deemed valid "despite its indirect burden on religious observance."[79] Justice William Brennan dissented, taking his cue from Justice Roberts' opinion in *Cantwell* in which Roberts modified the traditional distinction between protected belief and wholly unprotected action. Brennan wrote: "Religious freedom—the freedom to believe and to practice strange and, it may be, foreign creeds—has classically been one of the highest values of our society."[80] Ironically, those nineteenth-century Protestants who professed an almost theological faith in religious liberty and the separation of church and state had felt no compunction at all about using the legal power of the state to impose the Sunday observance on everyone, regardless of their religious convictions.

Two years later, however, in *Sherbert* v. *Verner,* the Court found for a Seventh Day Adventist who had been fired from her job for not working on Saturday and who was denied unemployment compensation by the state of South Carolina because she had failed, without good cause, to accept suitable work when offered it. The Court ruled that Ms. Sherbert's right to free exercise of religion had been violated by forcing her "to choose between following the precepts of her religion and forfeiting benefits, on the one hand, and abandoning one of the precepts of her religion in order to accept work, on the other."[81] Justice Brennan's dissent in *Braunfeld* became the controlling constitutional law.[82]

In 1985, in *Thornton* v. *Connecticut,* the Court invalidated a Connecticut law that gave employees an unqualified right not to work on their chosen Sabbath. Chief Justice Warren Burger argued that the state law imposed an undue burden on both employers and on nonreligious employees, who, he said, also had "strong and legitimate" reasons for wanting to avoid weekend work. The Chief Justice said that the state, by decreeing that "Sabbath religious concerns automatically control overall secular interests at the workplace," violated the constitutional principle that government "must take pains not to compel people to act in the name of any religion."[83]

THE CONSCIENTIOUS OBJECTOR CASES

In 1965, in *United States* v. *Seeger,* and, in 1970, in *Welsh* v. *United States,* the Court granted exemption from the draft to two conscientious objectors, even though both admitted that their objections had nothing to do with religious convictions or beliefs.[84] In the first case, the Court accepted a widened definition of religious belief to include any conviction that "is sincere and meaningful and occupies a place in the life of its possessor parallel to that filled by the orthodox belief in God. . . ."[85] In the second case, the Court accepted "readings in the fields of history and sociology" as sufficient basis for conscientious objection. The Court's broadened definition of religion was not without precedent. In a footnote to *Torcaso* v. *Watkins* in 1961, Justice Hugo Black had included under the umbrella of religion "Ethical Culture, Secular Humanism and others."[86] Although such an inclusive definition may have been sociologically and theologically indefensible, the Court at this time was concerned that the exemption be "tailored broadly enough that it reflects valid secular purposes."[87] Otherwise, the requirement of governmental neutrality regarding religion would not have been satisfied.

The Court, however, drew the line in a third case involving a conscientious objector. In 1971, in *Gillette* v. *United States,* the Court rejected an argument by a devout nonpacifist Catholic that he should be exempted from serving in a particular war which he deemed unjust. The Court said it was not prepared to allow individuals to make personal distinctions among the wars in which they were willing to serve. This is known as "selective conscientious objection," an option favored by the U.S. Catholic bishops.

THE AMISH CASE

In 1972, in *Wisconsin* v. *Yoder,* the Court allowed a member of the Old Order Amish community to remove his children from school after the eighth grade on the grounds that further schooling, whether public or private, would endanger their salvation. In one of its most dubious decisions, the Warren Burger Court found for Mr. Yoder on the grounds that the Amish community in Wisconsin and elsewhere had an exemplary record as law-abiding, hard-working, financially independent citizens. It was clear, therefore, that failure to comply with state attendance laws would have no adverse social effects.

The Amish, in effect, were declared a special class, defined by religion, exempt from some laws which apply to everybody else. Never before had the Court held that one's religious convictions entitle one to an exemption from a valid criminal statute.[88]

THE YARMULKE CASE

In 1986, in *Goldman* v. *Weinberger,* the Court ruled that the military can bar an Orthodox Jewish officer from wearing a yarmulke indoors while in uniform. Air Force regulations had drawn a line between religious apparel that is visible and religious apparel that is not. The 5–4 decision upheld a reprimand and other disciplinary action taken in 1981 against S. Simcha Goldman, an Air Force captain working as a psychologist, for insisting, as a matter of religious principle, on wearing his yarmulke while on duty.

Writing for the majority, Justice William Rehnquist noted that standardized uniforms encourage "the subordination of personal preferences and identities in favor of the overall group mission" as well as "a sense of hierarchical unity by tending to eliminate outward individual distinctions except for those of rank." Military officials, he continued, "are under no constitutional mandate to abandon their considered professional judgment," even in the face of complaints that military dress codes may violate one's religious beliefs.[89]

In a dissenting opinion, Justice William Brennan argued that the "practical effect" of this categorization is that, "under the guise of neutrality and evenhandedness, majority religions are favored over distinctive minority faiths." In other words, those religious groups that wear distinctive garb are penalized while mainstream Christians are not. Justice Sandra Day O'Connor also dissented, on the grounds that the government simply hadn't made its case that military discipline and esprit de corps would be harmed if Captain Goldman had been allowed to continue wearing his yarmulke.

Justice John Paul Stevens, in a concurring opinion, admitted Justice O'Connor's point, but argued that difficult problems would be created by any exception to the dress code. Even though yarmulkes are "the symbol of a distinguished tradition and an eloquent rebuke to the ugliness of anti-Semitism," he contended that the government cannot begin making distinctions between the practices of different religions. This would risk discriminatory enforcement and undermine "the interest in uniform treatment for the members of all religious faiths."[90]

In general, even some critics of the Court give it reasonably good marks for its handling of cases involving the "free exercise" clause, various inconsistencies notwithstanding.[91] Establishment cases are another story.

THE "NO . . . ESTABLISHMENT" CASES

Most of the following establishment cases would not have come before the U.S. Supreme Court were it not for the incorporation doctrine, by which First Amendment rights are incorporated into the Fourteenth Amendment and thereby made applicable to the states as well as the federal government. Various scholars have argued vigorously against that doctrine, insisting all the while that the "free exercise" of religion would not thereby be compromised in any way. They cite such examples as Great Britain, the Scandinavian countries, the Federal Republic of Germany, and Switzerland, where one or more religions (denominations) are established and/or financially supported by the government without prejudice to the universal freedom of religious expression.[92] Others have argued just as vigorously in favor of the incorporation doctrine.[93] The point, of course, is entirely moot because the U.S. Supreme Court, since *Cantwell v. Connecticut* in 1940, has accepted and abided by the incorporation doctrine in First Amendment cases.

The Court's acceptance of the incorporation doctrine has not made the interpretation of the "no . . . establishment of religion" clause any less difficult—for the Court *or* for analysts of the Court's decisions. One has the impression of a zigzagging rather than straight-line path, as will be obvious even in the highly abbreviated review which follows.

Chief Justice Warren Burger has acknowledged that the "course of constitutional neutrality in this area cannot be an absolutely straight line. . . ."[94] And Justice Byron White has given one of the most candid expressions of the problem in a decision rendered in a minor 1980 school-aid case, *Committee for Public Education and Religious Liberty v. Regan:* "Establishment Clause cases are not easy; they stir deep feelings; and we are divided among ourselves, perhaps reflecting the different views on this subject of the people of this country."[95]

SCHOOL-RELATED CASES

It is clear that the church-state/religion-state issue has been played out most dramatically, and most contentiously, in the public schoolhouse and the public schoolroom. With the weakening of the family, the neighborhood, and the churches, the schools have been under increasing pressure to undertake the tasks these other institutions once performed, especially with respect to moral development and the fashioning of public virtue.

"Supporting the public schools," William Lee Miller writes, "indicated the uncritical at-home-ness of Protestant Americans."[96] Significantly, as in the case of enforced Sabbath observance on Sunday, they did not see the anomaly of their approach. Committed in principle to voluntaryism, they nevertheless appealed to the state to do what the churches could no longer do by the power of persuasion and example alone. They sought to turn over to the state, through the public school system, culture-forming, commitment-making activities that belong properly to the churches themselves.

This was the case, that is, until Catholics became numerically powerful and their parochial school system began to rival the public system. Catholics are always to be found in the heart of the struggle because they are the ones with the largest private school system and the greatest financial needs. And where you find Catholics in great numerical strength, you also find anti-Catholicism, or at least fears of Catholic power and influence. So it is, and so it has always been in the United States of America.[97]

The U.S. Supreme Court, with support from mainline Protestants, Jews, and strict separationists of varying religious and nonreligious convictions (including not a few Catholics as well), has been concerned over the years not so much with the actualities of abuse, but with the potentialities, that is, with the possibility that religion could be promoted in schools and classrooms supported by government funds. This concern, however, has given rise to a dilemma. Any effort on the state's part to see to it that religion is *not* fostered requires the state to entangle itself with religious institutions.

Justice Byron White, in *Lemon v. Kurtzman* (1971), argued that the Court's fear regarding the promotion of religion through government funding of nonpublic schools, programs, or students created an "insoluble paradox" for the state and for parochial schools. "The State cannot finance secular instruction if it permits religion to be taught in the same classroom; but if it exacts a promise that religion not be taught—a promise the school and its teachers are quite willing and on this record able to give—and enforces it, it is then entangled in the 'no entanglement' aspect of the Court's Establishment Clause jurisprudence."[98]

Justice White's colleagues conceded his point, but insisted that there is no way out of the paradox. It is indeed "insoluble." Funding for church-related schools, Chief Justice Burger argued, is fraught with too much "divisive political potential," or for "divisive religious fragmentation in the political area."[99] It is as if nondiscriminatory aid to these schools could actually be justified by the First Amendment were it not for the political realities of modern American life.

Schools have indeed become *the* symbol of the ideal of church-state separation. "It is almost as if there were some tacit agreement, by a very large segment of society," Christopher Mooney writes, "that if an absolutely strict separation should be maintained here, an impregnable wall built wide and high, then the ideal will be secure, and movable lines, 'overlap' and accommodation may be more easily tolerated elsewhere, in order that our *other* American ideal of benevolence toward religion might also be secure."[100]

As is clear from the record, the Court is willing to allow some limited cooperation between church and state even in the educational area, insofar as the aim of such cooperation is the promotion of religious freedom. But the spirit of cooperation evaporates as soon as there is even a hint of a possibility of political divisiveness along religious lines. As Richard E. Morgan concludes, "Constitutional 'principles' are meaningless unless the values they are meant to serve are made explicit, and the whole attempt is bootless if the values are not widely shared."[101] This should be kept in mind as we review the complex course of school-related cases.

In 1907, in *Reuben Quick Bear v. Leupp,* the Court approved the payment of federal monies drawn from Indian treaty funds to support schools for members of the Sioux tribe operated by the Bureau of Catholic Missions, on the ground that the Indians had a right "to choose their own school and to choose it frankly because the education therein

is under the influence of the religious faith in which they believe. . . ."
Any other construction, the Court argued, would pervert the establishment clause "into a means of prohibiting the free exercise of religion."[102] Furthermore, the monies came from funds under the control
of the Commissioner of Indian Affairs and were not covered by recent
congressional legislation prohibiting as new national policy (not constitutional command) Indian education by sectarian schools.

In 1930, in *Cochran* v. *Louisiana State Board of Education*, the
Court upheld a Louisiana state law authorizing the Louisiana State
Board of Education to buy books for parochial school children. Chief
Justice Charles Evans Hughes noted, for a unanimous Court, that under
Louisiana law "the same books that are furnished for children attending
public schools shall be furnished children attending private schools."
Therefore, "none [could be] adapted to religious instruction." The
Chief Justice linked the state's general police power (including the
authority to provide for the public's education) with a "child-benefit"
theory, whereby the children and not the schools are the real beneficiaries of the aid.[103]

Following the 1940 *Cantwell* v. *Connecticut* decision, in which
Justice Owen Roberts had extended the establishment clause to the
states (in a case that had nothing to do with establishment), the first
major test of the establishment clause came in *Everson* v. *Board of
Education*, the so-called "Parochial School Bus Transportation" case
of 1947. Indeed, it has been called "the single most important American
constitutional law case in the realm of the Establishment of Religion
Clause."[104]

Everson was the first of a cluster of three important school-related
establishment cases. The other two were *McCollum* v. *Board of Education* in 1948 and *Zorach* v. *Clauson* in 1952. Each of these cases
has to be seen in a broader historical context.

From the beginnings of U.S. history until the end of the Second
World War, religion (of a Protestant kind) had been circulating through
every artery of the nation's school system. Religious instruction had
been one of the primary reasons for founding schools in the first place,
and pre-Revolutionary laws required it of every child. Following the
Revolution even those states without an established church continued
to support religious education in one form or another. With the increasing religious pluralism of the early nineteenth century, however,
there were some reductions in state and local support for religious
education in the schools. Prayer and readings from the King James
Version of the Bible, however, continued almost everywhere.

But the growing Catholic population of the Northeast objected to
the Protestant atmosphere of the public schools and established their
own schools, with some measure of financial support from local au-

thorities here and there. Expressions of anti-Catholic sentiment, including violence, marked the history of this period: the Nativist movement, the formation of the Know-Nothing party, and, in 1875, President Ulysses S. Grant's proposed constitutional amendment that "neither state nor nation, nor both combined, shall support institutions of learning other than those sufficient to afford every child growing up in the land of opportunity of a good common school education, unmixed with sectarian, pagan, or atheistical dogmas."[105]

In accordance with President Grant's wishes, the amendment was introduced into the House of Representatives by Congressman James G. Blaine (later speaker of the House and a Republican candidate for the presidency):

> No State shall make any laws respecting an establishment of religion or prohibiting the free exercise thereof; and no money raised by taxation in any State for the support of public schools, or derived from any public fund therefor, nor any public lands devoted thereto, shall ever be under the control of any religious sect, nor shall any money so raised or lands so devoted be divided between religious sects or denominations.[106]

In August 1876, the Blaine resolution was passed by the House by a 180–7 vote, with 98 not voting. In the Senate a much longer resolution was reported out of the Judiciary Committee. The final sentence discloses again the inconsistency of its Protestant supporters: "This article shall not be construed to prohibit the reading of the Bible in any school or institution. . . ."[107] The Senate vote for the resolution was 28–16, with 27 absent or not voting. Since the resolution lacked a two-thirds majority, it could not be submitted to the states for ratification. Nevertheless, the Republican platform in every presidential election from 1876 through 1892 contained a plank promising such an amendment, but the Republican leadership in Congress never again pressed the issue.

Between 1877 and 1913, however, 33 states amended their own constitutions to prohibit financial aid to church-operated schools. Other approaches were taken. "Released time" programs were inaugurated early in the twentieth century to allow students to leave school during class hours to receive religious instruction off-campus. By 1949 all except four states had such programs. In 1940, religious instruction, paid for and conducted by the religious bodies themselves, was permitted in the schools themselves during regular class time, most notably in Champaign, Illinois, where an arrangement had been worked out between school authorities and representatives of Catholic, Protestant, and Jewish religious communities. Participation was always voluntary, and required the approval of parents. The instructors were also subject to the approval and supervision of the superintendent of schools. This was the so-called Champaign plan (which would be declared unconstitutional by *McCollum* v. *Board of Education* in 1948).

The facts of the *Everson* case were fairly simple. In 1941, the New Jersey legislature passed a state statute authorizing the local school districts to provide for the transportation of children to and from school. The Board of Education of the township of Ewing, New Jersey, passed a resolution authorizing reimbursement to parents of monies spent sending their children to public or Catholic parochial schools "on regular busses operated by the public transportation system."[108] Mr. Everson challenged the constitutionality of both the state law and the school board resolution on various grounds, most notable of which was that the state law and school board resolution violated the establishment clause of the First Amendment made applicable to the states by the due process clause of the Fourteenth Amendment.

The Court voted 5–4 against Everson's complaint, even though it held at the same time that the establishment clause did indeed apply to the states. In this case, however, the purpose of the program was to protect children from traffic hazards and the dangers of the road. Such a program does not become unconstitutional merely because an incidental benefit is conferred upon churches.

More significant than the decision itself is the opinion expressed on behalf of the Court by Justice Hugo Black. For the first time in its history the U.S. Supreme Court set forth a comprehensive interpretation of the *minimal* prohibitions that the Court said were required by the clause, "Congress shall make no law respecting an establishment of religion. . . ." Although the vote had been split 5–4, no one challenged the Court's definition of minimal prohibitions, as presented in Justice Black's opinion:

> The 'establishment of religion' clause of the First Amendment means at least this: Neither a state nor the Federal Government can set up a church. Neither can pass laws which aid one religion, aid all religions, or prefer one religion over another. Neither can force nor influence a person to go to or remain away from church against his will or force him to profess a belief or disbelief in any religion. No person can be punished for entertaining or professing religious belief or disbelief, for church attendance or non-attendance. No tax in any amount, large or small, can be levied to support any religious activities or institutions, whatever they may be called, or whatever form they may adopt to teach or practice religion. Neither a state nor the Federal Government can, openly or secretly, participate in the affairs of any religious organizations or groups and vice-versa. In the words of Jefferson, the clause against establishment of religion was intended to erect a 'wall of separation between church and State. . . .'[109]

In 1948, in *McCollum v. Board of Education,* the Court declared the Champaign plan unconstitutional, appealing directly to its earlier *Everson* decision in which it ruled that the state may not pass laws that aid all religions. The Champaign plan had this effect by placing the public school system at the disposal of religious groups for the dissemination of their doctrines or ideals. "For the First Amendment rests upon the premise," the Court stated, "that both religion and government can best work to achieve their lofty aims if each is left free from the other within its respective sphere. Or, as we said in the Everson case, the First Amendment has erected a wall between Church and State which must be kept high and impregnable."[110]

The lone dissenter, Justice Stanley Reed, appealed to the historical precedents against the majority opinion and challenged his colleagues' interpretation of Jefferson's Regulations for the University of Virginia:

> Thus the 'wall of separation between Church and State' that Mr. Jefferson built at the University which he founded did not exclude religious education from the school. The difference between the generality of his statements on the separation of Church and State and the specificity of his conclusions on education are considerable. A rule of law should not be drawn from a figure of speech.[111]

In 1952, in *Zorach* v. *Clauson*, the Court drew back from its previous decision. It found a released-time program in New York City acceptable because it did not involve the use of public buildings. This is the case where Justice William O. Douglas made what was for him the astonishing observation that "we are a religious people whose institutions presuppose a Supreme Being. . . . When the state encourages religious instruction or cooperates with religious authorities by adjusting the schedule of events to sectarian needs, it follows the best of our traditions. . . . To hold that it may not would be to find in the Constitution a callous indifference to religious groups. That would be preferring those who believe in no religion over those who do believe."[112] William Lee Miller has been led to conclude that Justice Douglas' record on church-state cases resembles "the homeward journey of a New Year's Eve reveler."[113]

The school prayer issue burst upon the judicial scene in 1962 in the bitterly controversial *Engel* v. *Vitale* case. By the start of the decade fully one-third of the nation's public schools began the school day with some form of prayer, and nearly half required Bible reading (the percentages were highest in the South, lowest in the Far West). In the *Engel* case the Court ruled unconstitutional the use of a prayer composed in 1951 by the New York Board of Regents: "Almighty God, we acknowledge our dependence upon Thee, and we beg Thy blessings upon us, our parents, our teachers, and our country." Justice Black, writing for the majority, insisted that "the constitutional prohibition against laws respecting an establishment of religion must at least mean that in this country it is no part of the business of government to compose official prayers for any group of the American people to recite as part of a religious program carried on by the government."[114] The decision unleashed a torrent of criticism from religious leaders, including Catholics who had previously been suspicious of the influence of Protestantism in the public school system. But now there was a common enemy: secularism and its most virulent political form, "atheistic Communism."

In 1963, in *Abington School District* v. *Schempp* and *Murray* v. *Curlett* (one decision rendered for two cases), the Court struck down a Pennsylvania law requiring the reading of ten verses of the Bible at the beginning of each school day, and the practice of reciting the Lord's Prayer and passages from the Bible in the Baltimore public schools. The decision, written by Justice Tom Clark, introduced his often-cited test of any enactments regarding religion: what is their purpose and what is their primary effect? If the enactment either advances or inhibits religion, the enactment is unconstitutional. "That is to say," Justice Clark continued, "that to withstand the strictures of the Establishment Clause there must be a secular legislative purpose and a primary effect that neither advances nor inhibits religion. . . ."[115] The Abington, Pennsylvania, and Baltimore, Maryland, practices failed the test.

The Court challenged the counterargument, expressed in Justice Potter Stewart's dissenting opinion, that the effect of the Court's decision would be to establish a "religion of secularism." What is banned are only "religious exercises required by the States in violation of the command of the First Amendment that the Government maintain strict neutrality, neither aiding nor opposing religion." Indeed, Justice Clark insisted, "Nothing we have said here indicates that . . . study of the Bible or religion, when presented objectively as part of a secular program of education, may not be effected consistently with the First Amendment."[116] The Court also rejected the contention that the concept of neutrality collides with the majority's right to the "free exercise" of religion. The "free exercise" clause, the Court argued, has never meant that a majority could use the machinery of the state to practice its beliefs.[117] Few of the Court's arguments in religion-related cases have been more telling than that one.

Subsequent attempts by various states to circumvent the U.S. Supreme Court's decision were all struck down. Some of the Court's opponents launched a movement to pass a constitutional amendment to permit prayer in the schools, but their efforts in 1966, 1971, and 1984 (the last one with the full support of President Reagan) failed to achieve the necessary two-thirds vote in Congress.

In 1968, in *Epperson* v. *Arkansas*, the Court, in an opinion written by Justice Abe Fortas, struck down an Arkansas law, passed in 1928, prohibiting the teaching of evolution in the public schools. The "overriding fact" for the Court was that the Arkansas law proscribed the teaching of evolution "for the sole reason" that it was in conflict with "a particular religious doctrine; . . . a particular interpretation of the

Book of *Genesis* by a particular religious group." The law, therefore, was itself in conflict with the establishment and free exercise clauses of the First Amendment.

In the same year, in *Board of Education* v. *Allen*, the Court upheld a New York law requiring local school districts to lend textbooks free of charge to parochial school students. The Court ruled that such assistance was only indirect, and was justified because "private education has played and is playing a significant and valuable role in raising national levels of knowledge, competence, and experience."[118] Furthermore, according to Justice Byron White, the aid passed the test formulated by Justice Tom Clark in the *Schempp* case. Whatever financial benefit was involved in the free loan of textbooks went to parents and children, not the schools. Justice William O. Douglas issued a stinging dissent. "Can there be the slightest doubt," he asked, "that the head of the parochial school will select the book or books that best promote its sectarian creed?"[119]

In 1971, in *Lemon* v. *Kurtzman* (decided with *Earley* v. *DiCenso* and *Robinson* v. *DiCenso*), the Court ruled unconstitutional a Rhode Island law providing up to a 15% supplement from public funds for the salaries for private school teachers' salaries, textbooks, and instructional materials. A similar law in Pennsylvania was also struck down. In writing for the majority, Chief Justice Burger delivered himself of a broad judgment that, if given the force of constitutional law, could deny religious persons and religious institutions their constitutional right to participate fully in the political process: "Under our system the choice has been made that government is to be entirely excluded from the area of religious instruction and churches excluded from the affairs of government."[120]

On the same day, in *Tilton* v. *Richardson*, the Court saved the Higher Education Facilities Act of 1963, which in this case provided federal grants for the construction of buildings at four Catholic colleges and universities in Connecticut. There was no Court opinion as such because five of the nine justices could not agree on all points of a single opinion. Four of the justices did agree that the realm of higher education is different from elementary and high school education. There is significantly less potential for divisiveness because the student body is not primarily local but is drawn from many different parts of the country. Because Justice Byron White concurred separately, the law was sustained.

Two years later, in *Hunt* v. *McNair*, the Court also upheld a South Carolina statute aiding colleges, including church-related institutions, through the issuance of revenue bonds for construction of facilities expressly not used for sectarian purposes. The Court held that the statute met all three of the criteria: it did not have as its primary effect the advancing of religion; it had a valid public purpose, that is, the aiding of students attending institutions of higher education in the state; and it did not constitute excessive government entanglement with religion (a criterion added in *Lemon v. Kurtzman*).

Also in 1973, in *Committee for Public Education and Religious Liberty v. Nyquist, Commissioner of Education,* the Court ruled unconstitutional three New York state programs which provided (1) direct grants to private elementary and secondary schools in low-income areas for maintenance, repair, and equipment costs, (2) tuition reimbursements for low-income parents of private school students, and (3) tax deductions for parents whose income was too high to qualify for reimbursement. The Court held, in the opinion written by Justice Lewis Powell, that the New York law had the "impermissible effect of advancing religion," and, therefore, failed the second of the two tests for establishment which had been set down by Justice Tom Clark in the *Schempp* decision of 1963.[121]

In 1975, in *Meek v. Pittenger,* the Court sustained, in an opinion supported by only a plurality of three, with the necessary concurrence of three other justices, one Pennsylvania statute that allowed the use of public funds for acquiring and then loaning textbooks to nonpublic school children. On the other hand, it ruled unconstitutional another statute which provided "auxiliary services" (counseling, testing, psychological services, speech and hearing therapy, services for exceptional and remedial students, and so on) to nonpublic schools. This violated the establishment clause, the Court asserted, because the constant state supervision of these services would require significant "political entanglement together with administrative entanglement."[122] Also declared unconstitutional was a section of a statute allowing the direct loan of instructional materials and equipment to parochial schools, because the loan was seen as having the primary effect of advancing the religious character of the schools. In a dissenting opinion, Justice William Brennan added a fourth criterion to test the compatibility of state subsidies with the establishment clause: "the divisive political potential of these state programs."[123]

A year later, in *Roemer v. Board of Public Works of Maryland,* a plurality opinion, written by Justice Harry Blackmun, found that a Maryland statute which provided annual noncategorical grants to private colleges, including religiously affiliated institutions (on the condition that the funds not be used for "sectarian purposes"), passed the threefold *Lemon v. Kurtzman* test and so was not in conflict with the establishment clause.

In 1977, in *Wolman v. Walter,* the Court was shown to be "greatly divided, not only on the criteria to be used in examining a statute purportedly unconstitutional because it provided some public funding for nonpublic sectarian school children, but also in the most part as to which specific aids may be constitutionally provided and which may not."[124]

At issue was an Ohio statute that authorized the state to provide nonpublic school pupils with books, instructional materials and equipment, standardized testing and scoring, diagnostic services, therapeutic services, and field transportation. Justice Blackmun gave the major opinion in eight parts, in four of which he attracted a majority to his side. On the textbook issue, there were five different statements made by the nine justices. The provision was sustained. On the supplying of standardized tests and scoring, the vote was the same: four for upholding its constitutionality, two concurring, and three dissenting separately. On diagnostic services, six voted to uphold, two concurred, and one dissented. On therapeutic services, the vote was five to uphold, two concurring, and two dissenting. On instructional materials and equipment, a majority of five ruled the aid unconstitutional because it had the "primary effect of providing a direct and substantial advancement of the sectarian enterprise" of the parochial schools. One concurred with the majority, and three dissented. Finally, on field trips, a majority of five also found this aid unconstitutional, with four dissenting.

Little wonder that Justice John Paul Stevens should have declared: " 'Corrosive precedents' have left us without firm principles on which to decide these cases. As this case demonstrates the States have been encouraged to search for new ways of achieving forbidden ends. . . . What should be a 'high and impregnable' wall between church and state has been reduced to a 'blurred, indistinct, and variable barrier,' . . ."[125]

In 1980, in *Stone* v. *Graham*, the Court, by a surprisingly close 5–4 vote, ruled unconstitutional a Kentucky law ordering the posting of the Ten Commandments in public school rooms. And in the same year, the Court refused to hear an appeal from a lower court's approval of a Christmas display in the public schools of Sioux Falls, South Dakota.[126] The separatist spirit of the Warren Court was giving way to the more accommodationist temper of the Burger Court.

Also in 1980, in *Committee for Public Education and Religious Liberty* v. *Regan*, Justice White embraced the threefold test of *Lemon* v. *Kurtzman*, which he had attacked in the *Roemer* case, and wrote the opinion for a Court divided 5–4. The Court upheld a New York state statute authorizing the use of public funds to reimburse church-sponsored and secular nonpublic schools for performing various testing and reporting services mandated by state law. The statute's purpose and primary effect were secular and involved no excessive government entanglement with religion.

The next year, in *Widmar* v. *Vincent,* the Court ruled that the University of Missouri at Kansas City could not deny religious groups the use of school facilities that were made available to secular clubs.

In 1983, in *Mueller* v. *Allen,* the Court, in another 5–4 decision, upheld a Minnesota law which permitted state taxpayers to claim a deduction from gross income for some expenditures for tuition, textbooks, and transportation, whether their children attended public or private schools. The Court thereby crossed the firm line drawn in the *Nyquist* decision a decade earlier. Justice William Rehnquist, writing for the majority, argued that the Minnesota law did not constitute a support of religion because the deductions were available to parents of students in both public and private schools. This was the first time, Justice Thurgood Marshall stated in his dissenting opinion, that the Court had upheld financial support for religious schools without any reason to assume that the support would be restricted to the secular functions of these schools.

In 1985, the Court rendered three of its most controversial decisions in religion-related cases. In *Wallace* v. *Jaffree,* it ruled against an Alabama statute authorizing a one-minute period of silence in the public schools "for meditation or voluntary prayer." Justice Sandra Day O'Connor, in a concurring opinion, suggested that the practice might have been sustained if there had been no mention of prayer. And in *Grand Rapids* v. *Ball* and *Aguilar* v. *Felton,* it ruled unconstitutional programs in Grand Rapids, Michigan, and New York City through which public school teachers were providing remedial instruction in parochial schools to children with learning problems.

In 1986, in *Witters* v. *Washington,* the Court ruled, against the Washington Supreme Court, that the First Amendment does not forbid a state to grant vocational assistance to a blind college student who plans to study for the ministry in a Christian college, Inland Empire School of the Bible in Spokane. Although the decision was unanimous, there were four separate opinions, each giving somewhat different reasons for reaching the same result. Justice Thurgood Marshall concluded that the aid met the first two criteria of the Court's three-part test: the program clearly had a secular purpose and it would not have the primary effect of advancing religion. But he left open the possibility that such state aid might be barred by the third criterion: the danger of government "entanglement" with religion, since Mr. Witters would be using the money to study at a church-related institution.

In the same year, the Court left unresolved one of the most contentious constitutional issues before it during that particular term: whether student religious groups should be able to hold organized prayer meetings in the public schools. The case, *Bender* v. *Williamsport,* had been seen as a test of the constitutionality of the Equal Access

Act of 1984, which required schools to allow student meetings for "religious, political, philosophical" or other discussions on the same basis as other extracurricular activities.

The students had sued the Williamsport school board, arguing that they had a First Amendment right to hold prayer meetings when other extracurricular activities were taking place. In light of the Equal Access Act, a federal district court upheld the students' lawsuit and the school board decided to allow them to pray. One board member appealed the decision on his own, but his term expired while the appeal was pending. Meanwhile, a federal appellate court reversed the district court decision and ruled student prayer groups unconstitutional.

By a 5–4 vote, the U.S. Supreme Court ruled that the former school board member had no standing to appeal a federal district court decision that upheld student prayer rights. The effect of the U.S. Supreme Court's ruling was to reinstate that decision without passing on its correctness.

TAX-RELATED CASES

Bradfield v. *Roberts*, in 1899, was the first significant establishment case in the period following ratification of the Fourteenth Amendment. In this case the Court rejected a taxpayer's complaint that the appropriation of federal funds for the construction of buildings on the grounds of Providence Hospital, operated by the Sisters of Charity in Washington, D. C., constituted an establishment of religion. The Court ruled that a hospital run by a religious order was to be viewed as a secular corporation as long as it performed its purposes as stated in the articles of incorporation, despite the "alleged 'sectarian character of the hospital'."[127]

In 1970, in *Walz* v. *Tax Commissioner of the City of New York*, the Court upheld the right of the city of New York to grant tax exemptions for church property. There is room in the First Amendment, Chief Justice Warren Burger declared, for "benevolent neutrality" by government toward religion. Burger suggested that perhaps too much weight had been placed on a few words or phrases in Justice Hugo Black's opinion for the majority in the *Everson* case. To be sure, under the establishment clause, the state may not directly subsidize churches, but tax exemptions are simply acts by which the state "simply abstains from demanding that the church support the state."

Burger then added a third criterion to the two given earlier by Justice Tom Clark in the *Schempp* case. Beyond purpose and primary effect, the Court would now be attentive to the danger of "an excessive government entanglement with religion." Since the elimination of the tax exemption would establish a relationship of tax collector to taxpayer, the exemption passes this third test.[128]

The Chief Justice's notion of "benevolent neutrality" merits at least as much attention here as his criterion of "entanglement." Benevolent neutrality is to be distinguished from "strict neutrality," a concept proposed by constitutional scholar Philip B. Kurland. For Professor Kurland, "strict neutrality" means that the government is simply not to use religion as a basis for classification for purposes of government action, whether in the conferral of rights or privileges, or in the imposition of obligations. Justice John Marshall Harlan is the only member of the Court to have used Kurland's concept, and he did so in the *Walz* case.[129] Chief Justice Burger actually provided an answer to this theory in his *Walz* opinion:

> The course of constitutional neutrality in this area cannot be an absolutely straight line; rigidity could well defeat the basic purpose of these provisions, which is to insure that no religion be sponsored or favored, none commanded, and none inhibited. . . . Short of these expressly proscribed governmental acts there is room for play in the joints productive of a benevolent neutrality which will permit religious exercise to exist without sponsorship and without interference.[130]

In 1983, in *Bob Jones University* v. *United States,* the Court upheld the action of the Internal Revenue Service in denying tax-exempt status to Bob Jones University in North Carolina because of the school's policy of prohibiting interracial dating. According to the Court, the school based its policy on a particular interpretation of the Bible. Chief Justice Burger argued that "eradicating racial discrimination in education substantially outweighs whatever burden denial of tax benefits places on petitioners' exercise of their religious beliefs."[131] His successor, Justice William Rehnquist, dissented.

SUNDAY CLOSING LAW CASES

In 1961, there was a series of decisions on Sunday closing laws, most notably *McGowan* v. *Maryland,* in which the Court concluded that the Sunday observance had become so secularized that it no longer served any truly religious purpose. The real purpose of the Sunday observance is "to protect all persons from physical and moral debasement which comes from uninterrupted labor."[132] This time Justice Douglas occupied his usual libertarian high ground. "It is a strange Bill of Rights," he wrote, "that makes it possible for the dominant religious group to bring the minority to heel because the minority, in the doing of acts which intrinsically are wholesome and not antisocial, does not defer to the majority's religious beliefs. . . ."[133] He was alone in his dissent on these four cases.

THE LEGISLATIVE CHAPLAIN CASE

In 1983, in *Marsh* v. *Chambers,* the Court ruled in favor of the long-standing custom of the Nebraska state legislature to have a paid chaplain who opened each session with a prayer. Chief Justice Burger appealed to the nation's 200-year history and concluded that the practice of opening legislative sessions with a prayer had become "a part of the fabric of our society."[134] He also noted that only three days before it approved the Bill of Rights, including the First Amendment, the first Congress authorized the appointment of paid chaplains for both the House of Representatives and the Senate.

NATIVITY SCENE CASES

In 1984, in *Lynch* v. *Donnelly,* the Court upheld, by a 5–4 vote, the constitutionality of a Nativity scene display maintained by the city of Pawtucket, Rhode Island. The Court referred to the city's support as indirect only and saw the practice as no different from the celebration of Thanksgiving and Christmas as national holidays, the display of religious paintings in public art galleries, or the singing of Christmas carols and hymns in public schools.

In 1985, in *Board of Trustees of the Village of Scarsdale* v. *McCreary,* the Court split 4–4, thereby affirming a decision of the U.S. Court of Appeals for the Second Circuit that had invalidated a ban against a Christmas crèche put up by the Scarsdale (NY) Village Board.[135]

COMMENTARY

Although the preceding review makes no claim to constitutional expertise, some comment is in order here.

There is at least a hint of bias at opposite ends of the spectrum. On the left, supporters of an absolute "wall of separation between church and state" (more accurately, *religion* and state) resort to historical arguments that yield, at best, ambiguous conclusions. But they argue their views, with vigor and self-confidence, as if none except a fundamentalist or a financially strapped mainline religious group (read: Catholic), eager for access to the public treasury, could possibly disagree, so overwhelming is the evidence. Whatever the nature of the evidence, it is *not* overwhelming, as even a cursory review of these Court cases reveals.

Is it unfair to ask, therefore, if some advocates of an absolute "wall of separation" are at least as much influenced by their own philosophy of secularism as they are by legal and historical arguments? The secularist holds, as matter of principle, that religion has no legitimate place in public affairs, that it is essentially and exclusively a matter of private belief and practice.

Secularism is not an abstraction. Secularists exist.[136] And they can be as stubbornly ideological as some of the fiercely traditional religionists they criticize.

On the right are those traditional religionists, a group composed mainly of Protestant fundamentalists, conservative evangelicals, some conservative mainline Protestants, and a respectable minority of strongly-to-moderately conservative Catholics.[137] They think this nation was founded as, and should remain, a "Christian" nation. "Judeo-Christian" is their gesture toward ecumenism, but they'd have to look high and low for much Jewish influence in Convention Hall, Philadelphia, or in Thomas Jefferson's library, or just about anywhere else in the United States before the mass migration of Jews from eastern Europe in the 1880s.

For the right, the "wall of separation" can accommodate selective breachings. Religious organizations and their leaders can participate fully in the political process (running candidates, establishing political action groups, pressuring Congress, and so on), while government, in its turn, is obliged to support those religious initiatives which certain religious organizations and leaders urge it to support, like prayer in the schools, financial aid for religiously affiliated schools, municipally funded Nativity scenes on the courthouse lawn, and assorted laws banning, or at least severely restricting, behavior allegedly disapproved by the Bible. Anything less means that secularism rules America.

I should not agree, however, with Justice Potter Stewart's dissenting opinion in *Abington School District* v. *Schempp* (1963), which struck down Bible reading and the recitation of the Lord's Prayer in public schools, that such decisions establish "a religion of secularism, or at least government support for the beliefs of those who think that religious exercises should be conducted only in private."[138]

He, and those who agree with him, fail to make an important distinction between secularism and secularity. The former is an ideology which explicitly denies the reality of the sacred, or at least wishes to exclude it entirely from the realm of the world (thus, the word *secular*, taken from the Latin, *saeculum*, or world). The latter is a positive, or at least neutral, term, which affirms the integrity and independence of worldly realities in themselves. Secularity is opposed to the view, dominant in the medieval period, that the temporal is simply an instrument of the spiritual, the state an instrument of the church.[139]

Secularism and religious faith are antithetical, but secularity and religious faith are entirely compatible.

Neither do I agree with A. James Reichley and others who suggest that various Court decisions, including *Schempp*, have had, or can eventually have, the effect of banishing religion from the public life of "society."[140] The *state*, not society, is covered by these decisions. Religion continues to enjoy every right and opportunity to influence and even to permeate "society," especially by the force of its own example. If a tax-supported Nativity scene cannot be erected on public property, literally hundreds of them can be erected in front of churches, church-related schools, private corporations, and private residences.

Nor is religion banished from public life or civic life. There are many different ways in which religious organizations and leaders can, and do, participate in the public and civic life of the nation. What the First Amendment, as interpreted by the U.S. Supreme Court, forbids is any aid by the state to religion, which has as its purpose or primary effect an advancement of religion, or which "entangles" government with religion, or which has the potential for creating political divisions along religious lines. The First Amendment also clearly forbids the establishment of any religion or group of religions as the official religion(s) of the state, as well as any infringement on the right of individuals and groups to exercise their religion, or to profess and practice none at all. No more, no less.

Politically conservative scholars, like Robert L. Cord,[141] who take issue with various U.S. Supreme Court decisions in religion-related cases do so more on historical than on ideological grounds. They do not make the argument proposed by many nonscholars that, because this is a "Christian" nation, or at least one founded on "Judeo-Christian" principles, the state has an obligation to respect, preserve and nurture the nation's religious character, short of establishing any single religion as the state religion or of denying the rights of religious minorities to practice their own faith.

It is highly unlikely, therefore, that even so conservative a scholar as Professor Cord would agree with Education Secretary William J. Bennett's opinion that certain Court decisions have been "misguided" because they do not "reflect sufficiently on the relationship between our faith [sic] and our political order." For Secretary Bennett that relationship is clear: "Our values as a free people and the central values of the Judeo-Christian tradition are flesh of the flesh and blood of the blood."[142]

What Cord objects to is the quality of the Court's historical scholarship. Accordingly, his criticisms of certain religion-related Court decisions are not based on quasi-theological grounds, as Secretary Bennett's (and others') seem to be, but on the premise that the justices simply haven't provided "adequate reasons as to why nondiscriminatory aid to religion or religiously-affiliated institutions, in pursuit of a constitutionally valid public goal, violates the *Constitution* of the United States."[143] Indeed, Cord himself does not argue that religious observance must be preferred for its own sake. He has, in fact, disagreed with the Court's decisions in the "Sunday Closing Laws" because those decisions have "allowed a single religious tradition's 'day of rest,' in a religiously pluralistic society, to be legally prescribed, contrary to the Establishment Clause's prohibition of elevating any religion or religious tradition into an exclusively preferred position."[144]

I should not want to insert myself any more than I already have into the discussions regarding either the incorporation doctrine, whereby the Fourteenth Amendment is said to apply First Amendment rights and restrictions to the states, or into the historical argument between, let us say, Cord and Leo Pfeffer regarding the intentions of James Madison, Thomas Jefferson, and the other framers of the Constitution and the Bill of Rights.

These are constitutional, legal, and historical questions, not theological questions. John Courtney Murray was exactly right: the words and provisions of the First Amendment are "not articles of faith but articles of peace." They are "not invested with the sanctity that attaches to dogma, but only with the rationality that attaches to law."[145]

Nonetheless, some of the opposition to the U.S. Supreme Court's decisions in religion-related cases does indeed seem to be of a theological character, or at least of a politico-theological character. It is assumed by the Court's opponents on the right that the First Amendment, although immediately legal in nature, somehow embodies a theological principle, namely, that not only individuals and voluntary communities, but also states and governments have an obligation to acknowledge the sovereignty of God in some public way and to abide by the various dogmatic and moral truths that God has revealed. The argument collapses entirely the distinction between society and the state.

Some others, not necessarily associated with the political and religious right, seem to go even further, arguing that ours is a nation of a particularly religious character: a nation with a distinctive mission and destiny; a nation bound by a special covenant with God; indeed, a nation "with the soul of a church."[146] The state and its government are the political instruments whereby the nation fulfills its religious duties.

By insisting that no religion be preferred over others, it is argued, the First Amendment protects against excessive conflict among diverse religious groups, but it also guarantees the free exercise of religion. According to this view, the free exercise clause implies more than respect for the legal rights of dissenters. The government also assumes an obligation to support religious activity, giving special attention to "the central values of the Judeo-Christian tradition," because it is "flesh of the flesh and blood of the blood." But the "Judeo" part of the formula is open to historical question, and the "Christian" part of the formula *begs* a theological question: which *kind* of Christianity? Jimmy Swaggart's or Cardinal Bernardin's? Jerry Falwell's or Jesse Jackson's? Ronald Reagan's or Jimmy Carter's?

The left also employs politico-theological arguments, namely, that religion is essentially private and, therefore, must be treated legally and constitutionally as if it had no role to play in the social, economic, and political orders. Furthermore, because there is also something inherently divisive about religion, it must be treated legally and constitutionally with the greatest measure of skepticism and vigilance.

Since there is no truth whatever to the first assumption about the essentially private nature of religion, and since the desire to keep religion confined to "the sacristy" is already so widespread in our society, we should bend over backwards, in our interpretations of the First Amendment, to defend and protect the "free exercise" of religion by individuals and religious groups alike.

On the other hand, since there *is* some truth to the second assumption about the potentially divisive nature of religion, our interpretations of the First Amendment must resist every hint of an establishment of religion, including especially the use of the state as an instrument of religion.

James Madison offered sound advice in his *Memorial and Remonstrance*, namely, that to establish or to extend any privilege to the Christian religion (or to its "Judeo-Christian" surrogate) is "to weaken in those who profess this Religion a pious confidence in its innate excellence and the patronage of its Author; and to foster in those who still reject it, a suspicion that its friends are too conscious of its fallacies to trust its own merits."[147] A very important point indeed.

Thus, we should be far more concerned about state-sponsored prayer in public schools (which constitutes more than a hint of establishment) than about financial aid to students in church-sponsored schools (which might facilitate the free exercise of religion in a spirit of "benevolent neutrality").

By and large, the U.S. Supreme Court has been following this middle course between ideological secularism and (Judeo-) Christian preferentialism, albeit in a somewhat zigzagging fashion. That is why it has critics on the left and the right alike.

E Pluribus Unum

"There is an innumerable multitude of sects in the United States," Alexis de Tocqueville wrote a century-and-a-half ago. "They are all different in the worship they offer to the Creator. . . ."[148] Had Tocqueville said no more, we could have readily seen something of our own times in his. But there *is* more. "Each sect worships God in its own fashion," he continued, "but all preach the same morality in the name of God. . . . Moreover, all the sects in the United States belong to the great unity of Christendom, and Christian morality is everywhere the same."[149]

On two counts, therefore, Tocqueville's America differed very significantly from our own. First, there is no longer any national moral consensus. As the abortion issue alone has made clear, we have an extraordinary diversity of moral opinion today, even among Christians. Secondly, this is no longer a Christian nation, in any demographic sense. Not all the religious people in the United States "belong to the great unity of Christendom." While we still have, in these waning years of the twentieth century, an "innumerable multitude of sects," many of them are as likely to be non-Christian as Christian.

Accordingly, those who quote Tocqueville to buttress a case for governmental support of religious institutions and enforcement of religious values had better do so with care. In Tocqueville's view of America, religion meant Christianity, and Christians were supposedly in fundamental agreement about "the duties of men to one another," and preached "the same morality in the name of God."[150]

The *new* America was described by Governor Mario M. Cuomo, of New York, in his widely discussed lecture at the University of Notre Dame in September 1984. "We are a religious people, many of us descended from ancestors who came here expressly to live their religious faith free from coercion or repression," he declared. "But we are also a people of many religions, with no established church, who hold different beliefs on many matters."[151] So these are different times from Tocqueville's. Because there are many nonreligious as well as religious people in our society, and because even the religious people do not agree among themselves, public morality in America can no longer be identified simply with Christian morality nor even with that peculiar hybrid known as Judeo-Christian morality. The fact that certain values are religious (Christian, Judeo-Christian, or whatever) does not rule them out of court. But the fact that they *are* religious doesn't require their acceptability either. "The arguments start," Governor Cuomo suggested, "when religious values are used to support positions which would impose on other people restrictions they find unacceptable."

"The community must decide," he continued, "if what is being proposed would be better left to private discretion than public policy; whether it restricts freedoms, and if so to what end, to whose benefit; whether it will produce a good or bad result; whether overall it will help the community or merely divide it.

"The right answers to these questions can be elusive," Governor Cuomo conceded. "Some of the wrong answers, on the other hand, are quite clear." Those wrong answers come from those who say it's all very simple because this is, and always has been, a Christian nation. Our laws must reflect who we are and what we have been.

"But where would that leave the non-believers?" the Governor asked. Nonbelievers, after all, were not a very prominent part of the national scene in Tocqueville's day. "And whose Christianity would be law, yours or mine?" Again, Tocqueville would have been mystified by the question. For him, "Christian morality is everywhere the same." It may have been so in the first half of the nineteenth century although one doubts it, but it certainly isn't so today.

"This 'Christian nation' argument should concern, even frighten, two groups: non-Christians and thinking Christians," Cuomo continued. And it does, he said, because "[w]ay down deep, the American people are afraid of an entangling relationship between formal religions, or whole bodies of religious belief, and government. Apart from constitutional law and religious doctrine, there is a sense that tells us it is wrong to presume to speak for God or to claim God's sanction of our particular legislation and His rejection of all other positions."[152]

Two weeks later, at St. Francis College in Brooklyn, Governor Cuomo repeated his position, in light of some criticisms of the Notre Dame talk. He had *not* said at Notre Dame that religious and moral values have to be "surrendered to a popular consensus to avoid disagreement and foster harmony." Nor had he said that the community's consensus on what is right or wrong should never be challenged. "What I *did* say, and what I repeat is that if we are serious about making certain values a part of the public morality, part of the statutes and laws that bind everyone, there must first be a public consensus; that's the way laws are made in a democratic society."[153]

John Courtney Murray had articulated Cuomo's position, albeit in a somewhat more academic manner, 25 years earlier. No society or state can succeed in its purposes unless it is committed to what every society and state is committed to: justice. "Civic amity," as Murray called it, is possible only when it is grounded on a "commonly shared will to justice," and that "civic amity," in turn, is the ground of peace. "This unity, qualified by amity, is the highest good of the civil multitude and the perfection of its civility."[154]

Society and the affairs of state are "civil" when citizens are "locked together in argument" about three major themes: public affairs (matters which are, in Plato's ancient phrase, "for the advantage of the public"); the affairs of the commonwealth, which fall, in decisive measure, beyond the limited scope of government (such as education); and, what is most important and most difficult, the constitutional consensus, that is, about what it is that brings a people together into a political society and defines their larger aims.

The quest for civility in the United States is, of course, qualified by the nation's pluralistic character. Murray's analysis, however, is already dated. In his time, he spoke of four principal components of American pluralism: Protestant, Catholic, Jewish, and secularist. There are more than that now, and many "pluralisms" within each component as well.

Nonetheless, Murray's prescription remains pertinent. Although we cannot realistically hope for a perfect consensus, we *can* do at least two things: limit the warfare among various competing points of view (which he calls "conspiracies"), and enlarge the dialogue. In other words, we can lay down our arms and take up the argument.

It was for the sake of insuring such peace that the nation's founders proposed and ratified the First Amendment. This amendment is not a theological formulation, but a political one. It contains "not articles of faith but articles of peace." The establishment clause is not "a piece of ecclesiology" nor is the "free exercise" clause "a piece of religious philosophy."[155] Murray criticized both the Protestant tendency (not common to all Protestants, by any means) to elevate the freedom-of-religion and separation-of-church-and-state principles into doctrinal principles, and the secularist tendency to absolutize the same principles on philosophical, if not on theological, grounds.

In seeking an understanding of the First Amendment, Murray argued, "we have to abandon the poetry of those who would make a religion out of freedom of religion and a dogma out of separation of church and state. We have to talk prose, the prose of the Constitution itself, which is an ordinary legal prose having nothing to do with doctrinaire theories."[156] It was, in the words of John C. Calhoun, "the force of circumstances and not foresight or wisdom" which induced the framers of the Constitution to adopt its wisest provisions, including especially the First Amendment.[157] Its twin clauses were "the twin children of social necessity, the necessity of creating a social environment, protected by law, in which men of differing religious faiths might live together in peace."[158]

It was fortunate, Murray observed, that the framers of the First Amendment were for the most part lawyers. They had "a strong sense of that primary criterion of good law, which is its necessity or utility for the preservation of the public peace, under a given set of circumstances."[159] The "highest integrating element" of the common good, which is normative for all law, is "social peace, assured by equal justice in dealing with possibly conflicting groups. This legal criterion," he concluded, "is the first and most solid ground on which the validity of the First Amendment rests."[160]

A second legal criterion is embodied in Oliver Wendell Holmes' famous dictum, "The life of the law is not logic but experience."[161] The American experience itself has demonstrated again and again the practical wisdom of the framers. It has shown, first, that political unity and stability are possible without uniformity of religious belief and practice, and without the need for governmental restrictions on any religion. Secondly, the American experience has shown that stable political unity can be strengthened by the exclusion of religious differences from affairs of state and government, thereby preventing the factionalism which Madison and others warned against. And thirdly, the American experience has shown that religious communities themselves, not least the Catholic Church, have benefited by our free institutions and by the traditional separation of religion and state. Elsewhere, religions have been alternately the subject of privilege or persecution, as the political character of governments changed.

In the American experience the government has not tried to represent some transcendental truth that happens to be current in society. It represents only "the commonly shared moral values of the community," that is, "the truth of society as it actually is; and the truth is that American society is religiously pluralist."[162] And, Murray continued, it is not the function of government to resolve disputes among conflicting truths: "As representative of a pluralist society, wherein religious faith is—as it must be—free, government undertakes to represent the principle of freedom."[163]

Murray insisted that the unity of society, which is called peace, is "the highest good of the civil multitude and the perfection of its civility." In a society marked by pluralism, and especially religious pluralism, it is impossible to achieve this unity and peace apart from a dialogue which strives persistently for consensus.[164] The political dynamic is always from the many to the one, *e pluribus unum*.

FOUR

"WE HOLD THESE TRUTHS . . ."

THE history of the United States of America yields a complex and often ambiguous mix of data on the relationship between religion and politics. There is no single model or consistent pattern in the pre-Revolutionary colonies nor in the several states of the new Union. The intentions of the nation's founders as they drafted the Constitution and the Bill of Rights are open to varied interpretations, and so, too, is Thomas Jefferson's celebrated metaphor concerning the "wall of separation" between church and state.[1] It is impossible to construct a coherent synthesis of U.S. Supreme Court decisions in religion-related cases. And no consensus about the relationship between religion and politics exists even among or within America's major religious communities.

Nevertheless, the basic First Amendment questions remain on the table, to be addressed from the religious as well as from the political side of the line: What does the "free exercise" of religion require or imply? What is the proper relationship of religious bodies to the state? What, if anything, should religious bodies expect from the state by way of support? What are the limits of the involvement of the state with religion?

Although the American religious landscape includes more than Protestants, Catholics, and Jews, these are the nation's principal religious groups in terms of numbers and/or influence. For better or for worse, the public debate about the relationship between religion and

101

politics has not engaged, in any significant measure, the participation of Muslims, Buddhists, Hindus, Shintoists, and others.[2]

President Dwight D. Eisenhower was still in office when John Courtney Murray wrote that our "pluralist society, honestly viewed under abdication of all false gentility, is a pattern of interacting conspiracies."[3] A conspiracy, according to Murray, is literally a "breathing together," a united action for a common end taken by those who think alike. There are many such conspiracies in American society. Only by their conspiring together do the many become one: *e pluribus unum.*

Murray identified four major conspiracies: Protestant, Catholic, Jewish, and secularist. Although he recognized that in each camp "there [were] forces not fully broken to the authority of the high command,"[4] the composition of the three religious conspiracies was (and has since become) even more diversified than Murray thought.

When he engaged American Protestantism in debate about the natural law, for example, his commentary fit only two wings: the Social Gospel movement, whose principal figure was Walter Rauschenbusch, and the later school of Christian realism, personified by Reinhold Niebuhr.[5] Murray was critical, sometimes fiercely so, of both expressions of Protestant moral reasoning, but he understood mainline Protestantism as a partner with whom the civil dialogue of pluralism could be cultivated.[6]

He did not take into account the many millions of American evangelical and fundamentalist Protestants who have emerged in recent years as an important force on the political and religious scenes and for whom dialogue is not often the preferred form of public communication. Nor did he foresee, out of the debris of the liberal and mainline Protestantism with which he dealt, the gradual construction of a new ecumenical coalition of churches—mainline, evangelical, and Catholic alike—which Martin Marty has called "the public church."

Judaism is also different. Although there had always been large numbers of Orthodox and Conservative Jews in the American Jewish population, the public voice of Judaism, under the particularly negative impact of Prohibition and the Great Depression, had become increasingly liberal from the 1920s onward, and remained so in Murray's time. Political liberalism, as represented by the Roosevelt, Truman, Kennedy, and Johnson administrations, supported the principles of fairness and nondiscrimination that had opened political, economic, social, and professional doors for American Jews. Liberals had also been in the forefront of the fight against Nazi Germany and on behalf of the state of Israel.

The situation began to change, however, in the 1960s with the bonding of civil rights with "affirmative action" (including talk of quotas), the shift in liberal attitudes away from support for Israel and toward sympathy for Arab and other Third World causes, and, finally, the presidential candidacy of the Reverend Jesse Jackson, with its perceived overtones of anti-Semitism (reflected especially in the support which Jackson received and accepted from Minister Louis Farrakhan, leader of the Nation of Islam). Accordingly, some of the leading theoreticians of neoconservatism in the United States are Jewish: Norman Podhoretz, Nathan Glazer, Irving Kristol, Midge Decter, Daniel Bell, Ben Wattenberg, Seymour Martin Lipset, and columnists William Safire and Robert Novak.

To be sure, U.S. Catholicism has also changed since Murray's day. However, as an important participant in the Second Vatican Council and as a frequent commentator on its teachings in the period between its final adjournment on December 8, 1965, and his death on August 16, 1967, Murray actually witnessed the displacement of the traditional Catholic position on church and state and religion and politics by a new vision that promoted religious freedom for all and the independence of the Church from government.

Vatican II, of course, changed more than a theology. The council had also begun to reshape the character of the American Catholic community, introducing more democratic procedures in decision making, widening the range of lay participation in formal ministries, opening doors to other Christian denominations, and encouraging involvement in the struggle for peace, social justice, and human rights. Public and widespread dissent by American Catholics against Pope Paul VI's 1968 birth control encyclical, *Humanae Vitae,* demonstrated the depth of these vast internal changes. Murray, however, had barely begun to reflect on them before his death.[7]

What follows is an inquiry into each of these three conspiracies, as they exist today, without completely neglecting the fourth (secularism). How do they understand the American Proposition? What content do Protestants, Jews, and Catholics pour into the words, "We hold these Truths . . .?"

The Protestant Conspiracy

Ernst Troeltsch and H. Richard Niebuhr have given us the most widely cited typologies concerning the relationship of church and society in general, and of church and state in particular. These typologies apply principally, though not exclusively, to Protestant Christianity.

For Troeltsch, the history of the Church is best understood in terms of two opposing, yet complementary, tendencies: adjustment to, and accommodation with, the world, on the one hand, and rejection of, and protest against, the world, on the other. The first tendency he calls the church-type; the second tendency he calls the sect-type. Alongside these two types is a third, mysticism, which is an individualized response to the conflict between ideals and reality.

For H. Richard Niebuhr, there are five tendencies: sectarian (Christ against culture), liberal (Christ of culture), synthetic (Christ above culture), dualistic (Christ and culture in paradox), and conversionist (Christ, the transformer of culture).

There is some overlapping of the two sets. The sect-type in Troeltsch is the same as Niebuhr's Christ against culture. And Troeltsch's church-type combines Niebuhr's liberal, synthetic, dualistic, and conversionist models. Troeltsch's mysticism-type, however, has no parallel in Niebuhr.

Although each of these types or models has achieved some form of institutional expression in American Protestantism, there are today three especially important varieties: the "public church," fundamentalism and conservative evangelicalism, and individualism. The first corresponds to the church-type (and parallels), the second to the sect-type (and parallel), and the third to the mysticism-type. Only the first two, however, have any coherent answer to the questions posed by the American Proposition.

THE PUBLIC CHURCH

The public church, according to Martin Marty, is a family of Christian churches (a community of communities) which is "especially sensitive to the *res publica,* the public order that surrounds and includes people of faith."[8] It is a Christian embodiment of public religion in the United States. The churches that constitute the public church "contribute out of their separate resources to public virtue and the common weal."[9]

In the United States the constituency of this convergence of churches comes from elements within the old mainline Protestant communities, the newer Protestant evangelical communities, and the Catholic community. By mainline Protestant Marty means the collection of churches whose confessions affirm the historic core of Christian faith as it was re-formed in the sixteenth century, and who have given more attention "to nurture than to conversion."[10] By evangelical he means those Protestants who stress the personal experience of conversion, the high authority of the Bible, and the mandate to evangelize others. Finally, by Catholic he means the broad stream of faithful American Catholics who are not part of the polarized minorities.

The old mainline Protestants have participated more readily than others in the affairs of the public order, but at the same time have had greater difficulty than others with "being the church, with remaining intact as a center of loyalty to Christ."[11] The newer evangelicals have had less problem with "being the church" in the sense of being a community called out and set apart, but they have had more difficulties with public consciousness, "with discerning how they are called to serve God also beyond their specialized field of saving souls out of the world."[12] Finally, the Catholics "have lived with charters that give them access as Catholics to the public sphere while retaining a coherent churchly existence."[13] But not until the Second Vatican Council were they formally free to interact with other Christians in the fulfillment of their missionary agenda.

What are the challenges presently facing the public church in the United States? First, it is working out appropriate ways to live with secularity without abandoning the sacred or ignoring the marvelous staying power of religious impulses. Secondly, it is coming to a richer understanding of non-Christian religions and to the recognition of our need for one another in a world of increasing interreligious tensions. In America, the public church has the best chance of entering into honest and productive dialogue with Jews, for example. Thirdly, the public church is best situated within the network of religious communities to combat *totalism* (the tendency to impose a complete set of norms on lives), *tribalism* (the tendency of religious groups to close in on themselves over against other religious groups), and *privatism* (the tendency to view religion as a purely private affair, a matter of personal choice, without social consequence).

In summary, the public church is called upon to combine a special interiority with a specific openness. The former comes from its focus on Jesus Christ and its sensitivity to the presence of the Holy Spirit within the community of faith. The latter means that its worldly ties are mediated, focused, and disciplined. Its relations with the world are selective; the church "picks its shots."

The public church does not want to stand alone in the world. It should have natural allies in those humanists who fear persecution and dominance by religionists. But the humanist performance has been thus far disappointing. Humanists constantly underestimate the survival power of religion. Some of them believe that if you ignore it, it will simply go away. Other humanists assume that religion, by definition, must persecute. They even express a kind of awe for people whose faith is strong enough to lead them to kill or be killed in its name. These humanists "do not allow for loyalty to a God who does not license people to find value only in their totality, their tribe, their private zealotry," Marty observes. "To inform this humanist community of the probable terrors of the future and the need to find new forms of faith communities is a task that will occupy energies of the public church tomorrow."[14]

For Marty the stakes are high. Unlike the fundamentalists, with their talk of a "Christian nation," or the individualists, lost in their own world of consumer religion, adherents of the public church are committed to, and care about, the principle of religious liberty and the cultivation of religious pluralism. Both of these realities, however, have emerged very late in history and are still very rare, maintained as they are by a "gossamer-thin membrane of civility."[15] Many of the once civil no longer believe in civility, regarding it as a failed experiment.

"History gives no assurance of the survival of civility," Marty concludes, "and the promises of God by which Christians live do not picture their causes prevailing or the opposition to them disappearing inside history. Christians are only called to faithfulness, not to read the odds."[16]

FUNDAMENTALISM AND CONSERVATIVE EVANGELICALISM

Protestantism dominated the religious scene in America for the first two centuries, and the Bible played a major role in shaping American culture. Bible-centered preaching and devotional life had been especially strong among the Puritans, but it gained renewed significance in the revivalist movement of the nineteenth century, sparked by such prominent figures as Jonathan Edwards, Timothy Dwight, Lyman Beecher, and especially Charles Finney.

The revivalist believed that the universe is divided into the realm of God and the realm of Satan, the righteous and the unrighteous, the saved and the lost. Ambiguity was rare, and transitions were never gradual. The conversion experience involved a sudden, radical transformation from one condition to its opposite.[17]

Many Protestant fundamentalists, who form the core of the religious "new right," are evangelicals in the revivalist tradition. (Many others, however, are remarkably scholastic in their approach to the Bible.) Fundamentalism emerged as a definable movement in America in the late nineteenth century, appearing first in the so-called premillennial prophetic conferences which stressed the literal interpretation and complete accuracy of the Bible, and then appearing among traditionalist Northern Presbyterians and Northern Baptists who were alarmed at modern theological trends.

Many of the original adherents of the movement were loosely allied with Dwight L. Moody, who introduced a kind of free enterprise principle into the movement. If evangelists wanted to be successful, they had to work independently of the major denominations and build empires around evangelistic associations, Bible institutes, summer conference grounds, and affiliated ministries that could mobilize support for various causes.[18]

Fundamentalism, however, was not the only movement that came out of American revivalism. There were, first, the holiness denominations (the Nazarenes and the Salvation Army, for example) which stressed separation from the world in ethical behavior, and the dramatic experience of a "second blessing" and a subsequent life of perfect holiness; and, secondly, pentecostalism, which emphasized even more strongly those supernatural experiences that mark the believer's separation from the world (speaking in tongues and healing).[19]

Fundamentalism had much in common with these other two movements: acceptance of the complete authority of the Bible, the necessity of the conversion experience, and the importance of a holy life untarnished by vices such as drinking, dancing, gambling, and lasciviousness. Holiness and pentecostal groups, however, placed more stress on experiential and practical signs of personal separateness from evil. Fundamentalists, given their ties with scholastic Protestantism, placed greater emphasis on the necessity of right doctrine (the "fundamentals") and of organizing warfare against modern theology and worldly trends.

Fundamentalism took shape as a distinct movement in the aftermath of the First World War, in the midst of the cultural crises of the so-called "roaring '20s." Its first major battle, however, was a losing one: the anti-evolution crusade, culminating in the Scopes trial of 1925. Its champion, William Jennings Bryan, died the same year. But that campaign brought a significant southern component into the fundamentalist coalition for the first time.

The fundamentalists regrouped. The movement's centers shifted to individual congregations, independent of the major denominations, but held together by a network of transdenominational agencies, schools, and publications.[20] Fundamentalists were particularly adept at using the modern technology of radio. By the 1940s the most popular program in the United States was Charles E. Fuller's "Old Fashioned Revival Hour."[21] Nevertheless, the movement was "virtually overlooked or ignored by liberal culture and academics during this era."[22]

The fundamentalist movement was eventually split into conservative and moderate wings. The former were called "dispensationalists," because they saw the present dispensation, or "church age," as corrupt—a corruption infecting even the large mainline churches. The dispensationalists taught that only a small remnant of true believers would remain pure until Jesus returned to rule the nations from Jerusalem. The moderates, on the other hand, remained within the major denominations, insisting that this gave them a more effective base for evangelization. The split was institutionalized in the formation of rival fundamentalist national organizations: the strictly separationist American Council of Christian Churches, founded in 1941, and the less militant National Association of Evangelicals, founded in 1942, which would consolidate around the work of Billy Graham in the 1950s.

During the next 30 years the most influential spokesman for the militant wing was Carl McIntire, founder of the American Council of Christian Churches. Forced out of the (Northern) Presbyterian Church in 1936, McIntire engaged in constant attacks against the ecumenical and politically liberal National Council of Churches and the World Council of Churches, as well as the Catholic Church, which he regarded as a greater threat even than Communism.[23] Catholic and Communist conspiracies to undermine America became his chief theme. "Fundamentalist political concerns may have seemed inconsistent with their world-denying dispensationalism and their condemnations of the social gospel," George Marsden has noted, "but, whether in theology or politics, their world view had the unity of accounting for everything as part of organized forces for good or for evil."[24]

By the early 1960s fundamentalist political organizations found various nonfundamentalist groups moving along the same anti-Communist track. But leaders like Carl McIntire were too cantankerous to maintain large coalitions, and many fundamentalists, consistent with their dispensationalist and separatist principles, simply stayed out of politics. Indeed, the Reverend Jerry Falwell declared in 1965, "I would find it impossible to stop preaching the pure saving gospel of Jesus Christ, and begin doing anything else—including fighting Communism, or participating in civil-rights reforms."[25] The movement remained largely fragmented internally.

In the meantime, the division between fundamentalists and evangelicals continued. The latter, clustered around Billy Graham, sought to abandon the militancy of the fundamentalists for the sake of a broader evangelism, and to make the fundamentalist attack on modern theology and modern culture more intellectually sophisticated. Fuller Theological Seminary, founded in 1947 in Pasadena, California, became a center of evangelical theology, and *Christianity Today*, founded in 1956 by Carl Henry, one of Fuller's professors, provided a sense of unity to the new evangelical coalition by combining critiques of modern secularism with conservative theology, zeal for evangelical outreach, and moderately conservative anti-Communist politics. Although the evangelical movement leaned toward conservative Republicanism, it was careful to separate evangelism and church work, on the one hand, from the explicitly political activities of individuals and organizations, on the other.

These conservative evangelicals estimated their church member-

ship in the late 1950s at 24 million, or about half of all American Protestants, and the cultural crises of the 1960s accelerated their growth
even further. By the early 1970s religion was once again solidly "in"
on college campuses, and the evangelicals were exceedingly well-po-
sitioned to take advantage of the new wave of interest in spiritual values. They had not only a network of institutions but also skills in modern techniques of promotion and communication. The election of a
"born-again" Christian, Jimmy Carter, as president of the United States
in 1976 symbolized the new status of the movement, showing at the
same time that it wasn't uniformly conservative in politics.

But political conservatism remained the most widespread incli-
nation of the movement and Moral Majority was founded in 1979 to
give focus to it, particularly by way of reaction to the 1962 and 1963
U.S. Supreme Court rulings against school prayer and Bible reading,
the 1973 decision legalizing abortion, and the 1978 ruling by the Internal Revenue Service eliminating automatic tax exemptions for religious day schools and setting racial quotas as the general standard
for qualifying.

Significantly, the leadership of the new organization proudly called
itself fundamentalist rather than evangelical. Nevertheless, many hard-
line fundamentalists opposed its founder, the Reverend Jerry Falwell,
because he accepted Mormons, Jews, Catholics, Adventists, and others
into his moral-political crusade. "In this dispute," Marsden observes,
"the stricter fundamentalists are probably correct that Falwell's movement is similar to the neo-evangelical movement of the 1940s and
1950s. He is . . . torn between doctrines that demand separation and
ambitions for acceptance and influence that demand compromise."[26]

Moral Majority (now included, as of 1986, under the larger organizational umbrella of Liberty Federation) is a recombination of some
elements drawn from neo-evangelical and fundamentalist strains, particularly the emphasis on "secular humanism" as the enemy of Christianity and of all religion. The secular humanist idea has revitalized
the old conspiracy theory that Carl McIntire had promoted in the 1940s
and 1950s. Secular humanism, for many of today's fundamentalists, is
a concerted effort on the part of antireligious forces to drive God and
the Bible out of every facet of American life: the schools, the public
square, government, the health clinic, even the corner 7-Eleven convenience store.

Many Americans, however, are bothered by the way the term is
used. "Trying to define *secular humanism*," a spokesman for Norman
Lear's People for the American Way has remarked, "is like trying to
nail Jell-O to a tree."[27] For some, it is simply "a philosophy of ethical
behavior unrelated to a concept of God." For others, however, it is
nothing more than "an attempt to besmear political opponents by im-

pugning their faith in God."[28] But many fundamentalists have no doubts at all about its true meaning. For Florida pastor and television preacher D. James Kennedy, it is a "godless, atheistic, evolutionary, amoral, collectivist, socialistic, communistic religion."[29]

Some might think this a slightly oversimplified description, but it is not atypical of the fundamentalist way of defining reality. Fundamentalist Christianity has "no loose ends, ambiguities, or historical developments. Everything fits neatly into a system."[30] It is a message, too, that is peculiarly suited for large segments of society in a technological age. And fundamentalists have always been adept at handling mass communication, from their nineteenth-century beginnings, through the new era of radio, to today's world of television, satellites, and the mass-market paperback book. "If there is a rule of mass communications that the larger the audience the simpler the message must be," George Marsden suggests, "fundamentalists and similar evangelicals came to the technological age well prepared. Television ministries flourish best when they provide answers in simple polarities."[31]

For the fundamentalist and the conservative evangelical Protestant, America is a "Christian nation," or at least one founded on "Judeo-Christian" principles and values. The First Amendment may not warrant the establishment of any one religion, including Protestant fundamentalism and Protestant evangelicalism, as the official religion of the land. But according to many fundamentalists and conservative evangelicals, the Constitution does require that government support religion, through school prayer, tax exemptions and the like, and enforce religious values having to do with homosexuality, abortion, pornography, and even foreign policy, as it applies to the struggle against Communism and the defense of the state of Israel, to which Jesus is destined to return to initiate the final apocalyptic age. The religion that is to be supported and the religious values that are to be enforced, however, bear a striking resemblance to those of Protestant fundamentalism and conservative evangelicalism.[32]

INDIVIDUALISM

There is a third major strain in American Protestantism, but it cannot occupy us for very long because it has almost no interest in the relationship between religion and politics. Indeed, almost by definition it is simply *not* interested.

Fitting somewhat loosely within Troeltsch's mysticism-type of Christianity, this kind of individualism has been a part of American religious history from the beginning. Its "adherents" have included some of the nation's best known persons: Anne Hutchinson, Thomas Paine, Thomas Jefferson, Ralph Waldo Emerson, Henry David Thoreau, and Walt Whitman. At a less-celebrated level, their spirit is encapsulated in the remark, "I feel religious in a way. I have no denomination or anything like that."[33]

Common among religious individualists is criticism of organized religion rather than of religious beliefs or of the church as such. "Hypocrisy" is one of the most frequent charges levelled against organized religion. Traditional churchgoers fail to practice what they preach. "It's not religion or church that's going to save you," they say, "but what's in your heart, the quality of your personal relationship with God."

Mysticism-types, according to a recent sociological study, constitute "the commonest form of religion" in the United States. Indeed, "many who sit in the pews of the churches and the sects are really religious individualists, though many more never go to church at all."[34]

Critics of religious individualism in America have been severe. They speak of its "inner volatility and incoherence, its extreme weakness in social and political organization, and, above all, its particular form of compromise with the world—namely, its closeness to the therapeutic model in pursuit of self-centered experiences and its difficulty with social loyalty and commitment."[35] Discussions of the American Proposition or the First Amendment are beyond its immediate concern.

The Jewish Conspiracy

The traditional divisions within Judaism—Orthodox, Conservative, and Reform—do not provide an entirely satisfactory framework for understanding Jewish approaches to religion and politics in America.

Before the creation of the state of Israel in 1947, Orthodox Jews regarded themselves as a people in exile from their Palestinian homeland. They were not prone then, or now, to accommodate Judaism to modern American life. Reform Jews, on the other hand, have been engaged in precisely that kind of effort. They regard themselves as having been sent out into the world to apply the social teachings of the prophets, not to separate themselves from the world. Conservative Jews fall somewhere in between, retaining traditional elements of Jewish liturgy and moral practice, but committed at the same time to progressive social action, consistent with both the prophetic tradition and the principles of American democracy.[36]

Partly because of the congregational nature of Judaism and partly because of the high degree of secularization among ethnic Jews, Jewish involvement in the political order has been carried out through Jewish social action agencies rather than formally religious bodies: the American Jewish Committee, the Anti-Defamation League, and the American Jewish Congress. To the extent that American Jews have been engaged in First Amendment litigation and debates, it has been through the American Jewish Congress and its well-known constitutional lawyer, Leo Pfeffer, who has consistently articulated and defended a strictly separationist line of argument.[37]

A significant effort to understand the place of Jews and other non-Christians in the context of the First Amendment is that of Professor Morton Borden, of the University of California at Santa Barbara, in a work entitled, *Jews, Turks, and Infidels*.[38]

The primary historical fact with which Jews and other non-Christians have had to contend is the nation's long-standing Protestant bias. Some of the same early state constitutions that guaranteed religious liberty also contained provisions that restricted public office to Protestants. In several states these restrictions were maintained and defended well into the nineteenth century.

The expansion of religious liberty, therefore, did not come easily. It was the fruit of persistent efforts in state legislatures, constitutional conventions, the Congress, and in state and federal courts. "The Jewish presence in America and its vigilance," Borden argues, "were significant factors in broadening the definition of religious liberty."[39]

Viewing the early national period from a Jewish perspective, one can understand why Jews feared the potential of Protestant unity, and also why they looked in particular to Article VI, section 3, of the Constitution as a liberating force: "no religious test shall ever be required as a qualification to any office or public trust under the United States."

But the right to hold office was not the only issue that concerned American Jews. In the early nineteenth century Georgia law prevented Jewish clergymen from performing legal marriages. A law passed by Congress for the District of Columbia permitted only Christian congregations to be incorporated. An old Maryland law specified that the testimony of an Indian or a slave could not be heard in a court of law in any case involving a white Christian person. Attorneys in that state were required to take a Christian test oath. And a Jew could not be legally married outside the church.

When Governor James H. Hammond of South Carolina issued a Thanksgiving Day Proclamation in 1844, he did so with the words, "Whereas it becomes all Christian nations . . .," and exhorted "our citizens . . . to offer up their devotions to God their Creator, and his Son Jesus Christ, the Redeemer of the world."[40] William F. Johnston, the governor of Pennsylvania, issued a similar proclamation in 1848, but unlike Governor Hammond, apologized immediately. Thereafter, most governors were careful with their language, but there continued to be exceptions.

Although Catholics also labored under the same legal discrimination as Jews, they were bothered less because they were, after all,

Christians. Some Jews even supported the nativist attacks on Catholics because of their memories of Catholic persecution of Jews in Europe. But they came quickly to realize that the nativists were the common enemy because they would deny religious equality to all non-Protestants.

In 1863 a nondenominational National Reform Association was founded to promote a constitutional amendment placing the country under the sovereignty of Jesus Christ: "Recognizing Almighty God as the source of all authority and power in civil government, and acknowledging the Lord Jesus Christ as the Governor among the nations, His revealed will as the supreme law of the land, in order to constitute a Christian government. . . ."[41]

But the idea of a Christian amendment failed to gain the necessary political support. In spite of constant pressures on him, President Abraham Lincoln took no action endorsing or supporting the National Reform Association. It seems to have flourished only during periods of war, when even moderate Protestants were inclined to provide support, without thinking through the political and constitutional consequences. The movement finally dissolved in 1945, with the end of the Second World War.

At the same time, however, American Jews were not absolute separationists on the religion-and-state question. They had no objection to legislative prayers if their rabbis were occasionally selected to offer them, or to mentions of God in official proclamations, so long as God was not identified with Christ, or to tax exemptions for religious property and aid to religious schools, again so long as Jews received their fair share. Although some Jews argued against state Sunday laws as an unconstitutional infringement on their "free exercise" of religion, others simply advocated switching their religious services from Saturday to Sunday.

Indeed, Jewish responses to various assaults upon the principle of religious freedom and the non-establishment of religion have been diversified: from discreet silence to secular indifference to assimilationist strategies to an insistence on preserving their constitutional rights, especially in recent years through the efforts of Leo Pfeffer and the American Jewish Congress. For Professor Borden, this latter concern of a small number of Jews was an important factor that caused other Americans to think about the meaning of the First Amendment.[42]

The Jeffersonian "wall of separation between church and state" will always be important for Jews, but not only as a constitutional issue. It is, as Charles E. Silberman notes, "a metaphor for religious and cultural pluralism, for a society in which Christian symbols and rhetoric are sufficiently muted for Jews to be accepted as full and equal members."[43]

American Jews reacted negatively to the prominent role played by the Protestant fundamentalists in the 1984 Republican presidential campaign, because the fundamentalists' agenda reminded them of an earlier time in U.S. history when Jews were tolerated rather than accepted. Jews are convinced they are "safe only in a society acceptant of a wide range of attitudes and behaviors, as well as a diversity of religious and ethnic groups."[44]

That was the general idea behind the First Amendment.

The Catholic Conspiracy

"We [non-Anglicans] have all smarted heretofore under the lash of an established church," John Carroll, the first Catholic bishop in the United States, wrote to his friend Charles Plowden in England, "and shall therefore be on our guard against every approach towards it."[45]

Bishop Carroll had been angered when the Holy See had ignored the American clergy and had approached the new American government for its opinion on the appointment of a bishop. The overture had been made to Benjamin Franklin by the papal nuncio to France. The reply of Congress pleased Carroll and probably surprised Rome, which was not used to having governments declare themselves incompetent in ecclesiastical matters. Congress noted that "the subject of his [the nuncio's] application to Dr. Franklin being purely spiritual, is without the jurisdiction and powers of Congress, who have no authority to permit or refuse it."[46]

Much later, when the Ursuline sisters sued for damages incurred by the burning of their convent in Charlestown on August 11, 1834, a minority of representatives in the Massachusetts legislature argued that Catholics had no right to sue, given their spiritual loyalty to Rome. In response, the bishops of the United States issued a pastoral letter in 1837 rejecting that argument. Catholics owe no religious allegiance to any state nor to the federal government, and none of them claim supremacy or dominion over the Church or any citizens, of whatever religion, in spiritual and ecclesiastical concerns. The Church is free to give ecclesiastical supremacy "to whom we please, or to refuse it to every one, if we think so proper; but, they and we owe civil and political allegiance to the several States in which we reside, and also, to our general government."[47]

Therefore, in the exercise of this right to acknowledge "the spiritual and ecclesiastical supremacy of the chief bishop of our universal church, the Pope or bishop of Rome, we do not thereby forfeit our claim to the civil and political protection of the commonwealth. . . ."[48]

However, U.S. Catholics found themselves defending not only their Americanism to their fellow Americans, but also their Catholicism to their ecclesiastical superiors in Rome. The task on both fronts became more difficult after the publication in 1864 of Pope Pius IX's *Syllabus of Errors.* Among the condemned errors were the opinions that "the Church ought to be separated from the State, and the State from the Church," and that "in the present day, it is no longer necessary that the Catholic religion be held as the only religion of the State, to the exclusion of all other modes of worship. . . ."[49]

The most influential, and subsequently misunderstood, interpretation of the Syllabus came from Bishop Felix Dupanloup, of Orleans, France. Taking his cue from an article by a Jesuit theologian in the Roman periodical, *Civiltà cattolica,* Dupanloup applied to the Syllabus the distinction between "thesis" and "hypothesis."

According to the bishop, what Pope Pius IX had condemned in his Syllabus were absolute theses, or principles, from which there could never be any deviation. Thus, the pope had condemned not separation of church and state as such, but separation which takes religious indifferentism as its norm. For Dupanloup, the Catholic "thesis" was simply that harmony should exist between church and state. Such harmony could be achieved by a variety of "hypotheses," or practical applications of the thesis, one of which was the union of church and state.[50]

Later on, however, Dupanloup's careful distinction was misconstrued to mean that the Catholic "thesis" was the union of church and state, and the "hypothesis" was what was merely tolerable as long as the Church had its freedom.[51] In other words, there was only one right way ("thesis") for the Church to exist alongside the state, and that was the way of union. Every other arrangement ("hypothesis") would always be, at best, a temporary compromise.

This is how the distinction was drawn in the so-called Americanism controversy, which was precipitated in the 1890s by the publication of a French translation of the life of Father Isaac Hecker, the founder of the Paulists. The appearance of the biography only sharpened the division between two French Catholic camps: those who saw the tradition of American religious liberty as the basis for their own accommodation with the Third French Republic, and those who saw the American tradition as the basis for religious indifferentism or a creedless Christianity.

As the debate became more heated, Bishop Denis J. O'Connell, former rector of the American College in Rome and a leading liberal figure in the American hierarchy, addressed the issue in August 1897 at the Fourth International Catholic Scientific Congress, in Fribourg, Switzerland. It was in the course of this presentation that O'Connell confused Dupanloup's thesis-hypothesis distinction, equating the "thesis" with the state establishment of a church (rather than the principle of harmony between church and state) and the "hypothesis" with the American constitutional arrangement. O'Connell argued that if Americans were to establish a church, it would be Protestant, and that the state is incompetent in religious matters anyway. For O'Connell, not only was the American "hypothesis" acceptable; it was actually preferable to the "thesis."[52]

Although Bishop O'Connell's statement of the case was applauded by liberal Catholics in the United States, it was condemned as heresy by some on the other side: both of the issue and of the Atlantic. During the summer of 1898, Pope Leo XIII appointed a commission to investigate what was now known as Americanism. On January 22, 1899, the pope issued an apostolic letter, *Testem Benevolentiae*, in which he criticized "religious Americanism," while leaving intact American Catholic loyalty to the Constitution. "Religious Americanism" he defined as the tendency to carry over into the life of the Church the principles of constitutional liberty. Pope Leo XIII wanted to stress the difference between the Church, "which is of divine right, and all other associations which subsist by the free will of men." The pope was simply expressing the European fear that accommodation of the Church to democracy as a form of government might entail the introduction of democracy into the Church itself.[53]

After "an inchoate moment of native constructive theological thought," American Catholicism "slipped more or less peaceably into a half-century's theological hibernation."[54] It did not begin to emerge from its intellectual slumber until the end of the Second World War when the U.S. Catholic Church turned its attention to the rise of secularism in American society. To combat secularism, people like Father John Courtney Murray, S.J., were convinced of the need for "intercreedal cooperation" among Catholics, Protestants, and Jews. It was in this context that the resurfacing of the issues of church and state and religious liberty occurred.

At the same time that Murray began his own theological research into these issues, three prominent members of the American Catholic hierarchy were also becoming concerned with the problem of secularism: Archbishops John T. McNicholas, of Cincinnati, Samuel Stritch, of Chicago, and Edward Mooney, of Detroit. All were skeptical at first of the possibility of finding any theological common ground with Protestants and Jews.

In 1945 Murray prepared a paper for Mooney on the principles of religious liberty. Two years later Murray collaborated with the National Catholic Welfare Conference's legal and education departments in preparing their arguments in the *Everson* and *McCollum* cases before the U.S. Supreme Court. Probably in preparation for the Court's decision, Archbishop McNicholas, then chairman of the NCWC Administrative Board, issued a statement in early 1948 which fully endorsed the American constitutional system. "If tomorrow Catholics constitute a majority in our country," he wrote, "they would not seek a union of church and state. They would then, as now, uphold the Constitution and all its Amendments, recognizing the moral obligations imposed on all Catholics to observe and defend the Constitution and its Amendments."[55]

But others held to the point of view favoring the Catholic state. Father Francis J. Connell, C.Ss.R., at the time the nation's foremost Catholic moral theologian, and Father Joseph Clifford Fenton, the editor of the *American Ecclesiastical Review* and a professor at The Catholic University of America in Washington, D.C., were the leading exponents of the theory that the Catholic state, in which the activities of non-Catholic religions were restricted, was the ideal form of government. Fenton launched a series of attacks upon Murray, accusing him of Americanism.[56]

During the summer of 1950, however, Murray went to Rome where he received encouragement from Monsignor Giovanni Battista Montini, the substitute secretary of state, and the future Pope Paul VI. At the same time, he began to study seriously the encyclicals of Pope Leo XIII on church and state and religious liberty to see if they really did contradict the American Proposition.

Just as he sent his first article on Leo XIII off to the printer, Pope Pius XII named Alfredo Ottaviani a cardinal and appointed him prefect of the Holy Office (formerly the Inquisition and now the Sacred Congregation for the Doctrine of Faith). This was in January 1953. In March Cardinal Ottaviani spoke at the Rome's Lateran Seminary, where he argued that when Catholics are in the majority, they must create a confessional state in which the Catholic religion alone is legally protected. Where Catholics are in the minority, however, the Church has a right to be tolerated on an equal basis with other religious groups. He admitted that this manner of thinking involved a double standard: "one for truth, the other for error," as he put it. He then referred to the controversy between Fenton and Murray in the United States, and came down firmly on Fenton's side.[57]

On December 6, 1953, Pope Pius XII delivered a discourse to Italian jurists, *Ci riesce*, which seemed to modify Ottaviani's position. In seeking for world union, the pope recognized religious pluralism as a fact not only between states but also within them.[58] On March 25, 1954, Murray spoke at The Catholic University of America, arguing that the papal allocution laid to rest the proposition that Spain embodied the "thesis" (ideal) and the United States only the "hypothesis" (temporary compromise).[59] Murray mentioned Cardinal Ottaviani by name in his talk, and from that point on the cardinal sought to have Murray silenced.

Murray was required to have his writings submitted to Rome before publication. In July 1955 he learned that one of his articles had not been approved. A few days later, he received word that another article had been rejected. Murray informed his religious superior that he had cleared all the books on church and state and allied topics from his room, "in symbol of retirement," he said, "which I expect to be permanent."[60]

But the retirement was not permanent. On October 28, 1958, Angelo Roncalli, patriarch of Venice, was elected to the papacy, and took the name John XXIII. On January 25, 1959, the new pope announced his intention to call an ecumenical council, which would be known as Vatican Council II.

It is in this context that we take up John Courtney Murray's writings on religious liberty and church and state, the documents of Vatican II on both questions, and, finally, some recent statements, individual and corporate alike, of American Catholic bishops on the relationship between religion and politics.

RELIGIOUS FREEDOM

John Courtney Murray's understanding of religious freedom is of extreme importance because it became, in essence, the official teaching of the Catholic Church at the Second Vatican Council. Murray summarized his position in five points.[61]

First, it is not "incompatible" with the principle of religious freedom that there should exist an "orderly relationship" (a phrase taken from Pope Leo XIII) between government and the Church, even one based on a concordat. Nor is it contrary to religious freedom that the people of a particular nation should declare their common allegiance to the Catholic Church in some sort of constitutional document. Such a declaration would have no juridical consequences. It would have the value only of a statement of fact.

Secondly, in order that the relationship between church and state be truly orderly, three requirements of religious freedom must be observed:

1. There must be no infringement or inhibition of the Church's freedom as a spiritual authority and as the community of the faithful. The Church's internal autonomy must remain inviolable, and there must be no impediment to the free exercise of its apostolic mission. Moreover, the Church is not to be used in any way for the political purposes of the state.

2. There must be no confusion of religious unity and political unity. The state has no business trying to insure the unity of the Church by political or coercive means.

3. The relationship between church and state cannot be so conceived and executed that it would result in the kind of alienation of the people from the Church that was a prominent feature of the post-Tridentine and sectarian Liberal eras.[62]

Thirdly, the legal institution of religious intolerance is incompatible with religious freedom, which is an integral element of the freedom of the people. Religious freedom is not simply a necessary evil, as Murray's opponents always argued. It is a personal and political good.[63]

Murray's fourth point was that there is no such thing as an "ideal instance" of Catholic constitutional law. The twin institutions of establishment and intolerance certainly do not represent such an ideal.[64] On the contrary, there are two Catholic criteria, one proposed by Pope Pius XII and the other by Pope John XXIII: (1) that the constitutional order should guarantee the freedom of the Church to fulfill its spiritual mission; and (2) that the constitutional order should guarantee the personal rights of the citizen and promote the freedom of the people.

It was Murray's final point that the principle of religious freedom, as presently understood, is not simply a later and more perfect stage in the Church's tradition. It is explicitly the product of twentieth-century insight into the exigencies of the personal and political consciousness: specifically, "man's growing consciousness of his dignity as a person, which requires that he act on his own responsibility and therefore in freedom," and "man's growing consciousness of community, of that being with the others and for the others which is revealed, for instance, in the phenomenon of 'socialization' in the sense of *Mater et Magistra*."[65] Both of these "signs of the times" are approvingly described in Pope John XXIII's encyclical, *Pacem in Terris*.[66]

But this summary of John Courtney Murray's position makes sense only in light of various key distinctions and definitions that Murray also proposed.

The first is between "freedom of conscience" and "the free exercise of religion." These are the two dimensions of the right of religious freedom. *Freedom of conscience* corresponds to its personal content, and *the free exercise of religion* corresponds to its social implications.

Freedom of conscience is personal immunity from external coercion (all manner of compulsion, constraint, and restraint, whether legal or extralegal) in everything pertaining to the making of an act of religious faith or in the rejection of such faith. Freedom of conscience is based theologically on the freedom of the act of faith. A forced faith is no faith at all. It is a contradiction in terms.[67]

The free exercise of religion, which is the social side of religious freedom, includes three elements: (1) ecclesial or corporate religious freedom, that is, the right of religious communities to complete internal autonomy; (2) freedom of religious association, that is, immunity from coercion in founding, joining or quitting organized religious bodies (the old principle, *cuius regio, eius religio,* is totally incompatible with this freedom); and (3) freedom of religious expression, that is, immunity from coercion in what concerns public worship, public religious observances and practices, the public proclamation of religious faith, and the public declaration of the social, economic, and even political implications of religion and morality. The freedom of religious expression is the "free exercise of religion" in its most formal sense.

The free exercise of religion is defended on the basis of an indissoluble link, on the one hand, between the internal freedom of the Church and its external freedom to fulfill its spiritual mission, and, on the other hand, between personal freedom of conscience and social freedom of religious expression. The human person is essentially social. To grant personal freedom of conscience but deny its social expression would introduce a dichotomy into the human person, separating his or her personal-interior existence from his or her social-historical existence.

Furthermore, civil power, which has no right to coerce the religious conscience, has no corresponding right to coerce the social expressions of the religious conscience. Finally, history itself shows that constraints on the social expression of religion inevitably result in the destruction or diminution of freedom of conscience.

This is not to say that the state is absolutely incompetent in religious matters. It is competent, however, to do only one thing in respect of religion, which is, to recognize, guarantee, protect, and promote the religious freedom of the people.[68] This freedom can only be limited when it interferes with public order, that is, when the public peace, or commonly accepted standards of public morality, or the rights of other citizens are threatened. The application of this power must never be arbitrary.

"In what concerns religious freedom," Murray wrote, "the requirement is fourfold: that the violation of the public order be really serious; that legal or police intervention be really necessary; that regard be had for the privileged character of religious freedom, which is not simply to be equated with other civil rights; that the rule of jurisprudence of the free society be strictly observed, scil., as much freedom as possible, as much coercion as necessary."[69]

This is essentially the solution adopted by the framers of the Constitution and its Bill of Rights. "Religious freedom as a legal institution, which was formally created by the First Amendment," Murray noted, "stood in harmonious relation with the political conception of government as limited in its powers. . ."[70]

The concept of limited government is grounded, in turn, on three related sets of distinctions. The first distinction is drawn between the *sacred* and the *secular* orders of human life. The power of the state is limited to the latter. It cannot be used by the state to interfere with the spiritual purposes of religious bodies, *nor can it be used by religious bodies to further those spiritual purposes.* (This is an exceedingly important, and too often violated, principle.) Furthermore, there are aspirations of the human person that cannot be satisfied by the temporal institutions of society or the state. The Church, therefore, is always transcendent to any political system.

The second distinction, which is crucial for understanding the church-state issue in America, is between *society* and the *state*. The state exists within society, but is not identical to it. There are other orders of society—social, cultural, educational, economic, religious—which cannot be subsumed by the state. And this also means that exclusion of religion from the affairs of state does not necessarily entail the exclusion of religion from society itself.

Furthermore, when the distinction between society and the state is obliterated, the result is the totalitarian state. It is important to recall that this was the conception of the state that confronted Pope Leo XIII in the nineteenth century. Officially, the state was atheist and religion was a purely private affair, without public rights. The freedom of the Church was destroyed.[71]

Following from the distinction between society and the state is the distinction, finally, between the *common good* and the *public order*. The common good includes all the social goods, spiritual and moral as well as material, which people need to live. The pursuit of the common good devolves upon society as a whole. Public order, on the other hand, is a narrower concept and devolves upon the state. It includes three goods: *public peace*, which is the highest political good, *public morality*, as determined by moral standards commonly accepted among the people, and *justice*, which secures for the people what is due them. And the first thing due to the people, in justice, is their freedom, the proper enjoyment of their personal and social rights. This freedom is to be guaranteed by law, as embodied in a basic rule of jurisprudence: "Let there be as much freedom, personal and social, as is possible; let there be only as much coercion and constraint, personal or social, as may be necessary for the public order."[72]

It was this basic framework which Pope John XXIII adopted for his 1963 encyclical, *Pacem in Terris*. "Since by nature all men are equal in human dignity," he declared, "it follows that no one may be coerced to perform interior acts. That is in the power of God alone, who sees and judges the hidden designs of men's hearts."[73] Religion itself is covered by this immunity from coercion, grounded in the natural law: "Every human being has the right to honor God according to the dictates of an upright conscience, and therefore the right to worship God privately and publicly."[74] John XXIII, therefore, officially endorsed the concept of the limited state.

His second major contribution lay in his adding of freedom to the three spiritual forces which, according to Pope Leo XIII, sustain human society: truth, justice, and love. Catholic tradition, going back certainly to Pope Gregory VII in the eleventh century, had always asserted that the human quality of society depends on the freedom of the Church. But Pope John XXIII went beyond this, affirming that the human quality of society depends also on the freedom of *the people*. In fact, the two freedoms are inseparable, indeed identical. They stand or fall together.

Truth, justice, and love assure the stability of society, but freedom is the dynamism of social progress toward fuller humanity in communal living. Freedom is also *the* political method whereby the people achieve their highest good, which is their own unity as a people: "Human society is realized in freedom, that is to say, in ways and means in keeping with the dignity of its citizens, who accept the responsibility of their actions precisely because they are by nature rational beings."[75]

"Now religious freedom has a new basis in each of the dynamic spiritual forces that sustain society," Murray concluded. "It is an exigence of truth, justice, and civic friendship or love. In particular, it is acknowledged to be an integral element of the freedom of the people. It is not now a question of tolerating the institution as a lesser evil. . . . Now the Church positively affirms the validity of the institution of religious freedom."[76]

More than two-and-a-half years later, the Second Vatican Council issued its landmark document, *Dignitatis humanae* (Declaration on Religious Freedom).[77] It was a landmark document because it acknowledged the fact of the religiously pluralist society as the necessary historical context of the whole discussion; secondly, because it defined the role of government as constitutional and limited in function (namely, the protection and promotion of the rights of persons and the facilitation of the performance of civic duties), and at the same time disavowed any sacral function of government; and, thirdly, because it affirmed the freedom of the Church as "the fundamental principle in what concerns the relations between the Church and governments and the whole civil order" (n. 13).[78]

The Declaration pointed, as Murray had done, to two "signs of the times" which had brought about a fundamental change in the way this question of religious freedom would be discussed: (1) the "sense of the dignity of the human person . . . impressing itself more and more deeply on the consciousness of contemporary man," with the attendant demand for "responsible freedom" and immunity from "coercion"; and (2) the demand that "constitutional limits should be set to the powers of government, in order that there may be no encroachment on the rightful freedom of the person and of associations" (n. 1).

In fact, the whole teaching of the Declaration hangs suspended from the principle of the dignity of the human person.[79] Inherent in this dignity is the demand that human persons should act on their own initiative and responsibility, not under coercion. This demand, in turn, grounds the political principle that the freedom of the person is to be respected as far as possible and restricted only in cases of necessity. The equality of this demand in all persons who are equal in human dignity grounds the further juridical principle of the equality of all citizens before the law.

From these two principles of political and juridical equality together follow two sets of conclusions: (1) that the full immunity of the human person from coercion in religious matters is the object of a genuine human right; and that it is the duty of government itself to respect this right and to insure respect for it in society; and (2) that the exercise of the right to religious freedom is to be as free as possible; and that governmental or legal limitation of the exercise of the right is warranted only by the criterion of necessity.[80]

The Declaration also grounded its teaching in revelation. The act of faith is, of its very nature, a free act. Jesus Christ himself never compelled anyone to believe in him. His manner was always meek, humble, and patient. His miracles were intended to rouse faith in his hearers and to confirm them in faith, not to coerce them. Taught by Christ's example, the apostles followed the same way.[81]

"The Church therefore is being faithful to the truth of the gospel," the Declaration asserts, "and is following the way of Christ and the apostles when it recognizes, and gives support to, the principle of religious freedom as befitting human dignity and as being in accord with divine revelation" (n. 12).

It is clear that the official teaching of the Catholic Church, articulated in the Second Vatican Council's Declaration on Religious Freedom, is now entirely consistent with, and fully supportive of, the American Proposition and the First Amendment. John Courtney Murray deserves much of the credit for this remarkable shift.

CHURCH AND STATE/CHURCH AND SOCIETY

It is a matter of fundamental importance to recognize that the question of church and state was recast at Vatican II within the larger framework of church and society. John Courtney Murray, in fact, had characterized the church-state question as a nineteenth-century legacy in need of clarification, and insisted that the twentieth-century challenge was to see that "the inherent sense of the gospel summons the Church to the task of lifting man to his true dignity and of knitting the bonds of human community."[82]

The Second Vatican Council addressed both questions, church and state and church and society: the first in the Declaration on Religious Freedom *(Dignitatis humanae),* and the second in the Pastoral Constitution on the Church in the Modern World *(Gaudium et spes).* Our interest here is in the latter document since it provides the wider doctrinal framework for understanding the relationship between church and state as it exists in the United States.

Two major concerns pervaded the Pastoral Constitution: first, to reaffirm the traditional distinction between the sacred and the temporal orders, as well as the transcendence of the Church to the temporal order; and, secondly, to insist upon the active role of the Church in the world, so that "the earthly and heavenly city penetrate each other" (n. 40).

Regarding the first concern, that is, the distinction between the sacred and the temporal, and the transcendence of the Church to the temporal: The Church has "no proper mission in the political, economic, or social order. The purpose which [Christ] set before it is a religious one. . . . Moreover, in virtue of its mission and nature, it is bound to no particular form of human culture, nor to any political, economic, or social system." The Church asks only that, "in pursuit of the welfare of all, it may be able to develop itself freely under any kind of government which grants recognition to the basic rights of person and family and to the demands of the common good" (n. 42).

Regarding the second concern, that is, the freedom of the Church to take an active role in the world: The council restated the traditional paradox of a Church existing for a spiritual purpose and yet situated in, and committed to serve, a temporal world.[83] The Pastoral Constitution pointed to a resolution of the paradox in its notion of the Church as "a leaven and as a kind of soul for human society as it is to be renewed in Christ and transformed into God's family." The relationship between the two realms is captured in the word "compenetration," but it is a reality that is "accessible to faith alone" (n. 40).[84]

The Church not only "communicates divine life" to men and women, but also contributes toward making the human family and its history more human "by its healing and elevating impact on the dignity of the person, by the way in which it strengthens the seams of human society and imbues the everyday activity of people with a deeper meaning and importance" (n. 40). Everything is anchored now in the dignity of the human person. Indeed, "by virtue of the gospel committed to it, the Church proclaims the rights of man" (n. 41).[85]

If one were looking, however, for a single phrase in which to resolve the problem addressed in *Gaudium et spes,* namely, the relationship of Church and world, that phrase might be found in article 76: "For [the Church] is at once a sign and a safeguard of the transcendence of the human person." The text suggests that "the Church may neither be enclosed within the political order nor be denied her own mode of spiritual entrance into the political order. It indirectly asserts the rightful secularity of the secular order, at the same time that it asserts the necessary openness of the secular order to the transcendent values whose pursuit is proper to the human person."[86]

Indeed, the principle of cooperation of Church and state in the service of the human person is thus stated *as* a principle: "In their proper spheres, the political community and the Church are mutually independent and self-governing. Yet, by a different title, each serves the personal and social vocation of the same human beings. This service can be more effectively rendered for the good of all, if each works better for wholesome mutual cooperation, depending on the circumstances of time and place" (n. 76).[87]

The council acknowledges here that there are no ideal forms of church-state arrangements. The contingencies of history, and not some abstract theory (or "thesis"), must determine the institutional forms of church-state cooperation. Furthermore, the cooperation between the two is not required by some need of the Church, but by the dual nature of the human person: "For man is not restricted to the temporal sphere. While living in history he fully maintains his eternal vocation" (n. 76).

To fulfill its role in society, the Church asks only freedom to preach and to teach, and to pass moral judgment even on matters that belong to the political order, when human rights or the salvation of souls are at stake. On the other hand, the Church "does not lodge its hope in privileges conferred by civil authority," and is even ready to renounce those which have already been granted if they raise any doubts about the sincerity of the Church's witness.

Again, the Council's teaching, this time articulated in its Pastoral Constitution on the Church in the Modern World, is fully consistent with the First Amendment principles of non-establishment and free exercise.

THE U.S. CATHOLIC BISHOPS

Reference has been made above, in a broader historical context, to some earlier interventions of American Catholic bishops on issues pertaining to both church and state and church and society. Our attention here is focused on some of their more recent statements, which are firmly supportive of the American Proposition and the principles of non-establishment and free exercise as embodied in the First Amendment.

In an extremely important, although largely ignored, address on religion and politics at Georgetown University in the waning days of the 1984 presidential election campaign, Chicago's Cardinal Joseph L. Bernardin pointed out that, while John Courtney Murray had strongly defended the Church's right to speak in the public arena, he had also stressed the limits of its role. Following Murray's lead, Cardinal Bernardin argued that the Church must respect the complexity of public issues and recognize the legitimate secularity of the public debate.

Whether the issue be defense policy or health care, he declared, "the moral dimensions of our public life are interwoven with empirical judgments where honest disagreement exists." This is not to say that complexity should paralyze religious/moral analysis and advocacy of issues, but only that "we owe the public a careful accounting of how we have come to our moral conclusions."[88]

"I stand with Murray," Cardinal Bernardin continued, "in attributing a public role to religion and morality in our national life. But I also stand with him in the conviction that religiously rooted positions must somehow be translated into language, arguments and categories which a religiously pluralistic society can agree on as the moral foundation of key policy positions."[89] Bernardin explicitly criticized the religious right for its style of analysis and its mode of argument.

Bishop James W. Malone, of Youngstown, Ohio, and president of the National Conference of Catholic Bishops during the 1984 campaign (his term expired in November 1986), has generated a cluster of statements, some issued in his own name, others issued in the name of the Administrative Board of the United States Catholic Conference. A USCC Administrative Board statement, "Political Responsibility: Choices for the '80s," released on March 22, 1984, provides a useful framework for interpreting Bishop Malone's several pronouncements as Conference president.

The Board insisted that the Church has the responsibility and the right to "call attention to the moral and religious dimension of secular issues, to keep alive the values of the Gospel as a norm for social and political life and to point out the demands of the Christian faith for a just transformation of society."[90] These issues include, in alphabetical order: abortion, arms control and disarmament, capital punishment, civil rights, the economy, education, energy, family life, food and agricultural policy, health, housing, human rights, mass media, and regional conflict in the world.

While Christians and Christian organizations must participate in the public debate over alternative policies and legislative proposals regarding these issues, it is critical that the nature of their participation not be misunderstood. "We specifically do not seek the formation of a religious voting bloc," the Administrative Board statement declared, "nor do we wish to instruct persons on how they should vote by endorsing candidates. . . . Rather, we hope that voters will examine the positions of candidates on the full range of issues as well as their integrity, philosophy and performance."[91]

On August 9, 1984, a statement issued by Bishop Malone, as president of the National Conference of Catholic Bishops and on behalf of the Administrative Board, was prematurely released between the Democratic and Republican National Conventions. By its early release date, the statement gave the impression that it was composed as a refutation of Governor Cuomo, vice-presidential candidate Ferraro, and other Catholic Democrats who had been publicly at odds with New York's Archbishop O'Connor and other bishops.

On the one hand, the August 9 statement acknowledged that it would be "regrettable if religion as such were injected into a political campaign through appeals to candidates' religious affiliations and commitments."[92] This had already been done, blatantly, by the chairman of President Reagan's campaign committee, Senator Paul Laxalt, of Nevada, in a letter dated July 9 to 45,000 members of the clergy, primarily Protestants, in 16 states. The letter praised Mr. Reagan for his "unwavering commitment to the traditional values which I know you share," and asked the church leaders to "organize a voter registration drive in your church."[93]

On the other hand, Bishop Malone's statement seemed to chastise the view imprecisely associated with Governor Cuomo and Congresswoman Ferraro alike, without distinction, that "candidates satisfy the requirements of rational analysis in saying their personal views should not influence their policy decisions,"[94] thereby introducing a dichotomy between personal morality and public policy. Furthermore, the Malone statement seemed to suggest that, whereas sincere disagreement by Catholics and others is possible over most issues, abortion is not one of them. The statement made no distinction, however, between acceptance of the Church's teaching on the morality of abortion and agreement with a specific legislative proposal to deal with the problem of abortion in the public forum.

Bishop Malone issued a second, and much more carefully nuanced statement, on October 14, in which he repeated the principle enunciated in the March 22 statement; namely, that the bishops do not take positions on particular parties or individual candidates. In fact, his statement of October 14 was even more precise than the previous Board statement. The Board had declared only that the bishops would not *endorse* candidates. Bishop Malone toughened the language. "I repeat here a basic principle of these documents," he wrote. "We do not take positions for *or against* particular parties or individual candidates."[95] (By now it had become clear to many, inside and outside the Catholic community, that the Republican ticket had been endorsed, for all practical purposes, by Philadelphia's Cardinal Krol, New York's Archbishop O'Connor, Boston's Archbishop Law, and by others like Scranton's Bishop Timlin.)

In the October statement, however, Bishop Malone introduced a distinction that had been missing in his August 9 statement. Even on questions like abortion, he wrote, "we realize that citizens and public officials may agree with our moral arguments while disagreeing with us and among themselves on the most effective legal and policy remedies."[96] This would not exempt anyone from searching for political and public policy solutions to such problems as war and peace and abortion, even though the search-process will be long and difficult.

In his presidential address at the general bishops' meeting on November 12, 1984, in Washington, D.C., Bishop Malone embraced the challenge which John Courtney Murray set down: "In the public arena of a pluralistic democracy religious leaders face the same tests of rational argument as any other individuals or institutions. Our impact on the public will be directly proportionate to the persuasiveness of our positions. We seek no special status and we should not be accorded one."[97]

As in the previous statements issued over his name, Bishop Malone eschewed a single-issue approach, "because only by addressing a broad spectrum of issues can we do justice to the moral tradition we possess as a church and thereby demonstrate the moral challenges we face as a nation.[98] Cardinal Bernardin has referred to this as a "consistent ethic of life" or "seamless garment" approach.

Moreover, Bishop Malone endorsed Murray's principle of civility. "We should demonstrate that one can combine profound convictions of moral principle and abiding civil courtesy toward allies and adversaries in the public debate."[99]

On February 13, 1986, Bishop Malone addressed the Conference on Religion and Politics in the American Milieu at the University of Notre Dame. Drawing upon principles and themes expressed in his previous statements, he insisted that religion plays both a supportive and a prophetic role in a democratic society. It is supportive insofar as it articulates and defends those values that provide the moral foundation of a democracy (what follows the words, "We hold these Truths. . . ."), and it is prophetic insofar as it offers a critique of laws and social systems that pertain to social justice, human rights, and peace.

He rejected two extreme views of the religion-and-politics relationship: the theocratic ideal which would have religion dictate public policy, and the secularistic ideal which would have religion excluded from the policy debate. Notwithstanding the vociferousness of the religious right, Bishop Malone suggested that secularism poses a greater threat than theocracy. In constructing his case against the former, he drew upon the writings of John Courtney Murray and Vatican II's Declaration on Religious Freedom.

The points were familiar: the distinction between state and society, the empirically complex nature of public policy decisions, the limited moral aspirations of civil law, the right of the Church to offer guidance in the formation of the Catholic's conscience, and the distinction between moral principles and their application in the public order. On the last item, however, Bishop Malone laid down what has become a familiar challenge to Catholic politicians from their bishops: "Sincerity minimally requires that those who say they stand with the Church's teaching but reject the bishops' policy proposals offer genuine alternatives calculated to realize the same purposes."[100]

The Catholic politician's rejoinder is also familiar: "Ask those who demand a constitutional amendment what it would say precisely, and there is no reply," Governor Cuomo declared in a speech at St. Francis College, Brooklyn, on October 3, 1984. "The vague call for a constitutional amendment or a 'new law' is too often just an empty echo that, like the vague call of 'justice for all,' is well-intentioned and may soothe some consciences but avoids any effective argument for achieving its end."[101]

CATHOLIC PRINCIPLES AND THE FIRST AMENDMENT

The intramural Catholic debate continues, but at a much higher level than before the Second Vatican Council. Cardinal Bernardin's speech at Georgetown and Governor Cuomo's at Notre Dame provide compelling examples.

Nevertheless, the great majority of Americans, including Catholics themselves, remain generally uninformed about the substance of the debate. Either they are unaware of what Catholic doctrine and theology have to say about First Amendment issues, or they assume "the Catholic position" to be other than it is.

What follows is a synthesis of the relevant Catholic principles, drawn especially, although not exclusively, from Pope John XXIII's encyclical, *Pacem in Terris,* the Second Vatican Council's Declaration on Religious Freedom *(Dignitatis humanae)* and Pastoral Constitution on the Church in the Modern World *(Gaudium et spes)*, and the writings of John Courtney Murray. In their given form, these principles do not necessarily constitute *the* Catholic position, but no "Catholic" position can be constructed independently of them.

REGARDING THE "FREE EXERCISE" CLAUSE:

There are two levels of freedom at issue: freedom of conscience (which pertains to the personal aspect of religious faith) and freedom of religion (which pertains to the social implications of religious faith). The two levels are inextricably linked because of the social nature of the human person and of religious faith.

1. *Freedom of conscience* demands personal immunity from all manner of compulsion, constraint, and restraint in everything pertaining to the making or rejecting of an act of religious faith. This principle is based on the necessary freedom of the act of faith and on the dignity of the human person. (Vatican II, Declaration on Religious Freedom, n. 9.)

2. *Freedom of religion* demands (1) the complete autonomy of religious bodies in matters pertaining to their own organization, governance, and spiritual mission; (2) immunity from coercion in the founding, joining, or quitting of religious bodies; and (3) immunity from coercion in the public expression of religious faith, that is, in what concerns worship, religious observances and practices, the proclamation of religious faith, and the declaration of the social, economic, and political implications of religious faith. (Vatican II, Declaration on Religious Freedom, n. 13.)

3. *As much freedom as possible; only as much coercion as necessary.* The state's role with respect to religion is to recognize, guarantee, protect, and promote the religious freedom of the people, because freedom is the basis of the human quality of society (Pope John XXIII, *Pacem in Terris*). This freedom can only be limited when it interferes with public order, that is, when the public peace, or commonly accepted standards of public morality, or the rights of other citizens are threatened. (Vatican II, Declaration on Religious Freedom, n. 7.)

This first set of principles is entirely consistent with the "free exercise" clause of the First Amendment.

REGARDING THE "NO . . . ESTABLISHMENT" CLAUSE:

There are no ideal forms of constitutional relationships between religion and the state. Whatever relationship exists, it must be governed by the following principles:

1. Religious bodies cannot use the state to further their own spiritual purposes, that is, *the state cannot act as a church.* (It does so, for example, when it writes and/or mandates prayer in public schools.) This principle is based on the distinction between the sacred and the temporal orders. There is a rightful secularity to the temporal order, which must be open at the same time to sacred values. The Church, however, remains transcendent to every political system. (Vatican II, Pastoral Constitution on the Church in the Modern World, n. 40.)

2. *The state cannot use the Church for its purely political purposes.* This would violate the principle of the freedom of the Church.

3. On the other hand, *the Church must have an active role in society,* so that "the earthly and heavenly city penetrate each other" (Vatican II, Pastoral Constitution on the Church in the Modern World, n. 40). The Church must have the freedom, therefore, "to preach and to teach, and to pass moral judgment even on matters that belong to the political order, when human rights or the salvation of souls are at stake." (Pastoral Constitution, n. 76.)

4. *The Church seeks no special status and should be accorded none.* The Church always owes the public a careful accounting of how it came to its moral conclusions. Furthermore, if it is to influence the public debate and the formulation of public policy, the Church must translate its teachings into language, arguments, and categories which a religiously and politically pluralistic society can understand and agree upon as the moral foundations of key policy positions. Finally, the Church must address issues in a way that underscores their moral interrelatedness (Cardinal Bernardin's "seamless garment" and "consistent ethic of life" approach).

This fourth principle is the distinctive contribution of the U.S. Catholic bishops. It is drawn not only from their various public statements but also from the new teaching style they have adopted, especially in their recent pastoral letters on peace and the economy.

5. *The relationship between the Church and the state must be one of cooperation, for the sake of the common good.*[102] "In their proper spheres, the political community and the Church are mutually independent and self-governing. Yet, by a different title, each serves the personal and social vocation of the same human beings." (Vatican II, Pastoral Constitution on the Church in the Modern World, n. 76.)

This second set of principles is entirely consistent with the present tests used by the U.S. Supreme Court in establishment cases; namely, that (1) "the purpose" and (2) "the primary effect" of the enactment should not advance or inhibit religion, that is, there must be "a secular legislative purpose and a primary effect that neither advances nor inhibits religion" (Justice Tom Clark, in *Abington School District* v. *Schempp* [1963]), that (3) the law should not produce "an excessive entanglement with religion" (Chief Justice Warren Burger, in *Walz* v. *Tax Commissioner of the City of New York* [1970]), and that (4) the enactment should not have "divisive political potential" along religious lines (Justice William Brennan, in *Meek* v. *Pittenger* [1975]).

This second set of principles is also consistent with Chief Justice Burger's notion of "benevolent neutrality," in the *Walz* decision (employed by Justices Clark and Brennan in the 1963 *Schempp* case and by Justice Brennan again in *Sherbert* v. *Verner,* in the same year). Indeed, the Court has taken great pains on several occasions to insist that neutrality does not mean hostility.[103]

"The point is," John Courtney Murray argued, "that the goodness of the First Amendment as constitutional law is manifested not only by political but also by religious experience."[104] It cannot be emphasized enough that the preceding doctrinal and theological principles have grown out of *both* kinds of experience.

PART III

Applying the Principles

FIVE

ABORTION:
THE HARDEST CASE

HAD this book ended with the previous chapter, it might have been regarded, at best, as a comprehensive *theoretical* study of the relationship between religion and politics in the United States. Practitioners would have looked in vain for any specific discussion, much less guidance, on matters like abortion, gay rights ordinances, school prayer, aid to parochial schools, the sanctuary movement, the erection of Nativity scenes on courthouse lawns, war and peace, and the like.

My purpose in what follows is at once modest and perhaps wildly ambitious: to examine the discussion of several highly controversial issues, to identify manifest flaws where they exist, on whatever side of the argument, and to coax the debate onto a clearer and more coherent course. In the end, neither politician nor religious leader nor journalist nor "average citizen" will be told how to think about, much less resolve, any of these issues. But they might be encouraged to enter, or to reenter, the public argument in a manner that could at least improve the possibilities for intelligent and constructive solutions.

We begin with abortion, the hardest case of all, for two reasons: (1) it served as both the lightning rod and catch basin for the religion-and-politics issue during the entire 1984 presidential election campaign; and (2) it provides the most challenging test of the principles which have been identified and engaged throughout this study.

Abortion and the 1984 Campaign

On March 22, 1984, the Administrative Board of the United States Catholic Conference issued a statement entitled, "Political Responsibility: Choices for the '80s."[1] The statement defended the right and duty of religious leaders like themselves to enter public policy debates when the issues at stake involve human rights, peace, and justice. In other words, no issue is purely and exclusively "secular" if it touches human dignity and the common good, the twin pillars of Catholic social doctrine.

The bishops, however, placed strict limits on the mode of their participation in the political process: "We specifically do not seek the formation of a religious voting bloc; nor do we wish to instruct persons on how they should vote by endorsing candidates." Furthermore, they continued, "we hope that voters will examine the positions of the candidates on the full range of issues as well as their integrity, philosophy and performance."[2]

The pastoral leaders of the U.S. Catholic community, therefore, would not presume to tell their flock how to vote, except to say that they should vote for or against candidates on the basis of "the full range of issues." The statement listed some of the election year's principal issues in alphabetical order: abortion, arms control and disarmament, capital punishment, civil rights, the economy, education, energy, family life, food and agricultural policy, health, housing, human rights, mass media, and regional conflict in the world (Central America, the Middle East, and South Africa).

These straightforward principles would be violated or ignored during the campaign, even by some bishops.

The opening salvo of the intense, and sometimes bitter, intramural debate within U.S. Catholicism was fired not by Governor Mario Cuomo nor even by the pro-choice lobby within the Church, but by the newly installed archbishop of New York, John J. O'Connor. The occasion was a press conference, televised on WPIX, Channel 11, New York, on June 24, 1984.

The second question came from a reporter for *The Wanderer*, a national Catholic paper of strongly right-wing political and theological views. The reporter recalled that St. Ambrose, as archbishop of Milan, had threatened to excommunicate the Roman emperor for having "engaged in one act of slaughter against civilians, innocent civilians." (Ambrose did, in fact, excommunicate Theodosius I for a massacre at Thessalonica in the year 390.)

Then the reporter made a turn that was at once editorial and theological. Implying, first, that abortion is morally equivalent to the slaughter of innocent civilians in warfare and, secondly, that a public official's upholding of constitutional and other legal requirements in the funding of abortion is the moral equivalent of practicing abortion, he asked if Archbishop O'Connor still had "the juridical power to excommunicate Catholic heads of state if, as in the case of Governor Cuomo, they openly support assaults on innocent human life contrary to the teaching of the Church."

Instead of promptly ruling the question out of order on the grounds that its basic premise was unproven and even slanderous, Archbishop O'Connor dignified it with a long and circuitous response:

> The powers of an archbishop are so extraordinary I haven't even explored all of them yet. Would one, would an archbishop or a diocesan bishop (it wouldn't have to be an archbishop) have the power to levy excommunication under extraordinary circumstances? I would think he would. Church law governs excommunications, of course. But we have the Revised Code of Canon Law which has just been published on the 27th of November of 1983. And that lists areas for which people may be automatically excommunicated or for which an excommunication may be transmitted to them. [The Archbishop should have noted that penal canons always have to be interpreted strictly. The Code's provisions on abortion do not extend to politicians as such.[3]]
>
> The Church is extraordinarily careful about the use of the authority of excommunication. I would want to know precisely what the Governor or anyone else would say about these things. I would be awfully careful to think for a moment that the Governor feels that he is in any way involved in slaughter, massive or otherwise. Certainly one's intentions must always be considered very carefully and very prayerfully before the Church even dreams of levying any kind of censure. Since I haven't even had opportunity, neither his fault or my fault, to discuss the matter with the Governor because, since I have been here, as I just described, I've been running all over the atmosphere and the Governor is a very busy man. But I haven't had opportunity to talk with him personally and every impression I have been given, what people tell me, what I read by way of his interviews given to *The Catholic New York,* the Governor seems to feel that he is in good conscience and is following what he believes to be appropriate theological teaching. Perhaps when he and I discuss these issues, his position will be more clearly articulated. Then I will know whether, in accordance with my understanding of Catholic teaching, he is a, I'll know more clearly what his position is.[4]

He compounded the problem in his reply to the next question, from a reporter for *The Daily News.* In the Archbishop's opinion, the reporter asked, "can a Catholic, in good conscience, vote for a pro-abortion political candidate?"

> You're asking my personal opinion and I would have to answer, Bill, that I do not see how a Catholic in conscience could vote for an individual explicitly expressing himself or herself as favoring abortion. There may

be arguments that I haven't heard or that I haven't understood, but as far as I can see, there is no way, I don't see how it can be justified. I've read that you must take the totality of an individual's voting record or intentions and that there are those who are very faithful to try to take care of the homeless and the hungry and so on. And it, quotes, only on this single issue [sic]. But to me this single issue is an issue of life or death. And it's clearly a matter of belief in a great number of cases, if you believe as I believe, as the Catholic Church teaches, that from the moment of conception we are dealing with human life in the womb. Then I don't see how you can ever, under any circumstances, deliberately and intentionally take that innocent human life. And I think no matter what your record would be, you could be the finest person in the world, to argue that I do all these other wonderful things and they may be very, very wonderful things. . . .

We, the bishops, cannot accept the concept, "I personally am opposed to abortion, but . . ." . . . Now we say we cannot accept that concept, "I'm personally opposed, but . . .," which is the so-called pro-choice concept. Maybe one can distinguish, I don't see how you can. It seems to me that if you maintain that you're pro-choice, then you have to say you approve abortion if it is chosen. So that makes you pro-abortion. . . . It is a very crucial question in conscience and I think it is a very crucial question for voters.

Unless one is familiar with this press conference and, specifically, with these two answers to reporters' questions, the one on the possible excommunication of Governor Cuomo and the other on the moral obligation of voters to oppose so-called pro-choice candidates, one cannot understand why Governor Cuomo said what he said in an interview with The New York *Times* at his home in Holliswood, Queens, on July 31, 1984. Contrary to the charges of politically and theologically right-wing opponents, the governor did not pick a fight with his archbishop. He responded directly to a reporter's questions about Archbishop O'Connor's provocative remarks at that June 24 televised press conference.[5]

Recognizing that it has "always been safer not to talk about religious beliefs because religious beliefs are so personal that they tend to antagonize," Governor Cuomo noted, however, that "formal religion, more aggressively than ever before, is seeking to use the political process in the traditional way."[6]

The governor undoubtedly had in mind not only Archbishop O'Connor's entrance into the political arena but that of the Protestant fundamentalists and of the leadership of the national Republican Party. Only three weeks earlier, Senator Paul Laxalt, chairman of President Reagan's reelection campaign committee and a close personal friend of the president, sent a letter to 45,000 members of the clergy, mostly Protestant, in 16 states, urging them to "organize a voter registration drive in your church" in order to insure victory for a man who has given "unwavering commitment to the traditional values which I know you share."[7] (At the Republican National Convention in Dallas in early August, Laxalt shouted, "Shame on you, Mario Cuomo!" for challenging his archbishop.)

The Laxalt letter provoked criticism from both ends of the spectrum. James Reston characterized the gesture as "both bad religion and bad politics."[8] William Safire was even more keenly disturbed, not only with Senator Laxalt, but also with Archbishop O'Connor and President Reagan. "No President, not even born-again Jimmy Carter, has done more to marshal the political clout of these evangelicals than has Ronald Reagan—to his historic discredit."[9] As for Laxalt's letter, "That political proselytizing is surely so unethical as to be un-American." Archbishop O'Connor, meanwhile, finds himself "in strange bedfellowship with the Protestant evangelicals," who in 1928 defeated Al Smith in the most viciously anti-Catholic campaign in American history.

Governor Cuomo informed The New York *Times* in that interview of July 31 that he planned to do whatever he could to shift the public focus from selective moral tests, such as abortion and school prayer, to a broader debate over which political party best espouses universal religious values about peace and the poor. Thereupon, he directly challenged the archbishop's assertion that no Catholic could in good conscience vote for a so-called pro-choice candidate.

"Now you have the Archbishop of New York saying that no Catholic can vote for Ed Koch, no Catholic can vote for Jay Goldin, for Carol Bellamy nor for Pat Moynihan or Mario Cuomo—anybody who disagrees with him on abortion. He amends that by saying, 'I'm not telling anyone how to vote, that's my personal judgment.' But you're the Archbishop," Cuomo declared.

"If you took literally what he's saying," he continued, "he can only vote for a right-to-lifer. He can't vote for Reagan because Reagan signed the abortion statute." He was referring to the nation's first permissive abortion statute, signed by Mr. Reagan while serving as governor of California.

When Christ was asked to sum up everything he had been teaching, Governor Cuomo noted, he never mentioned abortion. "He wasn't terribly strong on negatives. He prescinded from politics—he refused to register in the zealot party. . . . And he said, 'The whole law is, love thy neighbor as thyself for the love of me'."

Anticipating some of the arguments he would make in September at the University of Notre Dame, Cuomo acknowledged that while he and the archbishop agreed on the morality of abortion, he had a responsibility to respect the law. And even if agreement could be reached on the scope of a constitutional amendment to ban abortion, "Is there any chance of its success? And, if not, what have you done except divide people?"

The battle was joined. In the next day's New York *Times*, Archbishop O'Connor accused Governor Cuomo of misinterpreting his stand on abortion.[10] He denied that he had ever said that Catholics could not vote for Mayor Koch, City Comptroller Harrison J. Goldin, City Council President Carol Bellamy or Senator Daniel Patrick Moynihan. To be sure, Governor Cuomo had been imprecise in his remarks. The archbishop did *not* mention any specific officeholders or candidates. What the governor should have said is that such was the unmistakably logical inference to be drawn from the archbishop's remarks. And indeed it was.

The archbishop also denied that he had ever said, "O.K., now I want you to insist that everybody believe what we believe." But as The *Times* pointed out, the governor apparently did not intend that it should be taken as a direct quotation of the archbishop. Cuomo had been, at that point in the interview, in "a kind of rhetorical dialogue with himself, as representing the position of the Archbishop."[11]

Archbishop O'Connor insisted, finally, that in his position as archbishop of New York, "it is neither my responsibility nor my desire to evaluate the qualifications of any individual of any political party for any public office, or of any individual holding public office." He would later skirt the edges of that self-imposed limitation in his public remarks about Congresswoman Geraldine Ferraro, the Democratic candidate for vice-president.

Governor Cuomo said that he was pleased by that part of the archbishop's statement. He accepted the possibility that he had misunderstood what the archbishop had said at his June press conference. "I'm delighted to have the clarification today where he is saying in effect we're not going to tell anybody to vote for anybody. That's wonderful," the governor continued. "If that came out of this dialogue, it was a good thing."[12]

At a press conference in Washington on August 3, before addressing the International Platform Association, he restated his reasons for entering the debate about religion and politics. He thought it "in danger of being co-opted by a single kind of religious group" and indeed by President Reagan himself, whom we see "repeatedly making much of religious issues like abortion, homosexuality. We see him in religious settings. All of this is not appropriate."[13] Significantly, Governor Cuomo identified abortion here as a "religious" issue. He would do so again, more than once, in his Notre Dame speech.

On the following Sunday, August 6, Congresswoman Ferraro reentered the debate. (In July she had challenged President Reagan for "calling himself a good Christian, but I don't for a moment believe it because the policies are so terribly unfair."[14]) "I try to separate my religious views from my standing on the issues," she said in an interview. And so began her slide down theology's slippery slope, into a position more akin to nineteenth-century Protestant and Enlightenment individualism than to Catholicism, and one sharply different from Mario Cuomo's, who, in his *Diaries,* had written that his "Catholic faith and the understanding it gives me of stewardship aren't a part of my politics. Rather, my politics is, as far as I can make it happen, an extension of this faith and the understanding."[15] The press, and just about everyone else, would miss this and other important differences between Ferraro's and Cuomo's views on religion and abortion.

Three days later, August 9, a statement by Bishop James W. Malone, president of the National Conference of Catholic Bishops, was prematurely released by a bishop or bishops unsympathetic with the Democratic ticket and/or with Governor Cuomo (advance copies of statements of this kind are routinely mailed to every U.S. Catholic bishop, with strict instructions that the document not be made public before the embargo date).

Bishop Malone's intention had been to release the statement after both national conventions had been completed, so that it would have an even-handed effect. Those who released it before the Republican convention in Dallas hoped to make it appear as a direct criticism of the Democratic platform and its candidates, and as a pointed reaction to the Cuomo–O'Connor debate. The statement, for example, rejected "the idea that candidates satisfy the requirements of rational analysis in saying their personal views should not influence their policy decisions; the implied dichotomy—between personal morality and public policy—is simply not logically tenable in any adequate view of both."[16]

Although the statement also repeated the assertion of the March statement issued by the Administrative Board, namely that the bishops' conference does not take positions for or against political candidates, the August document bore one very serious weakness. In listing the various issues of concern to them and to the American Catholic community, the statement acknowledged that there is "room for sincere disagreement by Catholics and others who share our moral convictions, over how moral principles should be applied to the current facts in the public policy debate." But then it seemed to exempt two issues: direct attacks on noncombatants in war, and abortion.

Since abortion, not military policy, had become the central issue in the debate about religion and politics, Bishop Malone was saying, in effect, that the Catholic politician had to accept, with an equal measure of assent, not only the bishops' teaching on the morality of abortion, but also their practical judgments about specific legislation (assuming those judgments were clear in the first place).

Bishop Malone's expressed hope that religion would not be injected into the political campaign fell on deaf ears, or perhaps was drowned out by the conservatives' applause for the other parts of the statement.

The next day, The New York *Times* quoted Brooklyn Auxiliary Bishop Joseph Sullivan in tacit support of Governor Cuomo's position. "The major problem the church has is internal," he said. "How do we teach? As much as I think we're responsible for advocating public policy issues, our primary responsibility is to teach our own people. We haven't done that. We're asking politicians to do what we haven't done effectively ourselves."[17] Governor Cuomo incorporated those lines in his Notre Dame address the following month.

On August 13, Governor Cuomo issued his first response to Bishop Malone's statement. "The question whether you ought to speak out to make [Catholic teaching on abortion] public policy is not dogma. It's a political judgment."[18] He insisted that the Church's own position on abortion has changed over the years (he cited Augustine and Aquinas and the Church's refusal, before the eighteenth century, to baptize an aborted fetus), and that the way to stop abortion is not by passing a law but by convincing people it's wrong. There were faint echoes here of an argument advanced in the 1950s and early 1960s by those, including President Eisenhower, who opposed civil rights legislation on the ground that a law was no substitute for a change of heart.

Whenever the discussion in the hour-long interview veered back toward abortion, however, the governor said he was reluctant to comment because he was in the midst of researching the subject of how a politician's private morality should influence public action. He also said that the problem was not limited to abortion but should include issues from birth control to nuclear war.

On the same day, August 13, Congresswoman Ferraro was drawn into a position from which she would never extricate herself for the remainder of the campaign. Her interviewer noted that, although she is "usually forthright and self-assured," she seemed "tentative and uneasy tackling the questions of politics and religion."[19] The vice-presidential candidate admitted that she felt "very uncomfortable discussing my religious views."

She acknowledged, in response to questions about the Malone statement, that she accepted the Church's teaching on abortion, but that she had no qualms about separating her religious beliefs from her political policies. "My religion is very, very private," she insisted. But she was wrong on at least three important counts.

First, abortion is not primarily, and certainly not exclusively, a religious issue. Secondly, religious beliefs are often relevant to political policies, as they were during the civil rights movement of the 1960s. Thirdly, religion is not "very, very private" (although hers apparently is). For good or for ill, it has social and even political ramifications.

Furthermore, the congresswoman's insistence that she accepted her Church's teaching on abortion was sometimes difficult to reconcile with some of her other public statements. She would not go on record, as Governor Cuomo had, to say that she opposed abortion on *moral* grounds. Indeed, the following year, speaking before the National Women's Political Caucus in Atlanta and relieved by then of the care of answering reporters' questions in the heat of a presidential campaign, she seemed to adopt an even stronger pro-choice position. She insisted, to much applause, that the right of women to choose an abortion "is inseparable from our struggle for political and economic independence," and she sharply criticized "male-dominated, conservative religious groups" that want to make "our decision for us."[20] The speech only accentuated again the difference between her views and those of Governor Cuomo, differences that were consistently ignored during the campaign.

On August 23, President Reagan gave his famous prayer-breakfast speech at the Republican convention in Dallas. It was one of the key moments of the entire campaign. The president attacked the U.S. Supreme Court's decisions on prayer and Bible reading in public schools and blamed the Court for a flood of lawsuits against tax exemptions for religious groups and references to God in the Pledge of Allegiance, in public documents, and on the federal currency. He charged that those who oppose prayer in the public schools, for example, are really "intolerant of religion."

He also forged an inextricable link between morality and religion ("The truth is, politics and morality are inseparable . . . . morality's foundation is religion . . ."), and implicitly confused the state with society. "A state," he said, "is nothing more than a reflection of its citizens. The more decent the citizens, the more decent the state."[21] He mentioned abortion only in passing.

On the same day on which President Reagan was speaking at the prayer breakfast, Archbishop O'Connor and Governor Cuomo had a 90-minute meeting at the archbishop's residence behind St. Patrick's Cathedral. Both men agreed that the meeting had been fruitful, although neither would reveal exactly what had been discussed. Later, however, Governor Cuomo admitted that he and the archbishop still disagreed over how to handle the issue of abortion, but that it was a disagreement over political tactics and not church teachings. The archbishop "won't say it's a sin" if you support Medicaid funding of abortions for poor women, the governor observed. "He won't say you're not a good Catholic if you do."[22] The governor said he believes it is discriminatory to permit abortion but then prevent poor women from obtaining them by denying funds.

The next day, August 24, Archbishop O'Connor said that he considered it his duty to correct politicians if they offered incorrect views on Catholic teachings. Governor Cuomo said later the same day that he had no quarrel with the archbishop on that point. Their disagreement on the abortion issue, the governor again insisted, is over political tactics, not church teaching. But that was not the archbishop's position. As he would say later, on October 15, "I recognize the dilemma confronted by some Catholics in political life. I cannot resolve that dilemma for them. As I see it, their disagreement, if they do disagree, is not simply with me; it is with the teaching of the Catholic Church."[23]

Thus, the archbishop erased the distinction between the authoritative proclamation of a moral principle and the recommendation of a particular practical application of that principle. For him, to disagree with the particular application is to dissent from the principle itself. Governor Cuomo took the opposite position, as did the National Conference of Catholic Bishops, particularly in its pastoral letter, "The Challenge of Peace" (and later in Bishop Malone's statement of October 14).

Both the archbishop and the governor had appeared together on August 24 in Albany's Catholic cathedral for the funeral of an auxiliary bishop. Many in the congregation seemed relieved by the archbishop's insertion of humor in his remarks at the end of the liturgy. He said that he hoped the governor would attend *his* funeral, but conceded that, if the governor did attend, he couldn't announce it beforehand because there would be a headline: "Governor Anxious to Go to O'Connor Funeral."[24]

The principal participants in the debate moved off center stage for a few days and the pundits filled the temporary vacuum. William Safire huffed about "the Reverend Reagan" and arched an eyebrow over Archbishop O'Connor's "strange bedfellowship" with anti-Catholic fundamentalists. James Reston asked who appointed the Republicans as "leaders under God's authority" (quoting from Senator Laxalt's letter), and William Shannon warned Catholics that, in spite of the president's energetic courting of their votes, there was "no realistic prospect" a reelected president could get two-thirds of Congress and three-fourths of the states to agree to ban abortion or restore prayer in the schools. "Nor is there any reason," Shannon continued, "that Reagan cares any more deeply about these issues than Nixon did."[25]

(Nixon, Shannon pointed out, also worked hard for the Catholic vote, and yet it was he who appointed the man, Justice Blackmun, who wrote the majority opinion in *Roe* v. *Wade*.) Shannon's prediction has not been contradicted by events.

A Catholic bishop, even more conservative than Archbishop O'Connor, also moved into the temporary vacuum. On September 4, Archbishop Bernard F. Law, of Boston, called a news conference in which he described abortion as "the critical issue in this campaign," and urged voters to make it their central concern when they cast their votes, in spite of the stated opposition of the Administrative Board of the National Conference of Catholic Bishops to single-issue voting. He read a strongly worded statement, signed by himself and 17 other Catholic bishops from Maine, Vermont, New Hampshire, and Massachusetts (the Boston ecclesiastical province) that reporters took as implicit criticism of Geraldine Ferraro and Mario Cuomo.

"To evade this issue of abortion under the pretext that it is a matter pertaining exclusively to private morality," the statement declared, "is obviously illogical."[26] The criticism may have applied to Ferraro; it certainly did not apply to Cuomo, although, clearly, in Archbishop Law's mind, it did. He had, for example, objected strongly when a Jesuit school, the College of the Holy Cross in Worcester, Massachusetts, invited Governor Cuomo to deliver its commencement address, and later expressed resentment over the invitation extended to the governor to speak at the University of Notre Dame. He had also been displeased when Boston College, another Jesuit institution, named its new library after one of its most distinguished alumni, Speaker of the House Thomas P. ("Tip") O'Neill.

The statement of the 18 New England bishops drove home a point central to Archbishop Law's thinking; namely, that abortion is an even more pressing moral issue than nuclear war. "While nuclear holocaust is a future possibility," the statement said, "the holocaust of abortion is a present reality. . . . we believe that the enormity of the evil makes abortion the critical issue of the moment."[27] That statement would not go unchallenged within the National Conference of Catholic Bishops.

Two days later, September 6, former Vice-president Mondale reentered the religion-and-politics debate in an address at the international convention of B'nai B'rith in Washington. He delivered a sturdy defense of religious liberty and a sharp reprimand to the fundamentalists: Jimmy Swaggart and Jerry Falwell, by name. He reserved his strongest criticism, however, for the president, focusing particularly on the prayer-breakfast speech in Dallas. "No President," he said, "should attempt to transform policy debates into theological disputes."[28]

But Mr. Mondale, like Ms. Ferraro (and unlike Mr. Cuomo), continued to display uncertainty on the religion issue. Mondale's embrace of the Jeffersonian "wall of separation between church and state" had a ring of absolutism to it, as if the two realms can never be allowed to overlap or intersect. Indeed, a week later, in Tupelo, Mississippi, he would insist, as Congresswoman Ferraro had, on the utterly private nature of religious faith.[29]

The point went to President Reagan. Religion and politics *do* mix. The question is: how? Mr. Mondale also tended, in his B'nai B'rith address, to confuse religious freedom with tolerance, celebrating "a religious faith that cannot be coerced and is tolerant of other beliefs." James Madison would not have been pleased.

President Reagan addressed the same audience later that day. Although he, too, made the mistake of confusing religious freedom, which is rooted in human and civil *rights*, with mere tolerance, the tone of his speech was far different from the one he had given in Dallas. He embraced the "wall of separation," even suggesting that it was to be found somewhere in the Constitution. "The unique thing about America," he said, "is a wall in our Constitution separating church and state." The president's breakfast audience in Dallas would not have been pleased with the B'nai B'rith speech.

The press and the electronic media would not, or could not, let go of the issue. Nearly every day there was a feature story or a special segment on television and radio.[30] Meanwhile, a certain measure of suspense started to build as Governor Cuomo prepared for his major address at the University of Notre Dame. Stories began appearing about the amount of time and effort he was putting into the speech. He was photographed often at his desk, a theological volume in hand or within reach. He seemed to be taking the Notre Dame speech as seriously as he had his keynote address two months earlier at the Democratic National Convention in San Francisco.[31]

The drama continued, this time in costume. On September 9, Archbishop O'Connor, still outfitted in his liturgical vestments following the celebration of Sunday Mass, gave an impromptu press conference on the steps of St. Patrick's Cathedral. The object of his attention had shifted by now to Geraldine Ferraro. (He had criticized her by name in a press conference two nights earlier, before addressing a Pennsylvania Pro-Life Federation convention in Altoona.) Congresswoman Ferraro, according to the archbishop, had been giving the impression that the teaching of the Catholic Church on abortion was not "monolithic," that there was a variety of legitimate opinions on the subject within the Church, and that Catholic teaching, therefore, is somehow divided over it.[32]

The congresswoman was perplexed. She couldn't recall having said anything of the sort during the campaign, and didn't know why the archbishop had suddenly decided to attack her. "I'd be very happy to provide you with any written statements that have been made that you'd like," the archbishop told reporters, "but these things are very complex." It would turn out that he was referring to a two-year-old letter sent, over her signature, to about 50 Catholic members of Congress, inviting them to a meeting to consider the political ramifications of the abortion issue. The letter of invitation was accompanied by some promotional material provided by Catholics for a Free Choice.

In the same spontaneous, open-air press conference, Archbishop O'Connor indicted her, albeit indirectly, for voting in favor of funding for abortion. "I cannot see how, in good conscience, a Catholic who believes the teaching of the Catholic church can vote to fund abortion." Asked if he was questioning Congresswoman Ferraro's support for such funds, the archbishop said he would have to leave the matter "to the conscience of the individual how he or she has come to a particular conclusion."

When pressed on the connection between personal morality and public policy, he replied, "That's—to me, that's an absolute."

"Does that mean," the reporter, Gabe Pressman, asked, "that our Government, any Governor or legislator, has a duty to persuade the people or other legislators, or whatever, to accept Catholic morality, if he is a good Catholic?"

Archbishop O'Connor fumbled the question. First, he failed to challenge the assumption that abortion is a matter only of "Catholic morality" rather than of natural law, binding everyone, Catholics and non-Catholics alike. And then, astonishingly, he answered the question with a flat, "No." He seemed to be siding, after all, with Congresswoman Ferraro and, to a slightly different degree, with Governor Cuomo.

A few moments later, however, he reversed himself. When asked if he thought that an officeholder who says "I'm personally against abortion" is obligated to try to persuade other people to be against it, the archbishop said, "I don't think there's any question about it."

Was this "I'm-personally-opposed-but" approach simply a "hypocritical device," therefore? "Well," the archbishop replied, "you get into a value judgment when you use the term hypocritical. I say it's wrong. And I think it's irrational. I think it's absolutely irrational."

The same day, President Reagan made a campaign stop at the National Shrine of Our Lady of Czestochowa in Doylestown, Pennsylvania. His host was Cardinal John Krol, of Philadelphia, who, much to the surprise even of some White House aides, praised the president for efforts to secure tax credits for parents with children in parochial schools and for supporting food aid to Poland. There were shouts of

"Four more years!" from the friendly crowd. In the president's remarks, he once again mixed religious symbols (praising Pope John Paul II, for example) with partisan political statements, but he made no reference to abortion or the issue of church and state.[33]

Two days later, September 11, Congresswoman Ferraro and Archbishop O'Connor were back on the front page of The New York *Times*, sharing space with Senator Edward M. Kennedy, of Massachusetts, who had also entered the debate.

The day before, Monday, September 10, the congresswoman and the archbishop had discussed their differences by telephone. She asked him, from a campaign stop in Indianapolis, what he had been referring to in his impromptu news conference outside of St. Patrick's Cathedral, and he mentioned the covering letter she had signed and circulated among the 50 or so Catholic members of Congress in 1982. Taken aback, she insisted that she had completely forgotten about the letter, and tried to explain how she had understood the term "monolithic." But her explanation wasn't persuasive.

It is meaningless, after all, to say that church teaching on the matter is clear, and presumably "monolithic," but that the personal beliefs of many laypersons differ from that teaching, and so are not "monolithic." (In an interview in Columbus, Ohio, the next day, September 11, this is how she phrased it: "I believe that the Catholic Church's position on abortion is monolithic. But I do believe that there are a lot of Catholics who do not share the view of the Catholic Church.") Congresswoman Ferraro was not the first, nor the last, person to be harmed by the calculated ambiguities of the Catholics for a Free Choice organization.

The waters were muddied even further by her press release of the same date (September 10). She said that she had told the archbishop she had a duty as a public official to uphold the Constitution, which guarantees "freedom of religion." She continued: "I cannot fulfill that duty if I seek to impose my own religion on other American citizens." So the distinction between morality and religion once again collapsed. Abortion was transformed from an issue of moral disagreement to one of religious conflict.

Senator Edward M. Kennedy, of Massachusetts, had joined the debate on the same day with a talk at a fund-raising event in New York City. This was not the first time he had addressed the issue, however. A year earlier he had spoken at Jerry Falwell's Liberty Baptist College in Lynchburg, Virginia, where he observed that people of religious faith are "tempted to misuse government in order to impose a value which they cannot persuade others to accept. But once we succumb to that temptation, we step onto a slippery slope where everyone's freedom is at risk."[34]

Like President Reagan and Walter Mondale, Senator Kennedy formulated the issue in terms of tolerance and intolerance rather than religious freedom and rights. "To stay the hand of mutual intolerance," he said in his New York City speech, "requires first of all a recognition that our political process is properly an area of disagreement among people of good will, but it is not an arena of combat between the forces of light and the forces of darkness. The choice we face is between Democrats and Republicans, not between good and evil."[35]

Kennedy showed himself more Catholic in his thinking than Ferraro. Religious faith is not "very, very private," as she had put it. In the face of ethical issues, the senator said, "Church leaders have the obligation to speak then, for that is their vocation." But there is a crucial distinction to be made between the proclamation of views in the public forum and the harnessing of governmental power to impose those views on the general populace.

"Religious leaders," he insisted, "may say anything they feel bound in conscience to say, but they may not ask Government to do something which it cannot do under the Constitution or the social contract of a pluralistic society." In cases like abortion, he continued, "the proper role of religion is to appeal to the free conscience of each person, not the coercive rule of secular law."

Referring explicitly then to the dispute between Archbishop O'Connor and Governor Cuomo, Senator Kennedy acknowledged the archbishop's constitutional right and religious duty to speak against abortion, but also Geraldine Ferraro's and Mario Cuomo's right, as "faithful Catholics, serving in public office," to agree with the archbishop's morality "without seeking to impose it across the board."

In the end, however, Kennedy came down on the side of those who place the abortion issue in the category of private morality. "Issues like nuclear arms are inherently public in nature. . . . The church can persuade an individual not to have an abortion; but the church cannot persuade an individual to restrain the nuclear arms race."

He disagreed with the August 9 statement issued by Bishop Malone which had asserted that separating personal morality and public policy is "not logically tenable." This "cannot mean that every moral command should be written into law," Senator Kennedy declared. Bishop Malone would have agreed. Indeed, he hadn't taken the position which Senator Kennedy criticized. Bishop Malone had been objecting specifically to the view that "candidates satisfy the requirements of rational analysis in saying their personal views should not influence their policy decisions." Such a view, according to Bishop Malone's statement, involves an "implied dichotomy—between personal morality and public policy," and it is that dichotomy which is "not logically tenable."

Senator Kennedy continued to insist that abortion is a matter of personal choice, and that, although such "questions" can be matters for "public debate," the "answers" cannot be matters for "public decision." The basis for such a distinction is, at best, elusive.

"The issues should be discussed before the widest audience, but they can be settled only in the depths of each individual conscience," he argued. Why? Because there is "a logical line of separation between private morality and public policy—and it is the line between the rule [sic] of Government and the role of individual rights."

In the final accounting, the abortion issue is not only inherently private but also inherently religious, according to Senator Kennedy. He implied that, if the government were to ban or restrict the practice of abortion, it would be imposing a particular religious doctrine on the general populace. And this, he said, was precisely what his late brother, President John F. Kennedy, had warned against in his address before the Greater Houston Ministerial Association during the 1960 campaign.

The next day, September 11, Congresswoman Ferraro was interviewed again, this time in Columbus, Ohio. "The Archbishop and I agreed to disagree," she said, "on the interpretation of that sentence" about the "monolithic" nature of Catholic teaching on abortion. When asked if she believed abortion to be immoral, The New York *Times* itself noted that "she skirted the question." She said, "I do not believe in abortion. I am opposed to abortion as a Catholic."[36]

For her, abortion remained a religious issue. Although opposed to abortion "as a Catholic," she would "not impose my religious views on others." She said that she felt "very, very strongly about the separation of church and state" and that she had no difficulty separating her religious views from her public policy position. Later, in a speech in Scranton, Pennsylvania, she made the same point, and was challenged within an hour by Archbishop O'Connor's successor as head of the Scranton diocese, Bishop James Timlin, who characterized her views as "absolutely ridiculous."[37]

But opposition to her position did not come only from the right. A fellow Catholic, Joseph A. Califano, secretary of Health, Education and Welfare under President Carter, had also challenged her on this very point in a column in The Washington *Post*. "If Ferraro in fact believes in the position of the church on abortion, then as a member of Congress, should she try to persuade others in a free and open political marketplace that her position is correct? I think so," he wrote. "She may disagree with the bishops on whether abortion under most circumstances is morally wrong. If so, she should clearly state that."[38]

Vice-president George Bush was in Columbia, South Carolina, that same day, September 11. He, like Ms. Ferraro, was drawn most reluctantly into the abortion debate. He said he would personally approve of abortion in the case of rape (a position at odds with Catholic teaching as well as the views of President Reagan and his Protestant fundamentalist supporters), but that he wouldn't favor the use of public funds to pay for such abortions. During the 1980 campaign, however, he had taken the opposite position.

Mr. Bush said he was hesitant to take questions on abortion because of the disagreement on the subject involving his vice-presidential opponent and Archbishop O'Connor, as if that had any bearing on his own right and responsibility to answer questions on the matter. He said that he wanted to exercise his right as an American "to remain silent."[39] When asked if he thought his credibility had been damaged by his assertion that his position on abortion had not changed, when indeed it had, he said, "No. There's an awful lot of things I don't remember."[40]

The next evening, September 13, Governor Cuomo delivered his much publicized address on religion and politics at the University of Notre Dame. Kenneth A. Briggs, of The New York *Times*, called it "one of the most anticipated exercises in theology ever presented by a member of the laity."[41] It proved to be a major turning point in the whole debate.

Governor Cuomo acknowledged at the outset that distinctions have to be made: for example, between matters of church and state, on the one hand, and religion and politics and morality and government, on the other. It was not always clear, however, whether these distinctions were consistently honored throughout the speech.

For example, unlike candidates Mondale and Ferraro, Governor Cuomo made clear his opposition to abortion, on *moral* grounds. "For me life or fetal life in the womb should be protected, even if five of nine Justices of the Supreme Court and my neighbor disagree with me. A fetus is different from an appendix or a set of tonsils. . . . the full potential of human life is indisputably there."[42] That was not the sort of remark to win him many votes from one of the newly assertive constituencies within the Democratic Party. On the other hand, the governor seemed, just as often as not, to cast the abortion issue in religious rather than moral terms.

A "morality-and-government" issue was several times transposed into a "church-and-state" and/or "religion-and-politics" issue. The Catholic who holds office in a pluralistic democracy like the United States of America bears a special responsibility to "help create the conditions . . . where everyone who chooses may hold beliefs different from *specifically Catholic* ones."[43] The governor gave three examples: divorce, birth control, and abortion. He made no distinction between moral requirements rooted in Catholic doctrine and binding only Catholics, for example, the obligation to attend weekly Mass, and moral requirements rooted in natural law and binding all persons, for example, the obligation to respect human life at every stage, including the fetal. The former applies to "specifically Catholic" beliefs, but the latter are universal in scope.[44]

Catholic officeholders, in fidelity to their oath to preserve the Constitution, the governor continued, gladly strive to guarantee the freedom of all citizens, "because they realize that in guaranteeing freedom for all, they guarantee our right to be Catholics: our right to pray, to use the sacraments, to refuse birth control devices, to reject abortion, not to divorce and remarry if we believe it to be wrong." Two categories were mixed: beliefs and behavior rooted in "specifically Catholic" doctrine, and beliefs and behavior rooted in natural law, and binding every human being: Catholic or not, religious or not.

Abortion, then, becomes a matter of religious freedom. To work and/or to vote for a law that would ban or restrict the practice of abortion is tantamount to seeking "to force our [religious] beliefs on others."[45]

The governor promptly got back on course, however, with another crucial distinction: between moral principle and practical application. One can accept the Church's teaching that abortion is immoral, as he does, but one is free to differ with the bishops on the most effective way to deal with the problem in the public arena, as he also does. Indeed, "there is no inflexible moral principle which determines what our political conduct should be." And he was right.

He contended, moreover, that the bishops themselves have honored this distinction. On divorce and birth control, for example, they adhere to the traditional teaching of the Church but abide by the civil law as it now stands. There are no efforts afoot to change the applicable laws nor to pass a constitutional amendment banning divorce and birth control.[46] Slavery was treated similarly in the nineteenth century. Furthermore, the bishops admitted in their 1983 pastoral letter on nuclear war that people may agree with them at the level of moral principles of peace and justice but sincerely disagree on the best practical approach to achieve them. "Abortion is treated differently," the governor noted.

In his mind, it shouldn't be. To abandon political realism for an all-or-nothing approach in the case of abortion is to retreat into a "moral fundamentalism." And yet, he noted, even the bishops themselves had to adjust to political realities in their quest for a constitutional amendment banning abortions. In 1981, much to the distress of hard liners in the pro-life movement, they changed strategy and supported the Hatch Amendment, which would have left the matter to the states.

Governor Cuomo rejected both approaches, the one interdicting abortions at the federal level and the other at the state level. Even if an amendment or a law could be passed, "it wouldn't work," he insisted. It would be " 'Prohibition' revisited, legislating what couldn't be enforced and in the process creating a disrespect for law in general."[47] Indeed, he argued, a constitutional amendment would permit people to ignore the root causes of abortion just as capital punishment is used to escape dealing more fundamentally and more rationally with the problem of violent crime.

But one could ask if the abortion and Prohibition cases are exactly parallel. The latter made the sale and use of all alcoholic beverages illegal. Would that not differ from a law that would only prohibit abortion-on-demand, while allowing abortion in the cases of rape, incest, danger of the mother's life, or radical fetal deformity? This is, of course, the principal point at which some of Governor Cuomo's most sympathetic critics parted company with him, including Father Theodore M. Hesburgh, C.S.C., president of the University of Notre Dame.[48]

The choice, they insisted, is not between a law banning all abortions and the present law, but between the present law and a law restricting abortions to the aforementioned special cases. There *is* a consensus in society for such a law, they argued. While most Americans oppose an absolute legal prohibition of abortion (a 1983 Gallup poll, for example, disclosed that only 16% favors an absolute prohibition, and more recent polls show a similar distribution of opinion), most also oppose abortion-on-demand (only 23% favor it, according to Gallup). A large majority, especially when the absolute prohibitionists are added in, favors some kind of restrictive legislation (58%, plus 16%, or about three-quarters of the population). Significantly, Catholic opinion isn't much different from that of other Americans, except perhaps on the matter of abortion-on-demand.[49]

"A remarkably well-kept secret," Father Hesburgh wrote, "is that a minority is currently imposing its belief on a demonstrable majority." He called upon Catholics to cooperate with "other Americans of good will and ethical conviction," who may not favor an absolute prohibition but who also clearly oppose abortion-on-demand. Catholics should continue to hold themselves "to a higher standard than we can persuade society-at-large to write into law." If Catholics were to help articulate this secret consensus, Father Hesburgh suggested, Catholic politicians would no longer be able, or feel compelled, to say, "I'm against abortion, but. . . ."

Even a denial of medicaid funding for abortion would not achieve the objective of preventing abortions, the governor continued. It would not prevent the rich and middle class from having abortions. It would not even ensure that the poor would not have them. It would "only impose financial burdens on poor women who want abortions." His critics, however, were not impressed with the poverty argument. Perhaps the principles of fairness and equal protection under the law would have provided a more compelling legal argument.[50] For whether one agrees with the U.S. Supreme Court or not, it has decided in *Roe v. Wade* that abortion is a constitutionally guaranteed right, rooted in the right of personal privacy.[51] It is not within the authority or the power of a governor, even the governor of so large and influential a state as New York, to revoke that decision or to circumvent it in the exercise of his office.

"The hard truth," Governor Cuomo contended, "is that abortion isn't a failure of government." No one is legally required to have an abortion. And yet Catholics don't seem to be much different from the rest of the population in their attitudes toward, and practice of, abortion.[52] If there is a failure, it is a failure that the Church must share, because we still have abortions despite "the teaching in our homes and schools and pulpits, despite the sermons and pleadings of parents and priests and prelates, despite all the effort at defining our opposition to the sin of abortion." (Auxiliary Bishop Joseph Sullivan, of Brooklyn, had made the same point.)

"We seem to be in the position," the governor said, "of asking government to make criminal what we believe to be sinful because we ourselves can't stop committing the sin.

"The failure here is not Caesar's. This failure is our failure, the failure of the entire people of God." That criticism has never been addressed by any of the governor's critics inside the Catholic Church.

This is not to suggest that the governor absolutely ruled out a legal remedy. What he said was that, apart from "example that is clear and compelling,. . . we will never convince this society to change the civil laws to protect what we preach is precious human life." Indeed, he argued only that "the moving strength of our own good example" would be "[b]etter than any law or rule or threat of punishment."

In the absence of legal prohibition, we can still take legislative initiatives to make abortion a less compelling option: programs to support impoverished mothers, to provide medical care for infants, or to establish a bill of rights for mothers and children. Indeed, even if abortion were outlawed, the work would still be there to do, including the task of "creating a society where the right to life doesn't end at the moment of birth."

And, as for Catholics, instead of trying to "make laws for others to live by," they can try "living the laws already written for us by God, in our hearts and our minds." In other words, Catholics must practice what they preach, and persuade others of the truth of their beliefs through the power of example.

"I hope that this public attempt to describe the problems as I understand them," the governor concluded, "will give impetus to the dialogue in the Catholic community and beyond, a dialogue which could show me a better wisdom than I've been able to find so far."

There is an extraordinary discrepancy between the actual text of Governor Cuomo's Notre Dame speech and the virulent attacks upon it, especially by politically and theologically right-wing Catholics. The latter either had never read the speech in full or, having read it, simply could not grasp concepts like public consensus and prudential political judgment, or the distinction between principle and the application of principle. Because the governor disagreed with their own political solutions (assuming they had clear-cut solutions to propose), they concluded that he denied the moral principle itself, even though he had made it abundantly clear, at the risk of alienating portions of his traditional Democratic constituency, that he opposes abortion on moral grounds.[53]

The next day, in fact, he was rebuffed in his effort to contribute his $1,500-check for the lecture and travel expenses to the Nazareth Life Center in Garrison, New York, a Catholic home for unwed mothers. The board of directors decided unanimously that it could not accept the gift "because it would seem we were disagreeing with the church," according to Sister Marita Paul, a member of the administrative staff. "We agree with the teaching of the church particularly as articulated by Archbishop O'Connor. I want to stand behind what he stands for."[54]

What "teaching of the church" she (and the board) thought Governor Cuomo had opposed is not clear. Indeed, nothing in his speech contradicted any Catholic doctrine. Nor were any of the differences between himself and the archbishop of a doctrinal nature. They differed on prudential, practical judgments. No doctrine was ever at issue, then or since.

If the right wing contributed confusion to the discussion, so, too, did the left wing. On the same day, Daniel C. Maguire, a professor of Christian Ethics at Marquette University and a leading critic of current official Catholic teaching on abortion, held a press conference in Washington, D.C., to announce that 55 Catholics had signed a statement which asserted that the Catholic Church's position was not "monolithic" (the word that had come back to haunt Geraldine Ferraro in her dispute with Archbishop O'Connor).[55] The statement was released under the auspices of Catholics for a Free Choice, a Washington-based Catholic group that takes a pro-choice position. Maguire had agreed with much in Governor Cuomo's speech, but thought him unduly conservative in his moral views.

The following month, the group published its statement, with just under 100 signers, most of whom were not theologians.[56] Fewer still were Christian ethicists or moral theologians. Of these, only Professor Maguire himself and Professor Margaret Farley, of the Yale Divinity School, could have been described as major Catholic figures in the field. The overwhelming majority of Catholic theologians refused to sign.

The liberal Catholic journal *Commonweal* called the full-page ad in the October 7 Sunday edition of The New York *Times* "a model of calculated ambiguity."[57] Its headline was factually accurate: "A DIVERSITY OF OPINIONS REGARDING ABORTION EXISTS AMONG COMMITTED CATHOLICS." But even that factually correct headline did not distinguish between the legal and moral dimensions of the issue. Many Catholics, like Governor Cuomo, support permissive legislation, while remaining firmly opposed to abortion on moral grounds.

The statement itself leapt from an assertion about the diversity of opinion among "committed Catholics," most of whom have never studied the issue in any depth, to a gratuitous and unfounded claim that a "large number of Catholic theologians" would approve of direct abortion in certain instances. Ambiguity again. The statement made no distinction between theologians who would approve of abortion in the highly extreme case where there is incontrovertible evidence of irreparable brain damage in the developing fetus, and theologians who would approve of abortion in a wide variety of cases, and even for reasons of convenience. The fact that the statement received the endorsement of so few Catholic theologians, major or otherwise, tended to substantiate the argument that it did not accurately reflect the current state of the discussion within the Catholic theological community.

The statement's sponsor, Catholics for a Free Choice, is indeed pro-choice, even to the extent of abortion-on-demand, according to the terms laid down by *Roe* v. *Wade*. Very, very few Catholic theologians favor abortion-on-demand, and national surveys show, again and again, that approximately three-quarters of the population, Catholics included, oppose abortion-on-demand.

Boston's Archbishop Law, a highly unsympathetic critic of Governor Cuomo's speech, was nevertheless accurate when he said a week later that the fall's debate about abortion was complicated because "there are several different arguments going on at once."[58] Chicago's Cardinal Bernardin, writing in his weekly column in *The Chicago Catholic,* made essentially the same point: "It is precisely because abortion is defined in such radically different ways that we have not been able to arrive at a consensus on this critical issue facing our society."[59] Both bishops insisted that abortion is an issue of public morality and not only private morality, and that it is a question of the human rights of the fetus, not the civil rights of the pregnant woman.

Archbishop Law, unlike Cardinal Bernardin, however, took public issue, by name, with leading Catholic Democrats: Congresswoman Ferraro, Senator Kennedy, and, of course, Governor Cuomo. He said in an interview at his residence on September 21 that all three were wrong in their arguments that Catholic politicians could support free choice as national policy while opposing abortion personally.[60] He also defended his focusing on the abortion issue, in apparent disagreement with Cardinal Bernardin's "seamless garment" approach. Finally, he directly challenged the position of Catholics for a Free Choice, saying that the organization's name had about the same ring to it as "Catholics for apartheid" or "Marxists for free enterprise." He insisted, "The church's position is monolithic from the prospective [sic] of the church." The assertion had a circular ring to it.

As the campaign moved toward the November election, religion, not the deficit, remained at the center of attention. On October 3, Governor Cuomo delivered another speech on the subject of religion and politics, at St. Francis College in Brooklyn. He devoted most of the talk to reactions to the Notre Dame address, but he also strongly endorsed Cardinal Bernardin's "seamless garment" approach to the various pressing human life issues.

At Notre Dame he had argued forcefully on behalf of the principle of consensus. We create our "public morality," he had said, "through consensus and in this country that consensus reflects to some extent the religious values of a great majority of Americans" But not all religiously based values have an a priori place in our public morality.

Governor Cuomo insisted at St. Francis College that many had misunderstood what he had said about consensus at Notre Dame. "I did *not* say that anyone's religious values or moral codes should be surrendered to a popular consensus in order to avoid disagreement and foster harmony.

"I did *not* say that what is popular must be good.

"Nor that the community's consensus on what is right or wrong should never be challenged.

"What I *did* say and what I repeat is that if we are serious about making certain values a part of the public morality, part of the statutes and laws that bind everyone, there must first be a public consensus: That's the way laws are made in a democratic society."[61]

He noted how many letters he had received from people, following the Notre Dame speech, arguing that Catholics (including the governor himself) had an obligation to make their view the public view and to have it adopted into law. "Very few, however, are suggesting specific ways of doing that. . . . Ask those who demand a constitutional amendment what it would say, precisely," he continued, "and there is no reply."

What was less persuasive, however, was his insistence that he had "tried to make clear at Notre Dame that the matter of abortion is not just a 'Catholic' issue or even just a religious one. I did it by pointing out that 'even a radically secular world must struggle with the questions of when life begins, under what circumstances it can be ended, when it must be protected and by what authority. . . .' "[62] He had indeed said that, but he had also said other things that tended to fuse the issue's moral and religious dimensions.

On October 14, Bishop James W. Malone, president of the National Conference of Catholic Bishops, issued a second statement on the religion-and-politics issue (the first had appeared between the two national conventions, in early August). What was remarkable in this second statement was its movement away from a crucial position adopted in the first; namely, that in the cases of abortion and the direct attack of noncombatants in war, a Catholic had to agree not only with the bishops' moral teaching but with their policy judgments as well. The distinction between principle and the application of principle had somehow been obliterated.

In the October statement, Bishop Malone conceded that "citizens and public officials may agree with our moral arguments while disagreeing with us and among themselves on the most effective legal and policy remedies." On the other hand, the statement continued, "a prudential judgment that political solutions are not now feasible does not justify failure to undertake the effort."[63] The statement also reaffirmed the bishops' opposition to single-issue politics.

By now, however, the tone of the campaign, and of the debate about abortion inside and outside the Catholic community, had already been established. Bishop Malone's statement came too late in the day to have had any major effect.

In any case, it had no discernible impact on the speech that Archbishop O'Connor delivered the next evening, October 15, before a group of medical professionals, nuns, and priests at Cathedral High School in New York City. His subject was "Human Lives, Human Rights." Without mentioning Governor Cuomo or Congresswoman Ferraro by name, the archbishop took issue with them on several points.

"You have to *uphold* the law, the Constitution says. It does not say that you must *agree* with the law, or that you cannot work to *change* the law," the archbishop declared.[64]

"What do we ask of a candidate or someone already in office? Nothing more than this: a statement opposing abortion on demand, and a commitment to work for a modification of the permissive interpretations issued on the subject by the United States Supreme Court.

"It will simply not do," he continued, in clear reference to Governor Cuomo's Notre Dame speech, "to argue that 'laws' won't work, or that 'we can't legislate morality.' Nor will it do to argue, 'I won't impose my morality on others.' There is nothing personal or private in the morality that teaches that the taking of unborn life is wrong."

The governor, of course, did not say that we cannot legislate morality. He said, rather, that before any morality can be translated into law, there must be a public consensus in its favor. To legislate a morality that lacks that public consensus would indeed be tantamount to imposing a morality on others.

"If we are going to argue [as Governor Cuomo did] that law must reflect a consensus," the archbishop declared, "we must admit that there was a strong, national consensus against abortion on demand before the Supreme Court issued its decree that the unborn is not a person whose life state law could legally protect." The archbishop had touched a weakness in his opponents' argument. Even if there were no clear public consensus in favor of an absolute ban on abortion, there was, and still is, a clear public consensus against abortion-on-demand.

But the archbishop seemed to throw away his advantage in the next several paragraphs. "There are those who argue," he continued, "that we cannot legislate morality [the Governor had not said that, and the argument is absurd on its face], and that the answer to abortion does not lie in the law. The reality is that we do legislate behavior every day." Of course, and no one could reasonably deny that, but the archbishop seemed to drive his argument into the ground, referring to murder, stealing, arson, child abuse, and so forth.

The most significant paragraph, however, came near the end of the archbishop's lengthy speech, when he referred to Father Hesburgh's observation that, while there is no public consensus for a law banning all abortions, there is a "secret consensus" against abortion-on-demand. Those who are part of this "secret consensus," on the other hand, do not want the law to prohibit abortion in special cases like rape, incest, danger to the mother's life, or radical fetal deformity. It was remarkable that Archbishop O'Connor did not challenge this approach. He acknowledged, without reproof, that "some may passionately believe" in these exceptions.

And then he concluded: "Whatever we may believe about such exceptions, however, we know that they constitute a fraction of the abortions taking place, so that at the very least we can come to grips with what is the real and the frightening issue of the day: abortion on demand." This was, in fact, the second time in the speech that the archbishop had made that point. Earlier he had said: "There is strong resistance by some to any change in the laws to make them less permissive or to reduce the possibility of 'abortion-on-demand' (for that is the real issue)."

If he really believes that abortion-on-demand is the "real issue," then Archbishop O'Connor will have some explaining to do with the pro-life community. For them, abortion is abortion, whether it follows a rape or whether it simply provides a convenient solution to an unplanned pregnancy. To endorse Father Hesburgh's proposal is, at the same time, to concede Governor Cuomo's main point; namely, that you can only put into law what a public consensus will support.

There is no public consensus for an absolute prohibition, Father Hesburgh admitted, but there *is* a "secret consensus" for legislation that would limit abortion to special cases. He implied, in fact, that Catholics ought to stop wasting their time on fruitless efforts to achieve a total ban on abortions, and instead "cooperate with others of good will to work for a somewhat more restrictive abortion law."[65]

Father Hesburgh's challenge was two-sided, of course. Governor Cuomo was challenged to modify the terms of his consensus argument, and Archbishop O'Connor was challenged to concede its applicability to the abortion debate.

On October 22, 23 Catholic bishops released a statement taking issue, although not by name, with Archbishop O'Connor and Archbishop Law for their heavy concentration on abortion during the election campaign. They cited the March statement of the Administrative Board of the National Conference of Catholic Bishops, the October 14 statement issued by Bishop Malone, as president of the Conference, the U.S. Catholic bishops' pastoral letter on nuclear war ("The Challenge of Peace"), and the "seamless garment" approach of Chicago's Cardinal Joseph Bernardin in support of their criticism.

"To claim [as Archbishop Law and some other New England bishops had] that nuclear war is only a potential evil and that abortion is actual neglects a terrible reality," the statement of the 23 bishops declared. "For indeed, there can be no possibility of exercising moral responsibility against nuclear war if we wait until the missiles have been released. Now is the time, the only time [we] have, to take a position on this moral issue. For right now we possess in our hands the means for the annihilation of the human race."[66]

"Further," they continued, "it is an illusion to think that the nuclear threat is not already taking a terrible human toll just as abortion." Citing the Holy See itself, the bishops reminded their colleagues that the arms race is an act of aggression against the poor because it deprives them of resources necessary for bare survival.

They challenged those bishops, like John J. O'Connor and Bernard Law, who had been implying throughout the campaign that Catholics should make abortion the crucial issue in voting for or against candidates for public office. Voters must bring "moral evaluation . . . to the entire spectrum of life issues . . . and then be free in their hearts to vote their conscience before God."

There was apparently no doubt in Archbishop Law's mind that the statement had been aimed at him. The next day he issued a statement of his own in which he suggested that the differences between himself and his 23 brother bishops involved "a practical judgment concerning emphasis."[67] But then he repeated his argument that this was an opportune time to concentrate on abortion because it had emerged in the campaign as a major issue. Again, there was a certain circular quality to the archbishop's reasoning. Abortion had become a central issue in the campaign, in large part because certain Catholic bishops, including himself, kept raising it, much to the discomfort of the Democrats and the delight of the Republicans.

"Obviously," he concluded, "such an emphasis on abortion must be without prejudice to the necessity of doing all we can to minimize and eliminate the threat of nuclear destruction. It may well be that the resolution of the issue of abortion will hasten the day when we will resolve the issue of possible nuclear holocaust. Both evils reflect the same moral fault: a failure to respect human life."[68]

But the question was begged: Hadn't his "practical judgment concerning emphasis" led him (and Archbishop O'Connor), *in fact*, to stress the abortion issue at the expense of the nuclear issue? Furthermore, was he suggesting at the end of his statement that the abortion issue has to be resolved *first*, before any progress can be made on nuclear disarmament?

Two days later, on October 25, Cardinal Bernardin delivered a major address on religion and politics at Georgetown University. It was undoubtedly the most sophisticated treatment of the subject given during the entire campaign year. "War and abortion," he said, "are linked at the level of moral principle. . . . The policy of abortion on demand needs to be resisted and reversed. But this does not mean the nuclear question can be ignored or relegated to a subordinate status."[69] Archbishop Law would have agreed.

But Cardinal Bernardin pressed his argument further. In the case of the nuclear threat, he said, "We are not confronting a hypothetical or speculative future danger. The possibility of nuclear war is a clear and present danger." Archbishop Law would not have agreed. Abortion is the more immediate danger, he had argued, because there are millions of them being performed right now.

"The value of the framework of a consistent ethic is that it forces us to face the full range of threats to life," Cardinal Bernardin continued. "It resists a 'one-issue' focus by the church, even when the urgent issue is abortion or nuclear arms."

"In the past year," he said, moving remarkably close to an open confrontation with archbishops Law and O'Connor, "some have questioned whether the linkage of the right to life with other human rights may unintentionally dilute our stand against abortion. On both moral and social grounds, I believe precisely the opposite. The credibility of our advocacy of every unborn child's right to life will be enhanced by a consistent concern for the plight of the homeless, the hungry and helpless in our nation, as well as the poor of the world."

On the other hand, there was no comfort for the secularist liberal in the Bernardin speech. Abortion, like the issues of war and poverty, is a question of "public morality." Contrary to *Roe* v. *Wade* and feminist ideology, abortion is not a matter of privacy or women's rights. Abortion involves "a direct attack on innocent life" and an assault upon society's weakest, at that. "The very vulnerability of the unborn tests our moral vision," he said, "for the moral quality of any society is measured not by how it treats the powerful, but how it respects the claims of the powerless."[70]

But there was also little comfort for the religious conservative. Although Cardinal Bernardin insisted that abortion is a question of "public morality," he also acknowledged that this claim is not self-evident. "Obviously, in a religiously pluralistic society, getting consensus on what constitutes a public moral question is never easy."[71] But it has to be done. We have to make "a rationally persuasive case" if we expect the authority of the state and civil law to be invoked on the issue. He suggested that case has been made with regard to abortion, given the "very magnitude of the problem."

He seemed to agree with Governor Cuomo on the point that there is no official Catholic teaching on how moral principles are to be implemented in the political order. Citing both the October 14 statement from Bishop Malone and the pastoral letter, "The Challenge of Peace," Cardinal Bernardin insisted on the distinction "between moral principle and political/legal strategies."[72]

And then he moved to endorse what he called, somewhat loosely, "the suggestion of both Archbishop O'Connor and Father Theodore Hesburgh that we initiate a national dialogue on steps to restrict the present policy of abortion on demand." Had Archbishop O'Connor really endorsed the Hesburgh suggestion? If he had, it would have moved him to a position closer to Governor Cuomo and away from Archbishop Law and the national right-to-life movement.

Cardinal Bernardin also implicitly supported Governor Cuomo's argument that the bishops themselves have recognized the need to make practical, prudential judgments when attempting to translate moral principles into law. To accept a restriction on abortion-on-demand without securing a total ban on abortions "is not to change Catholic teaching on the morality of abortion. It is to recognize the different roles played by moral law and civil law in a pluralistic society." One has to search for "what is possible and most effective in the civil arena."

"Whether we look at the problem of how to reverse the arms race or how to reverse the policy of abortion on demand," he concluded, "the beginning of the process is a series of conscious choices that something different must be done. Then the search for a deliberate policy can begin."

In his Georgetown speech, Cardinal Bernardin located himself precisely in the center of the abortion debate. On the left were those who kept insisting that abortion is a matter of private morality and personal choice, or who argued that the law cannot be changed because there is no consensus to change it; and that since there is no consensus to change it, there is nothing more to be done about it.

On the right were those who kept insisting that abortion is such an unmitigated evil, the greatest of evils, in fact, that only an absolute prohibition is morally acceptable. No political compromise is possible, because political compromise is tantamount to moral compromise. In the meantime, we must publicly oppose politicians, especially if they are Catholic, who may agree with "us" on the moral principles but disagree on their practical application in the political order.[73]

By then, of course, the 1984 election campaign was over, for all practical purposes. The polls were showing a landslide victory for President Reagan. Whether the unborn would be better or worse off under a Democratic administration was clearly moot. Walter Mondale and Geraldine Ferraro would not have the opportunity to prove themselves, one way or the other.

In his presidential address at a post-election meeting of the National Conference of Catholic Bishops in Washington, D.C., Bishop James Malone reiterated the Conference's opposition to a single-issue strategy and offered an implied criticism of those bishops [O'Connor and Law in particular] who tended to go their own way during the campaign.

"When a consensus has been established and expressed by the conference at the national level," he said, "a framework exists for the individual bishops or groups of bishops to articulate the implications of the position for specific choices and issues. I believe I am expressing the prevailing experience of bishops in saying that a conference statement on a particular question gives us as bishops a place in the public mind which is different from any single expression of the same position."[74]

He was right, of course. One only has to think of the reception accorded "The Challenge of Peace," the U.S. Catholic bishops' pastoral letter on nuclear war. In that letter, the bishops acknowledged that "Millions join us in our 'no' to nuclear war, in the certainty that nuclear war would inevitably result in the killing of millions of innocent human beings, directly or indirectly. Yet many part ways with us in our efforts to reduce the horror of abortion and our 'no' to war on innocent human life in the womb, killed not indirectly, but directly." Citing Pope Paul

VI's principle, "If you wish peace, defend life," the bishops pleaded "with all who would work to end the scourge of war to begin by defending life at its most defenseless, the life of the unborn."[75]

Framing the Debate

There are many (real or fabricated) dimensions to the abortion debate: feminism, concern for the weak and powerless in society, the right of personal privacy, the sociology of motherhood, even church and state.[76] Our concern here, however, is fixed at the point where morality intersects with the political order.

Whether abortion is defined as a civil rights issue (the pregnant woman's right to choose, or, as in *Roe* v. *Wade*, the right of privacy) or as a human rights issue (the fetus' right to life), it is always reducible to a question of law. Should the law allow abortions or not? Should the law authorize the use of tax monies to pay for abortions or not? Should the law be changed to reflect one moral view over others or not?

John Courtney Murray delivered himself of a grand understatement when he suggested that "the American mind has never been clear about the relation between morals and law."[77] The two orders are frequently confused. Either morality is thought to be determinative of law, or law is thought to be determinative of morality.

The mentality behind the first is that whatever is good should be enforced by law and whatever is evil should be prohibited by law. The mentality behind the second is that whatever is legal is by that fact moral, and whatever is not against the law is thereby morally acceptable. "From the foolish position that all sins ought to be made crimes," Murray argued, "it is only a step to the knavish position that, since certain acts . . . are obviously not crimes, they are not even sins."[78] In the case of abortion, which Murray never even mentioned, both positions are abroad.

Those who follow the first position tend to honor logic rather than jurisprudence and experience: "This is good, therefore. . ."; "this is evil, therefore. . . ." The social and political consequences and the possibility of enforcement are not taken into account, or are held to be of no *moral* account.

Thus, if drunkenness and alcoholism are social vices, the logical thing to do is to ban alcohol. Which is exactly what was done through the passage and ratification of the Eighteenth Amendment. So, too, with abortion: "There ought to be a constitutional amendment!"

But there is a difference between the moral law and the civil law. The former "governs the entire order of human conduct, personal and social; it extends even to motivations and interior acts." The latter "looks only to the public order of human society; it touches only external acts, and regards only values that are formally social."[79] Thus, the scope of civil law is limited, and its moral aspirations minimal. To have made the moral argument against abortion is not necessarily to have made the legal argument.

Civil law "enforces only what is minimally acceptable, and in this sense socially necessary," Murray continued. "Beyond this, society must look to other institutions for the elevation and maintenance of its moral standards—that is, to the church, the home, the school, and the whole network of voluntary associations that concern themselves with public morality in one or other aspect." In other words, even if the law cannot help, society is not bereft of resources in the fight against abortion.

Murray's view was entirely consistent with the Catholic tradition, as expressed, for example, in Thomas Aquinas. Although concerned with leading everyone to virtue, civil law does so gradually, not suddenly. "Therefore it does not lay upon the multitude of imperfect people the burdens of those who are already virtuous, namely, that they should abstain from all evil. Otherwise these imperfect ones, being unable to bear such precepts, would break out into yet greater evils. . . ."[80]

We have here a piece of the enforceability argument. Will the repressive law be obeyed? Can it be enforced against the disobedient? Is it prudent to undertake its enforcement, given the likelihood of harmful effects in other areas of social life? In other words, are we taking into adequate account the "condition of man, to whom different things are expedient according to the difference of his condition?"[81]

Enforceability is, in turn, part of the consent argument. And the issue of consent is, in turn, qualified by pluralism. In a pluralist society like the United States of America, winning consent for a law, necessary for its enforcement, is complicated by the existence of many different moral (and religious) points of views. What are we to do? Murray proposes four rules.

First, we can be mindful of the fact that each group retains the right to demand conformity from its own members. As Governor Cuomo said at Notre Dame, no one is compelled by law to have an abortion. And the Catholic Church can continue to tell Catholics that it's a mortal sin and it can continue to excommunicate Catholics for having an abortion. The government cannot interfere with that process. No law can impede it.

Secondly, no group in a pluralist society has the right to expect that government will impose or prohibit some act of behavior when there is no support for such action in society at large.

Thirdly, any group has the right to work toward a change in moral standards within the pluralist society, through the use of methods of persuasion and pacific argument.

Fourthly, no group has the right to impose its own religious or moral views on others, through the use of the methods of force, coercion, or violence. It would indeed be "incongruous" if certain religious bodies, concerned with values that are spiritual and moral, should pursue their ends by what appear to be the methods of power rather than of persuasion.

These rules were not "made in heaven," Murray insisted. They are "made on earth, by the practical reason of man. . . . Their supposition is the jurisprudential proposition that what is commonly imposed by law on all our citizens must be supported by general public opinion, by a reasonable consensus of the whole community."[82]

The key adjective here is "reasonable." The corresponding virtue, indeed a cardinal virtue, is prudence. We have to be people of justice and of fortitude, to be sure. To stand up for what is right. To defend the interests of the weak and the powerless. But we also have to be people of prudence, "who understand the art of procedure, and understand too that we are morally bound, by the virtue of prudence, to a concrete rightness of method in the pursuit of moral aims."[83]

Where does that leave us? With a consensus for restricting abortions to extreme cases: radical deformity of the fetus, rape, incest, danger of the mother's life. Can that consensus be translated into law? Only if two sides give ground: liberal politicians who pose the dilemma in terms of abortion-on-demand versus absolute prohibition, and conservative pro-lifers who do the same. There is a *tertium quid*. But absent any movement of these two forces, there will be no change in the situation.

In the meantime, each group that believes that abortion is evil can continue to exhort its own members to act in accordance with that belief, mindful of the fact that example remains the most effective form of teaching. And each group can continue to participate fully in the public debate, in a manner consistent with the tradition of civility.

Refining the Debate

The public debate over abortion, even when conducted in a civil manner, can neither promote clarity nor facilitate the resolution of conflict unless the debate honors the basic definitions, distinctions, and principles that have been engaged throughout this book.

The abortion debate, especially as it was carried on during the 1984 presidential election campaign, needs refinement in the following areas:

1. There has been a persistent tendency on the part of many (mostly on the left, but sometimes also on the right) to categorize abortion as a religious issue. Underlying that tendency is an assumption that morality and moral values are inextricably linked with religion and religious values.

   The argument that morality and religion can be distinct, one from the other, is not a theological argument. It is philosophical, which means that it is not derived from religious conviction or from religious doctrine. Indeed, one has only to read the work of the British philosopher, John Stuart Mill, no apologist for the Church, to appreciate this point. And if that is deemed insufficient, the preamble to the Declaration of Independence will do.

   Categorizing abortion as a religious issue serves only those who wish to maximize abortion rights. The debate is immediately transposed into one about religious freedom (with the we-cannot-impose-our-religious-beliefs-on-others argument), the dangers of religious factionalism, and even the separation of church and state.

   It is difficult to understand why some opponents of abortion concede, indeed even stress, the point that opposition to abortion is rooted in religiously-based values.

2. A relatively small number of people deny that morality, even private morality, is relevant to the abortion debate. Most, however, agree that abortion is at least partially, if not principally, a moral issue. But, of these, many argue that it is 'an issue of "private" morality, not subject to civil law.

   It is not self-evident, therefore, that abortion is a matter of public morality. The challenge facing the anti-abortion side is to develop the public morality argument already proposed by Cardinal Joseph Bernardin in his extremely important Georgetown University address of October 25, 1984. "Precisely because the unborn child represents the weakest member of our human community," he said, "there is an objective link to be made between unborn life and the lives of others who live defenseless at the margin of our society."[84]

3. Even if there were universal agreement that abortion is a matter of public morality, two questions would still require answers: *whose* version of morality?; and *by what process* is it to be incorporated into law?

Exclusive appeals to the Bible or to the teaching authority of the Catholic Church are the weakest forms of public argument in a religiously pluralist society. They are not even completely effective, as public opinion surveys demonstrate, when directed toward members of one's own religious community. And yet Protestant fundamentalists and some Catholic prelates persist in this unproductive course.

If the moral argument is to be compelling, it has to persuade people who do not share the same view of divine revelation or a particular moral tradition. There has to be a careful accounting of how the moral arguments have been derived and how the moral conclusions have been drawn from them. Again, the Bernardin lecture at Georgetown provides a model.

4. Disagreement over the political application of a moral principle does not necessarily imply disagreement over the moral principle itself. Many, indeed the majority, of those who oppose abortion on moral grounds also oppose an absolute legal prohibition. They want to leave *legal* room for abortion in the cases of rape, incest, danger of the mother's life, or radical deformity of the fetus.

The habit of absolute prohibitionists to lump that majority with the minority that favors abortion-on-demand obscures the existence of the "secret consensus" against abortion-on-demand, negates its political potential, and thereby sustains the legal status quo. The course proposed by Father Theodore Hesburgh, of the University of Notre Dame, has challenged both wings of the anti-abortion side: the politically conservative pro-lifers, for whom every single abortion is a moral tragedy, and the politically liberal politicians, who imply that they would act if only there were a consensus to support them.

Cardinal Bernardin knew whereof he spoke when, at Georgetown, he observed: "The questions which have run through this election—about the role of religion in our public life, the relation of political responses to moral issues—are broader and deeper than election politics can handle."[85]

SIX

OF SCHOOL BELLS AND MUSHROOM CLOUDS

ALTHOUGH abortion was surely the most prominent religion-related issue in the 1984 presidential election campaign, it is not the only issue of its kind in U.S. politics today. This final chapter touches upon some of the others: prayer in the public schools, financial aid and services to students and parents in private and parochial schools, religion in the public school curriculum, publicly supported Nativity scenes, legally mandated Sabbath observance, state-funded chaplaincies, tax exemptions for property owned by religious groups and for religious communities, military exemptions for conscientious objectors, the sanctuary movement, gay rights ordinances, pornography, and the morality of a nuclear deterrence policy. The list is not complete, but it is reasonably representative.

School Issues

Why has the schoolhouse become, for many Americans, the principal locus of conflict on matters of religion and politics? Because public schools have been, since colonial times, instruments of religious and patriotic indoctrination.[1] "The habit of looking to the school to produce learned piety and patriotism became so deeply ingrained in the American mind," Robert Michaelsen has written, "that few questioned its validity."[2]

Although the religion and piety of the public schools was, until the latter part of the nineteenth century, clearly and unmistakably evangelical Protestant (with a smattering of the founding fathers' enlightened Deism), their religio-patriotic purpose was taken for granted even by nonreligious educators like Horace Mann and John Dewey.

Mann regarded education as primarily a process of moral nurture supported by a kind of generic, nonsectarian religion. For Dewey, too, the school's role was religious insofar as it seeks to shape moral character and at the same time develop a sense of community, of a common identity as Americans.[3] But he always insisted on a distinction between religious and religion. The former, he said, refers to a quality of experience, a manner of valuing, a range of attitudes; the latter refers to something more institutionally substantive, to a body of beliefs and practices related to the supernatural order and to religious organizations.

Dewey summarized his views at the end of his *A Common Faith*, published in 1934:

> The things in civilization we most prize are not of ourselves. They exist by grace of the doings and sufferings of the continuous human community in which we are a link. Ours is the responsibility of conserving, transmitting, rectifying and expanding the heritage of values we have received that those who come after us may receive it more solid and secure, more widely accessible and more generously shared than we have received it. Here are all the elements for a religious faith that shall not be confined to sect, class, or race. Such a faith has always been implicitly the common faith of mankind. It remains to make it explicit and militant.[4]

Horace Mann's contemporary, Archbishop John Hughes, of New York, saw it somewhat differently. The school was a vehicle of religious education and even patriotism, to be sure, but the kind of religious education available in the public schools, he argued, was unacceptable for Catholic students. During the 1830s classes for Catholic children had been organized in crowded church basements, and by 1840 there were about 5,000 students enrolled.[5] When the Catholics of New York petitioned the Common Council for financial aid, the petition was denied. Archbishop Hughes began concentrating on building his own schools. By 1865, a year after his death, 75% of the parishes in the city had schools, with a total enrollment of 16,000 students, or about one-third of the Catholic school population. Two decades later, in 1884, the Third Plenary Council of Baltimore decreed that "near every church a parish school, where one does not exist, is to be built. . . ."[6]

The battle lines were drawn, and, with the rising rates of Catholic births and immigrations in the late nineteenth and early twentieth centuries and the concomitant expansion of the Catholic school system throughout the United States, the more sharply etched those lines be-

came. For some it was a battle to save, or eventually to restore, a Protestant America. For others it was a battle to preserve the principle of
absolute separation between church and state. For many Catholics it
was a battle for Catholic identity and for fairness in the distribution
of tax monies for education.

But, then, as the Second World War came to an end, the situation
took an ecumenical turn. Some members of the Catholic hierarchy
concluded that Catholics, Protestants, and Jews had a common enemy,
secularism in general and Communism in particular, and they enlisted
theologians like John Courtney Murray in the struggle against these
ideologies. It was out of this new assignment that Murray first developed his interest in church-state relations.[7]

Catholics, secure in their own school system and in their growing
political influence, became as concerned as many Protestants about
the declining influence of religious values in the public schools. They
reacted just as bitterly as Protestants, for example, to the *Engle* v. *Vitale*
U.S. Supreme Court decision in 1962, which ruled unconstitutional
the use of a prayer composed by the New York Board of Regents.[8] But
differences between Catholics and many other Americans persisted
over issues like tax credits and student aid.

PRAYER IN PUBLIC SCHOOLS

There have been at least five U.S. Supreme Court decisions related
directly or indirectly to prayer in the public schools. In 1962, there
was *Engle* v. *Vitale*, mentioned above. The Court was clearly correct
in its judgment. No governmental agency has any constitutional business composing prayers, however theologically bland they might be,
for use in public schools.[9] The state enjoys no competence whatever
in the theological or liturgical realms. To grant it that competence
would be to concede, at the same time, the possibility of its intruding
also into the internal doctrinal and liturgical activities of religious
bodies. No religious community wants that, and the First Amendment
forbids it, in any case.

Two other school prayer cases were decided the following year:
Abington School District v. *Schempp* struck down a Pennsylvania law
which required the reading of 10 verses of the Bible at the beginning
of each school day, and *Murray* v. *Curlett* struck down the practice
of reciting the Lord's Prayer and passages from the Bible in Baltimore's
public schools. These were the cases which evoked from Justice Tom
Clark the first two tests of enactments concerning religion: What is
their primary purpose, and what is their primary effect? According to
the Court, both laws failed these tests. The *Stone* v. *Graham* decision
in 1980 followed similar lines, ruling unconstitutional a Kentucky law

that ordered the posting of the Ten Commandments in public school rooms.

Again, the Court was on good ground. It is the churches' responsibility, not the state's, to encourage Bible reading and prayer and to remind Christians and Jews of the Decalogue's moral dictates. Moreover, the Bible, the Lord's Prayer, and the Ten Commandments are reflective of only two major religious traditions. To favor the liturgical, devotional, or moral beliefs and practices of those two traditions would be discriminatory toward all other religious traditions as well as toward those citizens with no religious affiliation at all. Furthermore, such outright favoritism would endanger the public peace, which was one of the original concerns of the First Amendment.

This is the point at which an appeal is usually made to the so-called Judeo-Christian character of the United States of America, as if a religion called Judeo-Christianity were, in fact, its established religion. There is no such religion. And if there were, the First Amendment would prohibit its establishment or even preferential treatment toward it.

Significantly, those who argue on behalf of Judeo-Christianity sometimes employ the language of "tolerance" when referring to religious or nonreligious citizens who happen not to be "Judeo-Christians."[10] Religious freedom, including immunity even from indirect coercion, is a matter of right, not of "mere toleration," as James Madison insisted in the debate over Article Sixteen of the Virginia Declaration of Rights.

Finally, in *Wallace* v. *Jaffree* (1985), the Court ruled against an Alabama statute authorizing a one-minute period of silence in the public schools "for meditation or voluntary prayer." Even Justice Sandra Day O'Connor concurred with the decision, noting that "there can be little doubt that the purpose and likely effect is to endorse and sponsor voluntary prayer in the public schools."[11]

In a dissenting opinion, Chief Justice Warren Burger made a point that has become commonplace in the arguments of those who support some kind of prayer activity in the public schools. "For decades," he wrote, "our opinions have stated that hostility toward any religion or toward all religions is as much forbidden by the Constitution as is an official establishment of religion."[12] It was a variation on the theme previously sounded by Justice Potter Stewart in the *Abington School District* v. *Schempp* case in 1963. Justice Stewart had interpreted that decision "not as the realization of state neutrality, but rather as the establishment of a religion of secularism, or at least as government support for the beliefs of those who think that religious exercises should be conducted only in private."[13]

Both justices were in error. A constitutional prohibition against the state's acting as a religious body is not an expression of hostility toward religion. It is an expression rather of the principle, rooted even more deeply in theology than in constitutional law, that the state has no competence in the area of religion in general and over such particular religious activities as calling people to prayer, silent or not.

Furthermore, not all defenders of the *Wallace* v. *Jaffree* decision believe that "religious exercises should be conducted in private." Church, synagogue, temple, and mosque services are not "private." If Catholic school children want to pray together in their parochial school classrooms, the state will not impede them. And if they want to have a religious procession up and down the streets of the parish, again the state would have no interest, so long as the appropriate permits had been obtained.

Once more, the distinction between the state and society is crucial. There is almost no limit to the kinds of nonprivate religious activities that are permitted, even encouraged, in American *society*. If the secularist does not like that, that is the price he or she has to pay for living in a society whose ethos is strongly religious, albeit of an indistinct sort. The secularist would have a basis for complaint, on the other hand, if the authority of the state were employed, however indirectly, to sponsor or enforce religious observances of any kind.

The power of the cultural ethos, it should be said, doesn't always work in religion's favor. Some expressions of American religious culture are distortions of authentic religious values. They convey a notion of religion as instrumentalist (religion is good for national unity) or therapeutic (religion makes you feel better about yourself and your lot in life) or manipulative (religion makes you feel guilty about forms of social, even political, behavior that are otherwise perfectly legitimate). Indeed, in a situation where the state places its legal authority at the service of religion and of religious interests, it is more likely that religion would be corrupted by the state than the state by religion.

Since Protestantism had always insisted on the voluntary nature of religious commitment, American Protestants were theologically inconsistent when, in the late nineteenth and early twentieth centuries, they supported prayer and Bible reading in the public schools. Catholics and Jews, not surprisingly, were uncomfortable with these practices because they tended to reinforce the Protestant, rather than public, nature of those schools.

With the growth of the Catholic population and its political influence, mainline Protestants tended to return to a more traditionally Protestant theological position. Protestant fundamentalists and conservative evangelicals, however, did not alter their view. In fact, they became more militant.

Catholics, on the other hand, were becoming increasingly ambivalent about the issue. As the Protestant character of the public schools lessened, as secularism and "atheistic Communism" loomed larger on the cultural and political horizons, and as the cost of operating a full-scale parochial school system spiraled upward, almost beyond control, Catholics began to look upon the public school with a different eye. Today, many of them, including some of their pastoral leaders, seem as prone to ignore their own theological principles and historical experience as their mainline Protestant brethren had been to ignore theirs at the end of last century and the beginning of this one.[14]

FINANCIAL AID AND SERVICES

Justice Byron White, in *Lemon* v. *Kurtzman* (1971), stated what was for him an "insoluble paradox" in financial aid cases before the Court: "The State cannot finance secular instruction if it permits religion to be taught in the same classroom; but if it exacts a promise that religion not be taught—a promise the school and its teachers are quite willing and on this record able to give—and enforces it, it is then entangled in the 'no entanglement' aspect of the Court's Establishment Clause jurisprudence."[15] His colleagues agreed, but saw no way out of the paradox. Indeed, the record of the Court on this matter has been difficult to track.

In 1907, in *Reuben Quick Bear* v. *Leupp,* it approved the payment of federal monies drawn from Indian treaty funds to support schools for members of the Sioux tribe operated by the Bureau of Catholic Missions. The Court said that the Indians had the right to choose their own school and even to choose it with religion in mind.

In 1930 *Cochran* v. *Louisiana State Board of Education* upheld a Louisiana law that authorized the Louisiana State Board of Education to buy books for parochial school children. Chief Justice Charles Evans Hughes argued that the same books were furnished to children attending public schools and that they could not be adapted to religious instruction. It was in this case that a "child-benefit" theory was developed, making a distinction between aid to children and aid to schools.

The famous *Everson* case in 1947, although it produced some of the most absolutely separationist opinions the Court has ever delivered, did resolve the dispute in favor of the parochial school children. Local school districts could continue to provide bus transportation to and from school, because the purpose of the program was to protect children from traffic hazards and dangers of the road. The benefit to the church sponsors of the parochial schools was only incidental, the Court argued.

In 1968, in *Board of Education* v. *Allen,* the Court upheld a New

York law requiring school districts to lend textbooks free of charge to parochial school students. Again, the argument was that the aid was only indirect. The financial benefit went to parents and children, not schools and churches.

But the Court veered away from its accommodationist view in *Lemon* v. *Kurtzman* (1971), ruling unconstitutional a Rhode Island law that provided up to a 15% supplement from public funds for private school teachers' salaries, textbooks, and instructional materials. It reached a similar conclusion in *Committee for Public Education and Religious Liberty* v. *Nyquist, Commissioner of Education* (1973), throwing out three New York state programs that provide money for school maintenance and equipment, tuition reimbursements for low-income parents, and tax deductions for parents with incomes too high to qualify for the reimbursements.

The decisions became even harder to track over the next few years: *Meek* v. *Pittenger* (1975) held that some benefits, for example, textbook loans, conferred by a Pennsylvania statute were constitutional while others, such as psychological services, were not; *Wolman* v. *Walter* (1977) contained an eight-part major opinion, with different votes on each part (books and diagnostic services, for example, were constitutional, but instructional materials, equipment, and field trips were not); *Committee for Public Education and Religious Liberty* v. *Regan* (1980) upheld a New York law authorizing reimbursements to church-sponsored schools for performing various testing and reporting services required by state law; and *Mueller* v. *Allen* (1983) upheld a Minnesota law permitting taxpayers to claim a deduction for some expenditures for tuition, textbooks, and transportation, even if their children attended a private school. (There were other decisions having to do with colleges and universities, but they are not of direct interest here.)

The most controversial cases of recent years, however, were *Grand Rapids* v. *Ball* and *Aguilar* v. *Felton,* both rendered in 1985. By a vote of 5–4, the Court ruled unconstitutional programs in both Grand Rapids and New York City in which public school teachers provided remedial and enrichment instruction to parochial school children with learning problems or from impoverished circumstances.

The state-funded program in Grand Rapids provided classes in mathematics, reading, and other subjects for about 11,000 children in 40 parochial schools. The city school system leased classes for six dollars per classroom, and required that each room be free of religious symbols and that a sign be posted stating that the room was a "public school classroom."

In New York City the program was federally funded under Title I of the Elementary and Secondary Education Act of 1965. About 300,000 children were involved, about 25,000 of whom were in parochial schools. New York City supervisors periodically checked the classrooms to insure that their instructors did not become involved in religious issues. As in Grand Rapids, religious symbols were temporarily removed from the classrooms.

Justice William Brennan, the only Catholic member of the Court at the time, wrote the majority opinion in both cases. In the Grand Rapids case he concluded that the program failed the second *Lemon* test because "it may impermissibly advance religion." He listed three specific dangers: that the public school teachers, under the influence of the "pervasively sectarian nature of the religious schools in which they work," may religiously indoctrinate students at public expense [not very likely, and indeed there was no evidence to substantiate this concern]; that, because a "symbolic union of church and state" is inherent in such a setting, the mere presence of these teachers on parochial school premises may, "at least in the eye of the impressionable youngster," convey a message of state support for religion [a bit more likely than the first danger, but still vague and speculative]; and that the public funding involved may have the effect of subsidizing the religious functions of the schools "by taking over a substantial portion of their responsibility for teaching secular subjects" [a not unreasonable conjecture].[16]

In the New York case, however, Justice Brennan focused on the third *Lemon* test, "excessive entanglement" with religion. Having state personnel walking the corridors of parochial schools, ready to make spot checks in the classrooms, not only entangles the state with religion, but also constitutes a form of intrusion by the state upon religion, through what the Court called a "permanent and pervasive state presence" in the parochial school.

Reactions to the decisions ranged from the secularists and absolute separationists (not all of whom are secularists) on the left, who applauded the Court for its defense of public education and of the "wall of separation" between church and state, to the "Judeo-Christianizers" on the right, who thought the decisions reflected "a hostility toward religion."[17] Closer to the center were those who judged the decisions simply too "doctrinaire," and not sufficiently attentive to the 19 conflict-free years of experience with the program in New York City.[18]

One is drawn, almost ineluctably, to the centrist view. Neither history nor theology lend much support to the principal assumptions of the other two camps. On the one hand, a flexible, Madisonian "line of separation" between religion and the state is a truer reflection of American history and of its religiously pluralist experience than is the immovable, Jeffersonian "wall of separation." An absolutist position is simply impossible to sustain. Absolute means absolute. No exceptions. But there have already been exceptions, however trivial they may seem or secularized they may have become, for example, "In God We Trust" on the currency; paid chaplains in the legislatures and in the military; the pledge of allegiance; tax exemptions for religious property, communities, and individuals.

On the other hand, an absolutist approach to the relationship between religion and the state isn't necessarily a reflection of hostility toward religion. Not all absolute (or strict) separationists are secularists. Many mainline Protestants and Jews are concerned about the intrusion of the state into religion, without being themselves hostile to religion. On the contrary.

Is the centrist critique the preferred one, therefore? Not necessarily. One has to think also of the fourth, albeit least established, test the Court has used in religion-related cases; namely, the concern for political and religious divisiveness. It is clear that many people in the United States feel strongly about the principle of separation between religion and the state, although for different reasons.

Secularists look upon government benevolence toward religion in any form as pressure upon themselves, as an implicit rejection of their own conviction that society and the republic can get on very well without religion. They believe their value system provides just as strong a basis for loyalty to country as belief in God.

Protestant and Jewish separationists, on the other hand, believe that nondiscriminatory aid to religious schools would inevitably discriminate in favor of the large Catholic school system.

"It is this conviction of a large segment of American society, both secular and sectarian," Christopher Mooney has written, "that any type of support to religious schools would be unfair to *them*, which is the basis for that potential for political division along religious lines which the Supreme Court seeks to avoid."[19]

Some limited cooperation may continue to be possible in the educational area if its aim is to promote religious freedom. But such cooperation is not possible if it serves to promote religious belief or the distinctive moral values of a particular religious group. Meanwhile, "the line separating the promotion of religious belief from the promotion of religious freedom is going to remain rather jagged for some time to come."[20]

CURRICULUM

In July 1925 public school teacher John T. Scopes went on trial in Dayton, Tennessee, for teaching Charles Darwin's theory of evolution, in violation of state law. The so-called "Monkey Trial" was one of those only-in-America events, with Clarence Darrow acting as defense attorney and William Jennings Bryan aiding the prosecutor. Scopes was convicted, but released on a technicality.

During this same period of fundamentalist militancy throughout the South, Arkansas adopted a statute similar to Tennessee's. In 1965 another young biology teacher, Susan Epperson, teaching in Little Rock Central High School, challenged the Arkansas law. As in the case of Tennessee, the Arkansas Supreme Court upheld the statute as a legitimate exercise of the power of the state to determine the curriculum of its public schools. This time, however, the case found its way to the U.S. Supreme Court. The arguments presented by Miss Epperson's lawyer, and by the American Civil Liberties Union and the National Education Association in *amicus* briefs, focused on her right of free speech and on academic freedom.

In its 1968 decision, *Epperson v. Arkansas*, the Court steered clear of any endorsement of the right of a public school teacher to teach what she or he liked (thus leaving untouched a state's right to prescribe public school curricula). Instead, Justice Abe Fortas, writing for himself and six others, ruled that since the Arkansas ban against teaching evolution was based solely on "a particular interpretation of the Book of *Genesis* by a particular religious group," the act was an impermissible establishment of religion.

But neither the Scopes trial nor the *Epperson* decision have set the issue to rest. From Hillsboro, Missouri, to Church Hill, Tennessee, and from Mobile, Alabama, to Dunn, North Carolina, the conflicts continue to multiply.

In Hillsboro, Missouri, a small group of fundamentalist parents filed suit against the town school board, accusing school officials of indoctrinating their children with an anti-God, atheistic philosophy known as "secular humanism." In November 1985 a judge dismissed the case when the parents refused to reveal the source of funding for their lawsuit. They had had more than casual contact with Phyllis Schlafly's Eagle Forum organization.[21]

In Church Hill, Tennessee, the local school board also stood firm against parents' complaints that the school's entire reading list, from kindergarten through eighth grade, promoted secular humanism by advocating witchcraft, sun worship, euthanasia, one-world government, and a disruption of "God-given roles for the different sexes" (one parent had objected, for example, to a text that portrayed a boy cooking while a girl read a book).[22] However, a federal judge ruled in the parents' favor.

In Mobile, Alabama, the parents also found a sympathetic federal district judge, Brevard Hand, who once stated that it was a matter of "common knowledge that miscellaneous doctrines such as evolution, socialism, Communism, secularism, humanism and other concepts are advanced in the public schools."[23] It was Judge Hand who, in January 1983, had upheld an Alabama law that authorized a moment of silent prayer in the public schools, saying that the U.S. Supreme Court had erred in finding that the Bill of Rights prohibited a state from establishing a religion (the incorporation doctrine). His decision was overturned in 1985 by *Wallace* v. *Jaffree*.

Judge Hand thereupon exercised the right he had reserved to himself in a footnote to his original decision. He had indicated in the footnote that, if he were overruled on the prayer issue, he would look into whether other forms of religion were being promoted in the curriculum. Since the original plaintiff, having won on appeal, dropped out of the case, Judge Hand realigned the case, making plaintiffs of the 624 parents, teachers, and students who had originally intervened to help defend the law on silent prayer. "What we are asking is that this strict neutrality concept be evenly applied," one of the lawyers for the plaintiffs said. "It's already been equally applied to remove Judaism and Christianity from the schools. We're asking that it be equally applied to remove humanism."[24]

But the curriculum issue cuts both ways. The family of a woman who had challenged the legality of Bible study in the public schools of Dunn, North Carolina, closed its business and left town after a barrage of harassing telephone calls and attacks published in the local newspaper. Mrs. Laurey Wyble, a practicing Presbyterian, had complained in August 1985 about classes on the Bible taught as part of the regular curriculum in Dunn's elementary and middle schools. The classes were financed by the Inter-Denominational Bible Fund, a local organization that paid teachers not employed by the public school to teach the classes. The organization had conducted its classes for 44 years.

School officials insisted that the classes were voluntary, and supporters of the program noted that they treated the Bible as literature, history, and poetry. One reader of the local paper wrote, "I'm tired of the Communists, humanists and the atheists ruling in our schools." Another suggested that the family that had complained about the program should be deported to Cuba or the Soviet Union.[25]

The Court has been right. Public schools have no business teaching a particular religious point of view, because the state has no competence in this area. And it is also wrong for the churches to appeal to the state to help them fulfill their religious mission. Religious bodies can and do function freely in American society: in their own houses of worship and assembly, in their own schools, in their own homes, through their own privately owned media, and so forth. A public school, however, is a state institution. And so the rules are different, not only legally but also theologically.

Does that leave the situation just about where it is now? No. Protestant fundamentalists and conservative evangelicals are not the only groups that are concerned about the absence of religion in public school curricula. Mainline Protestants, Catholics, Jews, and others are also troubled by the total shutout of religion from the public school curriculum, whether it be motivated by secularist ideology or by a fear of controversy.[26] And they are concerned about the lengths to which textbook writers sometimes go to deny the relevance of religion to historical events.[27]

Their argument is almost self-evident: one cannot adequately understand major news events or world history itself without giving serious attention to religion. A person totally ignorant of religion is only partially educated.

We are impelled, therefore, to reject not only the option proposed by Protestant fundamentalists and conservative evangelicals, but also that of secularists, doctrinaire separationists, and nervous public officials. What, then, are we left with?

In the *Abington School District* v. *Schempp* case of 1963, the Court struck down a Pennsylvania law requiring the reading of 10 verses of the Bible at the beginning of each school day. That was the case in which Justice Potter Stewart charged, in stinging dissent, that the Court had endorsed "a religion of secularism." Justice Tom Clark, writing for the majority, sought to rebut that charge. He conceded that "one's education is not complete without a study of comparative religion or the history of religion and its relationship to the advancement of civilization. It certainly may be said," he continued, "that the Bible is worthy of study for its literary and historic qualities. Nothing we have said here indicates that such study of the Bible or of religion, when presented objectively as part of a secular program of education, may not be effected consistently with the First Amendment."[28]

Justices William Brennan and Arthur Goldberg made the same point in concurring opinions. Justice Brennan noted that "the holding of the Court . . . plainly does not foreclose teaching about the Holy Scriptures or about the differences between religious sects in classes in literature or history."[29] Justice Goldberg's language was even stronger:

> Government must inevitably take cognizance of the existence of religion and, indeed, under certain circumstances the First Amendment may require that it do so. And it seems clear to me from the opinions in the present and past cases that the Court would recognize the propriety of . . . the teaching *about* religion, as distinguished from the teaching *of* religion, in the public schools.[30]

Over against those who share Justice Robert Jackson's caveat, expressed in the 1948 *McCollum* decision, that most teachers could not handle so sensitive an area satisfactorily, Robert Michaelsen has argued that religion is "no more sensitive than such areas as politics, economics, and, still in some communities, biology."[31] It *can* be done. In any case, the alternatives are worse.[32]

The Public Square and Its Environs

NATIVITY SCENES

Nowhere have the U.S. Supreme Court's decisions been more accommodationist than on the matter of Christmas decorations and Nativity scenes, whether in public schools or on the so-called town square.

In *Florey* v. *Sioux Falls* (1980) the Court declined to hear an appeal of a lower court decision approving the display of Christmas decorations, with clear religious content, in the public schools of Sioux Falls, South Dakota.

In *Lynch* v. *Donnelly* (1984), it upheld the constitutionality of a Nativity scene, maintained for some 40 years by the city of Pawtucket, Rhode Island, in a privately owned park in the business district. In 1980, Daniel Donnelly and other members of the local affiliate of the American Civil Liberties Union sued Mayor Dennis Lynch for violating the Establishment Clause. The District Court and the First Circuit Court of Appeals both ruled in favor of the ACLU's suit, on the grounds that the erecting of the Nativity scene had no secular purpose and had as its primary effect the advancement of religion. By a 5–4 decision, the Supreme Court overturned those lower court rulings.

Chief Justice Warren Burger, in the majority opinion, argued that the Constitution "affirmatively mandates accommodation, not merely tolerance, of all religions, and forbids hostility toward any. . . . The Court," he continued, "consistently has declined to take a rigid, absolutist view of the Establishment Clause. . . ."

Instead of "mechanically invalidating all governmental conduct or statutes that confer benefits or give special recognition to religion in general or to one faith—as an absolutist approach would dictate," the Court takes each case as it comes along. The process calls for "line-drawing," but without "fixed" rules. Without denying the relevance of the three tests (purpose, primary effect, and entanglement), the chief justice noted that "we have repeatedly emphasized our unwillingness to be confined to any single test or criterion in this sensitive area."[33]

Burger concluded that, if the Nativity scene in Pawtucket was of benefit to one faith or religion or to all religions, that benefit was indirect, remote, and incidental, on par, for example, with the display of hundreds of religious paintings in governmentally supported museums. Furthermore, the city did have a secular purpose in displaying this scene; namely, to engender "a friendly community spirit of good will in keeping with the season."[34]

Finally, in March 1985, the Court upheld, in a 4–4 vote, a decision by the Second Circuit Court of Appeals that invalidated a ban against a display by the Scarsdale [New York] Village Board.[35] Local officials had argued that they should be free to impose such a ban if the religious symbol offends some townspeople. (Scarsdale has a large Jewish population.) The Court could not muster a majority to agree with them. In *City of Birmingham* (Mich.) v. *American Civil Liberties Union* (1986), however, the Court upheld a similar ban.

What is to be said about these cases? First, no one can deny the constitutional right of Christians to erect Nativity scenes on private property and at private expense. It is the involvement of public funds, public sponsorship, and, as in three of the four cases, public property that creates the problem.

Secondly, a denial of the use of public funds or public property would not necessarily imply a hostility toward religion in general or toward any particular religion. No church or other Christian association has a legal right to public support for its Christmas displays, nor can it expect, as a matter of right, that a public authority take full financial and administrative responsibility for erecting such displays.

Thirdly, if no one in a particular community objects, public support for Christmas displays would not violate any fixed constitutional rule. The Madisonian "line of separation," unlike the Jeffersonian "wall of separation," is flexible. Experience rather than doctrinaire principle seems a more appropriate norm in cases of this sort.

Fourthly, however, if persons in the community *do* object on the grounds that such displays are offensive to their own religious or non-religious sensibilities, it would seem that the fourth test, that is, potential for political divisiveness along religious lines, becomes pertinent.

To be sure, accommodation is two-sided. One might hope that a small number of non-Christians, living in the midst of a very large number of Christians, would not press such an objection. But anyone is free to do so. If an objection is raised, the Christian majority should accept it with good grace—in keeping with the season.

The Nativity scene would not be lost to public view. Out of private resources it could be purchased from the local authority and erected on private property, even in some conspicuous location.

To allow differences over Nativity scenes to polarize a community is to make something of a mockery of a feast that heralds peace and good will.

SABBATH OBSERVANCE

There have been at least six U.S. Supreme Court cases having to do with Sabbath observance. In four cases decided in 1961, the Court took the position that, although Sabbath law originally did have a religious purpose, Sunday had become so secularized that laws restricting commerce and work on Sunday could no longer be construed as supportive of religion in general or of any particular religions. The purpose of such laws is "to protect all persons from the physical and moral debasement which comes from uninterrupted labor."[36]

Accordingly, in *Braunfield* v. *Brown* and *Gallagher* v. *Crown Kosher Super Market,* the Court denied the pleas of Orthodox Jewish merchants to remain open on Sunday since their religion required them to close on Saturday. Justices William Brennan and Potter Stewart, although in agreement with the Warren view that Sunday closing laws did not violate the Establishment Clause, nonetheless dissented in part on the grounds that the decision denied to members of the Orthodox Jewish faith their First Amendment right to the free exercise of religion.

Professor Robert L. Cord, a neoconservative constitutional scholar, has agreed: "Had these businessmen been of the religious faith in which Sunday was the 'day of rest,' they would not have clashed with state authority. . . . There is no place for this kind of religious discrimination in the United States if the principles of the Establishment Clause are to be respected."[37]

The matter is moot in many parts of the United States, where Sunday blue laws have disappeared. Unfortunately, many religious leaders, including some Catholic bishops, have openly resisted that development, not primarily out of concern for the physical and mental health of working people, but out of concern for the sacredness of the day. As the Court pointed out, however, if concern for the sacredness of the day were shown to be the present purpose of Sunday closing laws, then those laws would be in violation of the Establishment Clause.

It is not the state's business to ensure that the religious obligations of its citizens be fulfilled. That would indeed be in violation of the Establishment Clause. At the same time, the state cannot unreasonably impede religious people from fulfilling those obligations. That would be in violation of the guarantee of "free exercise." Indeed, the Court ruled two years later, in *Sherbert* v. *Verner* (1963), that a Seventh Day Adventist's right to the free exercise of religion had been violated by a company that fired her for refusing to work on Saturday.

However, in *Thornton* v. *Connecticut* (1985) the Court invalidated a state law that gave employees an *unqualified* right not to work on their chosen Sabbath. To sustain such an unqualified right, the Court concluded, would impose an unreasonable burden on both employers and on nonreligious employees, since many people like to avoid weekend work.

In its defense, the state of Connecticut had argued that because religion had a "special status" under the Constitution, the government could properly give favored treatment to workers motivated by religion rather than by "other strongly held beliefs." For the Court, this constituted a clear violation of the Establishment Clause because it impermissibly advanced a particular religious practice, and, in the process, forced others to conform their conduct to the religious necessities of co-workers.[38]

The relevant principles are clear:

1. Just as religious bodies cannot be used by the state to advance its political purposes, so the state cannot be used by religious bodies to advance their spiritual purposes.

2. Religious freedom *can* be limited when it interferes with the rights of others.

3. The state has to be theologically neutral at all times. It must grant equal rights to all.

4. Christians and Jews, whose Sabbaths are Sunday and Saturday respectively, do not have any *religious* claim on the state to designate one or both of those days as days of rest, any more than Muslims have a claim with regard to a Friday day of rest. (To live in Israel today, with its Jewish, Christian, and Muslim populations, is to experience a society with three successive days of rest, only one of which, of course, is legally established.)

5. In any case, even if the Sabbath observance were deemed by religious leaders as absolutely essential to the moral and spiritual health of the nation, it is not the task of civil law to safeguard or enforce every moral principle and spiritual value. The moral aspirations of law are limited by what is minimally acceptable (the matter of consensus) and socially necessary (the matter of public order).

STATE-FUNDED CHAPLAINCIES: MILITARY AND LEGISLATIVE

A rigid separationist view of the relationship between religion and the state would, logically, eliminate the government-funded chaplaincy program in the military, as well as government-funded chaplains in state and federal legislatures.

The first option has never seriously been advocated because insistence upon strict neutrality in this area would limit religious freedom and so violate neutrality. The basic aim of government neutrality in the matter of religion is to maximize religious freedom. But as Justice Tom Clark noted in the *Schempp* case, in military service "Government regulates the temporal and geographic environment of individuals to a point that, unless it permits voluntary religious services to be conducted with the use of government facilities, military personnel would be unable to engage in the practice of their faiths."[39]

The reasoning does apply to the use of government facilities, but would it necessarily apply also to salaries? On the other hand, if the religious bodies were required to fund chaplains from their own resources, would that impose upon them an unreasonable financial burden? Could they, in fact, supply a sufficient number of chaplains under those conditions? Some do now, of course, but could others?

The second option, regarding legislative chaplains, *has* been pressed at least once before the U.S. Supreme Court. In *Marsh* v. *Chambers* (1983), the Court ruled that the use of a paid chaplain to open each session of the Nebraska state legislature was not in violation of the Establishment Clause. Chief Justice Warren Burger appealed to the nation's 200-year history and concluded that practices of this sort had become "a part of the fabric of our society."[40]

Perhaps so, but certain questions can be raised:

1. Is the legislative "pulpit" open to members of every religious faith represented in the total population, as well as to those who, although not religious, have a moral point of view that could be embodied in some opening "reflection"?

2. Does the chaplain (permanent or guest) enjoy complete freedom in the composition of the opening prayer, or are there subtle pressures to produce prayers that would be least objectionable to the greatest number of legislators?

3. If the latter, on what grounds can the state make a determination of the suitability or nonsuitability of a *prayer?*

4. In any case, what function does the prayer serve, and what percentage of legislators is usually present to derive its benefits? Moreover, what function does the chaplain serve, beyond delivering the opening prayer, and what percentage of legislators takes advantage of that function?

TAX EXEMPTIONS

The principal tax exemption case, *Walz* v. *Tax Commissioner of the City of New York*, was decided in 1970, on grounds similar to *Marsh* v. *Chambers* (above). Chief Justice Warren Burger appealed here as well to the long-standing character of the practice.

Although tax exemptions provide an indirect economic benefit to religious institutions, Burger noted, they also keep government involvement with religion at a minimal and remote level. Involvement would be far greater, he argued, if all religiously owned property had to be assessed and taxed. A permanent relationship of tax collector and taxpayer would be established. Exemption, therefore, passed the "excessive entanglement" test.

It also allowed the government to "accommodate" itself to religion by including religiously owned property "within a broad class of property owned by non-profit, quasi-public corporations." Such accommodation neither interfered with the free exercise of religion, nor sponsored it. In short, it was neutral, albeit benevolently so. The state simply abstained from demanding that the church support the state.

But tax exemptions are not "perpetual or immutable," the chief justice continued. It happens that some tax-exempt groups "lose their status when their activities take them outside the classification and new entities come into being and qualify for exemption."[41] This judgment seemed to be confirmed in *Bob Jones University* v. *United States* (1983).

Bob Jones University and Goldsboro Christian Schools lost their tax-exempt status because of school policies that prohibited interracial dating. The Court discounted the argument that these policies were based on sincerely held religious beliefs. According to the Court, Congress intended that, in order to qualify as charitable, organizations "must demonstrably serve and be in harmony with the public interest." In this case, the religious interest in discriminatory school policies had to give way to the government's "compelling" interest in eliminating racial discrimination.[42]

What is to be said about tax exemptions for religiously owned property and for religious communities?

1. No fixed theological or constitutional principles are applicable. There are no principles by which a *right* to tax exemptions is established, and neither are there clear-cut principles that would rule them out.

2. If granted, such exemptions must be equally available to every religious and nonreligious institution and group that meets the legal norms.

3. The religious institutions and communities that benefit from these exemptions have to remain faithful nonetheless to their spiritual mission, even at the risk of jeopardizing their tax-exempt status. And they also have to remain faithful to their own basic moral principles in observing the requirements of law. Unfortunately, this isn't always the case.[43]

4. Not all institutions and groups that claim to be "religious" are, in fact, religious in any meaningful theological or sociological senses of the word. The Church of Scientology is a case in point.[44] The Court, however, has complicated the problem with its exceedingly broad definitions of religion in the 1963 *Torcaso* case,[45] and in certain conscientious objector cases (see below).

5. Although Chief Justice Burger noted in the *Walz* case that tax exemptions for religious groups have gone essentially unchallenged through the nation's 200-year history, the situation could change some day. Religious bodies could not, at that time, appeal to some doctrinaire principle in defense of their tax-exempt sta-

tus. The issue is one of accommodations, of moveable lines, and of prudential judgment. In the case of the First Amendment, we are dealing always with "articles of peace," not "articles of faith."

MILITARY EXEMPTIONS FOR CONSCIENTIOUS OBJECTORS

Section 6(j) of the Universal Military Training and Service Act of 1948 extended exemptions from military service to "anyone, who, because of religious training and belief and belief in his relation to a Supreme Being, is conscientiously opposed to a combatant military service or to both combatant and non-combatant military service."[46]

In two conscientious objector cases, one in 1965 and the other five years later, the U.S. Supreme Court granted exemptions from military service to two young men, even though both admitted that their objections had nothing to do with religious convictions or beliefs.

In *United States* v. *Seeger* the Court widened the definition of religious belief to include any conviction that "is sincere and meaningful and occupies a place in the life of its possessor parallel to that filled by the orthodox belief in God. . . ."[47] The Court not only inflated the meaning of religion, but also dropped a difficult challenge in the laps of every draft board; namely, "to decide whether the beliefs possessed by the registrant are sincerely held and whether they are, in his own scheme of things, religious."[48] The Court did not count on the registrant who refused to characterize his beliefs as religious in any sense. It confronted that problem in the next case.

In *Welsh* v. *United States* the Court accepted "readings in the fields of history and sociology" as a sufficient basis for conscientious objection. Only those registrants would be excluded "whose beliefs were not deeply held and those whose objection to war does not rest at all on moral, ethical or religious principle but instead rests solely upon consideration of policy, pragmatism, or expediency."[49]

The Court no longer made the still-common assumption that morality is rooted always and only in religion. On the contrary, it is possible to reach a morally "conscientious" decision independently of religious motivations or beliefs. Indeed, for Justice Hugo Black religion meant simply conscience, as it had for James Madison.[50]

In *Gillette* v. *United States* (1971), the Court decided, however, that exemptions could not be extended to those who objected to specific wars only. Seven months later, the United States Catholic Conference issued a "Declaration on Conscientious Objection" that supported the principle of selective conscientious objection.

For legal purposes, the Court has broadened the definition of religion to include any matter of conscience. Without quarrelling with the legal rationale, most theologians and many sociologists would dissent from the Court's all-embracing concept of religion. Rather than stretch the meaning of religion beyond recognition, it would be better to distinguish between morality and moral values, on the one hand, and religion and religious values, on the other. The bottom line would remain the same: it is possible to reach a conscientious decision, rooted in one's personal moral values, without any reference at all to religion.

Meanwhile, a more theologically defensible definition of religion would remain in place; namely, a personal, social, and institutional expression of some explicit faith in God. If the definition is not so broad that it can encompass any philosophy of life, neither is it so narrow that it can apply only to Christianity and Judaism, or to that nonexistent hybrid, Judeo-Christianity.

THE SANCTUARY MOVEMENT

The notion of sanctuary has its roots in biblical times, when people being pursued in vengeance found safety in special "cities of refuge" established by Moses at God's command (Numbers 35:9–15). Those who killed someone "without intent" were to be protected from the avenger until the congregation could hear the case. These places of refuge were also at the disposal of strangers and sojourners.

Christian sanctuaries were first recognized in Roman law toward the end of the fourth century. This was later adopted into English common law, so that a person accused of a felony could take refuge in a church for up to 40 days, after which time the accused would have to confess or face trial.

In the Middle Ages the institution of sanctuary was seen as protection from the absolute rule of kings. It helped prevent an excessive use of capital punishment, sometimes for minor crimes, and safeguarded against execution without trial. The provision was abolished in the eighteenth century.

The notion of sanctuary was employed just before the Civil War when northerners defied the Fugitive Slave Acts to harbor runaways. Churches in the South were an important part of the network of stops. There were also several instances of granting sanctuary to draft evaders and military deserters during the Vietnam War.

But the sanctuary movement in the United States did not begin officially until March 24, 1982, the second anniversary of the murder of San Salvador's Archbishop Oscar Romero. Outside his Southside Presbyterian Church in Tucson, Arizona, some 50 miles from the Mexican border, the Reverend John Fife nailed up a neatly painted sign that read (in Spanish): "This is a sanctuary for the oppressed from Central America." Since then more than 200 churches and synagogues in about 30 states have declared themselves sanctuaries, and stand ready to provide aliens with food, clothing, medical services, and temporary shelter.

The political and legal dispute is over the meaning and application of the 1980 Refugee Act passed by Congress. That law gives refugee status to every alien in the United States who claims a "well-founded fear" of persecution or death if he or she returns to his or her own country. Those active in the sanctuary movement argue that the law clearly applies to most of those coming to the United States from El Salvador, where even President José Napoléon Duarte has spoken of the "culture of terror" in his country. On the other hand, both the Immigration and Naturalization Service and the State Department claim that there is little evidence that the Salvadorans who are returned to their country are persecuted or even treated badly. Their real motive for coming to the United States is economic, not political.

The moral dispute has to do with the question of civil disobedience, and on this issue religious leaders themselves are divided. The movement is supported by the National Council of Churches, representing 32 denominations, the Presbyterian Church (U.S.A.), the Disciples of Christ, the United Methodist Church, the United Church of Christ, the American Lutheran Church, and the American Baptist Churches. In 1984 the Rabbinical Assembly, representing more than 1,200 Conservative rabbis around the world, passed a resolution in favor of sanctuary. The Assembly recalled that "millions of Jews were murdered by the Nazis because the nations of the world, including the United States, did not open their gates to those fleeing the Nazi onslaught."[51] Although the National Conference of Catholic Bishops has not taken a stand on the movement as such, individual bishops, like Archbishop Rembert Weakland, of Milwaukee, have declared their churches sanctuaries.

On the other side, Lutheran Pastor Richard John Neuhaus, a former activist against the war in Vietnam and now generally identified with neoconservative politics, dismissed the movement as "political theater."[52] The sanctuary workers, he charged, were not principally interested in sheltering people but rather to "score points" against the Reagan administration's policies in Central America. "It makes people cynical about the church," he said.[53] Elie Wiesel, a survivor of the Nazi Holocaust and a distinguished author, acknowledged his "great compassion" for the Central American refugees, noting that he, too, was a refugee. But he said that he did not favor breaking United States law by harboring the refugees in places of worship. "We should walk within the law and, if need be, change the law."[54] The National Association of Evangelicals, representing 42 denominations, has taken no formal position, but its executive director, the Reverend Billy A. Melvin, noted that "Evangelicals feel that there is a proper way to address the problem—through the law."[55]

One can go back and forth on the political, legal, and even moral aspects of the sanctuary movement, but none of these directly touches the concerns of the First Amendment. The government's infiltrating of churches with paid informers does.

Without a warrant and in all probability in violation of the regulations of the Justice Department, the Immigration and Naturalization Service hired two paid informants to attend and tape-record Bible study meetings, worship services, and a wide variety of activities carried on in Protestant and Catholic churches in Arizona. The government collected and produced 40,000 pages of secretly taped material. On the basis of that evidence, the government on January 14, 1984, indicted 16 persons (later reduced to 11) on 91 counts. On May 1, 1986, six defendants were convicted of conspiring to smuggle illegal aliens into the United States. Five defendants were cleared of this charge, but two of these were found guilty of lesser charges.

James Oines, pastor of Tucson's Alzona Lutheran Church, reported that an INS special agent sought to justify the infiltration by claiming that Bible study sessions and worship services at Alzona Lutheran were not religious services but political rallies. "When a government says that its agents are allowed the right to define religion," Pastor Oines said, "it can control any religious activity that questions its policies."[56]

Never in all of United States history has such a search been carried out against religious groups, not even against the Mormons at the end of the nineteenth century nor against the "Moonies" at the end of the twentieth. Theologians and jurists alike remained unimpressed with the INS's argument that it was investigating only the nonreligious aspects and activities of the churches.

Former congressman and now professor of law at the Georgetown University Law Center, Robert F. Drinan, S.J., argued that all the sanctuary workers' words and deeds, whether sacred or secular, merited privacy because they were done in a church-related context.[57] Robert McAfee Brown, professor emeritus at the Pacific School of Religion, condemned the government's action as a violation of the constitutional guarantee of the "free exercise" of religion. "People cannot exercise their religious faith freely in liturgical gatherings, prayer groups and Bible studies if they suspect that someone is taping their comments in order to bring legal suit against them."[58]

On January 13, 1986, the Presbyterian Church (U.S.A.), the American Lutheran Church, and four of their congregations in Arizona sued the government for what it termed unjustifiable intrusions on their religious services. The suit contended that the government violated constitutional guarantees of religious freedom. The plaintiffs acknowledged that religious groups have no right to act in a manner "above the law," but insisted that the government acted improperly and with a chilling effect on religion when it infiltrated the church services without a warrant. "The relationship between church and state has been threatened," the Reverend James E. Andrews, stated clerk of the Presbyterian Church, said at a news conference. "All American religious groups have a stake in this matter."[59] The suit was dismissed.

However one judges the merits or demerits of the sanctuary movement, it is important that its legal and political aspects (interpreting the Refugee Act of 1980, or American foreign policy in Central America) always be carefully distinguished from its moral and broader constitutional aspects (civil disobedience, and the "free exercise" of religion).

And the latter two must also be carefully distinguished. Whether the churches and synagogues (and other religious groups) ought to be providing sanctuary to refugees from Central America, even in violation of the law, is a debatable moral question, having to do with religious motivation and civil disobedience. Whether the government has the right to infiltrate religious meetings and secretly tape-record sermons, prayers, and conversations is a debatable constitutional question, having to do with the "free exercise" of religion.

The state, after all, is competent to do only one thing with respect to religion; namely, to recognize, guarantee, protect, and promote the religious freedom of the people. Religious freedom can be limited only when it interferes with public order; namely, when there is a threat to the public peace, or commonly accepted standards of public morality, or the rights of other citizens. The operating rule with regard to the limitation of religious freedom is always: as much freedom as possible, as much coercion as necessary.

It is a particularly dangerous course that government embarks upon, however, when one of its agents defends an act of intrusion on the grounds that the church events were political rather than religious. How does a government that is not competent to pass judgment on religious truth make such a determination?

GAY RIGHTS ORDINANCES

Wherever homosexuality is mentioned in the Bible, it is condemned. It is a crime worthy of death (Leviticus 18:22; 20:13), a sin "against nature" (Romans 1:27), that excludes one from the kingdom of God (1 Corinthians 6:9–10). And God is said to have visited a terrible punishment upon Sodom for this sin (Genesis 19:1–29).

For Christians and Jews who regard the Bible as the final authority in moral matters, the issue is clear. Homosexuality—or, more precisely, homosexual acts—is immoral because God has told us so through divine revelation.

For Catholics, however, the Bible is not the only source of moral authority. There is, in addition, the teaching authority of the Church, vested especially in the hierarchy, as well as the authority of natural law, "written on [human] hearts" (Romans 2:15) and binding every human being, Christian or not, religious or not. According to Catholicism, homosexuality stands condemned by all three sources of authority.

Enter again New York's Cardinal John J. O'Connor, and its Mayor, Edward I. Koch. In 1985 a conflict between two of New York City's most powerful figures erupted over the issue of discrimination against homosexuals, and specifically over Executive Order 50. The legal question was whether New York City could demand a pledge of nondiscrimination against homosexuals from agencies, including religious agencies, that contract to perform its social services.

An intermediate court ruled that the mayor had that power. The Archdiocese of New York contended that only the Legislature may define the rights of job applicants.

Mayor Koch insisted that a pledge not to discriminate would involve no doctrinal approval of homosexuality. But the Archdiocese noted that the mayor's regulations would require it to "actively recruit" in the homosexual community. It also expressed a concern that the city of New York would inevitably meddle in religious matters if it had to investigate too closely the hiring practices of Catholic agencies.

Significantly, the other major Catholic diocese within the city limits of New York, the diocese of Brooklyn, did not contest the Executive Order. Auxiliary Bishop Joseph Sullivan, episcopal vicar for human services, insisted that "conformity with Executive Order 50 does not imply any explicit or implicit approval of homosexual activity. The order says only that one's sexual orientation cannot be the basis for job discrimination.

"We hire people in child care," he continued, "on the basis of their moral character, training and experience. People are accepted or rejected on those criteria regardless of sexual orientation."[60]

Bishop Sullivan predicted that "if the court finds that the mayor has overstepped his authority, the matter will move to legislation in the City Council." And that is precisely what happened.

After Mayor Koch's Executive Order 50 was overturned by the State Court of Appeals, the matter did move to the City Council. This time, under strong and persistent pressure from both Cardinal O'Connor and the Vatican nuncio to the United States, Archbishop Pio Laghi, Brooklyn's Bishop Francis Mugavero joined with Cardinal O'Connor in opposing passage of the homosexual rights bill. They said in a statement that the bill, if passed, would be "exceedingly dangerous to our society," and that it would promote homosexuality and undermine Catholic teaching.

On January 9, 1986, Cardinal O'Connor met with 200 leaders of lay organizations to ask them to join in fighting the bill. He told them that he was opposed to the bill because it would "legitimize a life style that stands in direct contradiction to the teaching of the Catholic Church."[61] As on the abortion issue, the cardinal had once again reduced a question of natural law to one of Catholic doctrine.

The New York *Times* rejected Cardinal O'Connor's and Bishop Mugavero's reasoning. At the heart of their argument, The *Times* declared, is the supposition that "whatever is declared legal by that very fact becomes morally right." For The *Times* such reasoning "would enshrine an unacceptable confusion of the affairs of state and church. It is and should be legal to dissolve a marriage, but that does not make it always morally right. Atheism is legal but is morally contested from every pulpit."[62]

The bill, the editorial continued, went to extraordinary lengths to avoid exalting homosexuality and nowhere declared it "legal," as the bishops contended. "It is not the function of this civil rights statute to promote a particular group or community," the bill stated. And none of its provisions "shall be construed to . . . endorse any particular behavior or way of life." The bill also clearly incorporated exemptions that already existed in other civil rights laws, notably the right of religious institutions to consider an applicant's religion in hiring.

The bill passed on March 30, 1986, by a surprisingly wide margin of 21–14.

Exactly three months later, on June 30, a bitterly divided U.S. Supreme Court ruled in *Bowers* v. *Hardwick* that the Constitution does not protect homosexual relations between consenting adults, even in the privacy of their own homes. The Court held, by a 5–4 vote, that a Georgia law that makes it a crime for a person to engage in oral or anal sex could be used to prosecute homosexual conduct between men or women. Writing for the majority, Justice Byron White rejected the view "that any kind of private sexual conduct between consenting adults is constitutionally insulated from state proscription." Justice Harry Blackman said in dissent, "The right of an individual to conduct intimate relationships in the intimacy of his or her own home seems to me to be the heart of the Constitution's protection of privacy."[63] Indeed, as of the date of the Court's decision, 26 states had already decriminalized sodomy, and even Justice White insisted that the majority for which he spoke did not necessarily regard the Georgia law as "wise or desirable."

The gay community greeted the decision with dismay, viewing it as a serious setback to its efforts to win not only legal equality with heterosexuals but moral equality as well. The Reverend Jerry Falwell's reaction was perhaps typical of those on the religious right. "I applaud the decision for two reasons," he said. "The highest court has recognized the right of a state to determine its own moral guidelines, and it has issued a clear statement that perverted moral behavior is not accepted practice in this country."[64]

What is to be said about this issue?

1. In much of the public's mind, homosexuality is a moral issue, that is, it concerns right and wrong, good and evil. Since morality does not absolutely depend upon religion for its authority, moral judgments can be made independently of any particular religious tradition. Indeed, a convincing moral case against homosexuality cannot rely exclusively, nor even primarily, on the Bible or religious doctrines.

2. Only matters of public morality are subject to civil law. The burden rests with opponents of gay rights ordinances and supporters of state sodomy laws to show, again independently of religious arguments, that homosexuality and homosexual behavior fall within the range of public morality.

3. Only through public consensus can certain moral values become part of the public morality. That consensus, however, can only be achieved through public dialogue and public argument, consistent with the tradition of civility. That tradition is binding on both sides of the debate.

4. One cannot assume that the passage of sodomy laws, gay rights ordinances or the enforcement of executive orders are suppressive of religious freedom. On the other hand, if religious freedom *is* at issue here, such freedom is not unlimited, even under the First Amendment. It can be limited when the rights of other citizens are threatened.

5. The right of religious bodies and of religious leaders to participate in the public debate about such matters as these is beyond dispute, since they have the duty to pass moral judgment whenever human rights or the spiritual welfare of people are at stake. In those instances, however, religious bodies and religious leaders owe the public a careful accounting of how they have come to their moral conclusions.

6. In all such debates, a distinction is always to be made between moral principles and their application. People may agree on the moral principles pertaining to homosexual behavior, but disa-

gree in good conscience about the nature of executive orders and legislative ordinances in a pluralistic society.

7. In any case, it is not the task of civil law to safeguard or enforce every moral value and principle. The moral aspirations of law are limited by what is minimally acceptable (consensus) and socially necessary (public order).

Pornography

On July 9, 1986, the Attorney General's Commission on Pornography delivered a report that called for a national assault on the pornography industry through a combination of more vigorous law enforcement and increased vigilance by citizens groups. The report urged concerned citizens to band together into "watch groups" to file complaints, put pressure on local prosecutors, monitor judges and, if necessary, boycott merchants who sell pornographic material. The panel acknowledged that its conclusions were diametrically opposed to those of a presidential commission in 1970 that said that erotic material was not a significant cause of crime, delinquency, sexual deviancy or emotional disturbances.[65]

The same principles which apply to the preceding discussion of gay rights ordinances and sodomy laws would apply here as well. Indeed the two issues were joined in a statement by the National Organization for Women. Although NOW supported the commission's findings that pornography harms women and children, it expressed concern that the religious right might "use the revulsion that many Americans feel against the violence and subjugation of pornography as an excuse to spread bigotry and hatred against lesbians and gay men."[66]

The Bishops and the Bomb

The U.S. Catholic bishops' pastoral letter on war and peace, "The Challenge of Peace: God's Promise and Our Response," originated in November 1980 at the annual meeting of the National Conference of Catholic Bishops in Washington, D.C. The following January the Conference president, Archbishop John R. Roach, of St. Paul and Minneapolis, established an Ad Hoc Committee to prepare the document. Its members were: Archbishop Joseph Bernardin, of Cincinnati (now cardinal-archbishop of Chicago), Bishop Daniel P. Reilly, of Norwich, Connecticut, Bishop George A. Fulcher, of Lafayette, Indiana (now deceased), Auxiliary Bishop Thomas J. Gumbleton, of Detroit, and Auxiliary Bishop John J. O'Connor, of the Military Vicariate (now cardinal-archbishop of New York). Archbishop Bernardin was named chairman.

The Leadership Conference of Women Religious and the Conference of Major Religious Superiors of Men were invited to appoint representatives as consultants to the Committee: Sister Juliana Casey, I.H.M., and Father Richard Warner, C.S.C. Bruce Martin Russett, professor of Political Science at Yale University, was engaged as the principal consultant. Two others served as members of the Committee staff: Father J. Bryan Hehir, of the Office of International Justice and Peace in the United States Catholic Conference, and Edward Doherty, adviser for Political and Military Affairs in the same office. Father Hehir proved to be the key resource, and was largely credited with drafting the document.

The pastoral letter is a model of how religion and politics should, and can, intersect and interact in a pluralistic society like the United States of America, without prejudice to the spiritual integrity of religious bodies and religious leaders, on the one hand, or to constitutional principles, on the other.

DEFINING THE AUDIENCE

From the very beginning the Committee decided to address its document to two audiences: the U.S. Catholic community and the wider American public, including the government:

> Catholic teaching on peace and war has had two purposes: to help Catholics form their consciences and to contribute to the public policy debate about the morality of war. These two purposes have led Catholic teaching to address two distinct but overlapping audiences. The first is the Catholic faithful, formed by the premises of the gospel and the principles of Catholic moral teaching. The second is the wider civil community, a more pluralistic audience, in which our brothers and sisters with whom we share the name Christian, Jews, Moslems, other religious communities, and all people of good will also make up our polity. Since Catholic teaching has traditionally sought to address both audiences, we intend to speak to both in this letter, recognizing that Catholics are also members of the wider civil community.[67]

This decision to engage in dialogue with the wider civil community had ample precedent in recent Catholic teaching: the 1963 encyclical letter of Pope John XXIII, *Pacem in Terris*, had been addressed not only to Catholics but "to All Men of Good Will"; Pope Paul VI used the same formula in his own 1964 encyclical, *Ecclesiam Suam;* and the 1965 Pastoral Constitution of the Second Vatican Council, *Gaudium et spes*, had also been addressed "to the whole of humanity" (n. 2).

There were two major consequences of this decision to address two audiences simultaneously: the one regarding the method of moral argument and the other regarding the very process of drafting the document.

MAKING THE MORAL ARGUMENT

The bishops recognized that their own religious community shared a specific perspective of faith and could, therefore, be called to live out its implications. To reach this audience, the bishops could appeal to sacred scripture as well as the teachings of popes, bishops, and councils. Part I ("Peace in the Modern World: Religious Perspectives and Principles") and Part IV ("The Pastoral Challenge and Response") were directed explicitly to Catholics.

When the bishops did appeal to scripture, however, it was in a nuanced manner. The Bible, they noted, was written over a very long period of time and reflects many varied historical situations, all different from our own. It also speaks primarily of God's intervention in history, and contains "no specific treatise on war and peace."[68] Therefore, no one can appeal directly to scripture to justify a specific position on the issue of nuclear war: neither the just war theorist nor the pacifist. Instead, the Bible supplies a vision, a set a values, and a sense of moral direction.

Because the bishops addressed the wider civil community as well, including millions who did not share their own perspective of religious faith, they appealed also, perhaps even more, to human reason and human experience—what Catholics call natural law. According to Catholic teaching, natural law binds everyone, not just Catholics. The moral issue of war and peace, therefore, is not simply a Catholic issue. It is an issue that engages the consciences of all human beings.[69] Part II ("War and Peace in the Modern World: Problems and Principles") and Part III (The Promotion of Peace: Proposals and Policies") had this wider audience in mind.

To reach this wider audience, however, and especially the policymakers among them, the bishops knew they would have to engage in highly technical issues: the nature of the deterrent, targeting doctrine, negotiating positions.

And there had to be trade-offs. "To choose to speak to *both* the church and world," Father Hehir pointed out, "is to lose some of the 'prophetic edge' of the scriptures. To attempt to shape public policy leads inevitably to consensus positions which are not a clear witness against the evil threatened by nuclear war. . . .

"For some in policy circles," he continued, "the choices made by the bishops are beyond what can be followed. For some in the church the choices give away too much to the prevailing presumptions of policy."[70]

DEMOCRATIZING THE PROCESS

The principal drafter, Father J. Bryan Hehir, has described the pastoral-political style adopted by the bishops in producing the pastoral letter as "democratic" in process and in content. It was democratic in process not only because there were public hearings and witnesses from across the professional and ideological spectrum, but also because the drafts were circulated and criticisms and suggestions were invited from beginning to end. "Those who have followed this process know the significant impact such commentary has had," Father Hehir noted, not on the formulation of doctrine but on the manner in which the moral doctrine was conveyed, the quality of the empirical analysis, and the wisdom of the policy recommendations.[71]

The Committee formally began its work in July 1981. Over the next year it held 14 meetings or hearings in which a number of people, representing different occupations and different points of view, were invited to share their expertise and experiences. The witnesses included a panel of biblical scholars, a dozen moralists, a spectrum of arms control experts, two former secretaries of Defense, a physician, two retired military officers, and a panel of peace activists and specialists in nonviolent defense and conflict resolution. The hearing process closed with a full day of discussion with representatives of the Reagan administration: the secretary of Defense, the under secretary of State for Political Affairs, and the director of the Arms Control and Disarmament Agency.

In pursuing this course, the bishops were trying to be faithful to a principle enunciated by the Second Vatican Council; namely, that the Church must interpret the gospel only after "scrutinizing the signs of the times," that is, it must make a concrete examination of the moral questions to be addressed before moving to a theological reflection on them.[72]

A first draft of the pastoral letter was submitted for comments to the entire body of bishops in June 1982. The Committee met in July to revise the draft in light of the reactions. The volume of response had been so great that a planned November vote on the document had to be postponed. Instead a second draft was prepared for debate and discussion at the November General Meeting.

In January 1983 four representatives of the National Conference of Catholic Bishops (Cardinal Bernardin, Archbishop Roach, Father Hehir, and Monsignor Daniel Hoye, general secretary of the Conference) participated in a consultation on the second draft with representatives of several European episcopal conferences, at the Vatican.

Cardinal Bernardin and Archbishop Roach described the meeting as "positive and its results helpful" in preparing the third draft. They said the discussion in Rome had been primarily theological and ecclesiological, not political or strategic. There had been rumors, some of which were given credence by columnists Rowland Evans and Robert Novak, that in response to pressure from the Reagan administration, the Vatican was urging the U.S. bishops to moderate their criticisms of administration policy. There were also reports that the French and German bishops wanted a moderate statement, more in line with their own positions. They differed with the American bishops on the first use of nuclear weapons, which the Americans opposed, and about specific conclusions the Americans had drawn about deterrence policy.

But Cardinal Bernardin and Archbishop Roach had a different interpretation. The primary concerns expressed about the second draft were ecclesiological in nature. Cardinal Joseph Ratzinger, head of the Vatican Congregation for the Doctrine of Faith (formerly the Holy Office and, before that, the Inquisition), had chaired this meeting. He was especially troubled by the emergence of national conferences of bishops as a powerful source of authoritative teaching in the Catholic Church. What impact would this development have upon the authority of each individual bishop, and what impact would it have on the authority of the Vatican itself? Concern was also expressed about an intertwining of different levels of authority within the document. How would the individual Catholic reader be able to distinguish between what was binding in conscience and what was to be left to his or her own moral judgment?[73]

On March 23 Cardinal Bernardin announced that the Ad Hoc Committee had successfully completed its work on the third draft, after reviewing nearly 400 pages of comments from bishops and others, the consultation in Rome, and exchanges with administration representatives. The draft was made public during the first week of April.

Cardinal Bernardin and Archbishop Roach noted that the third draft was at variance with Reagan administration policy in several areas, most notably in its advocacy of a policy of "no first use" of nuclear weapons and in its support for an early and successful conclusion of negotiations on the Comprehensive Test Ban Treaty.[74] The draft also urged "clear public resistance" to "the rhetoric of 'winnable' nuclear wars, unrealistic expectations of 'surviving' nuclear exchanges, and strategies of 'protracted nuclear war.'"

The Committee met in the first week of April to consider some 700 submissions received since the publication and circulation of the third draft, and to devise a process for handling amendments at the General Meeting in Chicago.

The bishops convened at the Palmer House in Chicago on May 2–

3 to complete their work on the pastoral letter. The meeting was open to the press. Everything that went on is a matter of public record.

DEMOCRATIZING THE CONTENT

The content, too, had a "democratic" component. By distinguishing among various levels of teaching authority within the document, they left their Catholic readers free to make their own concrete policy options and invited debate within the church and society.

The bishops wrote:

> In this pastoral letter, too, we address many concrete questions concerning the arms race, contemporary warfare, weapons systems, and negotiating strategies. We do not intend that our treatment of each of these issues carry the same moral authority as our statement of universal moral principles and formal Church teaching. Indeed, we stress here at the beginning that not every statement in this letter has the same moral authority. At times we reassert universally binding moral principles (e.g., non-combatant immunity and proportionality). At still other times we reaffirm statements of recent popes and the teaching of Vatican II. Again, at other times we apply moral principles to specific cases.
>
> When making applications of these principles we realize—and we wish readers to recognize—that prudential judgments are involved based on specific circumstances which can change or which can be interpreted differently by people of good will (e.g., the treatment of "no first use"). However, the moral judgments that we make in specific cases, while not binding in conscience, are to be given serious attention and consideration by Catholics as they determine whether their moral judgments are consistent with the Gospel.[75]

The bishops wanted to hear the voice of the laity on secular questions and to engage in dialogue, at the same time, with the wider society. They believed that they had something to learn from, as well as to teach, the world. The "democratic" style of the pastoral letter, therefore, made the bishops themselves actors in the democratic process. Their initial arena of influence was their own religious community, but the pastoral's style, as well as the process employed in drafting it, made the bishops available to other constituencies. This was the arena of public opinion.

"Public opinion," Father Hehir has argued, "does not dictate public policy. But it does set a framework—establishing limits, giving weight to key values or issues—within which policy choices are made." By focusing on the moral dimensions of the public opinion and public policy debates, the bishops have followed "the invitation of Paul VI (to be actors in the development of Catholic social teaching), of Vatican

II (to dialogue in depth with the world) and John Courtney Murray (to assume responsibility for the moral consensus of a democracy)."[76] The bishops themselves saw their task in the same light:

> In a pluralistic democracy like the United States, the Church has a unique opportunity, precisely because of the strong constitutional protection of both religious freedom and freedom of speech and the press, to help call attention to the moral dimensions of public issues. . . . In fulfilling this role, the Church helps to create a community of conscience in the wider civil community. It does this in the first instance by teaching clearly within the Church the moral principles which bind and shape the Catholic conscience. The Church also fulfills a teaching role, however, in striving to share the moral wisdom of the Catholic tradition with the larger society.[77]

AN ASSESSMENT

1. Unlike sectarians, the bishops accepted responsibility for addressing not only their own fellow Catholics but also the wider civil community. As a consequence, they were required to develop arguments that they hoped would be compelling even for those who did not share Catholic, Christian, or any other religious faith.

2. Unlike fundamentalists, whenever the bishops appealed to the authority common to all Christians, that is, the Bible, they did so in a manner that reflected some of the complexities of modern biblical scholarship and of historical consciousness. They recognized, in other words, that the Bible does not yield ready-made answers to current political, economic, social, military, or even moral problems. Instead, it provides a vision, a set of values, a sense of moral direction.

3. Consistently with their commitment to the principle of dialogue, the bishops developed their pastoral letter through a process of openness—openness to the "signs of the times," openness to widely divergent points of view solicited through hearings and the circulation of drafts, and openness to the press, especially in the final meeting in Chicago where amendments to the letter were debated and voted upon and where the document itself was finally approved.

4. Sensitive to the special character of policy options, the bishops distinguished always between moral principles and their application, and distinguished also among various levels of moral authority. They made it clear, in other words, that it was possible to disagree with their practical conclusions and recommendations without fear of being labelled un-Catholic, un-Christian, or immoral.

5. Finally, the pastoral letter itself is a model of civility. James Madison and Thomas Jefferson would have been pleased.

And so should we all.

A Concluding Postscript

"The questions which have run through [the 1984] election—about the role of religion in our public life, the relation of political responses to moral issues—are broader and deeper than election politics can handle," Chicago's Cardinal Joseph Bernardin declared in a speech at Georgetown University on October 25, 1984.

This book has embodied one modest effort to address those questions without conscious regard for partisan political or denominational advantage. Its success can only be measured by its capacity to promote greater clarity, coherence, and civility in the public debate.

"Civility," John Courtney Murray reminded us, "dies with the death of dialogue."[78] We are either "locked together in argument" or locked together in combat. The former he thought to be "a rare spectacle." In the end, however, it is "the spectacle of a civil society."

APPENDIX I

Definitions, Distinctions, and Principles

Religion is a personal, social, and institutional expression of some explicit faith in God.

Religion is not so broad that it can encompass any "philosophy of life" (allowed for in *United States* v. *Seeger* in 1965 and in *Welsh* v. *United States* in 1970), nor so narrow that it can apply only, for example, to Protestant Christianity, or be reduced (by secularists, mainly) to the realm of the purely private, having no social or political consequence whatever.

The church is the network of organized Christian communities that together constitute American Christianity. In a less theologically precise sense, it may also include Judaism. Thus, the expression "church and state" is often applied to American Christianity and American Judaism together.

The concept of *religion*, however, is wider than that of the church, that is, wider than any one church or than all of the Christian churches and Jewish congregations combined.

Society is the network of social, political, cultural, religious, and economic relationships that is necessary for full human development. It is a system of social interaction composed of many diverse communities and groups: families, colleges and universities, small businesses, corporations, labor unions, religious organizations and communities, voluntary associations of every kind, and even governmental agencies.

Society is not equivalent to the state.

Society pursues the *common good*, which includes all the spiritual, moral, and material social goods that people need to live. The state, on the other hand, is immediately responsible for *public order*, which includes public peace, public morality, and justice.

The state is that part of society concerned with public order and the enforcement of social justice.

The relationship between religion (or church) and state, therefore, is narrower than that of religion (or church) and society.

Government is that portion of the state that exercises day-to-day responsibility for carrying out the purposes of the state.

Governments come and go; states (generally) remain.

Morality and *moral values* are not absolutely dependent upon, nor directly derived from, religion.

The Declaration of Independence affirms certain truths to be "self-evident," that is, not derived from revelation or from religious doctrine. These truths are "that all Men are created equal, that they are endowed by their Creator with certain unalienable Rights, among these are Life, Liberty, and the Pursuit of Happiness. . . ."

The Catholic tradition insists that these kinds of truths are part of the *natural law*, and as such are knowable by reason alone, apart from revelation and religious doctrines. Natural law is similar to, although not exactly congruent with, what others call *the public philosophy*.

It is possible, therefore, to be moral without being religious, and vice versa.

The failure to perceive the difference between morality and religion is at the root of most of the confusion in debates about religion and politics in general, and about specific issues like abortion.

Morality is concerned with *virtue*, that is, with the "power" to act in accordance with the dignity of one's human nature.

Virtue that equips a person to contribute to the quality of life in a political community is called *public virtue*. When that political community is a republic, it is also known as *republican virtue* or *civic republicanism*.

Not all morality is of a private nature. *Public morality*, that is, a morality that can be subject to civil law, is determined by the following criteria:

• It must be an issue of public order touching the values of public peace, justice (basic rights), or public moral sensibility.

• The law under consideration must be enforceable, that is, it has to pass the test of consent.

• The enforcement of the law must not disproportionately damage other values.

Morality and politics inevitably mix. Both are concerned with justice, peace, human dignity, and the common good.

The question is always: *whose* morality, and *by what process* are moral values incorporated by the political community (at which point they become part of the *public morality*)?

Only through public *consensus* can certain moral values become part of the public morality.

Public consensus, in turn, is achieved through public *dialogue* and public *argument.*

Striving for consensus through public dialogue and public argument rather than through any manner of compulsion is known as the *tradition of civility.*

Because a given public consensus is not necessarily morally right, it can be criticized and challenged.

A public consensus that is deemed morally deficient, however, can only be challenged in ways that respect the political process and the rights of others (the tradition of civility again).

Factionalism results when individual groups and constituencies within the political community refuse to pursue the way of public dialogue and public argument, consistent with constitutional principles, and when they press moral values upon the body politic on the sole basis of their own confessional understanding of revelation and religious doctrine.

Factionalism may look superficially like, but is the antithesis of, *pluralism.*

Legally, the United States of America is a secular, nonreligious, pluralist society and culture. *Actually,* however, it combines both religious and secular elements.

In this situation, there is a legitimate secularity of the political process, and there is a legitimate role for religious and moral discourse in national life.

There is an important distinction, however, between *secularism* and *secularity.* The former is an ideology that explicitly denies the reality of the sacred or that seeks to exclude it totally from the realm of the temporal. The latter is a positive, or at least neutral, term that affirms the integrity and independence of temporal realities in themselves.

Indeed, there has to be respect for the integrity and independence of *each* realm, the temporal and the spiritual. The one must not absorb or be absorbed by the other.

Religious bodies cannot be used to advance political purposes, nor can religious bodies use the state to further their own spiritual purposes.

Neither is there any absolute or impregnable "wall of separation" between the two realms since both share a common space and time, both are concerned with the common welfare, and both lay claim to the same citizens.

Therefore, the relationship between the religious and the political realms should be marked by *cooperation* rather than by hostility or indifference.

On the other hand, there *is* a "line of separation between the rights of religion and the Civil authority" (James Madison), which admits of movement, elasticity, and *accommodation*.

Neither the founders nor the Constitution nor even the U.S. Supreme Court has provided a single principle by which to determine the limits of such accommodation.

In addition to truth, justice, and love, *freedom* is what sustains human society, and is *the* political method whereby the people achieve their highest good, which is their own unity as a people.

The first thing due to people, in justice, is their freedom, the proper enjoyment of their personal and social *rights*.

Religious freedom and the *freedom of conscience* are not to be subsumed under the rubric of *toleration*, which assumes a superior/inferior relationship between the tolerant and the tolerated.

The state is competent, and in American Constitutional law is permitted, to do only one thing in respect to religion, which is to recognize, guarantee, protect, and promote the religious freedom of the people.

Religious freedom can only be *limited* when it interferes with public order, that is, when the public peace, or commonly accepted standards of public morality, or the rights of other citizens are threatened.

The operating rule with regard to the limitation of religious freedom is always: as much freedom as possible, as much coercion as necessary.

Government cannot pass judgment on religious truth. In a society that is religiously pluralist, it can only represent and enforce the principle of freedom, which means it must grant *equal* rights to all.

This is different from "mere toleration," whereby the tolerated group is assumed to possess no inherent right to freedom of association, worship, expression, and the like.

The United States of America is legally neither a Christian nor a "Judeo-Christian" nation.

All individuals and groups, religious and nonreligious alike, are absolutely equal before the law. Any political preference for Christian or "Judeo-Christian" moral values and practices, apart from a clear public consensus, would be discriminatory against those who do not share such moral convictions or freely engage in such practices.

The First Amendment religion clauses, therefore, are "not articles of faith but articles of peace" (John Courtney Murray).

They are the children of social necessity, of creating a social environment, protected by law, in which people of differing religious faiths (or of no religious faith at all) might live together in peace.

The wisdom of these religion clauses has been validated by political and religious experience alike.

The First Amendment religion clauses forbid only: (1) the establishment of any religion or religions as the official religion(s) of the state (federal and local alike); (2) any infringement on the right of individuals and groups to exercise or not exercise their religious prerogatives; and (3) any state aid to religion that has as its purpose or primary effect an advancement of religion, or that "entangles" government with religion, or that has the potential for creating political divisions along religious lines. (The U.S. Supreme Court, however, does not appeal so consistently to the last test ["creating political divisions"] as it does to the others.)

Religious bodies and religious leaders have a *constitutional right* to participate fully in the political process, consistently with the rights of others.

When they participate in the political process, however, religious bodies and religious leaders must rely upon their own powers of persuasion and especially the power of their own example, not upon the government's coercive power.

Examples of the latter would include enforced Sabbath observance on Sunday and mandated prayers or Bible reading in the public schools.

Religious bodies and religious leaders have the right and may rightfully claim a duty to pass moral judgment even on matters pertaining to the political order, when human rights or the spiritual welfare of people are at stake.

In those instances, however, religious bodies and leaders owe the public a careful accounting of how they have come to their moral conclusions.

In all debates involving morality/religion and politics, a distinction is always to be made between principles and their *application*.

People may agree on the moral/religious principles, but disagree, in good faith, about the most effective way to apply those principles in the political order.

In any case, it is not the task of *civil law* to safeguard or enforce every moral value and principle.

The moral aspirations of law are limited by what is minimally acceptable (*consensus*) and socially necessary (*public order*).

APPENDIX II

United States Supreme Court Cases

SUMMARIES

Abington School District v. *Schempp* and *Murray* v. *Curlett* (1963)
> In *Abington* the Court struck down a Pennsylvania law requiring the reading of ten verses of the Bible at the beginning of each school day.
>
> In *Murray* the Court struck down the practice of reciting the Lord's Prayer and passages from the Bible in Baltimore's public schools.
>
> Justice Tom Clark introduced his often-cited test of any enactments regarding religion: What is their primary purpose and what is their primary effect? There must be "a secular legislative purpose," and if the enactment advances or inhibits religion, the enactment is unconstitutional.

Aguilar v. *Felton* (1985)
> The Court ruled unconstitutional a program in New York City through which public school teachers were providing remedial instruction in parochial schools to children with learning problems.

Akron (1983)
> See *City of Akron.*

Babbitt v. *Planned Parenthood* (1986)
> The Court ruled that states may not deny family planning grants to private groups merely because they use money from other sources to offer abortions and abortion counselling.

Barron v. *Baltimore* (1833)

A landmark decision that the Bill of Rights applied only to the federal government and therefore placed no restrictions on the states.

Bender v. *Williamsport* (1986)

A test of the constitutionality of the Equal Access Act of 1984, which required schools to allow student meetings for "religious, political, philosophical," or other discussions on the same basis as other extracurricular activities.

Board of Education v. *Allen* (1968)

The Court upheld a New York law requiring local school districts to lend textbooks free of charge to parochial school students.

The Court ruled that whatever financial benefit was involved in the free loan of textbooks went to parents and children, not the schools.

Board of Trustees of Village of Scarsdale v. *McCreary* (1985)

A split court (4–4) affirmed an Appellate Court decision that invalidated a ban against a Christmas crèche erected by the Village of Scarsdale.

Bob Jones University v. *United States* (1983)

The Court upheld the action of the Internal Revenue Service in denying tax-exempt status to Bob Jones University in North Carolina because of the school's policy of prohibiting interracial dating, a policy based on a particular interpretation of the Bible.

Bowers v. *Hardwick and Doe* (1986)

The Court upheld a Georgia law that makes it a crime to engage in oral or anal sex. According to the Court, the Constitution does not protect homosexual relations between consenting adults, even in the privacy of their own homes.

Bradfield v. *Roberts* (1899)

The Court rejected a taxpayer's complaint that the appropriation of federal funds for the construction of buildings on the grounds of a hospital operated by the Sisters of Charity in Washington, D.C., constituted an establishment of religion. The Court viewed the hospital as a secular corporation as long as it performed its purposes as stated in the articles of incorporation.

Braunfeld v. *Brown* (1961)

The Court denied the plea of an Orthodox Jewish merchant to remain open on Sunday since his religion required him to close on Saturday. The Sabbath law, according to Chief Justice Earl Warren, was enacted to advance the state's "Secular goals."

Cantwell v. *Connecticut* (1940)

The Court overturned a breach-of-the-peace conviction of a Jehovah's Witness for playing an anti-Catholic record in a public street, and for lacking a religious solicitor's license.

An especially significant decision because the "incorporation doctrine" was applied for the first time to a major religion-related case.

City of Akron v. *Akron Center for Reproductive Health Inc.* (1983)
The Court struck down an Akron city ordinance requiring performance of all second-trimester abortions in a hospital, parental consent, informed consent, a 24-hour waiting period, and the disposal of fetal remains.

City of Birmingham v. *American Civil Liberties Union* (1986)
The Court let stand a federal appellate court's ruling holding unconstitutional the display of a Nativity scene on the front lawn of the Birmingham, Michigan, city hall.

Cochran v. *Louisiana State Board of Education* (1930)
The Court upheld a Louisiana state law authorizing the Louisiana State Board of Education to buy books for parochial school children.

The Chief Justice [Charles Evans Hughes] linked the state's general police power (including authority to provide for the public's education) with a "child-benefit" theory, whereby the children and not the schools are the real beneficiaries of the aid.

Committee for Public Education and Religious Liberty v. *Nyquist, Commissioner of Education* (1973)
The Court ruled unconstitutional three New York state programs that provided (1) direct grants to private elementary and secondary schools in low income areas for maintenance, repair, and equipment costs; (2) tuition reimbursements for low income parents of private school students; and (3) tax deductions for parents whose incomes were too high to qualify for reimbursement.

Committee for Public Education and Religious Liberty v. *Regan* (1980)
The Court upheld a New York state statute authorizing the use of public funds to reimburse church-sponsored and secular nonpublic services mandated by state law.

Davis v. *Beason* (1890)
Second Mormon case, which upheld an election law in the state of Idaho requiring voters to swear not only that they do not practice bigamy or polygamy, but that they do not belong to any group that favors it.

Justice Stephen Field, speaking for a united Court, maintained that the First Amendment protects opinions, not actions.

Earley v. *DiCenso* (1971)
See *Lemon* v. *Kurtzman*

Engle v. *Vitale* (1962)
The Court ruled unconstitutional the use of a prayer composed in 1951 by the New York Board of Regents.

Epperson v. *Arkansas* (1968)
The Court struck down an Arkansas law, passed in 1928, prohib-

iting the teaching of evolution in the public schools. The "over-riding fact" for the Court was that the Arkansas law proscribed the teaching of evolution "for the sole reason" that it was in conflict with "a particular religious doctrine."

Everson v. Board of Education (1947)

The Court upheld the constitutionality of a New Jersey state law and a Ewing township Board of Education resolution authorizing bus transportation for all children and reimbursement to parents for money spent on such transportation. The purpose of the program was to protect children from traffic and the dangers of the road.

For the first time in its history the U.S. Supreme Court set forth a comprehensive interpretation of the *minimal* prohibitions imposed by the Establishment Clause, including a prohibition against the granting of aid to religion, even when done on a non-discriminatory basis. The Court also agreed that the Fourteenth Amendment did incorporate the Establishment Clause.

Florey v. Sioux Falls (1980)

The Court refused to hear an appeal of a lower court decision that approved the display of Christmas decorations, with clear religious content, in the public schools of Sioux Falls, South Dakota.

Gallagher v. Crown Kosher Super Market (1961)

Companion case to *McGowan v. Maryland*

Gillette v. United States (1971)

The Court rejected an argument by a devout nonpacifist Catholic that he should be exempted from serving in a particular war which he deemed unjust ("selective conscientious objection").

Gitlow v. New York (1925)

Benjamin Gitlow, convicted of the crime of anarchy by the Supreme Court of New York, claimed that the Fourteenth Amendment placed First Amendment restraints on state legislation in the area of free speech and freedom of the press. In reviewing the case, the U.S. Supreme Court agreed that these rights "are protected by the Due Process Clause of the Fourteenth Amendment from impairment by the States."

Gobitis (1940)

See *Minersville School District v. Gobitis*

Goldman v. Weinberger (1986)

The Court upheld the Air Force's disciplining of an Orthodox Jewish officer for wearing a yarmulke while on duty, in violation of dresscode regulations. The officer had insisted on wearing the yarmulke as an expression of religious belief.

Grand Rapids v. Ball (1985)

The Court ruled unconstitutional a program in Grand Rapids through which public school teachers were providing remedial instruction in parochial schools to children with learning problems.

Grendel's Den (1982)

See *Larkin v. Grendel's Den*

Griswold v. Connecticut (1965)

The Court held that a Connecticut state law forbidding the *use* of contraceptives was unconstitutional on the grounds that it intruded on the right of marital privacy. The privacy argument was employed again in *Roe v. Wade* (1973).

Harris v. McRae (1980)

The Court upheld the Hyde amendment prohibiting the use of Medicaid funds for abortions.

Heffron v. International Society for Krishna Consciousness (1981)

The Court upheld the right of the Minnesota State Fair to require members of the Hare Krishna sect to confine their activities of selling literature and soliciting money to designated areas on the fairgrounds.

Hunt v. McNair (1973)

The Court upheld a South Carolina statute aiding colleges, including church-related institutions, through the issuance of revenue bonds for construction of facilities, expressly not used for sectarian purposes.

Jacobson v. Commonwealth of Massachusetts (1905)

The Court upheld the right of the state to force vaccinations even on those who resist for religious reasons.

Kedroff v. St. Nicholas Cathedral (1952)

The Court ruled that ownership and control of the Russian Orthodox Cathedral in New York belonged legitimately to the Patriarchs of Moscow.

Larkin v. Grendel's Den (1982)

The Court struck down a Massachusetts statute allowing churches to effectively veto the granting of liquor licenses within a 500–foot radius of their church building as a violation of the establishment clause.

Larson v. Valente (1982)

The Court struck down a Minnesota state law requiring religious groups receiving more than one-half their financial support from nonmembers to file an annual statement detailing their sources of income. The law had been directed primarily at the Unification Church.

Lemon v. Kurtzman (1971)

The Court ruled unconstitutional a Rhode Island state law providing up to a 15% supplement from public funds for private school teacher's salaries, textbooks, and instructional materials. A similar law in Pennsylvania was also struck down.

Lynch v. *Donnelly* (1984)
> The Court upheld the constitutionality of a Nativity scene display maintained by the city of Pawtucket, Rhode Island.

McCollum v. *Board of Education* (1948)
> The Court declared the Champaign, Illinois, "released time" plan unconstitutional. According to the Court, the Champaign plan had the effect of aiding religion by placing the public school system at the disposal of religious groups for the dissemination of their doctrines or ideals.

McDaniel v. *Paty* (1978)
> The Court struck down a Tennessee statute that disqualified ministers or priests from serving as state legislators, on the ground that the statute violated a clergyman's right of free exercise under the First and Fourteenth Amendments.

McGowan v. *Maryland* (1961)
> The Court upheld "Sunday Closing" laws (also known as "Blue Laws") on the ground that the Sunday observance had become so secularized that it no longer served any truly religious purpose. Sunday Closing laws are designed by the states to achieve a secular purpose: a uniform day of rest. The Court pointed out, at the same time, that such laws could be ruled unconstitutional if it could be demonstrated that their purpose "is to use the State's coercive power to aid religion."

Marsh v. *Chambers* (1983)
> The Court ruled in favor of the long-standing custom of the Nebraska State Legislature to have a paid chaplain who opened each session with a prayer. Chief Justice Burger appealed to the nation's 200-year history, arguing that the practice had become "a part of the fabric of our society."

Meek v. *Pittenger* (1975)
> The Court sustained one Pennsylvania statute that allowed the use of public funds for acquiring and loaning textbooks to nonpublic school children, but it ruled unconstitutional another statute that provided "auxiliary services" to nonpublic schools. Also declared unconstitutional was a section of a statute allowing the direct loan of instructional materials and equipment to parochial schools.

Meyer v. *Nebraska* (1922)
> The Court ruled unconstitutional a Nebraska law, passed in the aftermath of World War I, forbidding the teaching of any modern language except English before the ninth grade and mandating that all subjects be taught in English.
>
> What was important about this case was that the Court's ruling was based on the "incorporation doctrine."

Minersville School District v. *Gobitis* (1940)

The Court ruled against a Jehovah's Witness whose children had been expelled from public school for refusing to salute the flag.

Justice Felix Frankfurter, speaking for the Court, found an overriding state interest in instilling patriotic loyalty among the nation's youth.

Mueller v. *Allen* (1983)

The Court upheld a Minnesota law that permitted state taxpayers to claim a deduction from gross income for some expenditures for tuition, textbooks, and transportation, whether their children attended public or private schools.

The Court argued, in contrast with its earlier *Nyquist* decision (1963), that the Minnesota law did not constitute a support of religion because the deductions were available to parents of students in both public and private schools.

Murray v. *Curlett* (1963)

See *Abington School District* v. *Schempp*

Murdock v. *Pennsylvania* (1943)

The Court ruled that Jehovah's Witnesses must be exempted from a local ordinance requiring itinerant solicitors to pay a license fee.

Nyquist (1973)

See *Committee for Public Education and Religious Liberty* v. *Nyquist, Commissioner of Education*

O'Hair v. *Blumenthal* (1979)

The Court let stand a lower court decision that "In God We Trust" could remain on money and other governmental insignia.

Pierce v. *Society of Sisters* (1925)

The Court ruled unconstitutional an Oregon state law requiring all children between the ages of 8 and 15 to attend public schools.

In finding for the nuns, the Court declared that "a child is not the mere creature of the State; those who nurture him and direct his destiny have the right coupled with the high duty, to recognize and prepare him for additional obligations."

Presbyterian Church in the U.S.A. v. *Mary Elizabeth Blue Hull Memorial Church* (1969)

A decision by the Court favoring the preexisting governing authority (the Presbyterian Church in the United States) over a breakaway congregation.

Writing for the majority, Justice Brennan observed "there are neutral principles of law, developed for use in all property disputes, which can be applied without establishing churches to which property is awarded."

Prince v. *Massachusetts* (1944)

> The Court upheld the conviction of a Jehovah's Witness for bringing her nine-year-old niece along on sidewalk campaigns to sell the Witness publication, *Watch Tower*.
>
> The Court ruled that the state had wider power over the conduct of children than over adults.

Reuben Quick Bear v. *Leupp* (1907)

> The Court rejected a complaint that the payment of federal monies drawn from Indian treaty funds to support schools operated by the Bureau of Catholic Missions for members of the Sioux tribe constituted an establishment of religion.

Reynolds v. *United States* (1878)

> The first of the Mormon cases, in which the Court ruled against the practice of polygamy on the grounds that, while Congress has no legislative power over "mere opinion," it was "left free to reach actions which were in violation of social duties or subversive of good order."
>
> This was the first time the Court gave official recognition, in Chief Justice Waite's decision, to Jefferson's "wall of separation."

Robinson v. *DiCenso* (1971)

> See *Lemon* v. *Kurtzman*

Roe v. *Wade* (1973)

> The Court ruled that states may not ban abortion in the first six months of pregnancy. This ruling was based on the Fourteenth Amendment's protection of a woman from interference with her decision to have a child or not. The Court also held that a fetus was not a "person" under the terms of the Fourteenth Amendment. The decision did not make the right to abortion absolute—States may still regulate the second and third trimesters of a pregnancy—except where the woman's health is at stake.

Roemer v. *Board of Public Works of Maryland* (1976)

> A plurality opinion saved a Maryland statute that provided annual noncategorical grants to private colleges, including religiously affiliated institutions (on condition that the funds not be used for "sectarian purposes").

Sherbert v. *Verner* (1963)

> The Court found for a Seventh Day Adventist who had been fired from her job for not working on Saturday and who was denied unemployment compensation by the state of South Carolina because she had failed, without good cause, to accept suitable work when offered it.

Stone v. *Graham* (1980)

> The Court ruled unconstitutional a Kentucky law ordering the posting of the Ten Commandments in public school rooms.

Thornburgh v. *American College of Obstetricians and Gynecologists* (1986)

The Court struck down a Pennsylvania law as unconstitutional, on the ground that some provisions were designed to deter women from having abortions and others would require doctors to risk the health of pregnant women to save late–term fetuses.

Thornton v. *Connecticut* (1985)

The Court invalidated a Connecticut state law that gave employees an unqualified right not to work on their chosen Sabbath. Chief Justice Warren Burger argued that the state law imposed an undue burden on both employers and nonreligious employees, who, he said, also had "strong and legitimate" reasons for wanting to avoid weekend work.

Tilton v. *Richardson* (1971)

The Court saved the Higher Education Facilities Act of 1963, which, in this case, provided federal grants for the construction of buildings at four Catholic colleges and universities in Connecticut.

There was no Court opinion as such because five of the nine justices could not agree on all points of a single opinion.

Torcaso v. *Watkins* (1961)

The Court ruled that Maryland could not constitutionally disqualify atheists from public office. In a famous footnote, Justice Hugo Black included under the umbrella of religion, "Ethical Culture, Secular Humanism and others."

Two Guys from Harrison–Allentown v. *McGinley* (1961)

Companion case to *McGowan* v. *Maryland*

United States v. *Seeger* (1965)

A conscientious objector case in which the Court accepted a widened definition of religious belief to include any conviction that "is sincere and meaningful and occupies a place in the life of its possessor parallel to that filled by the orthodox belief in God. . . ."

Wallace v. *Jaffree* (1985)

The Court ruled against an Alabama statute authorizing a one-minute period of silence in the public schools "for meditation or voluntary prayer."

Walz v. *Tax Commissioner of the City of New York* (1970)

The Court upheld the right of New York City to grant tax exemptions for church property on the grounds that tax exemptions are acts by which the state "simply abstains from demanding that the church support the state."

This is the case in which Chief Justice Burger added a third criterion to the two given earlier by Justice Tom Clark in the *Schempp* case, that is, the danger of "an excessive government entanglement with religion."

Watson v. *Jones* (1871)

The Court ruled that the General Assembly of the Presbyterian Church in the United States held the general governing power and the right to determine property ownership in one of its own parishes.

The Court, in effect, removed itself from dealing with internal doctrinal controversies and limited itself to questions of fact.

Watson had the general effect of placing religious associations on a legal plane with other private associations.

Welsh v. *United States* (1970)

The Court granted exemption from the draft to a conscientious objector, even though he admitted that his objections had nothing to do with religious convictions or beliefs.

West Virginia State Board of Education v. *Barnette* (1943)

A Jehovah's Witness case in which the Court reversed itself [see *Minersville School District* v. *Gobitis*] in the name of freedom of expression, which included nonparticipation in flag-saluting exercises, rather than on the basis of the right to free exercise of religion.

Widmar v. *Vincent* (1981)

The Court ruled that the University of Missouri at Kansas City could not deny religious groups the use of school facilities that were made available to secular clubs.

Wisconsin v. *Yoder* (1972)

The Court allowed a member of the Old Order Amish community to remove his children from school after the eighth grade on the grounds that further schooling, whether public or private, would endanger their salvation.

The Amish, in effect, were declared a special class defined by religion, exempt from some laws that apply to everybody else, because of their exemplary record as law-abiding, hard-working, financially independent citizens.

Witters v. *Washington* (1986)

The Court upheld the right of a blind student to state vocational assistance grant money, even though he planned to use the grant to study for the ministry at a Christian college.

Wolman v. *Walter* (1977)

A very complicated case concerning an Ohio statute that authorized the state to provide nonpublic school pupils with books, instructional materials and equipment, standardized testing and scoring, diagnostic services, therapeutic services, and field transportation. The Court upheld everything except what applied to field trips and to instructional materials and equipment because these had the "primary effect of providing a direct and substantial advancement of the sectarian enterprise" of the parochial schools.

Zorach v. *Clauson* (1952)

 The Court found a released-time program in New York City acceptable because it did not involve the use of public buildings. This is the case in which Justice William O. Douglas made (what was for him) the astonishing observation that "we are a religious people whose institutions presuppose a Supreme Being. . . ."

TOPICS

ABORTION
 City of Akron v. *Akron Center for Reproductive Health Inc.* (1983)
 Babbitt v. *Planned Parenthood* (1986)
 Harris v. *McRae* (1980)
 Roe v. *Wade* (1973)
 Thornburgh v. *American College of Obstetricians and Gynecologists* (1986)
AMISH
 Wisconsin v. *Yoder* (1972)
BIRTH CONTROL
 Griswold v. *Connecticut* (1965)
CHAPLAINS, LEGISLATIVE AND MILITARY
 See *LEGISLATIVE CHAPLAINS and MILITARY CHAPLAINS,* below.
CHILD BENEFIT THEORY
 Cochran v. *Louisiana State Board of Education* (1930)
CHRISTMAS OBSERVANCE
 Board of Trustees of Village of Scarsdale v. *McCreary* (1985)
 City of Birmingham v. *American Civil Liberties Union* (1986)
 Florey v. *Sioux Falls* (1980)
 Lynch v. *Donnelly* (1984)
CLERGY IN POLITICS
 McDaniel v. *Paty* (1978)
CONSCIENTIOUS OBJECTION
 Gillette v. *United States* (1971)
 Torcaso v. *Watkins* (1961) (footnote)
 United States v. *Seeger* (1965)
 Welsh v. *United States* (1971)
DUE PROCESS
 Gitlow v. *New York* (1925)
FINANCIAL REPORTING
 Larson v. *Valente* (1982)
FREE EXERCISE
 Cantwell v. *Connecticut* (1940)
 Heffron v. *International Society for Krishna Consciousness* (1981)
 Minersville School District v. *Gobitis* (1940)
 Murdock v. *Pennsylvania* (1943)

1943 *Murdock* v. *Pennsylvania*
      West Virginia State Board
      of Education v. *Barnette*

1944 *Prince* v. *Massachusetts*

1947 *Everson* v. *Board of Education*

1948 *McCollum* v. *Board of Education*

1952 *Kedroff* v. *St. Nicholas Cathedral*
      Zorach v. *Clauson*

1961 *Braunfeld* v. *Brown*
      Gallagher v. *Crown Kosher Super Market*
      McGowan v. *Maryland*
      Torcaso v. *Watkins*
      Two Guys from Harrison–Allentown v. *McGinley*

1962 *Engle* v. *Vitale*

1963 *Abington School District* v. *Schempp*
      Murray v. *Curlett*
      Sherbert v. *Verner*

1965 *Griswold* v. *Connecticut*
      United States v. *Seeger*

1968 *Board of Education* v. *Allen*
      Epperson v. *Arkansas*

1969 *Presbyterian Church in the United States* v. *Mary Elizabeth Blue Hull Memorial Church*

1970 *Walz* v. *Tax Commissioner of the City of New York*
      Welsh v. *United States*

1971 *Earley* v. *DiCenso*
      Gillette v. *United States*
      Lemon v. *Kurtzman*

Robinson v. *DiCenso*
Tilton v. *Richardson*

1972 *Wisconsin* v. *Yoder*

1973 *Committee for Public Education and Religious Liberty* v. *Nyquist, Commissioner of Education*
      Hunt v. *McNair*
      Roe v. *Wade*

1975 *Meek* v. *Pittenger*

1976 *Roemer* v. *Board of Public Works of Maryland*

1977 *Wolman* v. *Walter*

1978 *McDaniel* v. *Paty*

1979 *O'Hair* v. *Blumenthal*

1980 *Committee for Public Education and Religious Liberty* v. *Regan*
      Florey v. *Sioux Falls*
      Harris v. *McRae*
      Stone v. *Graham*

1981 *Heffron* v. *International Society for Krishna Consciousness*
      Widmar v. *Vincent*

1982 *Larkin* v. *Grendel's Den*
      Larson v. *Valente*

1983 *Bob Jones University* v. *United States*
      City of Akron v. *Akron Center for Reproductive Health Inc.*
      Marsh v. *Chambers*
      Mueller v. *Allen*

1984 *Lynch* v. *Donnelly*

1985 *Aguilar* v. *Felton*
      Board of Trustees of Village of Scarsdale v. *McCreary*
      Grand Rapids v. *Ball*
      Thornton v. *Connecticut*
      Wallace v. *Jaffree*

1986 *Babbitt* v. *Planned Parenthood*
      Bender v. *Williamsport*
      Bowers v. *Hardwick and Doe*
      City of Birmingham v. *American Civil Liberties Union*
      Goldman v. *Weinberger*
      Thornburgh v. *American College of Obstetricians and Gynecologists*
      Witters v. *Washington*

NOTES

Notes to Preface

1. The less precise word "American" is used here, and elsewhere throughout the book, as shorthand for what pertains only to "the United States of America." As far as possible, however, the latter will be preferred to the former, out of respect for our American neighbors in Canada and throughout Central and South America.
2. I have outlined the genesis and development of this interest in an autobiographical essay, "Into the Political Kingdom," in *Journeys*, G. Baum, ed. (New York: Paulist Press, 1975), pp. 255–271.
3. (New York: Harper & Row, 1973).
4. For the quotation from *Tom Jones* and the Thwackum syndrome idea, see Robert McAfee Brown, "Religion and Politics: Fireworks in a Fog," *The Christian Century* 101 (October 24, 1984), p. 973. *Jews, Turks, and Infidels* is the title of a recent book on religion and politics in the United States by historian Morton Borden (Chapel Hill, NC: The University of North Carolina Press, 1984).
5. The terms Catholic and Catholicism refer here, and throughout the book, to that worldwide Christian community which, among other things, recognizes the Pope as the earthly head of the Church. Some Christians insist on calling Catholics "Roman Catholics," but that designation is too narrow. It does not encompass those millions of other Catholics who are also in communion with the Pope, but who do not worship according to the Roman liturgical rite: Melkites, Ukrainians, Maronites, and the like. Therefore, unlike our use of the words "America" and "American" as shorthand for what pertains to the United States of America, the terms Catholic and Catholicism are employed deliberately and consistently to refer only to that Christian community and tradition which do, in fact, recognize the supreme pastoral authority of the Pope. My colleague at the University of Notre Dame, James T. Burtchaell, makes the same argument in "Who Steals My Name Steals Not Trash," *The Christian Century* 100 (May 11,

1983) 444–445; and again in "Names," *The Tablet* [London] 239 (November 30, 1985) 1251–1252.

6. William Lee Miller has argued that "a personalistic communitarianism is the necessary base for a true republic in the interdependent world of the third century of this nation's existence. And the Roman Catholic community is the most likely single source of it—the largest and intellectually and spiritually most potent institution that is the bearer of such ideas." *The First Liberty: Religion and the American Republic* (New York: Alfred A. Knopf, 1985), pp. 288–289.

7. Christopher F. Mooney, *Public Virtue: Law and the Social Character of Religion* (Notre Dame, IN: University of Notre Dame Press, 1986), p. viii.

8. *The Federalist Papers*, no. 45 (New York: New American Library/Mentor, 1961), p. 289.

9. (Boston: Little, Brown and Company, 1955).

10. *Statecraft as Soulcraft: What Government Does* (New York: Simon and Schuster, 1983; Touchstone Edition, 1984).

11. (New York: Sheed & Ward, 1960).

Notes to Chapter 1

1. There are at least two reasons for the fundamentalists' success. First, they come out of the American revivalist movement of the nineteenth century, which, because of its organizational *and* financial independence of the major denominations, was forced to rely upon its own entrepreneurship for survival. The most successful evangelists then, as now, conducted large and carefully organized revival meetings, founded Bible institutes, established associations that could mobilize support for various causes, and made effective use of the media: the press, including mass-market paperback books, then radio, and eventually television. The derived income is subsequently reinvested to expand existing programs. Secondly, the so-called "televangelists" understand the first rule of mass communications— make it simple. Their uncomplicated biblical message clearly draws the line between good and evil (they call the latter "secular humanism"). There are no loose ends, and no ambiguities. One could not imagine a Greek Orthodox priest having the same success as Jimmy Swaggart, for example.

2. See, for example, Daniel Pipes, *In the Path of God: Islam and Political Power* (New York: Basic Books, 1983), pp. 3–10. According to Pipes, Western indifference to the religious dimension of world events can be attributed to three forces: secularization, materialism, and modernization. Secularized observers find it difficult to comprehend how anyone can take religion seriously, since they certainly do not. Materialists are convinced that nothing beyond economic self-interest can explain extraordinary or seemingly heroic behavior. Modernization theory, finally, postulates that all nations must follow the lines laid down by the first countries to become modernized, especially the United States and Great Britain. Religion is seen as an obstacle to modernization, but also as something that will grow inevitably weaker as modernization increases. The Iranian revolution of 1979, under the leadership of Ayatollah Ruhollah Khomeini, delivered the final blow to all these ideas, Pipes argues.

3. Ibid., p. 3. See also *Religion and Politics in the Modern World*, Peter H. Merkl and Ninian Smart, eds. (New York: New York University Press, 1983).
4. New York *Times*, June 10, 1985, p. A17.
5. Judith Miller, "The Embattled Arab Intellectual," New York *Times Magazine*, June 9, 1985, p. 72.
6. One might agree with Archbishop McNamara in principle, if not in its precise application. Thus, George Will: "Keats said the world is a 'vale of soul-making.' I say statecraft is soulcraft. Just as all education is moral education because learning conditions conduct, much legislation is moral legislation because it conditions the action and the thought of the nation in broad and important spheres of life." See *Statecraft as Soulcraft*, p. 19.
7. Boston *Globe*, August 27, 1985, p. 10.
8. The New York *Times*, September 14, 1985, p. A1.
9. Cited by Ben Bradlee, Jr., "Fanning the Flames with Religion," Boston *Globe*, October 20, 1985, p. 1.
10. "Is Israel's Soul Imperiled? Yes, by Liberal Jews," The New York *Times*, December 20, 1985, p. A31.
11. See Curtis Wilkie, "Mormon Center Spurs Dispute in Jerusalem," Boston *Sunday Globe*, December 29, 1985, p. 3. See also Thomas L. Friedman, "Israel's Uneasy Mix Of Religion And State," New York *Times*, June 22, 1986, p. E3.
12. See "Reform Group Faults Israel Orthodox Rabbis," New York *Times*, May 30, 1986, p. A3. See also William Claiborne, "Religious Tension and Violence Are on the Rise in Israel," Washington *Post National Weekly Edition*, June 2, 1986, p. 19.
13. Several months after the 1984 election, Father Theodore Hesburgh, C.S.C., president of the University of Notre Dame, with encouragement from Governor Mario Cuomo, tried to organize a three-day retreat for Catholic politicians, bishops, and theologians—away from the press and out of public view. The invited theologians agreed to participate. A few bishops expressed interest, but some had schedule conflicts. Two bishops whose presence would have been crucial to the meeting's success because of their own active involvement in the 1984 campaign thought it a bad idea. Furthermore, they didn't like the roster of invited guests. The politicians, for the most part, wouldn't touch it. They feared that such a meeting would degenerate into just another round on abortion, and wanted no part of it. Privacy and confidentiality would have been difficult to preserve in any case. One can only imagine how the media would have characterized such a gathering once word of it leaked out. Although the idea is still a good one, it may need a different mode of execution—in a public forum, with an ecumenical roster of participants.
14. The late Justice Potter Stewart lamented publicly when he retired in June 1981 that his epitaph could be his phrase from a 1964 obscenity case: "I know it when I see it."
15. *America: Religions and Religion* (Belmont, CA: Wadsworth Publishing Co., 1981), p. 1.
16. The theologian would say that we're all heretics, in the literal sense of the word (to choose or to prefer). We are limited by selective perception. Only God "sees" all reality, all at once, just as it is. We have to remain in dialogue with all of the other "heretics" of the world if we are to minimize the limitations imposed by our heretical perspectives. For another

angle of vision on it, see Peter L. Berger, *The Heretical Imperative: Contemporary Possibilities of Religious Affirmation* (Garden City, NY: Anchor Press/Doubleday, 1979), especially pp. 26–31.

17. Op. cit., pp. 5–7.

18. Ibid., p. 11.

19. See his classic work, *The Elementary Forms of the Religious Life* (London: Allen and Unwin, 1915).

20. See Thomas Luckmann, *The Invisible Religion* (New York: Macmillan, 1967); Robert Bellah, "Christianity and Symbolic Realism," *Journal for the Scientific Study of Religion* 9 (1970):89–96; and J. Milton Yinger, *The Scientific Study of Religion* (New York: Macmillan, 1970).

21. See his "Religion as a Cultural System," in *The Interpretation of Cultures* (New York: Basic Books, 1973), pp. 87–125. The definition is on p. 90.

22. 367 U.S. 488, 495, n. 11 (1961). The case involved a person in the state of Maryland who could not receive a commission as a notary public unless he took an oath affirming his belief in God. Justice Black held that the requirement violated Mr. Torcaso's "freedom of religion."

23. In *United States* v. *Seeger* (1965), a case involving a conscientious objector who had no explicitly religious motivation for his action, the U.S. Supreme Court accepted a widened definition of religious belief to include any conviction that "is sincere and meaningful and occupies a place in the life of its possessor parallel to that filled by the orthodox belief in God . . . " 380 U.S. 163 (1964). In 1970 the Court held that another young man, who specifically denied that religion had anything at all to do with his objection to military service and who based his rejection of war on various readings in the fields of history and sociology, must also be granted exemption. See *Welsh* v. *United States*, 398 U.S. 333 (1970).

   These decisions seem consistent with *Fowler* v. *Rhode Island*, 345 U.S. 67 (1953), in which the Court declared: "It is no business of the courts to say what is a religious practice or activity for one group is not religious under the protection of the First Amendment." On the other hand, the Court has accepted a more restricted definition of religion when it has been approved by lower courts, as in *Missouri Church of Scientology* v. *State Tax Commission of Missouri*, 439 U.S. 803 (1978). In that instance, the Court let stand a lower court ruling that the Church of Scientology could be taxed because it does not affirm a Supreme Being. See Robert Booth Fowler, *Religion and Politics in America* (Metuchen, NJ: The American Theological Library Association and the Scarecrow Press, 1985), pp. 265–267.

24. *We Hold These Truths: Catholic Reflections on the American Proposition*, pp. 18–24, especially p. 22.

25. See, for example, Rodney Stark, "A Sociological Definition of Religion" in *Religion and Society in Tension*, Charles Glock and Rodney Stark, eds. (Chicago: Rand McNally, 1965), pp. 3–17; Rodney Stark and William S. Bainbridge, *The Future of Religion: Secularization, Revival and Cult Formation* (Berkeley: University of California Press, 1985), pp. 1–14; Melford E. Spiro, "Religion, Problems of Definition and Explanation," in *Anthropological Approaches to the Study of Religion*, Michael Banton, ed. (New York: Praeger, 1966), pp. 85–126; and Peter L. Berger, *The Sacred Canopy* (Garden City, NY: Doubleday, 1967), pp. 175–178. For these authors, the category of the sacred is essential to any definition of religion, and they resist those who want to equate religion with the human *tout court*.

26. Stark and Bainbridge, op. cit., p. 3.
27. It is exceedingly difficult, if not impossible, to imagine how one could even begin to examine the relationship between religion and politics without adopting the more restricted definition of religion. A. James Reichley, senior fellow in the Brookings Governmental Studies program, evidently agrees. See his very useful *Religion in American Public Life* (Washington, DC: The Brookings Institution, 1985), p. 22.
28. See my "Roman Catholicism: *E Pluribus Unum*" in *Religion in America: Spirituality in a Secular Age*, Mary Douglas and Stephen M. Tipton, eds. (Boston: Beacon Press, 1983), pp. 179–189. The article appeared originally in *Daedalus: Journal of the American Academy of Arts and Sciences* 111 (Winter 1982) 73–83. See also my *Catholicism*, 2 vols. (Minneapolis: Winston Press, 1980; one-volume Study Edition, 1981), especially chapter 30.
29. *Letters and Papers from Prison* (London: Collins, 1959), p. 93 (letter of April 30, 1944).
30. See the Pastoral Constitution on the Church in the Modern World (*Gaudium et spes*), nn. 19–22; the Dogmatic Constitution on the Church (*Lumen gentium*), n. 16; and the Decree on the Church's Missionary Activity (*Ad gentes*), n. 7.
31. See Matthew 7:21, and also the parable of the sheep and the goats in Matthew 25:31–46. Paul Tillich always insisted that "there is no human being without an ultimate concern and, in this sense, without faith. Love is present, even if hidden, in a human being; for every human being is longing for union with the content of his ultimate concern." See *Dynamics of Faith* (New York: Harper Torchbook, 1958), p. 114. On his notion of religion, see *What is Religion?*, James Luther Adams, trans. (New York: Harper & Row, 1969), pp. 59–62.
32. For a fuller discussion, see my *Catholicism*, chapter 8, "Religion and its Varieties," pp. 245–281.
33. *Benjamin Franklin: Representative Selections*, F. L. Mott and C. E. Jorgenson, eds. (New York, 1936), p. 203. Cited by John F. Wilson, *Public Religion in American Culture* (Philadelphia: Temple University Press, 1979), p. 7. Franklin's vision, however, was not without tarnish. His proposal for the establishment of an academy included the stipulation that it would employ no "concealed papists" since these might lead the students to moral depravity. See Martin E. Marty, *Pilgrims in Their Own Land: 500 Years of Religion in America* (Boston: Little, Brown & Company, 1984), p. 155.
34. He also thought of it, however, in highly instrumental terms, "as a kind of public utility like the gas or water works." See William Lee Miller, *The First Liberty: Religion and the American Republic*, p. 28.

The best study of the Enlightenment's impact on America is Henry F. May's *The Enlightenment in America* (New York: Oxford University Press, 1976). May distinguishes among four Enlightenments: the Moderate Enlightenment (1688–1787), which defended balance and order in all things and indeed promoted the system of "checks and balances"; the Skeptical Enlightenment (1750–1789) of the so-called village atheists (the Clarence Darrow-type), which influenced America least; the Revolutionary Enlightenment (1776–1800), with its optimistic belief that men and women in the future would be morally better and politically freer than in the past or present; and the Didactic Enlightenment (1800–1815), which was the principal mode in which the Enlightenment was assimilated by the official American culture in the nineteenth century. This fourth and last form of

Enlightenment directly to affect the United States produced a tripartite national credo: the essential reality and dependability of moral values, the certainty of progress, and the usefulness and importance of "culture" in the narrower sense, especially literature.

35. Sidney Mead reminds us, however, of "the typically rationalist view that only what all the churches held and taught in common (the 'essentials of every religion') was really relevant for the well-being of the society and the state. Obversely this meant that they accepted the view that whatever any religious group held peculiarly as a tenet of its faith must be irrelevant for the general welfare. . . . Franklin exhibited his consistency when he rejected the minister whose sermons seemed aimed 'rather to make us Presbyterians than good citizens'—thus saying in effect that you really cannot do both." See *The Lively Experiment: The Shaping of Christianity in America* (New York: Harper & Row, 1963), pp. 65–66.

36. *Redeemer Nation: The Idea of America's Millennial Role* (Chicago: University of Chicago Press, 1968; Midway reprint, 1980).

37. *Righteous Empire: The Protestant Experience in America* (New York: Dial Press, 1970).

38. *A Christian America: Protestant Hopes and Historical Realities* (New York: Oxford University Press, 1971).

39. See Sidney E. Mead's essay of that title in *Church History* 36 (September 1967) 262–283. See also his classic work, *The Lively Experiment: The Shaping of Christianity in America,* cited above.

40. John F. Wilson, *Public Religion in American Culture,* p. 12. See also John P. Diggins, *The Lost Soul of American Politics: Virtue, Self-Interest, and the Foundations of Liberalism* (New York: Basic Books, 1984), pp. 296–333. "Lincoln," Diggins writes, "tried to instill in Americans what Santayana had aptly called the 'agonized conscience' of Calvinism. . . . In Lincoln American political thought ascended, and, ascending, reached spiritual ecstacy" (pp. 331, 333).

41. *Democracy in America,* George Lawrence, trans. (Garden City, NY: Doubleday/Anchor, 1969), pp. 292–293. Tocqueville's two-volume work was originally published in 1835. A final, thirteenth edition appeared in 1850.

42. John F. Wilson, op. cit., p. 14.

43. *Protestant-Catholic-Jew: An Essay in American Religious Sociology* (Garden City, NY: Doubleday, 1955). For an astute evaluation of this classic book, see Martin E. Marty, *Pilgrims in Their Own Land,* pp. 422–426.

44. Op. cit., p. 17.

45. *The Naked Public Square: Religion and Democracy in America* (Grand Rapids: William B. Eerdmans Publishing Co., 1984), p. 36. This is exactly the same argument advanced by Cardinal Joseph Bernardin of Chicago in his address, "Religion and Politics: The Future Agenda," given at Georgetown University on October 25, 1984: "From issues of defense policy through questions of medical ethics to issues of social policy, the moral dimensions of our public life are interwoven with empirical judgments where honest disagreement exists. I do not believe, however, that empirical complexity should silence or paralyze religious/moral analysis and advocacy of issues. But we owe the public a careful accounting of how we have come to our moral conclusions." *Origins: NC Documentary Service* 14 (November 8, 1984):324.

46. Ibid., p. 37. Christopher F. Mooney adds that what was "disruptive . . . in the interaction of religion and politics during the 1984 election year was not the *fact* of interaction but the *mode* of interaction; not the entry

of the Moral Majority into the public forum but the intolerance which they brought with them. It was their religious values and theirs alone which were to be normative for the nation." *Public Virtue: Law and the Social Character of Religion*, p. 15.

47. Ibid.

48. *We Hold These Truths: Catholic Reflections on the American Proposition*, p. 10. Elsewhere Murray reports that "the tradition of reason, which is known as the ethic of natural law, is dead" (p. 293). One has to keep in mind that this is a collection of essays, written at various times for various publications. What is constant in his argument is the conviction that natural law is, or must be once again, at the core of the national consensus.

49. The term is found in book 4, chapter 8, of Rousseau's *The Social Contract*. The "dogmatic" content of Rousseau's civil religion was almost identical with that of Franklin's "Publick Religion": the existence of God, the life to come, the reward of virtue and the punishment of vice, and the exclusion of religious intolerance. All other religious opinions, according to Rousseau, are outside the cognizance of the state and may be held freely by citizens.

50. See his "Civil Religion in America," *Daedalus* 96/1 (Winter 1967) 1–21 [reprinted in Robert N. Bellah, *Beyond Belief: Essays on Religion in a Post-Traditional World* (New York: Harper & Row, 1970), pp. 168–189], and his later monograph, *The Broken Covenant: American Civil Religion in Time of Trial* (New York: Seabury Press, 1975). See also Robert N. Bellah and Phillip E. Hammond, *Varieties of Civil Religion* (San Francisco: Harper & Row, 1980), especially pp. 3–23, where Bellah reflects on the discussion his original *Daedalus* article provoked. The term "civil religion" turned out to be more "tendentious and provocative" than he at first realized, but he still prefers it to such alternatives as "political religion," "religion of the republic," or "public piety." "Civil religion," he insists, has two thousand years of "historical resonance," going beyond Rousseau even to Plato. His coauthor, Phillip Hammond, argues in his turn that the analysis of civil religion in sociology has been influenced more by Emile Durkheim than by Rousseau (p. 138).

51. See, for example, the important remarks of James Madison during the debate in 1785 on the bill establishing religious freedom in Virginia, cited in Bellah and Hammond, pp. 10–11.

52. *Beyond Belief*, p. 176.

53. Ibid.

54. See especially Ernest Lee Tuveson, *Redeemer Nation: The Idea of America's Millennial Role*.

55. See John F. Wilson, op. cit., p. 18. Catherine Albanese makes the same point. She suggests that "in the Revolution Americans had found a kind of 'invisible' religion, that God was not so much the center of it as themselves. . . ." See *Sons of the Fathers: The Civil Religion of the American Revolution* (Philadelphia: Temple University Press, 1976), pp. 224–225. What is lacking, however, in so much of the myth making centered on the nation, on the part of left and right alike, is any sense of discrepancy and incongruity between claims and reality. See especially Reinhold Niebuhr, *The Irony of American History* (New York: Charles Scribner's Sons, 1952). "The prophets," he wrote, "never weary of warning both the powerful nations, and Israel, the righteous nation, of the judgment which waits on human pretension" (p. 159).

56. Martin Marty has suggested that Franklin's term "public religion" fits the

American pluralist pattern better than does Rousseau's "civil religion," because it takes into account the particularities of the faiths that would not disappear or lightly merge. Insofar as there is at least a partial Christian embodiment within America's public religion, Marty calls this the "public church." It includes the old mainline Protestant churches, the Catholic Church, and significant sectors of the evangelical churches. The public church offers a major alternative in American culture to radical religious individualism, on the one hand, and what Marty calls "religious tribalism," on the other. See his *The Public Church: Mainline-Evangelical-Catholic* (New York: Crossroad, 1981), p. 16.

On the other hand, Henry F. May speaks of a "national religion" in terms that try to bring together the insights of Bellah with those of Robert T. Handy. May suggests that, until early in the twentieth century, "Progressive Patriotic Protestantism" was the national religion. It has not yet been replaced, and may never be. It is possible that a new national religion is developing, and equally possible that America can get along without any national religion at all. See "The Religion of the Republic," in his *Ideas, Faiths and Feelings: Essays on American Intellectual and Religious History 1952–1982* (New York: Oxford University Press, 1983), pp. 163–186.

The mixture of terminology, however, seems endless. Christopher F. Mooney, for example, links the public church with civil religion rather than with public religion, as Marty himself does. See Mooney's *Public Virtue*, pp. 2–6.

57. Phillip E. Hammond, "Epilogue: The Civil Religion Proposal," in *Varieties of Civil Religion*, by Robert N. Bellah and Phillip E. Hammond (San Francisco: Harper & Row, 1980), p. 201. For a slightly different view, see Dick Anthony and Thomas Robbins, "Spiritual Innovation and the Crisis of American Civil Religion," in *Religion and America: Spirituality in a Secular Age*, Mary Douglas and Steven M. Tipton, eds. (Boston: Beacon Press, 1983), pp. 229–248. Anthony and Robbins suggest that "the present climate of moral ambiguity and the consequent polarization of monistic and dualistic world views are related to the *erosion* of a dominant American politico-moral ideology, or civil religion, that we call implicit legitimation" (p. 244, emphasis mine).

58. See *The Invisible Religion: The Problem of Religion in Modern Society* (New York: The Macmillan Company, 1967), pp. 22–23. One finds this tendency to collapse "religion" into "church" even in so sophisticated a work as A. James Reichley's *Religion in American Public Life*, pp. 2–4.

59. See *The Social Teaching of the Christian Churches*, 2 vols., Olive Wyon, trans. (New York: The Macmillan Company, 1931; New York: Harper & Row, 1960 [reprint]).

60. Ibid., pp. 999–1000.

61. See Robert N. Bellah, et al., *Habits of the Heart: Individualism and Commitment in American Life* (Berkeley: University of California Press, 1985), pp. 243–248. "Mysticism," Bellah writes, "is probably the commonest form of religion among those we interviewed, and many who sit in the pews of the churches and the sects are really religious individualists, though many more never go to church at all" (p. 246). See also his "Religion and Power in America Today," *The Catholic Theological Society of America: Proceedings of the Thirty-Seventh Annual Convention*, vol. 37, Luke Salm, ed. (New York: Manhattan College, 1982), especially pp. 20–25. In addition, Thomas F. O'Dea, *The Sociology of Religion* (Englewoods Cliffs,

NJ: Prentice-Hall, 1966), pp. 66–71. Finally, Rodney Stark, "Church and Sect," in *The Sacred in a Secular Age: Toward Revision in the Scientific Study of Religion*, Phillip E. Hammond, ed. (Berkeley: University of California Press, 1985), pp. 139–149.

62. For a scholarly analysis, see Hermann Strathmann's article in the *Theological Dictionary of the New Testament*, vol. VI, Gerhard Kittel, ed., Geoffrey W. Bromley, trans. (Grand Rapids: William B. Eerdmans Publishing Co., 1968), pp. 516–535. The word *polis* is employed many times in the Septuagint (the Greek Old Testament) and in the New Testament, but it has a much less elevated political meaning in biblical Greek than in non-biblical Greek. In the Bible it never refers to the state. However, when the New Testament was translated into Latin (the Vulgate), polis was rendered as *civitas*, which does mean "state". The shift in meaning, conveyed by the Latin translation, had an impact on Augustine. According to his own testimony, he gave his major work the title, *Civitas Dei* (The City of God), on the basis of various biblical references, where polis was rendered as civitas.

63. John Courtney Murray, *We Hold These Truths: Reflections on the American Proposition*, p. 8. For Murray, the opposite of the political community is one dominated by the barbarian, "who makes open and explicit rejection of the traditional role of reason and logic in human affairs" (p. 12).

64. *The Republic of Plato*, Allan Bloom, trans. (New York: Basic Books, 1968), p. 184 (504 b).

65. *The Politics*, T. A. Sinclair, trans. (Harmondsworth, England: Penguin Books, 1962), p. 191 (Bk. V, ch. 1).

66. Ibid., p. 128 (Bk III, ch. 13).

67. Ibid., p. 190 (Bk. V, ch. 1).

68. *De Re Publica*, Bk. III, ch. 22, sec. 33 (The Loeb Classical Library, Cambridge, MA: Harvard University Press, 1928).

69. *Sacrosanctum concilium*, n. 8 (p. 141 in the Abbott-Gallagher edition of *The Documents of Vatican II*).

70. See F. F. Bruce, "Render to Caesar," in *Jesus and the Politics of His Day*, Ernst Bammel and C. F. D. Moule, eds. (Cambridge: Cambridge University Press, 1984), pp. 249–263.

71. *The Later Christian Fathers*, Henry Bettenson, ed. and trans. (New York: Oxford University Press, 1970), p. 239. His treatment of the two cities is contained in Bk. XIV, ch. 28 through Bk. XV, ch. 5, of *The City of God*, David Knowles, ed., Henry Bettenson, trans. (Harmondsworth, England: Penguin Books, 1972), pp. 593–601.

72. See XIV, 2 and 4; XIX, 12; and XX, 9.

73. Aquinas' principal political writings are *On Kingship (De Regimine Principuum)* and his commentaries on Aristotle's *Ethics* and *Politics*.

74. See John Calvin, *On God and Political Duty*, John T. McNeill, ed. (Indianapolis: The Bobbs-Merrill Co., 1956), especially pp. 45 and 46.

75. *Martin Luther: Selections from His Writings*, John Dillenberger, ed. (Garden City, NY: Doubleday/Anchor, 1961), p. 372.

76. Ibid.

77. Ibid.

78. *The Prince*, George Bull, trans. (Harmondsworth, England: Penguin Books, 1961), p. 91. George Will is correct: "Until Machiavelli, the task of political philosophy was to solve man's fundamental problem, which was to answer the question 'How ought I to live?' With Machiavelli, political philosophy became concerned with solving the politician's problem, which was

understood to be keeping order and keeping power." See *Statecraft as Soulcraft*, p. 29.

79. Bernard Bailyn, *The Ideological Origins of the American Revolution*, (Cambridge, MA.: The Belknap Press of Harvard University Press, 1967), p. 161. And see again, Henry F. May, *The Enlightenment in America*.

80. *We Hold These Truths*, p. 32. On the relationship of constitutionalism and Catholicism, see Quentin Skinner, *The Foundations of Modern Political Thought. Volume Two: The Age of the Reformation* (Cambridge: Cambridge University Press, 1978), pp. 113–185; and Brian Tierney, "Roots of Western Constitutionalism in the Church's Own Tradition: The Significance of the Council of Constance," in *We, The People of God. . .: A Study of Constitutional Government for the Church*, James A. Coriden, ed. (Huntington, IN: Our Sunday Visitor Press, 1968), pp. 113–128.

81. Alexander Hamilton, James Madison, John Jay, *The Federalist Papers* (New York: New American Library/Mentor, 1961), p. 324 (No. 51).

82. Bernard Bailyn, op. cit, p. 319.

83. Robert A. Nisbet, *The Sociological Tradition* (New York: Basic Books, 1966), p. 6.

84. Robert Bellah, et al., *Habits of the Heart*, p. 333.

85. Ibid., pp. 152–155.

86. See, for example, Peter L. Berger, *Invitation to Sociology: A Humanistic Perspective* (Garden City, NY: Doubleday/Anchor, 1963), p. 26.

87. *We Hold These Truths*, p. 35.

88. Jacques Maritain, *Man and the State* (Chicago: University of Chicago Press, 1951), p. 10.

89. Ibid., p. 24.

90. Recent Catholic teaching on the relationship between society and the state is contained in Pope John XXIII's encyclical letter, *Pacem in Terris* (Peace on Earth), written just before his death in 1963, and in the Second Vatican Council's *Dignitatis humanae* (Declaration on Religious Freedom).

Notes to Chapter 2

1. Philosophers and theologians make a distinction between morality/moral values and ethics/ethical values. The former are derived not only from reason but also from religious faith and, therefore, are a matter for theological reflection, while the latter are derived from reason alone and are a matter for philosophical reflection. (But even specialists manage to complicate things, because there are disciplines known as "moral philosophy," on the one hand, and "Christian ethics," on the other). I am using the words "morality" and "moral values" in their dictionary sense, that is, to include the rational/ethical dimension, but without necessarily excluding the theological/religious. It will be clear from what follows, however, that religion is not an absolutely necessary precondition for morality.

2. See Ronald Reagan, "Politics and Morality Are Inseparable," *Notre Dame Journal of Law, Ethics & Public Policy* 1 (1984) 7–11. (Virtually all of the text was delivered as a speech to an ecumenical prayer breakfast in Dallas, Texas, on August 23, 1984.) "The truth is," he said, "politics and morality are inseparable. And as morality's foundation is religion, religion

and politics are necessarily related. . . . Without God there is no virtue because there is no prompting of the conscience. . ." (p. 10). For a rebuttal of President Reagan's argument, see Arthur Schlesinger, Jr., "Church-State Rift Is as Old as America," *The Wall Street Journal*, September 20, 1984, op-ed page.

On the other hand, see George F. Kennan's "Morality and Foreign Policy," *Foreign Affairs* 64 (winter 1985/86) 205–218, where he raises the question "whether there is any such thing as morality that does not rest, consciously or otherwise, on some foundation of religious faith, for the renunciation of self-interest, which is what all morality implies, can never be rationalized by purely secular and materialistic considerations" (p. 217).

Kennan's position is consistent with George Washington's in his Farewell Address of 1796: "And let us with caution indulge the supposition that morality can be maintained without religion. What ever may be conceded to the influence of refined education on minds of peculiar structure, reason and experience both forbid us to expect that national morality can prevail in exclusion of religious principle." Cited by William Lee Miller, *The First Liberty*, p. 245.

3. The question was evidently unimportant to President Dwight D. Eisenhower. "Our government," he once said, "makes no sense unless it is founded in a deeply felt religious faith—and I don't care what it is." Cited by Charles Krauthammer, *Cutting Edges: Making Sense of the 80's* (New York: Randon House, 1985), p. 102.

4. Such assumptions are common also in the field of education. William Honig, superintendent of public instruction in California, has found that his proposal for the teaching of moral and ethical values in schools is often opposed on the ground that it will hand the schools over to the Moral Majority, or some other religiously based group. See Fred M. Hechinger, "A Call for Teaching Morals and Ethics in Schools," New York *Times*, September 24, 1985, p. C9. See also Honig's *Last Chance for Our Children* (Reading, MA: Addison Wesley Publishing Co., 1985).

John Courtney Murray and Richard John Neuhaus have also made the point that even secularists have a morality that they want society to adopt. The issue, according to Murray and Neuhaus, is not a conflict between morality and secularism, but between competing moral systems. See Murray, *We Hold These Truths*, pp. 18–24; and Neuhaus, *The Naked Public Square*, pp. 125–126.

5. From his *Correspondence*, cited by George Will, *Statecraft as Soulcraft*, p. 79.

6. See also, for example, Christopher F. Mooney, "Public Morality and Law," *The Journal of Law and Religion* 1 (summer 1983) 45–58, and Joseph M. Boyle, Jr., "A Catholic Perspective on Morality and the Law," ibid., pp. 227–240.

7. "A Matter of Private, Not Public, Morality," letter to New York *Times*, October 23, 1984, p. A32.

8. "Excerpts From Speech by Kennedy," New York *Times*, September 11, 1984, p. A10. A fuller discussion of Senator Kennedy's and Congresswoman Ferraro's views follows in chapter 5.

9. *Moral Man and Immoral Society: A Study in Ethics and Politics* (New York: Charles Scribner's Sons, 1932; paperback ed., 1960), see especially pp. 23–50 and 231–277.

10. Ibid., p. 263.

11. Ibid., pp. 270–271.
12. See, for example, Rawls, *A Theory of Justice* (Cambridge, MA: The Belknap Press of Harvard University Press, 1971); Kohlberg, "Stage and Sequence: The Cognitive Developmental Approach to Socialization," in *Handbook of Socialization Theory and Research*, D. A. Goslin, ed. (Chicago: Rand McNally, 1969), chapter 6; Nozick, *Anarchy, State and Utopia* (New York: Basic Books, 1974); and Friedman, *Capitalism and Freedom* (Chicago: University of Chicago Press, 1962). Even Edmund Burke, the great opponent of the liberalism of the French Revolution, accepted a contractually based notion of society. See his *Reflections on the Revolution in France* (Garden City, NY: Anchor Press/Doubleday, 1973; originally published in 1790), p. 110.
13. "Religion and the Legitimation of the American Republic," in Bellah and Hammond, *Varieties of Civil Religion*, p. 9.
14. *Reconstructing Public Philosophy* (Berkeley: University of California Press, 1982), p. 15. For another critique of philosophical liberalism, see again John P. Diggins, *The Lost Soul of American Politics: Virtue, Self-Interest and the Foundations of Liberalism*.
15. See, for example, Morris Janowitz, *The Last Half Century: Societal Change and Politics in America* (Chicago: University of Chicago Press, 1979), and Lester C. Thurow, *The Zero-Sum Society: Distribution and the Possibilities of Economic Change* (New York: Basic Books, 1980).
16. Op. cit., p. 4. One liberal theorist, Daniel Bell, acknowledges the problem, but says that liberalism accepts the tension of the private and the public, and the individual and the group. On the other hand, he also acknowledges a contradiction within contemporary economic liberalism. American capitalism was once based on a moral system of reward for hard work, rooted in Protestant theology. Now it has substituted a hedonism that promises material ease and luxury, yet shies away from all the historic implications of such a "voluptuary system," with all its social permissiveness and libertinism. So now we have a truly mixed-up situation where today's political conservatives (including many who are philosophical liberals) want economic freedom but also moral regulation, and political liberals (including many who are also philosophically liberal) who want economic regulation and moral freedom. See *The Cultural Contradictions of Capitalism* (New York: Basic Books, 1978), pp. 80–84 and 275.
17. See *The Republic of Plato*, 427d–445e (Allan Bloom, trans.), and Aristotle's *The Politics*, book III, chapter 9.
18. *The Politics*, T. A. Sinclair edition (Penguin Books, 1962), p. 119. The antithesis of this classical tradition is "a shallow procedural democracy" that does not value the exercise of "public virtue." "Through its own exercise of public virtue," Christopher F. Mooney writes, "religion seeks thus to promote the political and social involvement of all citizens, to some extent at least, in the larger interests of the public weal." See again his *Public Virtue*, p. viii.
19. *On Liberty* (Indianapolis: Bobbs-Merill Company, 1956; original edition, 1859), pp. 61–62.
20. *Utilitarianism* in *Great Books of the Western World*, vol. 43, Robert M. Hutchins, ed. (Chicago: Encyclopedia Britannica, 1952), p. 455. (*Utilitarianism* was originally published in 1863.)
21. See, for example, "The Human Abode of the Religious Function" and "Morality Is Social," in *The Philosophy of John Dewey: The Lived Ex-*

perience, vol. II, John J. McDermott, ed. (New York: G. P. Putnam's Sons, 1973), pp. 696–723.

22. Garry Wills argues that Jefferson drew his ideas and words from Francis Hutcheson and other Scottish philosophers, "who stood at conscious and deliberate distance from Locke's political principles." See *Inventing America: Jefferson's Declaration of Independence* (New York: Vintage Books, 1979), p. 239.

23. Henry F. May, *Ideas, Faiths and Feelings: Essays on American Intellectual and Religious History 1952–1982* (New York: Oxford University Press, 1983), p. 113. May suggests that the Enlightenment came over from Europe in waves. In the first, pre-Revolutionary period the source was England, the principal theorist was Locke, and the impact on religion was in the form of supernatural rationalism: "the belief that intuition, experience, and reason will all prove to complement and confirm, rather than displace, the Christian revelation" (p. 119). In the second period (1784–1800) the source was France, the principal theorist was Voltaire, and the impact on religion was in the form of Deism, which held that God can be seen in nature and so there is no need for supernatural revelation and formal religion. In the third period (1800–1815) the source was Scotland, the principal theorist was Francis Hutcheson, and the impact on religion was in the form of moralism: "the belief that accepted moral dogmas are part of the framework of the universe" (p. 126).

24. *Democracy in America* (Anchor Books edition), p. 287.

25. Ibid., pp. 512–513.

26. Cardinal Joseph Bernardin, archbishop of Chicago, is entirely in line with this tradition when he writes, "The advocacy of moral argument in the public policy of the nation is not uniquely a religious task. It is incumbent upon all citizens and every social institution to feel a sense of moral as well as political responsibility for national policies." See "Morality and Foreign Policy," *Notre Dame Journal of Law, Ethics & Public Policy* 1 (winter 1985):291. This is also one of the principal underlying assumptions of the U.S. Catholic bishops' 1983 pastoral letter, *The Challenge of Peace,* to which a more detailed reference will be made later in the book.

27. *We Hold These Truths,* pp. 31 and 30. See also Christopher F. Mooney, *Public Virtue,* chapter 6, "Natural Law: A Case Study."

28. Op. cit., p. 335.

29. Ibid., p. 336. See the entire chapter, "The Doctrine Lives: The Eternal Return of Natural Law," pp. 295–336. Murray's linkage of the natural law tradition with the formulation of the American Proposition has been challenged from within the Catholic theological community. Charles E. Curran disagrees with the premise that the founding fathers accepted "the epistemological and metaphysical presuppositions which Murray sees as the basis for natural law," and he suggests that Murray "too readily sees in history the realities that support his own positions." See *American Catholic Social Ethics: Twentieth-Century Approaches* (Notre Dame, IN: University of Notre Dame Press, 1982), p. 230. John A. Coleman is similarly critical of Murray's "failure to admit that his own theory of natural law rests on particularistic Catholic theological principles and theories which do not command widespread allegiance. Were Murray to have made explicit the theological premises about revelation and reason, nature and grace, which ground his own understanding of natural law, it would turn out, I suspect, to be more theologically informed than

he claimed." See "A Possible Role for Biblical Religion in Public Life," *Theological Studies* 40 (December 1979):705. In Murray's defense, however, see John A. Rohr, "John Courtney Murray's Theology of Our Founding Fathers' 'Faith': Freedom," in *Christian Spirituality in the United States: Independence and Interdependence* (Villanova, PA: Villanova University Press, 1978), pp. 1–30; and J. Bryan Hehir, "The Perennial Need for Philosophical Discourse," *Theological Studies* 40 (December 1979):710–713.

30. (Chicago: University of Chicago Press, 1951), especially chapter 4, "The Rights of Man," pp. 76–107. It has been suggested that the lesser known Catholic philosopher, Yves Simon, provided a more cogent argument in his *Philosophy of Democratic Government* (Chicago: University of Chicago Press, 1951). For a more up-to-date exposition of the question of natural law, see Charles E. Curran, *Directions in Fundamental Theology* (Notre Dame, IN: University of Notre Dame Press, 1985), pp. 119–172.

31. That every person should be treated as an end and never merely as a means is, according to Glenn Tinder, "the primary intuition of Western moral consciousness and [is] indispensable to polities of the kind that recognize the needs and rights of every human being." See *Against Fate: An Essay on Personal Dignity* (Notre Dame, IN: University of Notre Dame Press, 1981), p. 1.

32. *Peace on Earth* (Huntington, IN: Our Sunday Visitor Press, 1963), pp. 12 and 14.

33. See note 29 above.

34. Public philosophy is to be distinguished from public theology. The former does not depend on insights or wisdom that can be derived only from some religious tradition. The latter *is* dependent on specific religious symbols and doctrines. John Coleman, for example, suggests that the more universal language of a public philosophy is "symbolically thin, with little power to stir human hearts and minds to sacrifice, service, and deep love of the community, while the 'thicker,' more powerfully evocative language of the Bible often becomes exclusive, divisive in public discourse, and overly particularistic . . . [and provides no] opening to those who stand as linguistic outsiders to its form of discourse. In the absence, however, of a vigorous retrieval of understanding of republican theory and virtue, there is little else available to correct the individualistic bias of American liberal philosophy." See again his article, "A Possible Role for Biblical Religion in Public Life," *Theological Studies* 40 (December 1979):706. See also David Hollenbach, "Editor's Conclusion: A Fundamental Political Theology," ibid., pp. 713–715, and J. Bryan Hehir, ibid., pp. 710–713. Hehir seems to make the stronger case. He acknowledges the power and richness of an evangelical ethic, but "the complexity of the major social issues we face, combined with the need to enlist allies who must be persuaded of both the justice and feasibility of specific proposals, requires the sophisticated structure of the kind of philosophically rigorous social ethic which the Catholic tradition has produced in the past" (p. 712). Martin Marty's notion of a public theology seems less biblically cast than Coleman's and more in harmony, therefore, with Hehir's concept of a public philosophy. See Marty's *The Public Church*, pp. 16–22.

35. *The Public Philosophy* (Boston: Little, Brown and Company, 1955), p. 101.

36. Ibid., p. 132.
37. Ibid., p. 134.
38. Ibid., p. 136. See also pp. 134–137.
39. *Reconstructing Public Philosophy* (Berkeley: University of California Press, 1982).
40. Ibid., pp. 9–10.
41. Ibid., p. 10.
42. Ibid., p. 13.
43. Robert N. Bellah, Richard Madsen, William M. Sullivan, Ann Swidler, and Steven M. Tipton, *Habits of the Heart: Individualism and Commitment in American Life* (Berkeley: University of California Press, 1985), p. 141. On this point, see also John W. Gardner, "Engagement of Values in Public Life," *Harvard Divinity Bulletin* 15 (October–November 1984), pp. 5–6.
44. Ibid.
45. New York *Times* (October 4, 1984), p. A17. The lecture, delivered on October 3, 1984, was entitled, "Religion and Politics—Some Personal Reflections." The full text is available in *Origins: NC Documentary Service* 14 (October 25, 1984) 301–303.
46. See, for example, Ellen K. Coughlin, "The Worlds of Morality and Public Policy Must Sometimes Clash, Scholars Agree," *The Chronicle of Higher Education* (October 31, 1984), pp. 5 and 8. See also "Religion and the Campaign" [editorial], *America*, August 25, 1984, p. 61, and Kenneth A. Briggs, "Catholic Theologians Have Mixed Reactions to Cuomo's Notre Dame Talk," New York *Times*, September 17, 1984, p. B12. For Governor Cuomo's reflections on the challenge of building a consensus, see "An Interview with Mario M. Cuomo," *Commonweal* 112 (May 31, 1985) 331–332. See also his rejoinder to such criticism in his address at St. Francis College, Brooklyn, on October 3, 1984: "Ask those who demand a constitutional amendment what it would say precisely, and there is no reply. The vague call for a constitutional amendment or a 'new law' is too often just an empty echo that, like the vague call of 'justice for all,' is well-intentioned and may soothe some consciences but avoids any effective argument for achieving its end." "Abortion and the Law," *Origins* 14 (October 25, 1984):303.
47. Federalist Paper No. 10, in *The Federalist Papers* (New York: New American Library, 1961; original edition 1788), p. 78.
48. Ibid., p. 84. Madison made the same point in Federalist Paper No. 51, p. 324. Chief Justice Warren Burger has noted that "political division along religious lines was one of the principal evils against which the First Amendment was intended to protect." *Lemon* v. *Kurtzman* 402 U.S. 602, 622 (1971). In constitutionally guaranteeing religious freedom, therefore, the government received something in return: freedom from religious strife.
49. "Freedom & Integrity in Church & State," *Commonweal*, October 16, 1985, p. 554.
50. *Reflections on the Revolution in France* (Anchor Press/Doubleday edition, 1973), p. 103.
51. Ibid., pp. 104–106.
52. *Democracy in America* (Anchor Books edition, 1969), p. 292.
53. Ibid., p. 293.
54. George Will, *Statecraft as Soulcraft*, p. 27.

55. Op. cit., pp. 444–445.
56. "Faith, Freedom, and Disenchantment: Politics and the American Religious Consciousness," in *Religion and America: Spirituality in a Secular Age*, Mary Douglas and Steven M. Tipton, eds. (Boston: Beacon Press, 1983), pp. 207–228, especially pp. 213–215. For a fuller statement of Kelly's views, see his *Politics and Religious Consciousness in America* (New Brunswick, NJ: Transaction Books, 1984). His is, according to his own words, "a pessimistic account" of the state of religion in the United States (see p. 276). For a more positive view of the relationship between religion and politics in America, see Paul Johnson, "The Almost-Chosen People," *The Wilson Quarterly* 9 (winter 1985):78–89.
57. "Civility and Psychology," *Daedalus* (summer 1980), p. 140. Cited by Kelly, p. 215.
58. (London: Watts, 1966).
59. "Religion and Politics in America: The Last Twenty Years," in *The Sacred in a Secular Age: Toward Revision in the Scientific Study of Religion*, Phillip E. Hammond, ed. (Berkeley: University of California Press, 1985), p. 301. See also Rodney Stark and William Sims Bainbridge, *The Future of Religion: Secularization, Revival and Cult Formation*, pp. 1–3, 429–431, 436–437, 454–456, et passim.
60. "From the Crisis of Religion to the Crisis of Secularity," in *Religion and America: Spirituality in a Secular Age*, Mary Douglas and Steven M. Tipton, eds. (Boston: Beacon Press, 1983), p. 14.
61. *Religion in the Secular City: Toward a Postmodern Theology* (New York: Simon and Schuster, 1984).
62. "Religion in America Since Mid-Century," *Religion and America*, p. 281.
63. Ibid., p. 285. See also his *The Modern Schism: Three Paths to the Secular* (New York: Harper & Row, 1969). Marty uses the term "schism" to indicate that "secularization did *not* mean the disappearance of religion so much as its relocation" (p. 11). Robert N. Bellah et al., address the same issue in *Habits of the Heart*, chapter 9, "Religion," pp. 219–249.
64. George Armstrong Kelly, art. cit., p. 208.
65. "Religion and Politics: The Future Agenda," *Origins* 14 (November 8, 1984):323. It is significant that Cardinal Bernardin used the word "church" instead of "religion" where the brackets appear. There is an astonishingly common tendency to equate religion and church in all First Amendment discussions. There may have been relatively few non-Christians in colonial America, but the Constitution nowhere limits itself to Christians or their churches.
66. Ibid.
67. Op. cit., p. 142.
68. Ibid., p. 153.
69. See also Daniel Bell, *The Cultural Contradictions of Capitalism*, p. 171. Bell is more concerned here with the tendency to fuse the two realms, in which case "the sacred is destroyed [and] we are left with the shambles of appetite and self-interest and the destruction of the moral circle which engirds mankind. Can we—must we not—reestablish that which is sacred and that which is profane?"
70. *We Hold These Truths*, pp. 56–63.
71. Ibid., p. 65.
72. Ibid., pp. 74–75.
73. The complete text is available in Appendix C of Theodore H. White's

The Making of the President 1960 (New York: New American Library, 1961), pp. 437–439.

74. Democratic vice-presidential candidate Geraldine Ferraro took exactly the same position some years later: "Personal religious convictions have no place in political campaigns or in dictating public policy. I have always felt that the spiritual beliefs of elected representatives are between them and their God, not their government." See her *Ferraro: My Story* (New York: Bantam Books, 1985), p. 211. In an interview with New York *Times* (August 14, 1984, p. A21), she insisted that her religion is "very, very private." Her running mate, former Vice-president Walter Mondale, came close to saying the same thing. He declared at Tupelo High School in Mississippi that "what makes America great is our faith is between ourselves, our conscience and our God. . . . More Americans go to church and synagogue, practice their faith than anywhere else, and I'll tell you why. Because from the beginning of America we drew a line, because from the beginning we told the government and the politicians keep your nose out of my own private religion and let me practice my faith." See Bernard Weinraub, "Mondale Defends Himself on Religion Issue in South," New York *Times* (September 14, 1984), p. A12.

75. See James S. Wolfe, "Exclusion, Fusion, or Dialogue: How Should Religion and Politics Relate?" *Journal of Church and State* 22 (winter 1980):89–105.

76. "The J.F.K.–Reagan Religion Irony," New York *Times*, September 11, 1984, p. A27.

77. The friendly Catholics—students, faculty, and those guests fortunate enough to get a reserved seat—were inside Notre Dame's Washington Hall that evening, giving him a standing ovation before and after the speech. The overflow crowd watched on closed circuit television. The unfriendly ones were just outside the building, picketing, handing out anti-Cuomo literature, and shouting their opposition.

78. Thus, Garry Wills: "All in all, it was a thoughtful performance—and a thousand times more nuanced than John Kennedy's simple distinction between his faith and his oath back in 1960." See "A Thoughtful Performance," *Notre Dame Magazine* 13 (autumn 1984):27. Wills was serving as a visiting professor at Notre Dame during that academic year.

79. See "Religious Belief and Public Morality: A Catholic Governor's Perspective," *Notre Dame Journal of Law, Ethics & Public Policy* 1 (inaugural issue, 1984):18. The text of the address, delivered on September 13, 1984, was also published in *Notre Dame Magazine* 13 (autumn 1984):21–30, with comments by the present author, Congressman Henry J. Hyde, Garry Wills, Ralph McInerny, a professor of Philosophy at Notre Dame, and Father Theodore M. Hesburgh, C.S.C., and in *The New York Review of Books*, October 25, 1984, pp. 32–37.

80. Ibid.

81. Ibid., p. 19.

82. Ibid. There were, of course, strong editorial endorsements for Governor Cuomo's position. See, for example, "A Faith to Trust," New York *Times*, September 15, 1984, p. A16, and "Commitment to Religious Freedom," *Jewish World*, September 21–27, 1984, pp. 4 and 61.

83. See, for example, James T. Burtchaell, "The Sources of Conscience," *Notre Dame Magazine* 13 (winter 1984/5):20–23. Father Burtchaell criticized both Governor Cuomo and Cardinal John J. O'Connor for making

abortion a Catholic issue, a matter of "tribal loyalty," as he had put it in an earlier interview. See Kenneth A. Briggs, "Catholic Theologians Have Mixed Reactions to Cuomo's Notre Dame Talk," New York *Times,* September 15, 1984, p. B12.

84. Governor Cuomo referred to the abortion issue several times in his Notre Dame speech as a matter of "Catholic morality." He also made clear, however, that, as far as he and his wife are concerned, Catholic doctrine on abortion is "in full agreement with what our hearts and our consciences told us."

85. I am using the word church here in its collective sense, to include all Christian churches: Catholic, Protestant, Anglican, Orthodox, and Oriental.

86. Columnist William F. Buckley, Jr., has taken it one step further. On a 1986 New Year's Day special edition of NBC's "Today" program, Buckley asserted that the Democratic Party had called President Reagan an "evil" man. When challenged by fellow panelist and former Congresswoman Barbara Jordan to offer evidence, Mr. Buckley cited the remark of the party's vice-presidential candidate, Congresswoman Geraldine Ferraro, that Mr. Reagan was un-Christian, given his approach to social programs. At least two of Buckley's fellow panelists were Jews, one of whom, moderator Gene Shalit, took exception to Buckley's fusing of Christianity and morality.

87. Secretary of Education William J. Bennett generated a controversy in a speech delivered to the Supreme Council of the Knights of Columbus, a Catholic men's organization, in Columbus, Ohio, on August 7, 1985. "Our values as a free people and the central values of the Judeo-Christian tradition," he said, "are flesh of the flesh, blood of the blood. . . . from the Judeo-Christian tradition come our values, our principles, the animating spirit of our institutions" (see *USA Today,* August 12, 1985, p. 8A).

The temptation to establish some form of Christianity as the official religion of the land has been present from pre-Revolutionary days (see Bernard Bailyn, *The Ideological Origins of the American Revolution,* pp. 246–272; Ernest Lee Tuveson, *Redeemer Nation: The Idea of America's Millennial Role;* and Henry F. May, *Ideas, Faiths, and Feelings: Essays on American Intellectual and Religious History 1952–1982,* especially "The Religion of the Republic," pp. 163–186). That form, however, was always Protestant, never Catholic, Orthodox, or Oriental Christian.

For a strong dissenting view against notions of a Christian nation or of a nation that is shaped and must continue to be shaped by Judeo-Christian principles, see especially Morton Borden, *Jews, Turks, and Infidels* (Chapel Hill, NC: The University of North Carolina Press, 1984); Sidney Blumenthal, "The Righteous Empire," *The New Republic,* October 22, 1984, pp. 18–24; and H. H. [Hendrik Hertzberg], "Washington Diarist," *The New Republic,* September 16 & 23, 1985, p. 50.

88. See J. Bryan Hehir, "The U.S. Catholic Bishops and the Public Policy Debate," a paper presented for the American Political Science Association Convention, New Orleans, LA, September 1, 1985.

89. This principle has been reaffirmed by the U.S. Supreme Court in *Walz v. Tax Commissioner of New York City:* "Adherents of particular faiths and individual churches frequently take strong positions on public issues including . . . vigorous advocacy of legal or constitutional positions. Of

course, churches as much as secular bodies and private citizens have that right." 397 U.S. 664, 670 (1970). On the other hand, section 501(c)(3) of the Internal Revenue Code stipulates that "substantial" efforts to influence legislation could provide grounds for revoking a religious organization's tax exempt status.

The Court interprets the First Amendment to mean that the government should not interfere with religion, without denying religion's right to interfere with government. The Internal Revenue Code seems to interpret the First Amendment to mean not only that government must not interfere with religion, but that religion must not interfere with government.

In 1980 a New York group calling itself the Abortion Rights Mobilization and 29 individual plaintiffs initiated a lawsuit against the Catholic bishops and the Internal Revenue Service, charging the latter with failing to enforce the law prohibiting overt political activity by tax-exempt groups. In 1982 the United States Catholic Conference and the National Conference of Catholic Bishops were dismissed as defendants in the suit, and only the U.S. Treasury Department, parent agency of the IRS, remained as a defendant.

On May 8, 1986, a federal district court judge in New York held the bishops in contempt of court for refusing to turn over documents concerning their opposition to abortion. Monsignor Daniel Hoye, general secretary of the bishops' Conference, noted at the time that the "case presents grave and fundamental constitutional issues that need to be resolved by an appeal to a higher court." See James L. Franklin, "Catholic bishops held in contempt," Boston *Globe*, May 9, 1986, p. 1.

90. See Robert N. Bellah, "Religion and Power in America Today," *The Catholic Theological Society of America: Proceedings of the Thirty-Seventh Annual Convention* (Bronx, NY: The Catholic Theological Society of America, 1982), pp. 15–25.

91. See *The Social Teachings of the Christian Churches*, vol. II, p. 1007. Bellah agrees, and calls especially upon Catholics to resist sectarianism and individualism, which reinforce privatization and depoliticization (see art. cit., pp. 24–25).

92. (New York: Harper & Row, 1951).

93. Thomas G. Sanders offers a slight variation on Niebuhr's schema in his *Protestant Concepts of Church and State* (New York: Holt, Rinehart and Winston, 1964; Garden City, NY: Anchor Books, 1965). For Sanders there are also five types, all of them Protestant: Lutheranism (which separates the functions of church and state, while uniting both institutions under God's sovereignty), the Anabaptist and Mennonite pacifist approach (counselling withdrawal from politics, while insisting that the state not violate Christian discipleship), the approach of the Society of Friends [Quakers] (which pursues a course of political action on behalf of peace), separationism (which absolutizes the separation of church and state), and transformationism (which relativizes the separation, leaving room for the church to bring its influence to bear upon the state).

94. "On the Structure of the Church-State Problem," in *The Catholic Church in World Affairs*, Waldemar Gurian and M. A. Fitzsimons, eds. (Notre Dame, IN: University of Notre Dame Press, 1954), p. 12.

95. Ibid., p. 31.

96. Op. cit., p. 69.

97. Ibid. There is, of course, a separate story to be told about Murray's conflict

with other, more conservative Catholic theologians and ecclesiastical leaders. They argued, over against Murray, that the American system is only tolerably "hypothetical," that is, it's something the church accepts for the time being because it cannot yet achieve the ideal, or "thesis," which is a state that formally and legally recognizes Catholicism as the one, true faith. See Gerald P. Fogarty, *The Vatican and the American Hierarchy From 1870 to 1965* (Wilmington, DE: Michael Glazier, 1985; original hardback edition, Stuttgart, Germany: Anton Hiersemann, 1982), pp. 368–385. See also Donald E. Pelotte, *John Courtney Murray: Theologian in Conflict* (New York: Paulist Press, 1976). The Catholic theologian most faithful to Murray's vision today is J. Bryan Hehir, of the United States Catholic Conference and Georgetown University, Washington, D.C.

98. *Models of the Church: A Critical Assessment of the Church in All Its Aspects* (Garden City, NY: Doubleday & Company, 1974).

99. See *A Church to Believe in: Discipleship and the Dynamics of Freedom* (New York: Crossroad, 1982), pp. 1–18.

100. Ibid., pp. 14–18.

101. What follows represents a synthesis of three sources: personal correspondence with Professor O'Brien; his essay, "The Future of Ministry: Historical Context," in *The Future of Ministry* (New York: Sadlier, 1985), pp. 34–65; and a paper given at the 1984 convention of the College Theology Society, "Choosing Our Future: American Catholicism's Precarious Prospects," published in the CTS's annual *Proceedings* (Chico, CA: Scholars Press, 1986).

102. See, for example, J. Brian Benestad, *The Pursuit of a Just Social Order: Policy Statements of the U.S. Catholic Bishops, 1966–80* (Washington, D.C.: Ethics and Public Policy Center, 1982).

103. The principal theological influences, however, are Protestant rather than Catholic. See Stanley Hauerwas, *A Community of Character: Toward a Constructive Christian Social Ethic* (Notre Dame, IN: University of Notre Dame Press, 1981); *The Peaceable Kingdom: A Primer in Christian Ethics* (Notre Dame, IN: University of Notre Dame Press, 1983); and *Against the Nations* (Minneapolis: Winston Press, 1985). See also John Howard Yoder, *The Politics of Jesus* (Grand Rapids: Eerdmans, 1972). For a pointed critique of sectarianism, by a fellow Protestant ethicist, see James M. Gustafson, "The Sectarian Temptation: Reflections on Theology, the Church and the University," *The Catholic Theological Society of America: Proceedings of the Fortieth Annual Convention* (Louisville: Catholic Theological Society of America, 1985), pp. 83–94.

104. See *Toward the Future: Catholic Social Thought and the U.S. Economy: A Lay Letter* (New York: Lay Commission on Catholic Social Teaching and the U.S. Economy, 1984). See also William Simon's "The Bishops' Folly," *National Review* 37 (April 5, 1985) 28–31, and Governor Mario Cuomo's response, "In Praise of Folly: The Bishops' Draft Pastoral and its Critics," a speech given at St. Peter's College, Jersey City, April 16, 1985.

105. See Richard V. Pierard, "Billy Graham and the U.S. Presidency," *Journal of Church and State* 22 (winter 1980):107–127; and Gerald P. Fogarty, *The Vatican and the American Hierarchy from 1870 to 1965*, pp. 237–345.

106. The Republican Party was embarrassed by a letter sent out over the signature of Nevada's Senator Paul Laxalt, chairman of the Reagan-Bush

reelection campaign, to 45,000 carefully selected fundamentalist ministers in 16 states, urging them to "help secure the re-election of President Reagan and Vice President Bush" because of the president's "unwavering commitment to traditional values." Senator Laxalt was severely criticized from all sides. See William Safire's "Christian Republican Party?" in New York *Times*, August 27, 1984, op-ed page, and James Reston's "Reagan's Political Religion," New York *Times*, August 29, 1984, op-ed page.

107. Father Hesburgh can "hardly remember a time during the last thirty years when [he] was not doing one or two or even three different tasks for the federal government. . . ." He views his service as that of a mediator and an ambassador. See "The Priest as Mediator and Ambassador," in *Between God and Caesar: Priests, Sisters and Political Office in the United States*, Madonna Kolbenschlag, ed. (New York/Mahwah, NJ: Paulist Press, 1985), pp. 282–290.

108. For an extraordinarily comprehensive and diverse collection of essays on this subject, albeit from a Catholic perspective, see again *Between God and Caesar: Priests, Sisters and Political Office in the United States*, Madonna Kolbenschlag, ed. See also *McDaniel* v. *Paty*, 435 U.S. 618 (1978), in which the U.S. Supreme Court struck down a Tennessee law denying clergy the right to be delegates to state constitutional conventions or to serve as members of the state legislature. The Court declared that such a law violated a clergyman's rights of free exercise of religion under the First and Fourteenth Amendments.

109. E. J. Dionne, Jr., "Pope Speaks out on Political Role," New York *Times*, September 22, 1984, p. A9.

Notes to Chapter 3

1. *Pilgrims in Their Own Land*, p. 423.
2. Catherine L. Albanese, *America: Religion and Religions*, p. 370. Albanese's book provides a comprehensive description of religious pluralism in the United States, pp. 19–243.
3. *The Federalist Papers*, no. 10 (Mentor Book edition), pp. 78–79.
4. Ibid., p. 82.
5. Ibid., p. 84.
6. Neoconservative authors are generally critical of the Court for not favoring religion more than it seems to do and for not allowing the state to assume some of religion's own roles, such as composing and/or mandating school prayers, or enforcing moral codes rooted in the so-called "Judeo-Christian" tradition. See, for example, Walter Berns, *The First Amendment and the Future of Democracy* (New York: Basic Books, 1970), and Robert L. Cord, *Separation of Church and State: Historical Fact and Current Fiction* (New York: Lambeth Press, 1982). Also concerned about the encroachment of secularism, but more moderate in criticizing the Court's overall record, is A. James Reichley, *Religion in American Public Life* (Washington, D.C.: The Brookings Institution, 1985).

   On the left side are the absolute separationists who applaud precisely what disappoints the neoconservative commentators, although even they worry sometimes about careless breaches of the wall. See, for example, Leonard Levy, *The Establishment Clause: Religion and the First Amendment* (New York: Macmillan, 1986), and Leo Pfeffer, *God, Caesar, and the Constitution: The Court as Referee of Church-State Confrontation* (Boston: Beacon Press, 1975).

At various points within the center are such diverse interpreters as Robert F. Drinan, *Religion, the Courts, and Public Policy* (New York: McGraw-Hill, 1963), which ends on a commendably ecumenical note; Philip B. Kurland, *Religion and the Law: Of Church and State and the Supreme Court* (Chicago: Aldine Publishing Co., 1962), which provides the most straightforward principle of interpretation of all—that religion not be used as a basis for classification for purposes of governmental action; and Richard E. Morgan *The Supreme Court and Religion* (New York: The Free Press, 1972), which warns against embracing principles of doctrinal coherence and consistency too quickly, especially when they leave out the factor of popular consensus.

7. *Tilton v. Richardson* 403 U.S. 678 (1970).

8. *Committee for Public Education* v. *Regan* 444 U.S. 646 (1981).

9. Documented rebuttal of arguments to the contrary is provided by Robert L. Cord, *Separation of Church and State: Historical Fact and Current Fiction,* especially chapter two, "Resurrecting Madison and Jefferson," pp. 17–47. Much is made of Madison's "Memorial and Remonstrance Against Religious Establishments, 1785," written to George Mason, July 14, 1826, in opposition to the use of Virginia's public funds to pay teachers of the Christian religion. Leo Pfeffer, for example, takes it as evidence that Madison held to a theory of absolute separation between church and state. See his *Church, State, and Freedom* (Boston: Beacon Press, 1967; rev. ed.). But Madison opposed the Assessment Bill because it was discriminatory, and thus placed Christianity in a preferred religious position. He did not necessarily oppose aid to religion as such, if such aid were not discriminatory. Furthermore, Cord argues, if Madison did hold to the absolute separation theory, why did he, as a member of the House of Representatives in 1789, recommend the chaplain system for Congress. And why, in his first draft of the Bill of Rights, did Madison use this language: "nor shall any national religion be established. . .," if he wasn't concerned about the establishment of a national religion rather than nondiscriminatory aid to religion as such? And why did he not object, one day after the House passed the First Amendment, to a proposed "Thanksgiving Day" proclamation? And why, on four separate occasions as president, did he issue Presidential Proclamations declaring days of "Thanksgiving and Prayer"?

Madison clearly backed away from these earlier positions in his so-called "Detached Memoranda," a document written after he left the presidency and not discovered until 1946. Should Madison be judged on his views as an author of the Constitution and Bill of Rights, as a member of the Congress, and as president, Cord asks, or on his views long after leaving these offices? "Indeed, the 'Detached Memoranda' is appropriately named, for it reflects ideas certainly 'detached' from views Madison expounded in the Congress and the White House" (Cord, p. 36).

See also William Lee Miller, *The First Liberty: Religion and the American Republic,* pp. 79–150. "If the word *religious* be broadened in the way that the U.S. Supreme Court in the twentieth century has been forced to broaden it," Miller writes, "then one might even say that Madison . . . was more religious than he knew" (p. 150).

10. 330 U.S. 1, at 15-16 (1947).

11. See A. James Reichley, *Religion in American Public Life*, pp. 53–114; and also Christopher F. Mooney, *Public Virtue*, pp. 24–25.
12. See, for example, Justice William Brennan's concurring opinion in *Abington School District* v. *Schempp* 374 U.S. 304 (1962); and Chief Justice Burger's in *Marsh* v. *Chambers*, slip no. 82-23 U.S. 5 (1983).
13. *God, Caesar, and the Constitution: The Court as Referee of Church-State Confrontation* (Boston: Beacon Press, 1975), p. 346.
14. From a letter to the Reverend Jasper Adams, written in 1832, and cited by Sidney E. Mead, "Neither Church nor State: Reflections on James Madison's 'Line of Separation'," *A Journal of Church and State* 10 (autumn 1968):349.
15. *The Ideological Origins of the American Revolution*, p. 247.
16. Ibid.
17. For a major examination of the whole question, see Leonard W. Levy, *The Establishment Clause*, especially chapters one and two.
18. Cited by Bailyn, ibid., p. 248.
19. Ibid., p. 251.
20. Ibid., pp. 253–254.
21. Ibid., p. 255.
22. Ibid., p. 261.
23. Ibid., p. 257.
24. Cited by Bailyn, ibid., p. 263.
25. Cited by Bailyn, ibid., p. 260.
26. For additional background on the role of religion in the original colonies and in the minds of the nation's founders, see A. James Reichley, *Religion in American Public Life*, pp. 53–114.
27. Such religious tests were imposed even in some states, including Pennsylvania, Delaware, and New Jersey, that never had any kind of establishment of religion. Yet no one at the time of the Constitutional Convention defined the scope of the protection granted by this clause.
28. Cited by Reichley, ibid., p. 108. I am indebted, in these several paragraphs on the Bill of Rights, to Reichley's study, pp. 106–114.
29. From the *Annals of the Congress of the United States*, cited by Reichley, p. 108.
30. Mentor Book edition, p. 513.
31. For a fuller discussion of these instances of de-establishment, see Leonard W. Levy, op. cit., chapter two.
32. See his "The Supreme Court as a National School Board," *Law and Contemporary Problems* 14 (1949):3–23; and also his *A Constitution of Powers in a Secular State* (Charlottesville, VA: The Michie Co., 1951), chapter 3, pp. 88–118. Levy examines and rebuts the nonpreferentialist school in *The Establishment Clause*, chapter five.
33. See his *The First Amendment and the Future of American Democracy*. "Liberal government," he writes, "protected the private realm, but there seems to have been an awareness that the health of liberal government required certain virtuous habits to be preserved in that realm. Stated otherwise, liberalism required both the subordination of religion and the maintenance of certain habits that religion alone could inculcate. This is why the First Congress, in drawing up the First Amendment, protected the right to be religious and, in forbidding laws respecting an establishment of religion, was careful to avoid language that would also forbid aid, including financial aid, to religion on a nondiscriminatory basis" (p. 31).

34. See his *Separation of Church and State*, p. 15, where Cord argues that the First Amendment had three purposes: first, to prevent the establishment of a national church or religion, or the giving of any religious sect or denomination a preferred status; secondly, to safeguard the right of freedom of conscience in religious beliefs against invasion solely by the national government; and, thirdly, to allow the states to deal, unimpeded, with religious establishments and aid to religious institutions as they saw fit. "There appears to be no historical evidence," he concludes, "that the First Amendment was intended to preclude Federal governmental aid to religion when it was provided on a nondiscriminatory basis." See also A. James Reichley, *Religion in American Public Life*, pp. 53–113; and William Lee Miller, *The First Liberty*, pp. 318–319.

35. *Church, State, and Freedom* (Boston: Beacon Press, 1967, rev. ed.), p. 149.

36. 330 U.S. 1, at 15–16. Cited in Robert L. Cord, *Separation of Church and State*, p. 109.

37. Letter of January 1, 1802, in *Writings of Thomas Jefferson*, Albert E. Bergh, ed. (Washington, D.C.: 1904–1905, 20 vols.), vol. XVI, pp. 281–282.

Jefferson, however, was not the first to employ the metaphor. In 1644 Roger Williams, of Rhode Island, wrote that when the Jews of the Old Testament and the Christians of the New Testament "opened a gap in the hedge or wall of separation between the garden of the church and the wilderness of the world, God hath ever broke down the wall itself, removed the candlestick, and made His garden a wilderness as at this day. And that therefore if He will ever please to restore His garden and paradise again, it must of necessity be walled in peculiarly unto Himself from the world; and that all that shall be saved out of the world are to be transplanted out of the wilderness of the world, and added unto His church or garden." See *The Complete Works of Roger Williams* (New York: Russell & Russell, 1963), vol. I, p. 392, and also Perry Miller, *Roger Williams: His Contribution to the American Tradition* (New York: Bobbs-Merrill, 1953), p. 98, from which this modernized version is drawn.

It would be a mistake, however, to interpret this text in any legal or constitutional sense. Williams was a sectarian Protestant. Sectarians believe that the world is evil, and that involvement of Christians in the world leads inevitably to the contamination of the church, not the transformation of the world. Williams, therefore, would not have wanted any governmental interference with the church, but neither would he have wanted any Christian participation in politics. The latter would have been a waste of time in any case, because he and his fellow sectarians expected the Second Coming of Christ and the end of the world in the very near future.

For Madison and Jefferson too much religion would corrupt the state. For Williams too much state would corrupt the church.

38. See, for example, J. M. O'Neill's *Religion and Education under the Constitution* (New York: Harper Brothers, 1949), p. 81; Edward S. Corwin, "The Supreme Court as National School Board," *Law and Contemporary Problems* 14 (winter 1949):14; and Robert L. Cord, *Separation of Church and State*, pp. 115–116. The last item (Jefferson's support for the Indian treaty) does pose a challenge to an absolutely separationist point of view. In this case, support was provided to a sectarian group, not to aid the group in its sectarian purposes, to be sure, but to achieve some secular end, that is, service to the Indian population.

39. "Query XVII: The Different Religions Received into That State?" reprinted in *The American Enlightenment: The Shaping of the American Experiment and a Free Society*, Adrienne Koch, ed. (New York: George Braziller, 1965), p. 390.

40. Cited by Robert N. Bellah, "Religion and Power in America Today," *The Catholic Theological Society of America: Proceedings of the Thirty-Seventh Annual Convention* (Bronx, NY: CTSA, 1982), p. 23.

41. Anchor Books edition, p. 295.

42. Ibid., pp. 300–301. For a different, but not contradictory, analysis, see H. Richard Niebuhr, *The Social Sources of Denominationalism* (Cleveland and New York: The World Publishing Co., 1957; orig. ed., 1929), pp. 206–208, 220–221. Niebuhr suggests that the separation of church and state benefits the church by stressing voluntary membership and personal immediacy in faith, unsupported by social authority. On the other hand, the separation of church and state also increases competition among the churches and other religions because none enjoys the advantage of official recognition.

43. Quoted by Sidney E. Mead, "Neither Church nor State: Reflections on James Madison's 'Line of Separation,' " *The Journal of Church and State* 10 (autumn 1968):349.

44. Ibid., p. 350.

45. Ibid.

46. From his "Mending Wall." Quoted by Mead, p. 351.

47. See *The Supreme Court: Views from Inside*, Alan F. Westin, ed. (New York: W. W. Norton & Co., 1965), pp. 43 and 52.

48. Ibid., pp. 43.–44.

49. 374 U.S. 203, 231, 294 (1963). This, and the next three references, are cited by Christopher F. Mooney, *Public Virtue*, pp. 31–32.

50. 392 U.S. 236, 242 (1968).

51. 397 U.S. 664, 669–70 (1970).

52. 403 U.S., at 612 (1971).

53. Some commentators insist that the Court took a wrong turn when it applied the Fourteenth Amendment to the First Amendment. The establishment and free exercise clauses were restrictions on Congress, not on the individual states. This is a position argued by Attorney General Edwin Meese and others. However, the point is now moot. "Even if we assume that the draftsmen of the Fourteenth Amendment saw no immediate connection between its protections against state action infringing personal liberty and the guarantees of the First Amendment," Justice William Brennan pointed out in *Abington School District* v. *Schempp*, "it is certainly too late in the day to suggest that their assumed inattention to the question dilutes the force of these constitutional guarantees in their application to the States." 374 U.S. 257 (1962).

54. See Charles Fairman, "Does the Fourteenth Amendment Incorporate the Bill of Rights?" *Stanford Law Review* 2 (December 1949):5–173. Fairman's documentation shows that the extension of the Bill of Rights to the states was not an issue in the state legislatures during the ratification debates. Furthermore, after the amendment was ratified, the governmental community gave no indication that the new amendment had somehow incorporated the Bill of Rights. Four months after ratification,

the New Hampshire Supreme Court did not feel inhibited from ruling on a controversy over the doctrinal orthodoxy of a Unitarian minister. The Court quoted Justice Joseph Story: "The whole power over the subject of religion is left exclusively to the State governments." When an Illinois state constitutional convention in 1868 debated a proposal for abolishing the grand jury, no one invoked the provision in the Fifth Amendment that makes a grand jury mandatory in cases involving a capital crime. And in 1876 when the Grant administration tried to pass a constitutional amendment prohibiting state aid to church-related schools, no one suggested that such aid might already be unconstitutional.

   A. James Reichley argues that the application of the First Amendment to the states was "neither constitutionally necessary nor consistent with American tradition." *Religion in American Public Life*, p. 156.

55. See Leonard W. Levy, *The Establishment Clause*, chapter seven, "Incorporation and the Wall."

56. 310 U.S. 296, 303–304 (1940).

57. 330 U.S. 1, 15–16. Cited by Robert L. Cord, *Separation of Church and State*, p. 109.

58. 330 U.S. I, 31–32, cited by Cord, p. 125.

59. Op. cit., p. 124. For Cord's full criticism of the Rutledge dissenting opinion, see pp. 124–133. By way of contrast, see Leonard W. Levy, *The Establishment Clause*, chapter five.

60. Stuart Taylor, Jr., "Meese, in Speech to A.B.A., Attacks High Court Rulings," New York *Times*, July 10, 1985, p. A9.

61. See Stuart Taylor, Jr., "Brennan Opposes Legal View Urged By Administration," New York *Times*, October 13, 1985, pp. A1 and A36; Stuart Taylor, Jr., "Justice Stevens, in Rare Criticism, Disputes Meese on Constitution," New York *Times*, October 25, 1985, pp. A1 and A11; Stuart Taylor, Jr., "Administration Trolling for Constitutional Debate," New York *Times*, October 28, 1985, p. A12. Justice Byron White has also expressed reservations about the "jurisprudence of original intent." Justice White has written in *Thornburgh* v. *American College of Obstetricians and Gynecologists* (1986): "This Court does not subscribe to the simplistic view that constitutional interpretation can possibly be limited to the 'plain meaning' of the Constitution's text or to the subjective intention of the Framers." See "The Abortion Dialogue at Court," New York *Times*, June 17, 1986, p. A26.

62. *Religion in American Public Life*, pp. 112–113.

63. "What Did the Founding Fathers Intend?" New York *Times Magazine*, February 23, 1986, p. 59.

64. Ibid., p. 68.

65. See Richard E. Morgan, *The Supreme Court and Religion*, pp. 34–35.

66. 344 U.S. 94 (1952). See also *Serbian Orthodox Diocese* v. *Milivojevich*, 426 U.S. 696 (1976).

67. 393 U.S. 440 (1969). Morgan refers to this case incorrectly as *Blue Hill Memorial Church*. In a related case the following year, *Maryland and Virginia Eldership of Churches of God* v. *Church of God at Sharpsburg, Inc.*, Justice William Brennan, citing *Blue Hull*, distinguished between the question of who exercises general governing power within a denomination, and the question of who the rules or laws of the denomination say exercises control over property. Only the first question, he said, is permitted to the courts. It is an objective question in that an outside

observer can see who, in fact, does most of the governing. The second question requires court interpretation of church rules, which brings the courts too close to interpreting and construing doctrine. The property follows the general governing authority no matter what the rules may say. 396 U.S. 367 (1970). Cited by Morgan, p. 54. On the other hand, in *Jones* v. *Wolf*, 443 U.S. 595 (1979), the Court maintained that if there are no doctrinal or central policy issues at stake, then the courts can decide property disputes.

68. 262 U.S. 402, 403 (1922). Cited by Reichley, p. 126.

69. 268 U.S. 535 (1924). Cited by Reichley, in ibid.

70. *Religion and the Law*, p. 27.

71. Ibid., p. 28. By contrast, Robert F. Drinan, while acknowledging that the case turned on the technical issue of property rights, concluded that *Pierce* established "the basic juridicial right of a Catholic school to exist" and that such a right is now "beyond dispute." See his *Religion, the Courts, and Public Policy*, p. 122.

72. *Reynolds* v. *United States*, 98 U.S. 150 (1878). For a discussion of this case in relation to Justice Black's opinion in the Everson decision, see Robert L. Cord, *Separation of Church and State*, pp. 119–120. For a succinct summary of this and many other religion-related cases that have come before the courts, see Anson Phelps Stokes and Leo Pfeffer, *Church and State in the United States* (New York: Harper & Row, 1964; rev. one-vol. ed.).

73. See A. James Reichley, op. cit., p. 122.

74. *Davis* v. *Beason*, 133 U.S. 334, 344 (1890). Cited by Reichley incorrectly as *Benson*, p. 122. Justice Field's reasoning, according to constitutional scholar Philip Kurland, "would have sustained outlawry of the mass . . . most of the Tudor legislation restricting Catholics and most of the legislation that forced religious dissenters to leave the shores of Europe for haven in the New World. . . ." The distinction between belief and action, Kurland argued, breaks down when applied to a meeting of a given religious group. A meeting is an action, not an opinion or belief, but such a meeting is surely protected by the First Amendment. See his *Religion and the Law: Church and State and the Supreme Court* (Chicago: Aldine Press, 1962), p. 24. Cited by Reichley, p. 123. Robert L. Cord also takes issue with Justice Field's opinion. See his *Separation of Church and State*, p. 103, n. 1.

75. In 1925, in *Gitlow* v. *New York*, the Court had laid down the principle that the Fourteenth Amendment did indeed incorporate the First Amendment, but ruled that the amendment's protection did not apply in this particular case where a political radical had been convicted for incitement to violence through the publication of a *Left Wing Manifesto*.

76. Cited by Richard E. Morgan, op. cit., p. 62.

77. 319 U.S. 112 (1942). Cited by Reichley, p. 129. See also *Jones* v. *City of Opelika II*, 319 U.S. 105 (1943).

78. Also in 1981, in *Heffron* v. *International Society for Krishna Consciousness*, the Court upheld the right of the Minnesota State Fair to require members of the Hare Krishna sect to confine their activities of selling literature and soliciting money to designated areas on the fairgrounds.

In 1982, however, the Court struck down, in *Larson* v. *Valente*, a Minnesota law requiring religious groups receiving more than one-half their financial support from nonmembers to file an annual statement detailing their sources of income. The law had been directed primarily at the Unification Church ("Moonies"). The Court held that the intimidating effects of this requirement violated the free exercise clause.

79. 366 U.S. 607 (1960). Cited by Reichley, p. 130. Even a conservative commentator like Robert L. Cord argues that the Court's decisions in favor of the Sunday closing laws allows "a single religious tradition's 'day of rest,' in a religiously pluralistic society, to be legally prescribed, contrary to the Establishment Clause's prohibition of elevating any religion or religious tradition into an exclusively preferred position" (*Separation of Church and State*, p. 211).

80. 366 U.S. 612 (1961).

81. 374 U.S. 404 (1962). Cited by Reichley, in ibid.

82. For some of the problems in the Brennan opinion, see Morgan, op. cit., pp. 148–149.

83. "Excerpts From Court Opinions on Law for Employee Time Off for Sabbath," New York *Times*, June 27, 1985, p. A14.

84. Section 6(j) of the Universal Military Training and Service Act of 1948 extended exemptions to "anyone who, because of religious training and belief and belief in his relation to a Supreme Being, is conscientiously opposed to a combatant military service or to both combatant and noncombatant military service." Cited by Morgan, op. cit., p. 166.

85. 380 U.S. 163 (1964). Cited by Reichley, p. 131. After this decision, Congress rewrote the statute to make it clear that religious exemption applied only to those who object to war on the basis of traditional religious beliefs in a Supreme Being.

86. 367 U.S. 488, 495, n. 11 (1961).

87. Justice Thurgood Marshall, writing for himself and seven others, in *Gillette* v. *United States* (1971). Cited by Morgan, op. cit., p. 176.

88. Walter Berns called this decision "a palpable and unprecedented misconstruction of the Constitution." See his *The First Amendment and the Future of American Democracy* (New York: Basic Books, 1976), p. 38.

89. "Excerpts From Opinions of Justices in Case Involving Military Dress Code," New York *Times*, March 26, 1986, p. A13. But see Robert F. Drinan, "The Supreme Court, Religious Freedom and the Yarmulke," *America*, July 12, 1986, pp. 9–11.

90. Stuart Taylor Jr., "Curb On Yarmulke Upheld By Court," New York *Times*, March 26, 1986, p. 13. See also "Excerpts From Opinions. . .," in ibid.

91. See, for example, Reichley, pp. 134 and 167. But see also Richard E. Morgan, op. cit., pp. 161–162. As a rule, the Court's presumption is in favor of religious freedom except where the government has an important secular reason to interfere. The classic case was *Jacobson* v. *Massachusetts*, 197 U.S. 11 (1905), in which the Court decided that the state may force vaccinations even on those who resist for religious reasons. More recently, the Court has determined that religious belief cannot allow an individual to gain exemption from the Social Security program and that the government may use Social Security numbers for citizens in its administrative procedures even if it conflicts with their religious beliefs. See, respectively, *United States* v. *Edwin O. Lee*, 155 U.S. 252 (1982) and *Bowen* v. *Roy*, No. 84–780 (1986).

92. See, for example, Edwin S. Corwin, *A Constitution of Powers in a Secular State* (Charlottesville, VA: Michie, 1951). A. James Reichley singles out Justice Owen Roberts for special criticism for his extension, without

elaboration, of the establishment clause to the states in *Cantwell* v. *Connecticut* (1940). See *Religion in American Public Life*, p. 135.

93. See Leonard W. Levy, *The Establishment Clause*, chapter seven.
94. *Walz* v. *Tax Commissioner of New York City* 397 U.S. 664 (1970).
95. 444 U.S. 646 (1981). Cited by Reichley, p. 156. The recently appointed Justice Antonin Scalia made a similar observation in his pre-confirmation testimony before the U.S. Senate Judiciary Committee in August, 1986. "If I had to pick a whole area of constitutional law that's in an unsettled state, that would be one. The problem arises because of basic conflict between the establishment clause and the freedom of religion clause. That's the problem that runs through these cases." See *The Catholic Messenger* (Davenport, Iowa), August 14, 1986, p. 6.
96. *The First Liberty*, p. 261.
97. Richard E. Morgan writes: "On the whole, however, Protestant America (which conceived itself as "America period") was implacably hostile to Catholicism and particularly to its schools. In the words of Josiah Strong, a leading *liberal* Protestant and participant in the founding of the Federal Council of Churches (predecessor of the National Council): 'Manifestly there is an irreconcilable difference between papal principles and the fundamental principles of our free institutions. . . . it is as inconsistent with our liberties for Americans to yield allegiance to the Pope as to the Czar.' " *The Supreme Court and Religion*, p. 52.
98. 403 U.S. 668 (1971).
99. Ibid., at 622–623. And *Tilton* v. *Richardson* 403 U.S. 688 (1971).
100. *Public Virtue*, p. 50.
101. Op. cit., p. 202.
102. 210 U.S. 76 (1907). Cited by Reichley, pp. 123–124.
103. 281 U.S. 375 (1930). Cited by Cord, pp. 106–107.
104. Robert L. Cord, *Separation of Church and State*, p. 109.
105. Cited by Reichley, p. 139.
106. Cited by Stokes and Pfeffer, *Church and State in the United States*, p. 434.
107. Ibid.
108. Cited by Cord, p. 110.
109. 330 U.S. 1, 15–16. Cited by Cord, p. 109. For Cord's criticism of Justice Black's opinion, see pp. 111–124.
110. Cited by Stokes and Pfeffer, *Church and State in the United States*, p. 133. For a particularly critical review of the McCollum decision, see Edward S. Corwin, *A Constitution of Powers in a Secular State*, pp. 88–118.
111. 333 U.S. 203, at 247. Cited by Cord, p. 139. Cord calls a small portion of Justice Robert Jackson's concurring opinion "a spark of refreshing candor." Justice Jackson wrote: "It is idle to pretend that this task is one to which we can find in the Constitution one word to help us as judges to decide where the secular ends and the sectarian begins in education. Nor can we find guidance in any other legal source. It is a matter on which we can find no law but our own presuppositions. . . ." See 333 U.S. 203, at 237–238, and Cord, p. 143.
112. 343 U.S. 313 (1951). Cited by Reichley, p. 143, although he cites the case incorrectly as *Clausen*. For a discussion of the *Zorach* v. *Clauson* decision, see Cord, pp. 167–174.
113. *The First Liberty*, p. 303.
114. 370 U.S. 425 (1961). Cited by Stokes and Pfeffer, pp. 142–143. Local and

regional opposition to the Court's decision was intense, and compliance has been uneven ever since. See David M. O'Brien, *Storm Center: The Supreme Court in American Politics* (New York: W. W. Norton & Company, 1986), pp. 298–299.

115. 374 U.S. 222 (1962). Cited by Stokes and Pfeffer, p. 146.
116. 374 U.S. 25.
117. See Stokes and Pfeffer, p. 147.
118. 392 U.S. 247 (1967). Cited by Reichley, p. 154.
119. 392 U.S. 236, at 256. Cited by Cord, p. 196.
120. 403 U.S. 625 (1970). Cited by Reichley, p. 155. After 1973 the justices referred to this case as *Lemon I* because a case involving the same litigants came twice before the Court on appeal, involving different issues.
121. 413 U.S. 794 (1972). Cited by Reichley, p. 156.
122. 421 U.S. 349, 372 (1975). Cited by Cord, p. 202.
123. 421 U.S. 349, 374 (1975). Cited by Cord, p. 203.
124. Robert L. Cord, *Separation of Church and State*, p. 207.
125. 433 U.S. 229, 266 (1977). Cited by Cord, p. 207.
126. *Florey* v. *Sioux Falls*, 449 v. 987 (1980).
127. 175 U.S. 291 (1899). Cited by Cord, p. 104. Here and elsewhere, the Court uses the word "sectarian" in a legal rather than theological sense. For the Court, any definable religious group is sectarian in nature. For theology, a sect is a particular kind of religious group, one that resists every form of accommodation with the world and that practices its faith in a manner that sociologists would characterize as "counter-cultural."
128. 397 U.S. 669, 670, 674 (1969). Cited by Reichley, p. 153. According to Robert L. Cord, only in this case and in the earlier *Epperson* v. *Arkansas* did the Court "correctly employ the historical concept of separation of Church and State that the Framers of the First Amendment embraced" (*Separation of Church and State*, p. 211).
    The "entanglement" test has not been without detractors outside the Court. See, for example, Kenneth F. Ripple, "The Entanglement Test of the Religion Clauses—A Ten Year Assessment," *UCLA Law Review* 27 (August 1980) 1195–1239; and Paul J. Weber, "Excessive Entanglement: A Wavering First Amendment Standard," *The Review of Politics* 46 (October 1984) 483–501.
129. 397 U.S. 694.
130. 397 U.S. 664, 669–670.
131. Slip no. 81-3 U.S. 29 (1983). Cited by Reichley, p. 154.
132. *McGowan* v. *Maryland* 366 U.S. 436 (1961). Chief Justice Earl Warren is quoting here Justice Stephen Field from an 1885 decision. Cited by Cord, p. 183.
133. 366 U.S. 575 (1961). Cited by Reichley, p. 145. For a fuller summary, see Cord, pp. 182–185. The companion case was *Two Guys from Harrison–Allentown* v. *McGinley*. There were also two other cases, *Braunfield* v. *Brown* and *Gallagher* v. *Crown Kosher Super Market*. Only one member of the Court in any of the four "Sunday Closing Laws" cases was of the opinion that the state statutes in question violated the establishment clause. For the other eight justices, even the accommodation of religion by the state's selection of Sunday as the common day of rest was, in the *McGowan* opinion, not considered an establishment of religion. See also *Larkin* v. *Grendel's Den*, 459 U.S. 116 (1982), in which the Court struck down a Massachusetts statute allowing churches to effectively veto the granting of liquor licenses within a 500-foot radius of their church building as a violation of the establishment clause.

134. Slip no. 82-23 U.S. 5 (1983). Cited by Reichley, p. 162. According to Professor Robert Booth Fowler, every challenge to "a clearly established civil religion in the United States" has failed, including this one. In *O'Hair* v. *Blumenthal*, 442 U.S. 930 (1979), the Court let stand a lower court decision that "In God We Trust" could remain on money and other governmental insignia. In *O'Hair* v. *Clements*, order 80-1908 (1981), the Court dealt similarly with the presence of Nativity scenes and menorahs in the Texas State Capitol during the December holiday season. And in *O'Hair* v. *Cooke*, order 80-1907 (1981), the Court upheld a lower court ruling that the Austin, Texas, city council could have a nondenominational prayer at its meetings. See *Religion and Politics in America*, pp. 268–269.

135. 105 S.Ct. (1985) no. 84-277. In *City of Birmingham* v. *American Civil Liberties Union*, No. 86-389 (1986), the Court reached a different conclusion because there were no secular symbols of Christmas in the display, e.g., Santa Claus and reindeer.

136. Even Leo Pfeffer has acknowledged what anyone familiar with the academy, the news media, and the entertainment industry already knows; namely, that secularism is "a cultural force which in many respects is stronger in the United States than any of the major religious groups or any alliance among them." See his "The Triumph of Secular Humanism," *Journal of Church and State* 19 (spring 1977):211.

137. I am deliberately leaving out here those politically active Christians, Protestant and Catholic alike, for whom constitutional questions seem not to matter at all. They do not even take sides on the various questions that have come before the U.S. Supreme Court. Their attention is completely focused on their respective social, economic, and political agenda: civil rights, the fight against poverty, nuclear disarmament, and the like.

138. 373 U.S. 313 (1962). Cited by Reichley, p. 149.

139. One of this century's most prominent Catholic theologians, Yves Congar, O.P., adopted precisely this position in his highly influential, *Lay People in the Church: A Study for a Theology of the Laity*, Donald Attwater, trans. (Westminster, MD: Newman Press, 1959), pp. 15–21. For Congar, to be secular is to affirm the value of the world for its own sake, and not simply as a stepping-stone to heavenly realities. Indeed, he writes, "To be secular is to use all the resources within us in that pursuit of justice and truth for which we hunger, the very stuff of human history" (pp. 19–20). Theologically, this attitude is rooted in the doctrine of creation. The world is good, although fallen, because it comes from the creative hand of God.

140. See *Religion in American Public Life*, p. 165.

141. The designation "conservative" is hardly misplaced. His book, *Separation of Church and State*, has a Foreword by William F. Buckley, Jr., and a jacket endorsement from one of my colleagues at Notre Dame, Professor Charles E. Rice, who is probably to the right of Mr. Buckley.

142. See Susan F. Rasky, "Bennett Assails Curb on Aid to Parochial Schools," New York *Times*, August 8, 1985, p. A18.

143. *Separation of Church and State*, p. 239. George Will makes a similar point in his syndicated column: "Perhaps the court's policy is intrinsically preferable to that of the framers. Perhaps the evolution of America has made the framers' intentions anachronistic. What is passing strange is the argument that the court is faithful to the framer's intentions." "Liberals are Short on History," Hartford *Courant*, August 15, 1985, op-ed page.

144. Ibid., p. 211.
145. *We Hold These Truths: Catholic Reflections on the American Proposition*, p. 49.
146. See again, for example, Robert N. Bellah, *The Broken Covenant: American Civil Religion in Time of Trial* (New York: Seabury Press, 1975); Sidney Mead, *The Lively Experiment: The Shaping of Christianity in America* (New York: Harper & Row, 1963) and *The Nation with the Soul of a Church* (New York: Harper & Row, 1975); and Ernest Lee Tuveson, *Redeemer Nation: The Idea of America's Millennial Role* (Chicago: University of Chicago Press, 1968). See also Winthrop S. Hudson, *Nationalism and Religion in America: Concepts of American Identity and Mission* (New York: Harper & Row, 1970).

It would be a serious mistake, however, to confuse Evangelical Protestantism with Protestant Fundamentalism on this important point. The former is a broader category than the latter. Not all Evangelicals are fundamentalistic in their interpretation of the Bible, and certainly they are not all conservative in their political views. Evangelical scholars, Mark A. Noll, Nathan O. Hatch, and George M. Marsden, for example, insist that a "blanket endorsement of early America as 'biblical,' 'Judeo-Christian,' or 'Christian' leads to serious misunderstandings. It attributes to the Bible things that are not drawn from the Bible. Moreover, the idea that a more-or-less generally Christian culture prevailed in America until very recent times lowers the guard of Christians to distinguish what is truly biblical from what is merely part of their cultural heritage." See their *The Search for Christian America* (Westchester, IL: Crossway Books, 1983), p. 133.
147. Cited by William Lee Miller, *The First Liberty*, p. 361. For the full text, see pp. 359–364.
148 *Democracy in America* (Anchor Books edition), p. 290.
149. Ibid., pp. 290–291.
150. Ibid., p. 290. Nor could he have written the following today without some second thoughts: "Nonetheless, America is still the place where the Christian religion has kept the greatest real power over men's souls. . ." (p. 291). Poland and Ireland would have to be part of those second thoughts, and so, too, would those national surveys which show repeatedly that many American Christians know little about their faith and that their behavior is influenced more often by the current secular ethos than by Christian moral precepts.
151. The speech was widely reprinted. See, for example, *Notre Dame Journal of Law, Ethics & Public Policy* (inaugural issue 1984), pp. 13–31. Excerpts were published the following day in New York *Times*, September 14, 1984, pp. A21–A22, and in other newspapers.
152. Ibid., pp. 18–19.
153. New York *Times*, October 4, 1984, p. A17. The full text is in *Origins* 14 (October 25, 1984) 301–303.
154. *We Hold These Truths: Catholic Reflections on the American Proposition*, p. 8.
155. Ibid., p. 51.
156. Ibid., p. 56.
157. Cited by Murray, p. 56.
158. Ibid., p. 57.
159. Ibid. The circumstances that exerted this sort of pressure on the framers included the great mass of the unchurched, the multiplicity of denom-

inations, economics (persecution and discrimination were bad for business), and the widening of religious freedom in England itself.

160. Ibid., p. 58. Why the First Amendment commends itself specifically to the Catholic conscience will be discussed in the next chapter. For Murray's reasons, see pp. 56–71.

161. Cited by Murray, p. 72.

162. Ibid., p. 74. See also Christopher F. Mooney, *Public Virtue*, pp. 21–54.

163. Op. cit., pp. 74–75.

164. John Murray Cuddihy, on the other hand, has argued that tolerance and civility are sometimes valued by people who feel some measure of distance from their faith, mixed with some doubt and uncertainty perhaps. Accommodation to another's religion, therefore, is relatively easy. Cuddihy's criticism may apply to some, but not to John Courtney Murray, nor to the Second Vatican Council, for that matter. See Cuddihy's *No Offense: Civil Religion and Protestant Taste* (New York: The Seabury Press, 1978).

Notes to Chapter 4

1. See, however, the interpretation given by the signers of an interreligious statement issued in New York on September 5, 1984, during the presidential election campaign: "If the principle of separation of church and state is to have substance in America, it must mean this: The state should not behave as if it were a church or a synagogue. It should not do for citizens what, in their rightful free exercise of religion, they are perfectly capable of doing for themselves." *Origins* 14 (September 20, 1984), p. 216. The signers included Howard I. Friedman, president of the American Jewish Committee, Dr. Claire Randall, general secretary of the National Council of Churches of Christ in the United States, Sister Margaret Ellen Traxler, SSND, founder of the National Coalition of American Nuns, Rabbi Mordecai Waxman, president of the Synagogue Council of America, and the Reverend James M. Dunn, executive director of the Baptist Joint Committee on Public Affairs.

2. This is not to suggest, however, that American citizens who are neither Christian nor Jewish have little interest or personal stake in the discussion. Adherents of other religious traditions are beginning to raise questions, for example, about customs governing prayers at political conventions and at commencement exercises at secular institutions. Is it still appropriate that these prayers should be "pronounced exclusively by Christian priests and ministers, with an occasional rabbi breaking the monotony?" See Jagdish N. Bhagwati and Padma Desai, "America Grows Roots Outside the Old Testament," *The Wall Street Journal*, December 2, 1985, p. 20.

3. *We Hold These Truths: Catholic Reflections on the American Proposition*, p. 22. The essay had been originally published in 1958.

4. Murray used military metaphors to describe the various conspiracies (see pp. 18–24). The reference here is to the diversity that exists within individual conspiracies. Murray's conspiracies were unified, but not necessarily uniform. For an excellent collection of essays on the state of

these religious conspiracies today, see *The Annals of the American Academy of Political and Social Science: Religion in America Today* 480 (July 1985). See also Robert Booth Fowler, *Religion and Politics in America*, pp. 77–110 and 293–316.

5. See Charles E. Curran, *American Catholic Social Ethics: Twentieth Century Approaches* (Notre Dame, IN: University of Notre Dame Press, 1982), p. 184. Curran's entire fifth chapter is devoted to Murray's writings (pp. 172–232).

6. See *We Hold These Truths*, chapters 12 and 13, pp. 275–336.

7. See especially his "Freedom, Authority, Community," *America* 115 (December 3, 1966) 734–741.

8. *The Public Church: Mainline—Evangelical—Catholic*, p. 3.

9. Ibid., p. 16. See also Christopher F. Mooney, *Public Virtue: Law and the Social Character of Religion*, pp. 1–20.

10. Ibid., p. 13.

11. Ibid., p. 3. Liberals within the mainline churches have had the greatest difficulty of all with "being the church." Liberals, in fact, would seem to constitute only a small minority of the public church. In disarray during the years of the cold war when accusations of being "soft on Communism" flew about, liberal Protestantism began breaking apart during the socially disruptive 1960s (when they bore the brunt of criticism for the racism and elitism of American Christianity), and then sealed its own doom, as it were, with its embrace of one form or another of death-of-God theology, what Edwin Scott Gaustad called "the ultimate capitulation." See his "*Did* the Fundamentalists Win?" in *Religion and America: Spirituality in a Secular Age*, Mary Douglas and Steven M. Tipton, eds., pp. 175–176. It's not clear, Professor Gaustad writes, that the fundamentalists have won. It *is* clear, however, that liberal Protestantism has lost—"This round" (p. 178).

12. Ibid.

13. Ibid.

14. Ibid., p. 9.

15. Ibid., p. 10.

16. Ibid. Robert N. Bellah and others follow a similar line of argument from outside the fields of theology and church history. See, for example, Bellah's "Religion and the Legitimation of the American Republic," in *Varieties of Civil Religion*, Robert N. Bellah and Phillip E. Hammond, eds., pp. 3–23, and his original piece on civil religion in the May 1966 issue of *Daedalus*, reprinted in his *Beyond Belief*, pp. 168–189. Marty's argument is that the public church is distinguished by its commitment to the values of civic republicanism, as articulated and defended by Bellah and others.

For a discussion of the public church in relation to the widespread phenomenon of religious individualism in the United States, see Bellah et al., *Habits of the Heart: Individualism and Commitment in American Life*, pp. 243–248.

17. See George M. Marsden, *Fundamentalism and American Culture: The Shaping of Twentieth-Century Evangelicalism, 1870–1925* (New York: Oxford University Press, 1980), pp. 11–21 and 221–228. For a study of the Catholic counterpart of this movement, see Jay P. Dolan, *Catholic Revivalism: The American Experience, 1830–1900* (Notre Dame, IN: University of Notre Dame Press, 1978).

18. This is exactly what the Reverend Jerry Falwell, Pat Robertson, Jimmy Swaggart, Oral Roberts, and others have done in recent years, creating

colleges, television networks, hospitals, political organizations, and the like.

19. Pat Robertson, head of the Christian Broadcasting Network, based in Virginia Beach, Virginia, host of its *700 Club* program, and an active candidate for the presidency in 1988, is closest to the pentecostal wing of the evangelical movement. For a comment on Robertson's mixing of politics and religion, see William Saletan, "Teflon Telepreacher," *The New Republic*, January 20, 1986, pp. 9–11.

20. The Reverend Jerry Falwell's ecclesiastical base, for example, is not in any denomination. He has his own church, the Thomas Road Baptist Church in Lynchburg, Virginia, and depends completely on his own ability to raise funds for his assorted enterprises, including Liberty University.

21. The Reverend Jerry Falwell calls his own weekly television program "The Old Time Gospel Hour."

22. George M. Marsden, "Preachers of Paradox: The Religious New Right in Historical Perspective," in *Religion in America: Spirituality in a Secular Age*, Mary Douglas and Steven M. Tipton, eds., p. 153. Most of the historical background for this section of the chapter is drawn from Marsden's essay and from the book on which the essay is based, *Fundamentalism and American Culture*. For a broader view of fundamentalism, see James Barr, *Fundamentalism* (Philadelphia: The Westminster Press, 1977).

23. Anti-Catholicism, in fact, has been a constant theme of Protestant fundamentalist preaching, from the days of Billy Sunday on. Among present-day fundamentalist television preachers, however, only Jimmy Swaggart allows this to slip through on occasion, much to the chagrin of his fellow fundamentalist evangelists who receive considerable financial support from Catholics.

24. Ibid., p. 154.

25. Cited by Marsden, ibid., p. 155.

26. Ibid., p. 158.

27. Cited by William Safire, "On Language: Secs Appeals," New York *Times Magazine*, January 26, 1986, p. 6.

28. Ibid., , p. 8.

29. Ibid., p. 6.

30. Marsden, "Preachers of Paradox," p. 164.

31. Ibid. See also "Power, Glory—and Politics," *Time* 127 (February 17, 1986):62–69. This is a cover-story on televangelists, with special attention to Pat Robertson.

32. For a popular survey of the history and political activity of Protestant fundamentalism, see the cover story, "Jerry Falwell's Crusade," in *Time* 126 (September 2, 1985):48–57, and the companion piece, "Jerry Falwell Spreads the Word," pp. 58–61.

33. Robert N. Bellah, et al., *Habits of the Heart: Individualism and Commitment in American Life*, p. 233.

34. Ibid., p. 246.

35. Ibid.

36. See, for example, Robert M. Seltzer, *Jewish People, Jewish Thought: The Jewish Experience in History* (New York: The Macmillan Publishing Company, 1980), pp. 720–766.

37. See his *Church, State, and Freedom* (Boston: Beacon Press, 1953; rev. ed., 1967); *The Liberties of an American* (Boston: Beacon Press, 1956); *This Honorable Court* (Boston: Beacon Press, 1965); *God, Caesar, and*

The Constitution (Boston: Beacon Press, 1975); and, with Anson Phelps Stokes, *Church and State in the United States* (New York: Harper & Row, 1950; rev. ed., 1964). Professor Pfeffer, who has participated in more than half of the establishment cases before the U.S. Supreme Court since the *Everson* case in 1947, believes that, on the whole, the American people and the Court have been "faithful to the constitutional command to Caesar not to meddle in God's affairs, either to help Him or to hurt Him . . ." (*God, Caesar, and the Constitution*, p. 358). See also Leonard W. Levy, *The Establishment Clause: Religion and the First Amendment* (New York: Macmillan, 1986).

38. (Chapel Hill, NC: The University of North Carolina Press, 1984.)
39. Ibid., p. x.
40. Cited by Borden, p. 142, n. 2.
41. Pittsburgh *Dispatch*, January 28–29, 1864. Cited by Borden, p. 63.
42. Ibid., pp. 128–129.
43. *A Certain People: American Jews and Their Lives Today* (New York: Summit Books, 1985), p. 349.
44. Ibid., p. 350.
45. Letter of February 27, 1785. Cited by Gerald P. Fogarty, "American Catholic Influence on Church-State Relations," an unpublished paper given at the Conference on Religion and Politics in the American Milieu, University of Notre Dame, February 14, 1986, p. 2.
46. Cited by Fogarty, in ibid.
47. *Pastoral Letters of the American Hierarchy, 1791–1970* (Huntington, IN: Our Sunday Visitor Press, 1971), pp. 66–67.
48. Ibid.
49. Nn. 6 and 10. See *Documents of the Christian Church*, Henry Bettenson, ed. (London: Oxford University Press, 1963; 2nd ed.), p. 273.
50. See Roger Aubert, "Monseigneur Dupanloup et le Syllabus," *Revue d'histoire ecclésiastique* 51 (1956) 117–122.
51. Gerald P. Fogarty, *The Vatican and the American Hierarchy From 1870 to 1965*, p. 155.
52. See Gerald P. Fogarty, *The Vatican and the Americanist Crisis: Denis J. O'Connell, American Agent in Rome: 1885–1903* (Rome: Università Gregoriana Editrice, 1974) pp. 319–326.
53. See Gerald P. Fogarty, *The Vatican and the American Hierarchy From 1870 to 1965*, pp. 178–179.
54. James Hennesey, *American Catholics: A History of the Roman Catholic Community in the United States* (New York: Oxford University Press, 1981), p. 203.
55. Cited by John Tracy Ellis, "Church and State—An American Catholic Tradition," *Harper's* 207 (November 1953):67.
56. See Donald E. Pelotte, *John Courtney Murray: Theologian in Conflict* (New York: Paulist Press, 1976), pp. 154–160.
57. Gerald P. Fogarty, *The Vatican and the American Hierarchy from 1870 to 1965*, pp. 371–372.
58. See *Acta Apostolicae Sedis* 45 (1953) 794–802.
59. This was difficult for many American Protestants to believe in those pre-Vatican II years. Frederick A. Olafson's observation was typical: "To speak bluntly, many Americans believe that the leadership of the Roman Catholic Church in this country accepts the religious neutrality of the state only provisionally and lives in expectation of demographic shifts that will make other more congenial arrangements politically feasible." Olafson even worried about Murray's acceptance of pluralism, suggesting

that it retained "the very flavor of reluctance and conditionality which he seems to have wished to avoid." See "Two Views of Pluralism: Liberal and Catholic," *The Yale Review* 51 (June 1962):528.

60. Gerald P. Fogarty, *The Vatican and the American Hierarchy*, pp. 380–381.

61. See "The Problem of Religious Freedom," *Theological Studies* 25 (December 1964):503–575, especially 565–568. This is one of Murray's most important works. No serious student of these questions can afford to ignore it.

62. The references here are to the Council of Trent, which adjourned in 1563 and which was the dominant influence on Catholic theology, catechesis, worship, and devotional life until the Second Vatican Council opened in 1962; and to the spirit of the Jacobins, an antiecclesiastical political movement given expression in the French Revolution

63. The distinction between religious freedom and toleration is an important one. The latter implies condescension, as if the superior group were simply granting a privilege to a lesser group. Religious freedom, on the other hand, implies full respect for all religious and nonreligious groups and individuals. It was James Madison who successfully amended the Virginia Declaration of Rights, changing the wording of Article Sixteen from "all men shall enjoy the fullest Toleration in the Exercise of Religion according to the Dictates of Conscience" to "all men are *equally* entitled to the full and free exercise of religion, according to the dictates of conscience" (my emphasis). See William Lee Miller, *The First Liberty*, pp. 3–5.

64. Murray, of course, was not alone in arguing his case. An extraordinary meeting of French and Belgian Catholic theologians took place in October 1951 to discuss the issue of religious pluralism and religious freedom. Some of the Church's leading scholars contributed papers: Lucien Cerfaux, Roger Aubert, Augustin Léonard, Yves Congar, and others. See *Tolerance and the Catholic*, George Lamb, trans. (New York: Sheed & Ward, 1955). The book circulated under a cloud of suspicion and was soon out-of-print and unavailable. In my one and only meeting with Father Murray, he and I sat side-by-side at a lecture at the graduate house of the North American College in Rome during the Second Vatican Council. The speaker referred at one point to this book, noting how difficult it was to obtain, and Murray reached into his briefcase to show me his copy.

65. "Freedom, Authority, Community," *America* 115 (December 3, 1966):735.

66. See the passages in Murray's *Theological Studies* article, p. 513.

67. Thomas Jefferson held that religious freedom is an "unalienable" right because one cannot relinquish the responsibility for exercising it even if one wants to. "The care of every man's soul belongs to himself," he wrote in his *Notes on Religion*. "The magistrate has no power but what the people gave," and they "have not given him the care of souls because they could not; they could not, because no man has *right* to abandon the care of his salvation to another." Cited by Sidney Mead, *The Lively Experiment: The Shaping of Christianity in America*, pp. 57–58.

68. See Murray, art. cit., p. 528. This is obviously an important principle, given the views of many religious leaders that the state has an obligation to provide support of various kinds to religiously sponsored enterprises, such as schools.

69. Ibid., p. 530.

70. Ibid., p. 534.
71. See ibid., pp. 536–542.
72. Ibid., p. 521.
73. *Acta Apostolicae Sedis* 55 (1963):270. English translation, *Peace on Earth* (Huntington, IN: Our Sunday Visitor, 1963), p. 18.
74. *AAS* 55 (1963):260. *Peace on Earth*, p. 8.
75. *AAS* 55 (1963):266. *Peace on Earth*, p. 14.
76. Op. cit., p. 557.
77. This document followed a winding path toward ratification. It began as a chapter on church-state relations in the council's original document on the Church (which became the Dogmatic Constitution on the Church, or *Lumen gentium*). Since that document on the Church was originally drafted by Cardinal Ottaviani's committee, the chapter followed the old thesis-hypothesis approach. At the same time, the Secretariat for Promoting Christian Unity, under the liberal Cardinal Bea, included a section on religious freedom (as opposed to mere toleration) in its schema on ecumenism. At the council's first session, however, the subject wasn't even discussed. Murray was not present because he had been excluded by Ottaviani's forces. In April 1963, Cardinal Spellman, of New York, named Murray an adviser *(peritus)* at the council, and Pope John XXIII issued his encyclical, *Pacem in Terris*, which substantially altered the state of the discussion.

John XXIII died in June, but was succeeded by the progressive Cardinal Montini, who took the name Paul VI. At the start of the council's second session in September 1963, Cardinal Spellman insisted that the question of religious liberty be restored to the conciliar agenda. In November Murray went before Cardinal Ottaviani's Theological Commission to explain the chapter on religious liberty as it appeared in the schema on ecumenism. The Commission approved the chapter by a vote of 18–5. But the second session ended without any final action, thereby giving the Secretariat for Promoting Christian Unity time to strengthen the document.

By the beginning of the third session, religious liberty had been separated from the schema on ecumenism and became a schema of its own. After two days of debate in September 1964, the bishops voted to have the Secretariat revise the document. Murray was designated with Monsignor (now Cardinal) Pietro Pavan, of the Lateran University, to draft a new text. The bishops were scheduled to vote on it in November, but Pope Paul VI withdrew it from consideration. Murray later admitted it was the weakest of the possible schemata. Since discussion of the issue had been so long repressed in the Church, the council could not easily find the proper vocabulary to express its proposed teaching.

During the summer of 1965 a new draft was prepared. On September 21, after six days of debate in which the American bishops took a leading role, the council voted overwhelmingly to close the discussion and submit the text to the Secretariat for final revision. (Murray was in a Rome hospital and took no part in this process.) On December 7, 1965, the day before the final adjournment of Vatican II, the Declaration on Religious Freedom was passed by a vote of 2308–70.

According to Murray, the main reason for opposition to the Declaration had nothing to do with the issues of religious freedom or of church and state. What always lay below the surface was the theological issue of the development of doctrine. Those who opposed the document to the end could not see how the Church could explain the change from the teaching of Pope Pius IX's *Syllabus of Errors* to that of Vatican II. And yet that is precisely what the Declaration admitted it was doing: ". . .in taking up the matter of religious freedom this sacred Synod intends to develop the doctrine of recent Popes on the inviolable rights of the human person and on the constitutional order of society" (n.1). See Murray's brief commentary in *The Documents of Vatican II*, Walter M. Abbott and Joseph Gallagher, eds. (New York: America Press, 1966), pp. 672–674.

78. At the close of the council, Pope Paul VI emphasized this third point in an address to various statesmen and diplomats accredited to the Vatican: "And what is it that the Church asks of you, after almost two thousand years of all manner of vicissitudes in her relations with you, the powers of earth—what is it that she asks of you today? In one of the major texts of the Council she has told you what it is. She asks of you nothing but freedom—freedom to believe and to preach her faith, freedom to love God and to serve Him, freedom to live and to bring to men her message of life." *AAS* 58 (1966):10–11. Cited by Murray, "The Issue of Church and State at Vatican Council II," *Theological Studies* 27 (December 1966):593.

79. This principle has also been central to much of the teaching of Pope John Paul II. In his first encyclical, *Redemptor hominis* (Redeemer of Man), he declared that human dignity is at the heart of the Gospel and is "part of the content of that proclamation." See *Redeemer of Man* (Washington, D.C.: United States Catholic Conference, 1979), p. 36. See also p. 28.

80. See John Courtney Murray, "The Declaration on Religious Freedom," in *Vatican II: An Interfaith Appraisal*, John H. Miller, ed. (Notre Dame, IN: University of Notre Dame Press, 1966), pp. 565–585, especially p. 576.

81. See chapter 2 of the Declaration, especially nn. 9–12.

82. "The Issue of Church and State at Vatican Council II," p. 585.

83. There is a whole body of theological literature on the mission of the Church in the world. One might start with Joseph Komonchak's "Clergy, Laity, and the Church's Mission in the World," in *Between God and Caesar: Priests, Sisters and Political Office in the United States*, Madonna Kolbenschlag, ed., pp. 149–173. A sample of Catholic works would include: Yves Congar, *Lay People in the Church* (Westminster, MD: Newman Press, 1957); Avery Dulles, *Models of the Church* (Garden City, NY: Doubleday, 1974); Gustavo Gutierrez, *A Theology of Liberation* (Maryknoll, NY: Orbis Books, 1972); Eugene Hillman, *The Church as Mission* (New York: Herder and Herder, 1965); Hans Küng, *On Being a Christian* (Garden City, NY: Doubleday, 1976); Johannes B. Metz, *Theology of the World* (New York: Herder and Herder, 1969); Karl Rahner, "Church and World," in *Sacramentum Mundi: An Encyclopedia of Theology* (New York: Herder and Herder, 1968), vol. I, pp. 346–357; and Edward Schillebeeckx, *The Mission of the Church* (New York: Seabury Press, 1973). Samples from other Christian traditions include: Dietrich Bonhoeffer, *Letters and Papers from Prison* (New York: Macmillan, 1962); Robert McAfee Brown, *Frontiers for the Church Today* (New York: Oxford University Press, 1973); Martin Luther King, Jr., *Stride Toward Freedom* (New York: Harper & Row, 1958); Jürgen Moltmann, *The Church in the Power of the Spirit* (New York: Harper & Row, 1977); Wolfhart Pannenberg, *Theology and the Kingdom of God* (Philadelphia:

Westminster Press, 1969); John A. T. Robinson, *The New Reformation?* (Philadelphia: Westminster Press, 1965); Alexander Schmemann, *Church, World, Mission* (Crestwood, NY: St. Vladimir's Seminary Press, 1979); and Dorothy Soelle, *Political Theology* (Philadelphia: Fortress Press, 1974). For a Protestant sectarian view, see Stanley Hauerwas, *A Community of Character* (Notre Dame, IN: University of Notre Dame Press, 1981); and John Howard Yoder, *The Politics of Jesus* (Grand Rapids: Eerdmans, 1972).

84. The paradox also gives rise to a dilemma. How can church leaders, such as the U.S. Catholic bishops, speak convincingly to the wider American public, without moving too far from the language of scripture and traditional doctrine, or speak compellingly to the faithful, without losing the wider public in the process? See, for example, David J. O'Brien, "American Catholics and American Society," in *Catholics and Nuclear War*, Philip J. Murnion, ed. (New York: The Crossroad Publishing Co., 1983), pp. 16–29.

85. Murray acknowledges that there is "more than a hint of triumphalism" in the document, since most of the victories won in the West for the cause of constitutional government and human rights "owed little to the Church." See "The Issue of Church and State at Vatican Council II," p. 601.

86. Ibid., pp. 602–603.

87. The Third International Synod of Bishops' document, *Iustitia in mundo* (Justice in the World) provides the clearest statement that the Church's mission includes the struggle for social justice and human liberation: "Action on behalf of justice and participation in the transformation of the world fully appear to us as a constitutive dimension of the preaching of the Gospel, or, in other words, of the Church's mission for the redemption of the human race and its liberation from every oppressive situation." See *Synod of Bishops: The Ministerial Priesthood/Justice in the World* (Washington, D.C.: National Conference of Catholic Bishops, 1971), p. 34.

88. "Religion and Politics: The Future Agenda," *Origins* 14 (November 8, 1984):324. The address was delivered on October 25, 1984.

89. Ibid.

90. *Origins* 13 (April 12, 1984):733.

91. Ibid.

92. "Religion and the '84 Campaign," *Origins* 14 (August 23, 1984):163.

93. Full text in *Origins* 14 (September 20, 1984):215.

94. Op. cit., p. 163.

95. "USCC Says Bishops Non-Partisan," *Origins* 14 (October 25, 1984):291 [my emphasis].

96. Ibid.

97. "Intersection of Public Opinion and Public Policy," *Origins* 14 (November 29, 1984):386. J. Brian Benestad, however, has been severely critical of the bishops' record. He has accused them of ignoring evangelization, of downplaying education, of usurping the rightful role of the laity, of acting in a politically partisan manner, of neglecting the principle of subsidiarity by favoring too much governmental action, and of granting too much authority to partisan and insufficiently competent staff personnel. See *The Pursuit of a Just Social Order: Policy Statements of the U.S. Catholic Bishops, 1966–80* (Washington, D.C.: Ethics and Public Policy Center, 1982). In a remarkably uncritical Foreword, Avery Dulles,

S.J., expressed his gratitude to the author "for introducing some distinctions that greatly help to clarify the current controversies about the mission of the Church" (p. xiii). I should describe them rather as "false dichotomies" than as "distinctions": between evangelization and public teaching on social justice, human rights, and peace; between the teaching and practice of virtue, on the one hand, and the struggle for justice, on the other; between the role of the clergy and the role of the laity; and between the other-worldly and this-worldly aspects of the Kingdom of God.

98. Ibid., p. 387.
99. Ibid., p. 390.
100. "Religion and Politics," a paper given at the Conference on Religion and Politics in the American Milieu, University of Notre Dame, February 13, 1986. See "Relating Church Moral Teaching to Politics," *Origins* 15 (February 27, 1986):601, 603–607. Citation is from p. 606.
101. "Abortion and the Law," *Origins* 14 (October 25, 1984):303.
102. References to the common good in Catholic social teachings are too numerous to cite. The following is representative: "The political community exists for that common good in which the community finds its full justification and meaning, and from which it derives its pristine and proper right" (Vatican II, Pastoral Constitution, n. 74). It is a theme, as William Lee Miller notes, that runs down through the Catholic ages, and it "may bring to this excessively individualistic American Protestant culture that sense of . . . 'solidarity,' . . . of the interweaving of human beings in community." See his *The First Liberty,* p. 288.
103. See Justice Clark's opinion in *Schempp,* 374, U.S. at 225; Justice Brennan in the same opinion, ibid., at 256, 295; Chief Justice Burger in *Lemon* v. *Kurtzman,* 403 U.S. at 615 (1971); and Burger again in *Marsh* v. *Chambers* 463 U.S. 783, 786, 788, 792 (1983).
104. *We Hold These Truths: Catholic Reflections on the American Proposition,* p. 76.

Notes to Chapter 5

1. The complete text is available in *Origins* 13 (April 12, 1984): 732–736.
2. Ibid., p. 733.
3. The canons on abortion and on excommunication are narrowly drawn. Canon 1398, which stipulates that "A person who procures a completed abortion incurs an automatic excommunication," is a penal canon and must be interpreted strictly (see canon 18: "Laws which establish a penalty or restrict the free exercise of rights or which contain an exception to the law are subject to a strict interpretation"). Only a loose interpretation of canon 1398 would expand its scope to include legislators, governors, and other public officials. See my syndicated column on the subject, "Excommunication: The Larger Issue," *The Catholic Transcript* (weekly paper of the Archdiocese of Hartford, Connecticut), January 21, 1986, p. 5.
4. Transcribed from a tape recording of the press conference.
5. In an interview with *Commonweal* magazine in 1985, Governor Cuomo insisted that this was, in fact, the case: "Let's get the context: I'm here minding my own business, tortured as everybody is by the subject of abortion, a governor who isn't even at the national level. All of a sudden the issue arises and the archbishop says, 'You might be excommunicated.'

(At least that's the way it sounds on TV—with my wife and son watching the program.)" See "An Interview with Mario M. Cuomo," *Commonweal* 112 (May 31, 1985): 331.

He expressed an even stronger reaction in an earlier interview for *Notre Dame Magazine*: "I felt sick. I felt like throwing up. I hoped the Archbishop would say, 'That's ridiculous.' He didn't say that. He said, 'Well, we'd have to be very careful, and we'd have to think about it, and we'd have to explore it'—which was, by acquiescence, by nonrebuttal, a kind of acceptance of the remark."

Governor Cuomo also revealed that Archbishop O'Connor called him subsequently and said that he had regretted that "it didn't come over the way he'd wanted it to," but for Cuomo "it was too late." He leaned back in his chair and shook his head, "It was a punishing, punishing blow. Not politically. . . .Personally it was a very heavy hit." Joan Barthel, "The Education of a Public Man," *Notre Dame Magazine* 13 (winter 1984/85): 13.

6. Sam Roberts, "Cuomo to Challenge Archbishop over Criticism of Abortion Stand," New York *Times*, August 3, 1984, p. A1.
7. Reprinted in *Origins* 14 (September 20, 1984): 215.
8. "Reagan's Political Religion," New York *Times*, August 29, 1984, op-ed page.
9. "Christian Republic Party?" New York *Times*, August 27, 1984, op-ed page.
10. Robert D. McFadden, "Archbishop Asserts That Cuomo Misinterpreted Stand on Abortion," New York *Times*, August 4, 1984, pp. A1, A7.
11. Ibid., p. A7.
12. Jane Perlez, "Cuomo Praises Archbishop's Statement," New York *Times*, August 4, 1984, p. A7. A later nationwide Harris Survey, taken between September 21 and 25, 1984, showed that Catholics reacted negatively, 69 to 23 percent, to Archbishop O'Connor's statement that he could not see how a Catholic in good conscience could vote for a candidate who favored abortion. Archbishop O'Connor had no comment on the results. See "Harris Survey Says Catholics Disagree with Archbishop O'Connor," NC News Service, October 18, 1984.
13. Jane Perlez, "Cuomo Praises Archbishop's Statement," New York *Times*, August 4, 1984, p. A7.
14. Cited in New York *Times*, August 3, 1984, p. A10.
15. *Diaries of Mario M. Cuomo: The Campaign for Governor* (New York: Random House, 1984), p. 464.
16. The full text was reprinted in New York *Times*, August 10, 1984, p. B4. It is also available in *Origins* 14 (August 23, 1984): 161, 163.
17. Kenneth A. Briggs, "Politics and Morality: Dissent in Catholic Church," New York *Times*, August 11, 1984, p. A7.
18. Michael Oreskes, "Cuomo Adds to Debate with Church on Policy," New York *Times*, August 14, 1984, p. A21.
19. Jane Perlez, "Ferraro Says Politicians Need Not Follow Church," New York *Times*, August 14, 1984, p. A21.
20. Phil Gailey, "Ferraro Defends Right to Abortion," New York *Times*, June 29, 1985, p. A8.
21. "Remarks by President at the Prayer Breakfast," New York *Times*, August 24, 1984, p. A11.
22. Michael Oreskes, "Archbishop Cites Duty to Correct Politicians on Church Teaching," New York *Times*, August 25, 1984, p. A27.
23. Kenneth A. Briggs, "Fight Abortion, O'Connor Urges Public Officials," New York *Times*, October 16, 1984, p. A1.

24. Ibid., pp. 1, 27.
25. "Reagan Woos the Catholic Voters," *Boston Globe*, September 5, 1984, p. 15.
26. Fox Butterfield, "Boston Archbishop Cites Abortion Issue," New York *Times*, September 6, 1984, p. B13.
27. "The Responsibilities of Citizenship," *The Pilot* (Boston), September 7, 1984, p. 5. Also available in *Origins* 14 (September 20, 1984): 217–218.
28. "Excerpts From Candidates' Addresses to B'nai B'rith Meeting," New York *Times*, September 7, 1984, p. A14.
29. Bernard Weinraub, "Mondale Defends Himself on Religion Issue in South," New York *Times*, September 14, 1984, p. A12.
30. See, for example, Kenneth A. Briggs, "Political Activism Reflects Churches' Search for a Role in a Secular Society," New York *Times*, September 9, 1984, p. A17.
31. See, for example, Michael Oreskes, "Cuomo Drafts Talk on Theology and Politics," New York *Times*, September 9, 1984, p. A17.
32. Robert D. McFadden, "Archbishop Calls Ferraro Mistaken on Abortion Rule," New York *Times*, September 10, 1984, pp. A1, A15.
33. Steven R. Weisman, "Roman Catholic Shrine Is Site for Reagan Rally," New York *Times*, September 10, 1984, p. B9.
34. Phil Gailey, "Kennedy Speaks about Tolerance at Virginia School Run by Falwell," New York *Times*, October 4, 1983, p. A17.
35. "Excerpts From Speech by Kennedy," New York *Times*, September 11, 1984, p. A10.
36. Jane Perlez, "Ferraro Acts to Still Abortion Dispute," New York *Times*, September 12, 1984, p.B9.
37. Ed Magnuson, et al., "Pressing the Abortion Issue," *Time*, September 24, 1984, p. 19. On September 25, Bishop Timlin wrote Geraldine Ferraro an apologetic note in which he said, "After the election—win, lose or draw—you still have a friend in Scranton, Pennsylvania, one whom you may have thought is an enemy." Boston *Globe*, "Campaign '84: Political Notebook," October 21, 1984.
38. See "Moral Leadership Is Not Partisanship," Washington *Post National Weekly Edition*, September 3, 1984, p. 3. The column was reprinted as "Moral Leadership and Partisanship" in *America*, September 29, 1984, pp. 164–165. Mr. Califano praised Governor Cuomo for seeing the issue as one of practical, political judgment, a question of "what steps you take" to persuade the rest of society to accept your position. As a chief executive of a state, former Secretary Califano argued, Cuomo "faces the hardest case." Once a law is in effect, a governor either has to enforce it or resign. "To assign greater moral value to resignation," he noted, "would eliminate many Catholics (and others) from the very arenas of public policy where bishops want their views espoused. Politics is not a game where you pick up your marbles and go home. It is a process of compromise and persistence, as advocates on all sides of the abortion issue have learned."

Mr. Califano also criticized Archbishop O'Connor for seeming to make abortion a political litmus test. Labor and business groups do that all the time, but the Catholic Church isn't just another political or economic group. He noted that the National Conference of Catholic Bishops, through Bishop Malone's statement of August 9, had urged against any expression of partisanship and had left room for Catholics to make individual decisions about voting for candidates. The statement, Califano wrote, urged "Catholics in public life to put their political capital where they claim their beliefs are—in campaigns, in legislative debates, in votes on the floor of Congress." But it also left "Catholics in executive branch positions the ability to fulfill their public responsibility to enforce the law of the land or the state, even when it conflicts with their personal beliefs." The statement, he concluded, "positions the bishops about where they ought to be in a free, pluralistic America."

39. Gerald M. Boyd, "Bush, in the South, Becomes Embroiled in Abortion Dispute," New York *Times*, September 12, 1984, p. B9.

40. "Pressing the Abortion Issue," *Time*, September 24, 1984, p. 19.

41. "Cuomo vs. Bishops: A Sharp Distinction Between Politician and Hierarchy," New York *Times*, September 14, 1984, p. A13.

42. Michael Novak, resident scholar at the American Enterprise Institute and a syndicated columnist, felt that Governor Cuomo "did not make a very convincing case," although Novak was obviously pleased that he had tried. The governor, he said, should have called attention to recent scientific evidence "which has shown conclusively that the unborn fetus from extremely early stages: (a) has a human form, with fingers, arms, legs, etc.; (b) has an individual genetic code, different from the mother's (and so cannot at all be described as 'part of the woman's body'); and (c) feels pain. In short, whatever else it is, the fetus is a sensitive human individual." On the other hand, Novak was one of the few people on the right who praised the Notre Dame speech, calling Governor Cuomo "courageous to take on such a complex theme" and describing the event as "a good night for the country, for Catholics, and perhaps, especially for all of us unmeltable ethnics, proud of a country such as this." See "Let Cuomo join debate on morality of abortion," New York *Post*, September 22, 1984.

43. "Excerpts From Cuomo Talk on Religion and Public Morality," New York *Times*, September 14, 1984, p. A13 (my emphasis).

44. Later, in a public exchange of correspondence with a professor from the University of Notre Dame, Governor Cuomo made clear that he was not equating abortion with birth control and divorce, but that he was comparing these three moral issues "only to demonstrate that the Roman Catholic Church itself has been flexible, not on the morality of these acts, but in its attempts to deal with them in the American political arena." "Letters," New York *Times*, October 23, 1984, p. A32. The governor was responding to David L. Schindler's own letter, "Begging the Abortion Question," September 29, 1984 [editorial page].

45. Although many critics took Governor Cuomo to task for categorizing the abortion issue as "religious," there were others, at opposite ends of the spectrum, who seemed to be in agreement with him on the point. New York *Times* editorialized two days later that the lecture had stated "a thoughtful politician's analysis of how his private religion guides his public life. He can be devout without imposing *religious beliefs* on others. . . ." See "A Faith to Trust" [editorial], New York *Times*, September 15, 1984, p. A16 (my emphasis).

On the other side of the abortion question, John T. Noonan, professor of Law at the University of California Law School, Berkeley, and now a federal judge on the 9th Circuit Court of Appeals, observed that "Pro-life activists are, for the most part, religious persons; those on the other side are not. The *religious conviction* that human life is sacred animates and unites the defenders of the unborn." Professor Noonan did not argue that "religious persons should be imposing their beliefs on others," but noted that "the morals which are embedded in our society are of Jewish or

Christian origin and these *religiously-derived* precepts have always been imposed by law." See "Abortion 1985," *The Pilot* (Boston archdiocesan newspaper), October 18, 1985, p. 5 (my emphasis).

Congressman Henry J. Hyde (R-Illinois), another strong opponent of abortion, seemed more ambivalent about it. On the one hand, he insisted, against Governor Cuomo, that "abortion is not, at bottom, a 'Catholic issue,' but rather a moral and civil rights issue, a humanitarian issue and a constitutional issue of the first importance." Elsewhere, however, he referred to abortion as "at once the hardest and the most typical case involved in the whole complex area of *religiously based* values and public policy. . . . Until we re-establish the legitimacy of an appeal to *religiously based* values in the conduct of the public debate over the public business, the abortion debate will remain a case of barely restrained 'civil war carried on by other means.' " "The Hardest Case," *Notre Dame Magazine* 13 (autumn 1984): 24 (my emphasis). For the full text of his speech at the Notre Dame Law School, September 24, 1984, see "Keeping God in the Closet: Some Thoughts on the Exorcism of Religious Values from Public Life," *Notre Dame Journal of Law, Ethics & Public Policy* 1 (inaugural issue 1984): 33–51.

46. On the contrary, the last two birth control laws to disappear had been on the books in two states with a predominantly Catholic population: Massachusetts and Connecticut. Neither Boston's Cardinal Richard J. Cushing nor Hartford's Archbishop Henry J. O'Brien protested. Cushing, in fact, issued a statement that followed a line of reasoning almost identical with Governor Cuomo's: "Catholics do not need the support of civil law to be faithful to their own religious convictions and they do not seek to impose by law their moral views on other members of society." New York *Times* called it an "admirable statement . . . a declaration of conscience that has applications far beyond birth control." See "Cushing on Law and Morality" [editorial], March 4, 1965, p. A30.

Cushing's letter had been directly influenced by a four-page, single-spaced memorandum that he had privately solicited from Father John Courtney Murray, S.J. At the time, Cushing and Murray were allies in the struggle to produce a document on religious liberty at the Second Vatican Council. The document was overwhelmingly approved the following December.

In 1948, however, spurred on by his auxiliary bishop, John J. Wright, Archbishop Cushing had mounted a successful archdiocesan-wide campaign to defeat a referendum that would have repealed the Commonwealth's law prohibiting the sale of birth control devices. For an account of that 1948 campaign, see James M. O'Toole, "Prelates and Politicos: Catholics and Politics in Massachusetts, 1900–1970," in *Catholic Boston: Studies in Religion and Community, 1870–1970*, Robert E. Sullivan and James M. O'Toole, eds. (Boston: Archbishop of Boston, 1985), pp. 15–65.

The Connecticut law, ruled unconstitutional in *Griswold* v. *Connecticut* (1965), had also banned the *use* of contraceptives! It was the classic case of an unenforceable law. In *Griswold*, the Court anticipated the central argument of *Roe* v. *Wade* by pointing to a "zone of privacy" that must be immune from governmental intrusion. See 381 U.S. 479 (1965).

47. Rhode Island state Senator David R. Carlin, Jr., a contributor to *America* and *Commonweal* magazines, noted that Governor Cuomo had advanced two arguments in the Notre Dame speech: the weaker attracted attention; the stronger one did not. The first argument assumes that opposition to

abortion is rooted in religious faith. Since we are a religiously pluralist nation, we cannot impose our own religious beliefs on others. Carlin insisted that this argument is irrelevant to the abortion debate because opposition to abortion is a matter of "moral insight arrived at pretty much the same way we arrive at other moral insights." The second argument, however, has "considerably more merit." It is the "impracticality of enforcement" argument, "the sort of position a reasonable person of good will might take." Carlin himself disagreed with the argument, and tried to show how the passage of the Hatch Amendment, leaving the matter to the states, would have the effect of reducing the number of abortions without necessarily eroding respect for law, as would be the case were there an absolute ban across the whole nation. See "Mario Slips Through," *Commonweal* (July 12, 1985): 392–393 [quotations are from p. 393]; and "Abortion, Religion and the Law," *America* (December 1, 1984): 356–357.

48. A few weeks after Governor Cuomo's Notre Dame speech, Father Hesburgh distributed, through the Universal Press Syndicate, an 800-word column that was carried in many papers throughout the United States. He had entitled it, "Reflections on Cuomo: The Secret Consensus." He made the same points in a much shorter piece, "A Well-Kept Secret," *Notre Dame Magazine* 13 (autumn 1984):30. Archbishop O'Connor gave favorable mention to Father Hesburgh's views in an October 15 speech on abortion in New York City: "As Father Hesburgh of Notre Dame has observed: tragically, in essence, we may never again come to an agreement in our land that all abortion should be declared illegal, and some may passionately believe that exception should be made in cases of rape, of incest, of truly grave threat to the actual physical survival of the mother. Whatever we may believe about such exceptions, however, we know that they constitute a fraction of the abortions taking place, so that at the very least we can come to grips with what is the real and the frightening issue of the day: abortion on demand." See "Key Portions of Archbishop's Speech on Abortion and Politics," New York *Times*, October 16, 1984, p. 14. The paragraph appears in *Origins* 25 (October 25, 1984):301.

49. Data released in December 1984 by the Notre Dame Study of Catholic Parish Life disclosed the following breakdown of answers to the question, "Which of the following comes closest to your views about abortion?" Abortion is always acceptable (.6%). Abortion is acceptable under most conditions (4.6%). Abortion is acceptable under certain extreme conditions, like a threat to the mother's life, rape, incest (69.1%). Abortion is never acceptable (25.8%). The high percentage of Catholics willing to allow abortions "under certain extreme conditions" is of greatest significance.

50. Jesuit Father Robert F. Drinan, a five-term member of Congress, had cast votes in favor of medicaid-funding of abortions on those very grounds of fairness and equal protection under the law. He had also worried about imposing the moral views of his own Catholic tradition upon others, citing the Second Vatican Council's Declaration of Religious Freedom, n. 10. See ". . .Or Exhortation to Consider Abortion Above All?" *The National Catholic Reporter*, August 31, 1984, p. 9.

Father Drinan paid a political price for his votes, however. Under pressure from antiabortion forces inside as well as outside the Congress, the Vatican ordered him not to stand for reelection to a sixth term. The order came so late in the primary campaign that no other Democratic candidate could get on the ballot. Each aspirant had to run what they call in Massachusetts a "sticker" campaign. Representative Barney Frank won.

51. The Court ruled, in a decision written by Justice Harry Blackmun, that states may not ban abortion in the first six months of pregnancy. This ruling was based on the Fourteenth Amendment's protection of a woman from interference with her decision to have a child or not. The Court also held that a fetus was not a "person" under the terms of the Fourteenth Amendment. The decision did not make the right to abortion absolute, however. States may still regulate the second and third trimesters of a pregnancy, except where the woman's health is at stake. See 410 U.S. 113 (1973). For excerpts from the Blackmun opinion, see *A Documentary History of the United States*, Richard D. Heffner, ed. (New York: New American Library/Mentor Book, 1985 [4th ed.]), pp. 367–371. *Roe* v. *Wade* has been reaffirmed by *City of Akron* v. *Akron Center for Reproductive Health Inc.*, 462 U.S. 416 (1983), and in a 5-4 decision, by *Thornburgh* v. *American College of Obstetricians and Gynecologists*, handed down on June 11, 1986. Both decisions held that statutory discouragement of abortions is unconstitutional. On the other hand, the Hyde amendment, which prohibited the use of federal Medicaid funds for abortions, was upheld by the U.S. Supreme Court in *Harris* v. *McRae*, 448 U.S. 297 (1980).

52. According to some statistics, Catholic women account for nearly 30% of all abortions in the United States. See, for example, "Harper's Index," *Harper's* 272 (May 1986):11.

53. A very different kind of critical response came from a professor of Theology at the University of Notre Dame, James T. Burtchaell, C.S.C. (See "The Sources of Conscience," *Notre Dame Magazine* 13 [winter 1984/85]:20–23.) He chastised both Governor Cuomo and Archbishop O'Connor for making abortion a matter of Catholic tribal loyalty and for failing in responsibilities peculiar to their respective offices.

The archbishop had failed as a teacher because he simply invoked official doctrine, as if it were something akin to "a sectarian house rule." In the process, he came across with "the mien and the manner of a party whip, when what is needed is the authenticity of an eyewitness. He informs us of the official teaching with the air of a redneck sheriff informing a black suspect of his rights: He is not quite speaking heart to heart."

The governor, in his turn, was unconvincing when he appealed to a lack of consensus to justify his own inaction. "The active question today," Father Burtchaell argued, "is not whether all abortions should be outlawed but whether all should be lawful, as is now the case. Here the Governor has failed to discern a genuine consensus" against abortion-on-demand, and even against government funding for abortion except to save a woman's life.

Father Burtchaell's argument lost its way, but not its tone, after that. The "voting laity of every church . . . will call him to account," he wrote. "They will not ask after his personal childbearing choices . . . . They instead will ask what he does when he takes up the gubernatorial pen, to see if he is sincere when he claims that he, like them, regards the extermination of the unborn as a crime."

First, Governor Cuomo doesn't have the option of lifting his "gubernatorial pen" on this issue. The New York State law providing for funding for abortion was on the books before he became governor. He has not had any opportunity to sign or veto any legislation on the matter. Secondly, abortion is not a "crime." It may be a "sin," and a mortal one at that, but it is legal.

The article's ending is clever, but perhaps unfair. Father Burtchaell

compares Archbishop O'Connor to Friar Laurence of *Romeo and Juliet,*
who is "supposed to be a man of words, and he is always devising political
strategies." Governor Cuomo he compares to Prince Escalus, the Duke
of Verona, who is "supposed to be a man of action, and he is always giving
sermons." He concludes: "The man empowered with force is afraid to
act; the man empowered with truth is afraid to speak."

54. Michael Oreskes, "Home for Unwed Mothers Rebuffs Cuomo over Offer
of $1,500 Gift," New York *Times,* September 15, 1984, p. A29. The press
incorrectly calculated the honorarium at $1,500. The stipend for the lecture
was $1,000. The governor was also given $500 for travel expenses, even
though he travelled in a state airplane.

55. John Herbers, "55 Scholars Say Church's Abortion Stand Is Not Monolithic," New York *Times,* September 15, 1984, p. A29.

56. Among the signers were twenty-four nuns who were later threatened with
expulsion from their religious communities unless they retracted. See
Kenneth A. Briggs, "Nuns Say They Got a Vatican Threat," New York
Times, December 15, 1984, pp. A1 and A9. The dispute was eventually
settled "out of court," and none of the sisters was expelled.

57. "To Admit Diversity & Endorse Discussion" [editorial], 112 (November
1, 1985) 599.

58. James L. Franklin, "Archbishop: debate recasts abortion issue," Boston
Globe, September 21, 1984, p. 51.

59. "Religion and politics—again (part 2)," September 28, 1984, p. 2.

60. John Herbers, "Archbishop Explains Abortion Stand," New York *Times,*
September 22, 1984, p. A34.

61. "Religion and Politics—Some Personal Reflections," St. Francis College,
Brooklyn, New York, October 3, 1984. Full text in *Origins* 14 (October
25, 1984):301–303. Citation is from p. 302. For a news analysis of the St.
Francis College speech, see Kenneth A. Briggs, "Cuomo Finds Chicago
Prelate an Ally in a Debate," New York *Times,* October 6, 1984, p. A11.

62. See also "An Interview with Mario M. Cuomo," *Commonweal* 112 (May
31, 1985):331. Abortion, he said, "is not purely a religious proposition."

63. "Text of Bishops' Statement on Role of the Church in Politics," New York
Times, October 15, 1984, p. A13. Full text is also available in *Origins* 14
(October 25, 1984):289, 291.

64. "Key Portions of Archbishop's Speech on Abortion and Politics," New
York *Times,* October 16, 1984, p. A14. Full text available in *Origins* 14
(October 25, 1984):291–301.

65. "A Well-Kept Secret," *Notre Dame Magazine* 13 (autumn 1984):30.

66. Full text available in *Origins* 14 (November 1, 1984):311.

67. *The Pilot* (Boston archdiocesan weekly newspaper), October 26, 1984.

68. Archbishop Law's immediate predecessor in Boston, Cardinal Humberto
Medeiros, had taken a similar stand during the 1980 congressional elections. In a strongly worded statement published in his archdiocesan weekly
newspaper, *The Pilot,* Cardinal Medeiros clearly implied that Catholics
should not vote for candidates who opposed a constitutional amendment
to restrict abortions and/or who supported medicaid funding of abortions.
The statement was taken as an endorsement of Robert Hatem over Representative James Shannon in the Democratic primary for the Fifth
Congressional District, and of Waltham's Mayor Arthur J. Clark over Barney Frank, in the Democratic primary for the Fourth District seat being
vacated by Father Robert F. Drinan, S.J., upon direct orders from the
Vatican. Both Shannon and Frank won, the latter with Father Drinan's

endorsement. See "Abortion and the Elections: Cardinal Medeiros," *Origins* 10 (September 24, 1980):239.

69. "Religion and Politics: The Future Agenda," *Origins* 14 (November 8, 1984):321, 322–328. This citation and the next several as well are from p. 326.

70. Ibid., p. 325.

71. Ibid., p. 326.

72. Ibid., p. 327. The remaining citations from the Bernardin address are to be found on the same page.

73. This tactic continues to be employed. Governor Cuomo withdrew as keynote speaker at the 1985 annual convention of the National Conference of Catholic Charities, to be held in San Francisco in October, after the Pennsylvania bishops protested the invitation. Once again, Bishop James Timlin, Archbishop O'Connor's successor in Scranton, took the lead: "On this crucial issue of abortion it cannot be business as usual with politicians who take a pro-choice position." (New York *Post*, September 10, 1985.) Governor Cuomo had been invited to speak on "A Just Tax System and the Church." For a critical reaction to this development, see "To Admit Diversity & Endorse Discussion" [editorial], *Commonweal* 112 (November 1, 1985):597–599.

74. "Intersection of Public Opinion and Public Policy," *Origins* 14 (November 29, 1984):387. See also New York *Times*, November 13, 1984, pp. 1 and 16. In a later talk at the University of Notre Dame in February 1986, Bishop Malone mounted an implicit challenge to the other side as well: "Sincerity minimally requires that those who say they stand with the Church's teaching but reject the bishops' policy proposals offer genuine alternatives calculated to realize the same purposes." See "Relating Church Moral Teaching to Politics," *Origins* 15 (February 27, 1986):606.

75. *The Challenge of Peace: God's Promise and Our Response* (Washington, D.C.: United States Catholic Conference, 1983), p. 89.

76. For an intelligent, balanced, and sensitive attempt to address some of these other dimensions of the issue, see Sidney and Daniel Callahan, "Breaking Through the Stereotypes," *Commonweal*, October 5, 1984, pp. 520–523.

77. *We Hold These Truths*, p. 156.

78. Ibid., p. 158.

79. Ibid., p. 166.

80. See the *Summa Theologica* II-I, q. 96, a. 2.

81. II-I, q. 97, a. 1.

82. Ibid. *We Hold These Truths*, p. 169.

83. Ibid., p. 171.

84. "Religion and Politics: The Future Agenda," *Origins* 14 (November 8, 1984):326.

85. Ibid., p. 328.

Notes to Chapter 6

1. See especially Robert Michaelsen, *Piety in the Public Schools: Trends and Issues in the Relationship Between Religion and the Public School in the United States* (New York: Macmillan, 1970). The literature on the subject is vast. See also, for example, Rockne McCarthy, et al., *Society,*

State, & Schools: A Case for Structural Pluralism (Grand Rapids: William B. Eerdmans, 1981), pp. 79–92, et passim. This book advances the unusual thesis that, because the public schools themselves are not religiously neutral (at the moment they are inculcating a secular religion known as humanism), the state should adopt a multiple school system. The choice of schools would be left entirely to the individual parents, and the state would provide funding across the board, on a nondiscriminatory basis. See pp. 133–135.

2. Op. cit., p. 51.

3. See, for example, "Religion and Our Schools," *The Hibbert Journal* 6 (July 1908):796–809.

4. *A Common Faith* (New Haven: Yale University Press, 1934), p. 87.

5. See Jay P. Dolan, *The American Catholic Experience: A History from Colonial Times to the Present* (Garden City, NY: Doubleday, 1985), p. 263. See the entire tenth chapter, "Schools," pp. 262–293.

6. Neil G. McCluskey, ed., *Catholic Education in America: A Documentary History* (New York: Teachers College, Columbia University, 1964), pp. 90–94.

7. See again Gerald P. Fogarty, *The Vatican and the American Hierarchy from 1870 to 1965* (Wilmington, DE: Michael Glazier, 1985), pp. 355 and 369.

8. The alliance has been altered in recent years. Mainline Protestants, Jews, and moderate-to-progressive Catholics are now generally opposed to mandated prayer in the public schools. On the other side, Protestant fundamentalists and conservative evangelicals are often joined by conservative Catholics.

9. This is also the point that Justice Hugo Black made in writing for the majority. 370 U.S. 425 (1961).

10. See, for example, William J. Bennett, "We Are a Religious People," Washington *Post National Weekly Edition*, September 16, 1985, p. 28. "Some of my critics," he wrote, "seem to believe that Americans are a people primed for a campaign of *intolerant* oppression. . . . And they assume that describing the intimate relationship between the Judeo-Christian tradition and our public life is a step down the path toward Lebanon, or Iran. This vision seems to me to say more about its beholders than about America. America is both religious and *tolerant* . . ." [my emphasis]. For a sharp rejoinder to the "Judeo-Christian nation" argument, see H. H. [Hendrik Hertzberg], "Washington Diarist," *The New Republic*, September 16 & 23, 1985, p. 50.

11. "Excerpts From Opinions and Dissents in School Prayer Case," New York *Times*, June 5, 1985, p. B5.

12. Ibid.

13. Cited by A. James Reichley, *Religion in American Public Life*, p. 149.

14. On September 19, 1973, for example, the Administrative Board of the United States Catholic Conference called for a constitutional amendment permitting prayer and religious instruction in public schools. The bishops' statement noted the acute concern of parents for "the faith and morality of their children." Secularism, too, raised its ugly head. Parents are "rightly concerned," the bishops declared, "lest the religious heritage of the nation be supplanted by a pervasive secularism." Indeed, the bishops interpreted the Court's school prayer decisions as a suppression of religious freedom. The passage of their amendment, they assured their opponents, would

do "no violence to the views and rights of non-believers." See "Bishops Propose Constitutional Amendments," *Origins* 3 (October 4, 1973):231.

The Administrative Board's statement made several untenable assumptions: (1) that morality and moral values are absolutely dependent upon religion and religious values; (2) that there is no real distinction between secularism and secularity; (3) that religious bodies can, and even must, use the state to further their own spiritual ends; (4) that government is in a position to pass judgment on theological and spiritual matters, and, therefore, would be competent to administer and supervise a program of daily prayer in the public schools; and (5) that there are no limits to the moral aspirations of civil law.

The statement is remarkable for its political and theological naivete.

15. 403 U.S. 668 (1971).
16. Linda Greenhouse, "Public Teachers Can't Hold Class in Church Schools," New York *Times,* July 2, 1985, pp. 1, 11 [with excerpts from opinions in the Grand Rapids case].
17. Edward B. Fiske, "Ruling Means Cities Must Work out How to Get Help to Parochial Pupils," New York *Times,* July 2, 1985, p. 11. The brief quotation is from Education Secretary William J. Bennett. Officials of the Roman Catholic Archdiocese of New York and the United States Catholic Conference also spoke against the decisions. Those who were pleased with the decisions included Norman Redlich, dean of the New York University Law School, speaking for the American Jewish Congress, Scott Widmeyer, on behalf of the American Federation of Teachers, and Florence Fast, chair of the Committee for Public Education and Religious Liberty, a coalition of 50 organizations that had coordinated legal efforts in the New York case.
18. For arguments against the Court's "doctrinaire" position, see Nathan Glazer, "Church-State Bargain," *The New Republic,* October 21, 1985, pp. 16–18, and Harry J. Byrne, "Tragic Paranoia: The Supreme Court and Parochial Schools," *America,* October 5, 1985, pp. 185–189.
19. *Public Virtue,* p. 53. Rockne McCarthy, et al., would solve this problem by recognizing that the public schools are already "religious," in that they are committed to, and teach, the secular "religion" of humanism. They propose, therefore, that all schools, public and private, be placed on an equal legal footing, and that government money and services be available to all accredited schools on an equal basis. See again *Society, State, & Schools,* pp. 107–144 and 169–208.

Mooney's fellow Jesuit, John Courtney Murray, argued a position closer to the preceding than to Mooney's. "The doctrine that public aid should be denied by law to certain schools simply on the grounds that they teach a particular religion," Murray wrote, "was never in conformity with the moral canon of distributive justice." *We Hold These Truths,* p. 146. He would have agreed with Mooney that governmental responsibility is limited to the care for religious freedom, never for religious belief. However, for Murray, education is a special case. He wrote that "it is precisely in this area of education that the spiritual needs of a religious people are today being sharply felt. Government," he continued, "cannot ignore these needs. . . .for the fortunes of free government are intimately linked to the fact of a religiously informed and virtuous citizenry" (p. 153). Had Murray, usually so careful about making the proper distinctions, collapsed religion and morality (virtue) here? How does government's legitimate concern for civic virtue justify government aid to private schools operated by religious bodies?

20. Mooney, ibid., p. 54.
21. Keith B. Richburg, "Public Schools and the Politics of Curriculum," Washington *Post National Weekly Edition*, January 20, 1986, pp. 14–15.
22. Dudley Clendinen, "Conservative Christians Again Take Issue of Religion in Schools to Courts," New York *Times*, February 28, 1986, p. A11. See also Dudley Clendinen, "Fundamentalist Parents Put Textbooks On Trial," New York *Times*, July 15, 1986, p. A14.
23. Ibid.
24. Ibid.
25. "Bible Study Fight in Carolina Town," New York *Times*, December 16, 1985, p. A13.
26. See, for example, Jacob Neusner, "The Campus Conspiracy Against the Religious Order," *The National Review*, March 14, 1986, pp. 41–42. See also Warren A. Nord, "Liberals Should Want Religion Taught in Public Schools," The Washington *Post National Weekly Edition*, July 21, 1986, pp. 23–24.
27. See, for example, George W. Cornell, "Analysis of Public School Textbooks Finds Religion, Family Downplayed," *Hartford Courant*, February 1, 1986, p. D6. See also Leslie Maitland Werner, "Religion Lack in Texts Cited," New York *Times*, June 3, 1986, pp. A19, 22.
28. 374 U.S. 203, 225 (1963). Cited by Robert Michaelsen, *Piety in the Public School*, pp. 213–214.
29. 374 U.S. 300 (1963). Cited by Michaelsen, p. 214, n. 60.
30. 374 U.S. 306 (1963). Cited by Michaelsen, p. 214.
31. Ibid., p. 215.
32. Teaching about *religion* in the public schools is not to be confused with teaching *values* in the public schools. The two are related, of course, but not identical. Proposals for reintroducing a "moral content" to the curriculum have come from President Reagan, Education Secretary Bennett, and various business leaders, on the one hand, and, on the other, from William Honig, California's superintendent for public instruction, who attacked value-free education in his book, *Last Chance for Our Children* (Reading, MA: Addison-Wesley Publishing Co., 1985).

Honig vigorously resists the charge that his proposal embraces the agenda of Bible Belt evangelism. There is a difference between religion and morality. Among the nonreligious moral issues his proposal would touch upon are "the sanctity of human life, respect for the dignity of the individual, and the importance of the family and personal moral effort," as well as "an understanding of the guarantees of freedom of speech, religion, association and the press and of equality before the law." Such values can be taught through literature.

"Are you a laissez-faire capitalist?" he asks. "Then read Frank Norris' *The Octopus*, and squirm. An unregenerate Bolshevik? Try Arthur Koestler's *Darkness at Noon*. Pacifists should be sure to read *The Diary of Anne Frank* or William Shakespeare's *Henry V*. And Marine Corps recruits should study Stephen Crane's *The Red Badge of Courage* or Erich Maria Remarque's *All Quiet on the Western Front*." See Fred M. Hechinger, "A Call for Teaching Morals and Ethics in Schools," New York *Times*, September 24, 1985, p. C9. See also Jonathan Friendly, "Ethics Classes Avoid Teaching Right and Wrong," New York *Times*, December 2, 1985, p. B2.

33. 104 S.Ct. 1355. 1359-62 (1984). Cited by Christopher F. Mooney, *Public Virtue*, p. 46.
34. For a different view, from the U.S. District Court Judge whose decision had been overturned, see Raymond J. Pettine, "Warning from the Bench: Federal Judge Speaks out on Church-State Relations," *Journal of Church & State* 38 (May 1985):7–10.
35. *Board of Trustees of the Village of Scarsdale v. McCreary*, 105 S.Ct. (1985) no. 84-277.
36. Chief Justice Earl Warren, quoting from an 1885 opinion by Justice Stephen Field. 366 U.S. 436 (1961). Cited by Robert L. Cord, *Separation of Church and State*, p. 183.
37. Op. cit., pp. 193–194.
38. Linda Greenhouse, "High Court Voids Connecticut Sabbath Law," New York *Times*, June 27, 1985, pp. 1 and 14.
39. *Abington School District v. Schempp*, 374 U.S. at 222 (1963). Cited by Christopher F. Mooney, *Public Virtue*, p. 47.
40. Slip no. 82-23 U.S. 5 (1983). Cited by A. James Reichley, *Religion in American Public Life*, p. 162.
41. 397 U.S. at 673 (1970). Cited by Mooney, *Public Virtue*, p. 45.
42. 461 U.S. 574, 591–92 (1983). Cited by Mooney, p. 45.
43. See Robert Lindsey, "The Difficulty in Regulating Religions That Turn a Profit," New York *Times*, February 9, 1986, p. E5.

    As Judge Richard R. Cardamone, of the Second Circuit Court of Appeals, argued in rejecting an appeal from Unification Church leader Sun Myung Moon in 1983, the First Amendment does not excuse religious ministers from paying taxes on personal income any more than it bestows immunity from any other criminal offense. "To allow otherwise," he wrote, "would be to permit church leaders to stand above the law." Michael Isikoff, "New Moon," *The New Republic*, August 26, 1985, p. 16.
44. Ibid. The group was founded by the late Lafayette Ronald Hubbard, a science fiction writer who in the 1950s established a network of mental health clinics that he later renamed the Church of Scientology. At the time of his death in January 1986, the Internal Revenue Service was nearing the end of an investigation into allegations that he had secretly diverted more than $100 million of Scientology's assets to foreign bank accounts during the early 1980s. In 1979, he, his wife, and nine other members were convicted of burglary, wiretapping, and other crimes in connection with the operations of a secret group (the "Guardian's Office") he had established to break into government offices and harass and intimidate reporters and others who tried to examine the organization.
45. This is the case in which Justice Hugo Black contributed his famous footnote that "among religions in this country which do not teach what would generally be considered a belief in the existence of God are Buddhism, Taoism, Ethical Culture, Secular Humanism and others." 367 U.S. 488, 495, n. 11 (1961).
46. From Senate Report No. 1268, 80th Congress, 2nd session. Cited by Richard E. Morgan, *The Supreme Court and Religion*, p. 166.
47. 380 U.S. 163 (1964).
48. 380 U.S. 163, 184–185 (1965).
49. 398 U.S. 333, 342 (1970). Cited by Mooney, p. 35.
50. See John Paris, "Toward an Understanding of the Supreme Court's approach to Religion in Conscientious Objector Cases," *Suffolk University Law Review* 7 (1973):449. Cited by Mooney, p. 163, n. 41.

51. Ari L. Goldman, "U.S. Clerics Debating Ethics of Giving Sanctuary to Aliens," New York *Times*, August 23, 1985, pp. A1 and B18.
52. "Bringing Sanctuary to Trial," *Time*, October 28, 1985, p. 69.
53. Ari L. Goldman, art. cit., p. B18. Such cynicism may be evident in Charles Krauthammer's syndicated column on the subject. See "Declaring Sanctuary from the Laws of the United States," *The Hartford Courant*, May 11, 1986, p. E3.
54. Ibid.
55. Ibid.
56. "Events and People," *The Christian Century* 102 (November 13, 1985):1024.
57. See Robert F. Drinan, "The Sanctuary Movement On Trial," *America*, August 24, 1985, pp. 81–83.
58. "Paid Informers, Deception and Lies," *The Christian Century* 102 (November 13, 1985):1028.
59. Wayne King, "Churches Sue U.S., Alleging Illegal Acts in Inquiry on Aliens," New York *Times*, January 14, 1986, pp. A1 and A47.
60. Cited by Howard Basler, "Care of Children Must Be Priority in Current Gay Rights Controversy," *The Tablet* [Brooklyn], July 7, 1985.
61. Joseph Berger, "The O'Connor Way: Assertive, Heard," New York *Times*, February 17, 1986, p. A12.
62. "Church, State and Homosexuality" [editorial], New York *Times*, February 10, 1986, p. A20.
63. See Stuart Taylor, Jr., "High Court, 5-4, Says States Have The Right To Outlaw Private Homosexual Acts," New York *Times*, July 1, 1986, pp. A1 and A11. For excerpts from the Court's opinions, see p. A10.
64. See Larry Rohter, "Friend and Foe See Homosexual Defeat," New York *Times*, July 1, 1986, p. A11. For other reactions, see Paul Gewirtz, "The Court Was 'Superficial' In the Homosexuality Case," New York *Times*, July 8, 1986, p. A21; Anthony Lewis, "A Rage to Judge," New York *Times*, July 10, 1986, p. A23; and David R. Carlin, Jr., "Two Doctrines of Privacy," *America*, August 9, 1986, pp. 50–51.
65. See Robert Pear, "Panel Calls on Citizens to Wage National Assault on Pornography," New York *Times*, July 10, 1986, pp. A1 and B7.
66. See Barbara Gamarekian, "Report Draws Strong Praise and Criticism," ibid., p. B7.
67. Para. 16. The entire document was published in booklet form in 1983 by the United States Catholic Conference, Washington, D.C. It is also available in *Origins* 13 (May 19, 1983):1–32.
68. Para. 28.
69. See para. 17. See also Charles E. Curran, "The Moral Methodology of the Bishops' Pastoral," in *Catholics and Nuclear War*, Philip J. Murnion, ed. (New York: The Crossroad Publishing Co., 1983), pp. 45–56.
70. "From the Pastoral Constitution of Vatican II to *The Challenge of Peace*," in Murnion, *Catholics and Nuclear War*, p. 81. For examples of such reactions, see "Bishops and the Bomb" [editorial] New York *Times*, May 6, 1983, p. A30; and Gordon C. Zahn, "Pacifism and the Just War," in *Catholics and Nuclear War*, pp. 119–131. The award for the most acerbic reaction, however, may go to Patrick Buchanan: "For those reared in Catholic traditions, the assemblage in Chicago was less redolent of tragedy than burlesque. . . . [The pastoral letter] leaves the American bishops as moral freeloaders—conscientious objectors of the Cold War, whose right to preach, publish and speak is protected by the political leaders and professional soldiers—whose morality they are free to fly-speck from their

perches in the pulpits, far above the real world which Ronald Reagan has to lead." See "Bishops are moral freeloaders," Boston *Herald*, May 9, 1983, op-ed page.

71. See "The U.S. Catholic Bishops and the Public Policy Debate," a paper prepared for the American Political Science Association Convention, New Orleans, September 1, 1985, p. 21. See also his "Moral Aspects of the Nuclear Arms Debate: The Contribution of the U.S. Catholic Bishops," in *The Nuclear Arms Debate: Ethical and Political Implications*, Robert C. Johansen, ed. (Princeton: World Order Studies Program Occasional Paper #12, 1984), pp. 7–40.

72. Pastoral Constitution on the Church in the Modern World (*Gaudium et spes*), n. 4.

73. For Cardinal Bernardin's and Archbishop Roach's assessment of the Vatican meeting, see "January Meeting in Rome on the War and Peace Pastoral" and "A Positive and Helpful Exchange of Views," *Origins* 12 (April 7, 1983):690–691, 695–696. For the Vatican's own report on the consultation, see Jan Schotte, "A Vatican Synthesis," ibid., 691–695.

74. "How the Proposed Pastoral Relates to U.S. Policy," *Origins* 12 (April 21, 1983):738–739. The bishops of the United Methodist Church, in a pastoral letter of their own in 1986, rejected any use of nuclear weapons and the entire concept of nuclear deterrence. See Eric Pace, "Ban on A-Arms Urged in Study By Methodists," The New York *Times*, April 27, 1986, pp. A1 and A17.

75. Para. 10. The bishops considered themselves to be on good ground in making such distinctions. The Second Vatican Council itself, in its Pastoral Constitution on the Church in the Modern World (*Gaudium et spes*), had made the same point; namely, that "with equal sincerity some of the faithful will disagree with others on a given matter." Solutions proposed by one side or the other to specific moral problems "may be easily confused by many people with the Gospel message. Hence it is necessary for people to remember that no one is allowed in the aforementioned situations to appropriate the Church's authority for his opinion. They should always try to enlighten one another through honest discussion, preserving mutual charity and caring above all for the common good" (n. 43).

76. "The U.S. Catholic Bishops and the Public Policy Debate," op. cit., p. 23.

77. Para. 328.

78. *We Hold These Truths*, p. 14.

SUGGESTED READINGS

The following list is not for scholars. It represents a sample of the books and articles that I found most helpful in completing this complex project.

Probing the Foundations

The three books whose audiences I have especially hoped to reach are Walter Lippmann's *The Public Philosophy* (Boston: Little, Brown and Company, 1955); George Wills' *Statecraft as Soulcraft: What Government Does* (New York: Simon & Schuster, 1983); and John Courtney Murray's *We Hold These Truths: Catholic Reflections on the American Proposition* (New York: Sheed & Ward, 1960; reprinted 1985).

In a review of Lippmann's book some three decades ago, John Courtney Murray succinctly expressed the concern that binds each of these three works together, including Murray's own: "At the moment when we are witnessing this upsurge of public religion in America, we are notified that there has occurred a decadence of the public philosophy of America. . . . Our task . . . is the re-creation of the tradition itself through an understanding of its inner substance and through an adaptation of this substance to the society in which we live. . . ."

Religion and Politics in U.S. History

Martin E. Marty's *Pilgrims in Their Own Land: 500 Years of Religion in America* (Boston: Little, Brown and Company, 1984; Penguin paperback ed., 1985) offers a richly detailed and exceedingly fair-minded historical account. Marty himself recommends Sydney E.

Ahlstrom's *A Religious History of the American People* (New Haven: Yale University Press, 1972; Garden City, NY: Doubleday, 1975), as "the most expansive and successful attempt to tell the story of American religion."

Bernard Bailyn's *The Ideological Origins of the American Revolution* (Cambridge, MA: The Belknap Press of Harvard University Press, 1967) won both the Pulitzer Prize and the Bancroft Prize. It has been described justly as a modern classic.

The best book on the impact of the Enlightenment in the United States is Henry F. May's *The Enlightenment in America* (London: Oxford University Press, 1976). This and Bailyn's work are indispensable for understanding the social and intellectual roots of the Declaration of Independence and the U.S. Constitution.

The Federalist papers, especially numbers 10 and 51, remain the most important contemporary commentary on the new U.S. Constitution. Alexis de Tocqueville's *Democracy in America* is still regarded as a masterpiece of political and social interpretation, covering the early decades of the nineteenth century. Both works are available in various paperback editions.

William Lee Miller's *The First Liberty: Religion and the American Republic* (New York: Alfred A. Knopf, 1986) is brightly written, sometimes distractingly so. The portrait of James Madison is excellent, and the concluding chapter, "Reflections After Two Centuries," is original and insightful. I'm glad I used it, in spite of an unfairly negative review in The New York *Times*. (The absence of footnotes is its most serious drawback.)

For more traditionally scholarly studies, see Sidney E. Mead's *The Lively Experiment: The Shaping of Christianity in America* (New York: Harper & Row, 1963); and Ernest Lee Tuveson's *Redeemer Nation: The Idea of America's Millennial Role* (Chicago: University of Chicago Press, 1968; Midway reprint, 1980). The first is a classic. Serious students should know both, however.

The best treatment of fundamentalism is George M. Marsden's *Fundamentalism and American Culture: The Shaping of Twentieth-Century Evangelicalism 1870–1925* (New York: Oxford University Press, 1980). See also his essay, "Preachers of Paradox: The Religious New Right in Historical Perspective," in *Religion and America* (below), pp. 150–168.

Religion and Politics in America Today

The book that comes closest in kind to my own is A. James Reichley's *Religion in American Public Life* (Washington, D.C.: The

Brookings Institution, 1985). This is an intelligent and generally well-balanced work, one that *America* magazine said was "unlikely to warm the hearts of secularists or give the green light to fanatical pietists." Its neoconservative tilt, however, is evident here and there, and especially in the final chapter.

Robert Booth Fowler's *Religion and Politics in America* (Metuchen, NJ: The American Theological Library Association and the Scarecrow Press, 1985) is also worth looking at to fill in some of Reichley's gaps, particularly regarding court cases.

One of the best collections of essays on the central topic and related issues is *Religion and America: Spirituality in a Secular Age,* Mary Douglas and Steven M. Tipton, eds. (Boston: Beacon Press, 1983). Don't be distracted or put off by the subtitle. It is totally misleading. The book contains some of the meatiest and most insightful articles on one or another aspect of the subject, for example, by Peter Berger, George Marsden, Edwin Scott Gaustad, George Armstrong Kelly, and Martin E. Marty. The collection appeared originally, in almost identical form, in the winter 1982 issue of *Daedalus: Journal of the American Academy of Arts and Sciences.* Kelly has produced a fuller statement of his position in *Politics and Religious Consciousness in America* (New Brunswick, NJ: Transaction Books, 1984). He's not always easy to follow, however.

Catherine L. Albanese's *America: Religions and Religion* (Belmont, CA: Wadsworth Publishing Company, 1981) provides a comprehensive overview of the field, and includes chapters on Judaism, "Public Protestantism," Catholicism, and civil religion.

Varieties of Civil Religion, by Robert N. Bellah and Phillip E. Hammond (San Francisco: Harper & Row, 1980) is an important collection. The brief opening chapter by Bellah is a clearly written contextual piece. Bellah's original call for a "civil religion" appears in *Beyond Belief: Essays on Religion in a Post-Traditional World* (New York: Harper & Row, 1970), pp. 168–189. It was initially published in the winter 1967 issue of *Daedalus.*

John F. Wilson's *Public Religion in American Culture* (Philadelphia: Temple University Press, 1979) is equally important for understanding that phenomenon.

Martin E. Marty's *The Public Church: Mainline—Evangelical—Catholic* (New York: Crossroad, 1981) applies the above to the church itself. What emerges is a Christian community with "a special interiority and a specific openness," one that fully affirms the principles of American constitutionalism without loss of Christian identity or commitment. Marty's proposal, both in substance and in style, is very different from that of his fellow Lutheran, Richard John Neuhaus, whose *The Naked Public Square: Religion and Democracy in America*

(Grand Rapids: William B. Eerdmans Publishing Company, 1984) tries to mark a neoconservative path between political fundamentalism and mainline Christian liberalism. Neuhaus seems more exercised over the latter, however.

For a useful insight into the place of non-Christian Americans in this pluralist nation, see Morton Borden, *Jews, Turks and Infidels* (Chapel Hill, NC: University of North Carolina Press, 1984).

For more sociologically oriented studies, see *The Sacred in a Secular Age: Toward Revision in the Scientific Study of Religion*, Phillip E. Hammond, ed. (Berkeley: University of California Press, 1985), especially Bryan Wilson's "Secularization: The Inherited Model" (pp. 9–20), Rodney Stark's "Church and Sect" (pp. 139–149), and Benton Johnson's "Religion and Politics in America: The Last Twenty Years" (pp. 301–316); *The Future of Religion: Secularization, Revival and Cult Formation*, Rodney Stark and William Sims Bainbridge, eds. (Berkeley: University of California Press, 1985); and *Habits of the Heart: Individualism and Commitment in American Life*, by Robert N. Bellah, Richard Madsen, William M. Sullivan, Ann Swidler, and Steven M. Tipton (Berkeley: University of California Press, 1985), especially chapter 9, "Religion," pp. 219–249. Sullivan has contributed a monograph of his own to the discussion: *Reconstructing Public Philosophy* (Berkeley: University of California Press, 1982). The nonspecialist will find the style a bit difficult, however.

For a still broader perspective, see *Religion and Politics in the Modern World,* Peter H. Merkl and Ninian Smart, eds. (New York: New York University Press, 1985).

Religion and the U.S. Supreme Court

Unfortunately, a good up-to-date compendium of U.S. Supreme Court cases doesn't exist (which is why I had to expend so much effort on Chapter 3 of this book). But there are several commentaries, many of which carry a bias, whether secularist or neoconservative.

Neoconservative authors who are generally critical of the Court's decisions for not favoring religion more than it seems to do include: Walter Berns, *The First Amendment and the Future of Democracy* (New York: Basic Books, 1970); and Robert L. Cord, *Separation of Church and State: Historical Fact and Current Fiction* (New York: Lambeth Press, 1982). A. James Reichley is also concerned about the encroachment of secularism, but is more moderate in his criticism of the Court's general record. See again *Religion in American Public Life*, chapter 4, "Interpreting the First Amendment," pp. 115–167.

On the left are the absolute, or strict, separationists who like what the neoconservatives deplore. See, for example, Leonard Levy, *The Establishment Clause: Religion and the First Amendment* (New York: Macmillan, 1986); and Leo Pfeffer, *God, Caesar, and the Constitution: The Court as Referee in Church-State Confrontation* (Boston: Beacon Press, 1975).

At various points in between are such diverse interpretations as Robert F. Drinan's *Religion, the Courts, and Public Policy* (New York: McGraw-Hill, 1963); Philip B. Kurland, *Religion and the Law: Of Church and State and the Supreme Court* (Chicago: Aldine Publishing Co., 1962), which alone among all commentaries suggests a hard-and-fast principle for dealing with religion-related cases in the courts; namely, that religion not be used as a basis of classification for purposes of governmental action; Richard E. Morgan, *The Supreme Court and Religion* (New York: The Free Press, 1972), which warns precisely against such hard-and-fast doctrinal principles of interpretation; and Christopher F. Mooney, *Public Virtue: Law and the Social Character of Religion* (Notre Dame, IN: University of Notre Dame Press, 1986), especially the first two chapters, pp. 1–54.

For a very capable analysis of school-related issues and cases, see Robert Michaelsen, *Piety in the Public School: Trends and Issues in the Relationship Between Religion and the Public School in the United States* (New York: Macmillan, 1970). This is the best book on the subject and introduces the reader to a larger body of literature.

Although no up-to-date compendium of religion-related cases exists, there is still some value in *Church and State in the United States,* by Anson Phelps Stokes and Leo Pfeffer (New York: Harper & Row, 1964; revised one-volume edition). One historian has called it "a good garbage dump" for material on this subject.

A good general book on the U.S. Supreme Court is David M. O'Brien's *Storm Center: The Supreme Court in American Politics* (New York: W.W. Norton & Company, 1986).

The Wisdom of Catholicism

The Catholic Church's current official teaching on religious liberty and church and state respectively is contained in the Second Vatican Council's Declaration on Religious Freedom (*Dignitatis humanae*) and in its Pastoral Constitution on the Church in the Modern World (*Gaudium et spes*). Both are available in *The Documents of Vatican II,* Walter M. Abbott, ed. (New York: America Press, 1966). Pope John XXIII's widely honored encyclical *Pacem in Terris* (Peace on Earth) is emphatic in its defense of human rights, including the right to religious liberty.

John Courtney Murray was the chief architect of the Second Vatican Council's teaching on religious liberty and the Catholic Church's leading authority on matters of church and state. Although much of the book is dated, the essence of his thought is available in *We Hold These Truths: Catholic Reflections on the American Proposition* (New York: Sheed & Ward, 1960; reprinted 1985), especially the Introduction and chapters 1, 2, and 7. His most important scholarly articles on the subject are: "The Problem of Religious Freedom," *Theological Studies* 25 (December 1964):503–575; and "The Issue of Church and State at Vatican II," *Theological Studies* 27 (December 1966):580–606. Both essays challenge the intellect. They are digested and synthesized in Chapter 4 of this book. (J. Bryan Hehir is the clearest and most faithful interpreter of Murray today. All of Hehir's writings on the general topic are worth reading.)

The U.S. Catholic bishops' pastoral letter, "The Challenge of Peace," is a model of how religion can most effectively, and civilly, interact with the political order. It is published as a booklet under the title, *The Challenge of Peace: God's Promise and Our Response* (Washington, D.C.: United States Catholic Conference, 1983). For an unsympathetic critique of the bishops' recent initiatives, see J. Brian Benestad, *The Pursuit of a Just Social Order: Policy Statements of the U.S. Catholic Bishops, 1966–80* (Washington, D.C.: Ethics and Public Policy Center, 1982). I don't necessarily recommend the book, but fairness requires that it be mentioned.

Jacques Maritain's *Man and the State* (Chicago: The University of Chicago Press, 1951) is a distillation of the pre-Vatican II Catholic tradition. Books of this sort only succeed, however, if they motivate us to delve more deeply into the primary source material, like Augustine's *City of God*, Thomas Aquinas' *On Kingship (De Regimine Principuum)* and his commentaries on Aristotle's *Ethics* and *Politics*, Thomas More's *Utopia*, or Dante's *Divine Comedy*. And they, in turn, might prompt us to go all the way back to Plato's *Republic* and Aristotle's *Politics*, both of which are available in various paperback editions.

For a richly diverse collection of essays on the participation of clergy and sisters in politics, see *Between God and Caesar: Priests, Sisters and Political Office in the United States*, Madonna Kolbenschlag, ed. (New York: Paulist Press, 1985).

The best source of current and recent documents pertaining especially, but not exclusively, to Catholic contributions to the subject is *Origins: NC Documentary Service*, published weekly (except during

July and August when biweekly) by the National Catholic News Service, 1312 Massachusetts Ave., N.W., Washington, D.C. 20005.

Some Protestant Approaches

Ernst Troeltsch's *The Social Teachings of the Christian Churches,* Olive Wyon, trans. (New York: Harper & Row, 1960; originally published 1911), 2 vols., is a modern classic. Every serious attempt to understand the relationship between church and society has to take this work into account.

Thomas G. Sanders' *Protestant Concepts of Church and State* (New York: Holt, Rinehart and Winston, 1964; Garden City, NY: Doubleday Anchor Books, 1965) is dated, but still useful as a straining out of several different strands of thought.

INDEX